Democracy and Expertise

Democracy and Expertise

Reorienting Policy Inquiry

Frank Fischer

OXFORD
UNIVERSITY PRESS

OXFORD
UNIVERSITY PRESS

Great Clarendon Street, Oxford OX2 6DP

Oxford University Press is a department of the University of Oxford.
It furthers the University's objective of excellence in research, scholarship,
and education by publishing worldwide in

Oxford New York

Auckland Cape Town Dar es Salaam Hong Kong Karachi
Kuala Lumpur Madrid Melbourne Mexico City Nairobi
New Delhi Shanghai Taipei Toronto

With offices in

Argentina Austria Brazil Chile Czech Republic France Greece
Guatemala Hungary Italy Japan Poland Portugal Singapore
South Korea Switzerland Thailand Turkey Ukraine Vietnam

Oxford is a registered trade mark of Oxford University Press
in the UK and in certain other countries

Published in the United States
by Oxford University Press Inc., New York

© Frank Fischer 2009

British Library Cataloguing in Publication Data
Data available

Library of Congress Cataloging in Publication Data
Data available

Typeset by SPI Publisher Services, Pondicherry, India
Printed in Great Britain
on acid-free paper by
the MPG Books Group

ISBN 978–0–19–928283–8 (Hbk.)
       978–0–19–956524–5 (Pbk.)

1 3 5 7 9 10 8 6 4 2

To the memory of my father,
architect, painter and poet

Acknowledgments

It is never possible to account for all of the influences that go into a work of this kind, part theoretical, part empirical, and part speculative. It is important, however, to identify and acknowledge a number of people who have helped along the way, in some cases reading and commenting on various chapters, and discussing the issues with me in ways that enlarged my understanding of their nature and implications. In my case, I have to express special thanks to Susan Fainstein, Carmen Sirianni, Hubertus Buchstein, Alan Mandell, Mara Sidney, Navdeep Mathur, Douglas Torgerson, Tim Forsyth, Michael Orsini, Kathrin Braun, Jeanette Hofmann, Nick Turnbull, Laureen Elgar, Alexander Goersdorf, Lew Friedland. Gabriela Kuetting, Linda Soneryd, John Dryzek, Susan Owen, Rob Doubleday, Jan-Peter Voss, Thomas Greven, and Paul Dorfman for commenting on parts of the manuscript. My appreciation also goes Maarten Hajer, Carolyn Hendrix, Dieter Plehwe, Dvora Yanow, Mark Warren, Patsy Healey, Yrjo Haila, Herbert Gottweis, Bron Szerszynski, Jack Stilgoe, Judith Innes, Ian Walsh, Chris Rootes, Eric Griessler, Sandra Yenwen Peng, Rob Hoppe, Les Levidow, Wayne Parsons, and Christoph Scherrer; they helpfully discussed particular issues with me at various points along the way. All assisted me in one way or another but none of them—to apply the standard disclaimer—bear any responsibility for what does or doesn't appear in the pages that follow. In addition, I extend my thanks to Wendy Godek for editorial assistance, as well as to Shunsaku Komatsuzaki and Rakhi Poonia for their many trips to the library on my behalf. Thanks also goes to the University of London, Queen Mary College, and the Research School of the Social Sciences of the Australian National University for providing me with comfortable, quiet places to work during periods of writing and editing, as well as to members of workshop on "Traveling Knowledge" at Cambridge University for providing me with the opportunity to discuss various chapters with them in some detail. As has always been the case, the editorial staff at Oxford University Press were most helpful, Elizabeth Suffling, Susan Beer, Louise Sprake, and Joy Mellor in particular. I extend my gratitude to them as well. And, not least important, I also express my deep appreciation to Sabine Braun-Fischer for her steady patience and support.

Contents

Contents

Introduction

This book explores the role of policy expertise in a democratic society. Focusing on the relationships among experts, politicians, and citizens, the approach is primarily normative, although the arguments are grounded in empirical examples. From the perspectives of political and policy theory, the chapters work out the implications of deliberative democratic governance for professional expertise and extend them to specific policy practices. Toward this end, emphasis is placed on the relation of the professional policy expert to the citizen. The challenge is to restructure professional practices in ways that can assist citizens understand and discuss the complex policy issues that affect their lives. In doing so, it also examines ways in which experts and citizens can do this through more cooperative forms of policy inquiry.

The idea for the book emerged as part of a continuing interest in the relation of science to politics, citizens to experts in particular (Fischer 2000). More specifically, it was motivated by an interest in problems of expert knowledge, complexity, and citizen deliberation. Given the technical and social complexity of most contemporary policy issues, a significant degree of competence is required of citizens and their politicians to participate meaningfully in policy discussions. If they are unable to understand and make intelligent judgments on the issues, as many would argue, this poses a worrisome problem. Putting democratic rhetoric aside, it would suggest the need to rethink the meaning and applicability of democracy in contemporary times. It is scarcely a new question, but it is all the more pressing in an "age of expertise."

A second and related issue has to do with the proliferation of work on deliberative democracy in political theory. As interesting and significant as this work has been, most of it has failed to devote sufficient attention to the role of expertise. Moreover, beyond the normative realm of theory, the same can be said of the many experimental research projects designed to promote and facilitate citizen deliberation, such as citizen juries, scenario workshops, and stakeholder deliberations. It is not that experts play no role; they are typically asked to make themselves available, one way or another, to citizens in need of professional opinion—clarification and explanation—on the complex problems being deliberated. But these interactions, it is argued here, largely rest on a problematic understanding of the role of knowledge and expertise.

The study has also been motivated by the new interest in participatory modes of governance in Western liberal polities over the past couple of decades, especially in Europe. These initiatives, both theoretical and practical, have given rise to an encouraging degree of innovation and experimentation with the devolution of political power to citizens and citizen-based nongovernmental organizations. Such efforts, moreover, have come as much from the bottom up as the top down. Along the way, however, this new emphasis on democratic governance has raised numerous questions. To what degree do state institutions take these activities seriously? Are they merely introducing and accommodating them to achieve their own pre-established interests and goals? In what way does it relate to standard hierarchical models of policymaking? How do values such as equity and justice fare in these participatory processes? And not least of all, what is the role of expertise in such participatory processes. Indeed, it is to this latter question that the present work is largely addressed.

The issue comes into sharper focus when we turn to an examination of other kinds of participatory projects in the public sphere, especially those organized by social movements and progressive professionals. In many of these cases, experts can be found helping citizens to understand and discuss the issues at hand, as well as doing it actively in ways that assist members of the public to organize and facilitate their own deliberative processes. In fact, some professionals have labored to develop deliberative practices—methods and procedures—for doing just this. Such efforts suggest a new role for expertise and expert practices, one that not only assists citizens to engage in deliberation, but helps at the same time to promote deliberative democracy more generally.

To be sure, questions about the relation of expertise to democracy and citizen participation are scarcely new. Indeed, it is one of the classical issues in politics and sociology (Ezrahi 1990; Fischer 1990: 59–76). Today, given the dominance of expertise in the decision processes, the topic stands out more than ever. The institutions and practices of modern societies are anchored to professional knowledge, leaving decisionmakers highly dependent on expert judgments. Politicians and policy decision-makers, along with citizens, are left to depend on and trust the validity of the knowledge and competencies of the experts who make them. Sur-rounded by expert systems whose validities are said to be independent of time and context, there is little choice but to rely on the decisions of faceless authorities. It is one of the main reasons that trust has emerged as an important sociopolitical issue. Modern life depends fundamentally on trusting experts we don't know—professionals who often move in elite circles socially distant to the lives of everyday citizens and speak languages that can be difficult to understand. It has led Dahl (1989: 337) to speak of a "quasi-guardianship" of "elite public policy specialists" no longer accountable to the general public.

A troublesome indicator of this malaise is the decline of citizen engage-ment in Western democracies. While the interpretation of this reality is subject to considerable disagreement, it reflects in part the difficulties citizens have engaging complex policy issues. It has led many to raise the question: Do citizens—as well as many of their political representa-tives—have the capacity and competence to make judgments on issues such as nuclear power, environmental degradation, abortion, and AIDS? And if they do not, how should we understand the political systems in which we live? Are we destined to head toward ever more technocratic forms of governance? Or can we in some way rejuvenate the citizen's role and revitalize our traditional understandings of a democratic society?

Technocratic governance has surely had its enthusiasts and many today are privately—and sometimes not so privately—of the belief that decisions by experts would be preferable to the sort of manipulated, distorted forms of politics that all-too-often define contemporary political systems, espe-cially Western-style electoral processes. Given that unsolved problems only continue to mount up, why not turn things over to those who know how to go about solving them?

This view, however, has its own problems. It might be one thing if the knowledge elites were able to handily dispose of the myriad of problems that confront contemporary societies. But we have come to learn over the past decades that the experts are themselves incapable of answering many of the pressing questions, at least with sufficient degrees of certainty, not to mention supplying workable solutions. To further dampen enthusiasm for such a politics we have also learned that scientific expertise is not the neutral, objective phenomenon that it has long purported to be. Indeed, professionals have all too often served the ideological function of legitimating decisions made elsewhere by political rather than scientific means.

Recognition of these limitations, moreover, has led to a politicization of expertise that pits one set of experts against another. Unable to sort out many of the questions themselves, the citizen's role under these circumstances is little more than that of an audience watching experts debate the issues, typically removed from direct public encounter. The matter becomes even more important as a growing number of citizens are unwilling to uncritically accept the trained judgments of professional experts. Numerous writers have described a lack of trust in experts as one of the critical issues of our time (Giddens 1990; Beck 1995; Jasanoff 2006).

The situation presents a genuine dilemma. If citizens are in need of specialized expertise, but have lost confidence and trust in experts, how are they to grapple with the issues they confront? It is a question that can best be dealt with from an alternative, constructivist approach to knowledge—in terms of both how knowledge is obtained and how it applies to the public realm. The "postempiricist" perspective can assist us in initiating new and more productive efforts to rethink the relationship of expert discourses to citizens.[1] This involves the complicated task of not only dealing with expert findings related to sophisticated technical issues, but also understanding how citizens and experts make judgments about such questions.

The approach taken here has roots in the political writings of John Dewey. Concerned with the increasing technological complexity in the early twentieth century, Dewey (1927) worried that citizens would be unable to fulfill their cornerstone role in the democratic process. In face of the unfolding techno-industrial society, he saw the need for a new relationship between experts and citizens. Toward this end, he called on experts to play a major role in helping citizens understand the issues, thus permitting them to perform their democratic assignment. Experts would assist citizens in improving their abilities to deliberate and debate public issues.

The challenge, in Dewey's view, rested on a paradox. As the role of the citizen grew in the political sphere—resulting in significant part from the expansion of basic political and legal rights in the nineteenth

---

[1] "Postempiricism," used here interchangeably with "postpositivism," does not deny the importance of the empirical. It rather seeks to transcend the ideology of "empiricism," which fails to recognize the normative social context in which the empirical is embedded. In the postempiricist approach, the empirical is only one of a number of components in constituting that which is called knowledge (Fischer 2003: 117–38).

and twentieth centuries—there was at the same time a growth in the size and power of large corporate enterprises and government bureaucracies directed by managerial and technical expertise. In the very period when the political potential for citizen influence was emerging, it was being undermined by the expansion of large organizations and a more instrumental orientation to politics, deepening what Max Weber described as the rationalization of modern economic and social life. This elevated concerns about an informed citizenry and the future prospects of democratic governance.

For many, to be sure, the ability to increase the quality of public opinion and thus citizen judgment in the face of modern-day complexities is limited at best. Others ask if it not better to rely those who are better informed? Setting aside the fact that the experts do not always know best, as ample experience makes clear, the answer to those who question the need to worry about and improve public opinion is not as difficult as it might first appear. Public opinion, simply put, is basic to democratic politics and has an unavoidable impact on competitive electoral processes. In so far as the opinions of the citizens influence the positions taken by the politicians who seek their support, opinion plays an important role—even when in the longer run—in shaping the direction of politics and the society of which it is a part. Given this political reality, a higher quality of public judgment can only be better than the lower levels we often experience today. In all ways, the quality of democracy depends on it.

For this reason, Dewey asked if we can find ways to overcome the challenge presented by an unprecedented level of technical and social complexity? The answer for him was to be found in a new cooperative division of labor between citizens and experts. On the technical front, experts would identify and analyze basic social and economic problems. On the political front, citizens and their political representatives would democratically set out an agenda for dealing with them. The two processes could be integrated, Dewey argued, through improvements of the methods and conditions of debate, discussion, and persuasion. Public debate would require the participation of experts, but they would serve in a special way: rather than just rendering advice they would analyze and interpret their findings in ways helpful to citizens. Acting as teachers and interpreters, professional experts—social scientists in particular—would decipher the techno-industrial world for citizens and other political actors, enabling them to make intelligent political judgments. In the process, democratic politics could be revitalized in a world of large-scale technologies, big organizations, and technocratic expertise.

The central goal of this work, in the tradition of Dewey, is to examine this tension between experts and citizens. The chapters explore how the contemporary "expert–public gap" might be restructured through deliberative forms of interactive inquiry (Yankelovich (1991: 91)). As the effort depends on an understanding of both the political and epistemological developments that have evolved over the past few decades, these foundations need to be addressed before directly turning to specific practices. In particular, we take advantage of a more contemporary social constructivist understanding of inquiry that facilitates a different orientation to knowledge production. Such work, as we shall see, permits us to approach the challenge as involving different ways of seeing and knowing rather than simply a matter for technical competence. This opens new possibilities for bringing together citizens and experts that can increase the quality of public deliberation and the judgments which would emerge from it.

The various chapters are set in the context of numerous contemporary efforts, both theoretical and practical, designed to improve the methods of deliberation and debate. The perspective, in this regard, is informed and motivated by thriving theoretical exchanges in political theory on deliberative democracy, practical work with deliberative experiments, the theory and practices of democratic governance, and participatory research, all dedicated to revitalizing the citizen's role in civil society. Within deliberative democracy and deliberative experimentation, the focus has largely been on rules and procedures related to deliberative practices and institutional processes. This has involved questions of how the participants are selected, group size, the scope of the deliberation, institutional structures, specific goals (advisory capabilities, problem-solving orientation, educational potentials, etc.), institutional level of participation (large or small scale), issues of empowerment, democratic legitimacy, contributions to civic engagement, quality of deliberation, relationships to official political processes, accountability, popular mobilization, and the like. As already noted, however, a more fundamental consideration of the role of expertise in such deliberative processes has been missing. In significant part, the failure rests on a continuing reliance on conventional understandings of the role of the expert. This is attributable to both the experts themselves and to those who organize deliberative projects. While experts typically make contributions to deliberative fora—such as citizens, juries, consensus conferences, scenario workshops, stakeholder deliberations—they generally work from traditional—largely outdated—conceptions of knowledge and expertise. By turning to a more sophisticated constructivist interpretation of expertise, as is argued here, new possibilities emerge for making the expert–citizen relationship more participatory, if not democratic per se.

Many contemporary deliberative projects have emerged as a way to offset the dominant role accorded to experts in policy discussions. This, however, does not offset the fact that the issues are complex and that citizens are in need of expert advice to engage them meaningfully, both to explain issues and to facilitate the discursive processes. Work on participatory governance, on the other hand, has in some cases made an effort to address the problem. This has mainly resulted from the use of participatory action research, especially as it has evolved in developing countries. Participatory research offers a great deal of information and experience about expert–citizen interactions.

The specific approach advanced here is grounded in emerging work on deliberative policy inquiry and the participatory practices that support it (Fischer and Forester 1993; Hajer and Wagenaar 2003). Some of this investigation is designed to help policy decision-makers and politicians deal more collaboratively with the issues they confront. Other contributors have focused more explicitly on efforts to move beyond the conventional practices of liberal democracy to a stronger, more participatory conception of democracy, or what has been described as the struggle to "democratize democracy" (Santos 2005). In this book, deliberative policy inquiry seeks to reorient the theory and and practices of public policy analysis to include the facilitation of public participation and citizen deliberation. Although much of deliberative policy inquiry still remains a project in the making, it is not without practical examples, the practices of the Danish Board of Technology being a primary example (which we take up in Chapter 3).

The task is thus to broaden the policy-analytic assignment. Whereas policy analysis evolved to narrowly assist government officials with information and analysis relevant to public decision-making, a deliberative-analytic approach redirects and extends the effort to include the public more generally. Grounded in a commitment to public enlightenment, a deliberative orientation seeks to assist affected political actors—politicians, administrators, and citizens—at various levels of governance to think about and discuss the pressing political and policy issues of the day. As such, it promotes a form of practical knowledge that brings technical findings together with the political values and social assumptions to which they relate, as well as the action-oriented narratives required for decision-making.

On one hand, it speaks to the need to extend democracy for its own sake; it recognizes democratic participation to be a virtue unto itself. Not only does it offer citizens an opportunity to learn about the world in which they live, it presents them with a chance to develop their own communicative competencies and sense of self-efficacy. As such, it offers schooling in citizenship and democratic self-governance. On the other hand, it seeks more pragmatically to address the limits of contemporary government. It understands that both electoral democracy (based only on periodic election of representatives) and bureaucratic administration (operating through hierarchy and rules) stumble in the face of modern-day complexities. Centralized governments—their representatives and administrators—are recognized to deal poorly with political uncertainty, risky situations, lack of hard evidence, and unexpected consequences that surround many contemporary policy issues; their top–down practices are unable to offer effective solutions. As part of participatory governance, deliberatively oriented policy inquiry thus seeks where appropriate to link existing institutional arrangements with more informal processes of decision-making, and in other cases, to shape new institutional relationships. In the process, it brings forth new issues, actors and arenas.

One of the virtues of deliberative policy analysis, as Hajer and Wagenaar (2003: 2) have pointed out, is that it offers a new vocabulary of governance that helps us to open up and reflect on "the cognitive commitments implicit in the thinking about governing and political decision-making." It helps both theorists and practitioners "to unlearn embedded intellectual reflexes and break out of tacit patterns of thinking." Not only does a deliberative-analytic model of policy inquiry assist in interpreting many of the difficult political and policy issues, through participation among interdependent citizens it can facilitate the building of public trust in government.

What follows offers no explicit propositional claims. It rather seeks to deepen and extend a discussion about policy expertise and citizen participation. Focusing on issues that have failed to receive sufficient attention, at the most general level the discussion brings together several literatures that can benefit from more interaction—the postempiricist orientation in policy analysis, deliberative democracy, deliberative experimentation, participatory governance, and participatory research. More specifically, the work seeks to situate the postempiricist practices of deliberative policy analysis in the context of the theoretical issues posed by deliberative democratic politics and the practical tasks involved in facilitating citizen deliberation, particularly in citizen juries, scenario workshops, and stakeholder deliberations. Stressing the benefits of mutual interaction among these fields of inquiry, the primary focus is on the reorientation of professional policy practices. It emphasizes the need to better understand the epistemic relationships that shape citizen–experts interactions. Along the way, it brings these perspectives to bear on theoretical and practical debates in the discipline of policy analysis, including their implications for education and training.

The study, as such, takes the professional policy expert—present and future—as a primary audience. It argues the case for a new role on the part of experts—policy analysts and planners in particular—in public deliberation and seeks to outline its essential features. While it is not a practical how-to-do-it book, it attempts to offer guidance in a number of ways to experts involved in organizing and facilitating deliberative fora. In the process, it places particular emphasis on the need to attend to the intersubjective nature of communication, including the expression of emotional sentiment. Because it recognizes the contributions of a wider range of participants in policy deliberations—including politicians, administrators, citizens, journalists, and scholars—the text refers more generally to "policy inquiry" than to the standard disciplinary terminology (such as policy science or policy analysis). This is to underscore the fact that others in addition to professional policy analysts have contributions to make to policy decision processes, a point that becomes all the more important in the effort to forge cooperative relationships between experts and lay citizens.

The position here, it is also important to make clear, is not that the professional disciplines need to be redesigned to focus exclusively on facilitation of public deliberation and debate. Instead, these deliberative practices are seen as a *component part* of the professional activities of those in the policy-related disciplines. The discussion thus calls for a new specialization in the field, one that investigates the "policy epistemics" of expert–citizen/client relationships and, at the same time, the ways in which such knowledge can inform new deliberative arrangements. How might expert knowledge and public judgment be brought into a more efficacious balance. The practice would, of course, be relevant for all who might engage with citizens, but more specifically it would be a topic of specialization for some. For those who take on the assignment, it would involve research into the nature of these interactions as part of deliberative research more generally—which should not only involve what citizens can do, but also how they can be helped to do it. It would secondly examine the epistemic nature and process of such policy communication—how its messages are interpreted, how it moves from one knowledge domain to another, etc.

Plan of the book

Part I of the book focuses on issues related to professional expertise and citizen engagement in the public realm. Chapter 1 examines the evolution of the professional orientation to public responsibilities, in particular civic engagement. The traditional commitments to serve the public are seen to have given way to more technical market-oriented approaches that emphasize the delivery of services on a contractual basis. The turn away from public commitments was challenged by progressive movements within a number of the major professions in the late 1960s and 1970s, but these efforts failed in part because of a problematic understanding of the relation of expert knowledge to the politics of community struggle and change. The chapter concludes by examining the less radical orientation that replaced the approach of these earlier movements, emphasizing newer forms of collaborative relations between citizens and experts professionals.

Chapter 2 turns to citizen deliberation—understood to be a normative core component of civic engagement—and outlines its worrisome decline in Western democratic societies. It does this by way of asking if most citizens can meaningfully deliberate policy issues in the modern age of complexity. And if they cannot, should we be talking about a more participatory, deliberative form of democracy? Pointing to various practical experiences, the question is answered affirmatively, but the difficulties involved in extending participation are underscored. After discussing the implications of contemporary theories of citizenship and governance for participation, the chapter concludes by arguing that there is nothing obvious or straightforward about participation. In important ways, it has to be facilitated, even nurtured.

The discussion then moves on to examine deliberative democratic theory and various deliberative experiments that can inform it. Chapter 3 illustrates how these efforts pose questions of expertise and complexity that have yet to be adequately taken into account. Deliberative democratic theory, largely abstract and impractical, has mainly neglected—if not ignored—these problems and their implications. At the same time, a parallel body of experimental research is shown to have usefully worked out practical deliberative designs. While these contributions generally recognize the need for expertise, they too have failed to move beyond standard understandings of expertise which has long hindered citizen participation. Emphasizing the expert–citizen relationship, the discussion points to the need to bring both of these theoretical and practical pursuits together in a more fruitful interaction.

Part II seeks to advance our understanding of policy expertise by placing it in the social context of which it is a part. Moving beyond the traditional conceptions of value-neutrality and context independence that have dominated the epistemology of the policy sciences, Chapter 4 offers a social constructivist interpretation of real-world practices. Introducing the constructivist perspective, the chapter presents an alternative dialectical understanding of knowledge and its relation to practical reason in policy deliberation. Here the postempiricist expert, as deliberative policy analysis, is posited as an interpretive mediator operating between the available analytic frameworks of social science, particular policy findings, and the differing perspectives of the public actors, both those of policy decisionmakers and citizens.

Chapter 5 turns to the difficult question of who should have the authority and legitimacy to speak about the technical dimensions of policy issues. Toward this end, the analysis engages the seminal effort of Collins and Evans to develop a contributory theory of technical expertise. Developing their theory to assist public policy deliberation in matters related to science and technology, they fail understand a crucial dimension of their project—namely, that there is no direct bridge from the technical sphere to the public realm across which such knowledge can travel. While technical knowledge is important for deliberation in public decision-making, it is not processed in the public realm by the same epistemological rules employed in the techno-scientific realm. The discussion thus examines the way in which the application of technical knowledge is situated in particular social contexts governed by the logic of practical reason. The chapter concludes with a call for the study of the epistemics of public deliberation and policy decision-making.

Having introduced the social context in which policy expertise operates, the analysis turns to the nature of public policy itself. Chapter 6 demonstrates how a public policy is more fundamentally a sociopolitical construct than technical/instrumental tool, as it is approached in much of policy science. Employing a constructivist sociology of knowledge, the discussion illustrates the ways in which a policy is the product of multiple realities and, as such, is as much a matter for interpretive analysis as it is techno-empirical assessment. To clarify the theoretical position, the second half of the chapter demonstrates the point through the political struggle over sustainable development in environmental policy. Beyond technical knowledge, the case points to how policies are socially experienced—in particular, how they supply citizens with the social sense of collective participation in mutual ventures with fellow members of their own communities.

The first chapter of Part III returns to an important issue introduced in Chapter 5; it elaborates on how policy findings are fitted into competing sociopolitical narratives. Presenting the narrative form as the primary mode of social understanding, the ways narrative stories are judged to be good or bad is examined. Here the emphasis is on the relation of narration to practical reason and the giving of good reasons. Not only does the explication demonstrate how policy narratives relate to factual information, but also to group identities and collective action. Offering an example of the use of narrative story-lines in climate change policy research, the chapter closes with a discussion of the concept of validity as understood in narrative analysis.

Chapter 8, co-authored by Alan Mandell, takes up an essential contention of deliberative democracy, namely the idea that citizens can improve their communicative competencies in ways that lead to self-transformative learning. It explores this argument by examining the nature of critical social learning, in particular the way it turns on underlying assumptions and tacit understandings. Toward this end, the text employs theoretical contributions from the field of adult education, especially work on "transformational learning" pioneered by theorists such as Freire and Mezirow. In the process, it speaks to the role of differences in deliberative theory—especially those related to culture, gender, class, or race—and their crucial function in the dialectical processes of argumentation. The chapter concludes with a discussion of the implications of tacit knowledge for expert practices and the facilitation of democratic dialogue.

Chapter 9 takes up the design of deliberative fora. It begins by introducing the influential theory of "empowered participatory governance" put forward by Fung and Wright, which is seen to focus mainly on procedural and material factors. Enabling participation, it is argued, require more attention to the underlying social conditions necessary for participatory deliberation to work. Drawing on contributions from postmodern cultural politics, as well as experiences from participatory research, democratic structures and procedures are seen to offer an opening for participatory empowerment, but cannot in and of themselves ensure authentic deliberation. Deeper political and social-psychological factors related to the intersubjective aspects of participation are involved as well. The argument is illustrated through several theoretical and practical contributions, including a more detailed analysis of the "People's Planning Campaign" in Kerala, India.

The final chapter explores one of the most difficult questions facing citizen participation and deliberative democracy: What is the role of emotion in political deliberation and public policy? The fact that emotional passion is basic to politics is clear, but the question of how to handle it both analytically and procedurally in the deliberative process is not easy to answer. In search of a better understanding of emotion in reason and politics, the chapter examines a range of perspectives, from Aristotle's theory of rhetoric to contributions from modern neuroscience. All show emotion and reason to be tied together in a complex relationship. The insight leads to the consideration of emotional expression in terms borrowed from drama and performativity. Emotion is then explored through experiences drawn from efforts by urban planners to revitalize depressed communities. The chapter concludes by suggesting a two-step process for dealing with "passionate reason."

Finally, the book closes with a brief Afterword on the implications of the theoretical and practical arguments contained in the preceding chapters. Given that they are designed for a world that does not yet fully exist, this closing discussion re-emphasizes the fact that the interrelated discussions are presented as part of an effort to help stimulate professional change and renewal, to promote a better understanding of expertise in deliberative democracy, to advance expert practices conducive to real-world deliberative fora, and to think about how these practices might be brought into the professional policy curriculum.

Part I

Policy Expertise and Citizen Participation in the Public Realm

1

Between Technical Knowledge and Public Responsibility: Professional Expertise in Critical Perspective

The discussion in this chapter seeks to set the social and political context for an examination of professional policy expertise in a democratic society.[1] As such, it lays out the issues posed by professional expertise in general, which serve as a background for subsequent chapters. To begin, it is important to note that the topic of professional expertise is scarcely new in the social sciences. But most of the scholarship on the professions has been written from a sociological perspective on occupations and work. In contrast to sociology, however, political science has largely ignored the professions (Dzur 2008). Despite the central role of professional expertise in the policy decision-making process, political scientists have traditionally considered this subject to fall outside their jurisdiction. There is thus little about the professions in the study of politics, although there have been some recent exceptions. The topic of policy expertise, if not the professions per se, has gained attention the field of public policy. It is increasingly recognized that as societies become more complex so does the importance of expert advice in matters related to governance. But professional expertise is also seen as a barrier to meaningful citizen participation. None of the more recent work, however, comes close to filling the gap in our understanding of the role of professional expertise

---

[1] There is no one firm definition of expertise. In general, it refers to a widely acknowledged source of reliable knowledge, skill, or technique that is accorded status and authority by the peers of the person who holds it and accepted by member of the larger public. The expert is a well-informed person, skilled in a particular field of knowledge or practice. He or she is distinguished from the less experienced novice (see Ericsson *et al.* 1991, 2006).

and its relation to the public realm. To help rectify this situation, it is important and useful to cast the question as part of a broader examination of the development of professional expertise in Western societies generally.

The modern professional society: From praise to critique

Western society has evolved as a "professional society" dominated by expert disciplines that speak to and regulate all aspects of contemporary life in Western societies.[2] Professional experts have a high degree of influence in most of the sectors of modern social systems; their skills are essential to the functioning of the complex institutions of industry, government, law, health care, and education, among others (Carr-Saunders and Wilson 1964). But this is not to imply that the professions are a relatively new phenomenon; the traditional professions emerged as part of the legacy of the seventeenth and eighteenth-century Enlightenment in Europe, which called for the development of technical and social knowledge for human betterment (Tawney 1921; Perkins 1989). In the classical professions such as medicine and law, authority over the respective field is granted by the state through a process of licensing designed to ensure both competency and a commitment to act responsibly in the interests of those served (Friedson 1986).

A profession, as such, is an applied field founded on more fundamental sources of knowledge. The practice of medicine, for example, is based on the sciences of anatomy and physiology. A professional is thus someone who applies this particular body of knowledge, skills, and techniques to the problems confronting his or her clients. Today, professional associations and their practitioners leave few economic and social issues untouched. One measure of the significance of this development is found in the commonplace fact that the word "professional" is now so prominent that it is often used more simply to identify good conduct or practices.

The professions are thus the direct and indirect product of a long line of developments, moving from the Enlightenment in Europe through the Progressive Era in the United States to the modern administrative state in both Europe and the US (Wagner 2006). In both parts of the world the professions emerged to deal with particular problems that relate to the application of knowledge to society, although the patterns have differed.

---

[2] Especially important here has been the path-breaking work of Michael Foucault, whose historical and sociological research has revealed the deep-rooted "disciplinary power" of expertise and its role in the shaping and guidance of modern society.

In Europe, the professions have evolved in close relation to the modern state and its institutions, often taking their identities from their service to these bodies. By contrast, they have developed in the US more as free standing bodies with a market relationship to their clients.

In continental Europe the professions grew up under the tutelage of the established institutions of church and state (MacDonald 1995: 66–99). As in the United States, modern European nations developed in response to both expanding economies and new state institutions. In both parts of the world scientific scholarship and professional expertise were embraced by the leading groups. But where the US has typically resisted the expansion of the state, European states have traditionally served as the carriers of collective purposes and values. In this respect, the state in Europe has a higher degree of relative autonomy than the American state. As such, European states have over centuries developed a core of institutions designed to deal with economic and social complexity. In the United States, this came only as late as the 1930, and even then in much weaker form. Since then, moreover, conservative groups have regularly sought to ensure that government remains weak.

From the late eighteenth century forward, European nations established new universities, or reoriented older ones to educate a new professional class: medical doctors, lawyers, religious pastors, career military officers, university professors, and civil servants; the latter group holding much higher status than their counterparts in the US. With great emphasis placed on higher education, typically elite education, the civil service in Germany, France, or Britain is widely considered a prestigious occupation and is sought after as a path to both social standing and economic security (MacDonald 1995). These public professions drew their authority more from the elite institutions and agencies that they served than to free standing associations and, as such, were "professions of office." Still today, professional civil servants in Europe tend to identify themselves with state institutions and the universities closely related to those institutions.

By the end of the Second World War, the contemporary professions had emerged in full blossom. Talcott Parsons (1968), the leading sociologist of the time, spoke of a "professional complex" as the guiding model of the new techno-industrial society. Indeed, he sought to redefine or characterize modern Western society in terms of professionalism rather than capitalism; a discussion to which we return. Somewhat later, Daniel Bell (1960) wrote of the "end of ideology," envisioning a new world in which the classic tensions between socialism and capitalism were beginning replaced by converging systems in which the central questions became technical rather than political. Later Bell wrote of the coming of post-industrial society which he described as a professional society. This was a society characterized as based on codified knowledge administered by professionals, who specialized in placing knowledge in larger applied contexts than do the scientists generating it.

The professions can be credited with fostering many important advances. About this there can be no doubt. Not only have they advanced the quality of life, they have been the carriers of particular social values. Because of the medical profession we live longer; because of the practice of law we can defend our basic political and social rights in court. Owing to the application of their skills for societal betterment, professionals have been the beneficiaries of high expectation and social trust on the part of the public. Professional practices, in short, have traditionally rested on a set of understandings about trust and good faith between the practitioners and the general citizenry. Where professions are formally licensed by the state, this compact may be quite explicit.

Despite their accomplishments, however, the professional experts have in recent decades confronted growing criticism (Rampton and Stauber 2001). This was especially the case in both popular and academic literatures in the 1980s and 1990s, although there is no sign that opinion has changed in the first decade of the new century. Often they have been accused of betraying their basic social responsibilities to society. Many complain that the professions have self-interestedly turned to earning money and perpetuating their own social status and power, a charge not taken lightly. Indeed, the classical professions, as licensed occupations, are legally accepted by governments and publics on the basis of their formal fiduciary responsibilities to protect and serve society at large. It is part of the bargain that grants them the power to practice in particular domains, medicine, law, architecture, and education being among the most important examples.

More specifically, the authority of professional expertise has been periodically challenged in the form of public protests against what is seen as self-serving and arrogant interventions in both public and private life. There is no shortage of examples to illustrate the point. They include concerns about chemical tests on unknowing citizens, doctors performing abortions, the genetic engineering of plants and animals, the irradiation of foods, the installation of hazardous waste incinerators, doctors denying their patients' wishes to die, professional educators busing children to distant neighborhoods, psychologists and social workers telling families how to raise their kids, lawyers helping corporations to hide excessive earnings through illegal tax schemes, accountants fixing the books of business firms, journalists uncritically reporting the information that government supplies to them, and more.

In the case of the science-related professions, some of this might be associated with a larger techno-pessimism in modern society. Polls, in fact, show a large percentage of the adult population in Western societies to be skeptical about the increasing embrace of high technology and the professional emphasis on "technological fixes" to pressing societal problems, opposition to genetically modified foods being one of the most recent examples (Murphy and Levidow 2006). The percentage is even higher in Europe than in the United States, as documented by shelves of books, documents, and reports. Although open protests have tended to occur only sporadically, surveys show a steady decline in the public's confidence in and respect for the professions and their practices. This underlying lack of confidence is one of the primary reasons why otherwise isolated reports of professional malfeasance can excite dramatic displays of moral outrage.

The degree of intrusion of professional influence in modern social and political life has led many to express concern about an emphasis on status and gain over social responsibility. While the professions have traditionally been considered to be "competent, dependable, accountable, trustworthy, honest and loyal," as Berube (1996) put it, they are today seen by many as "arrogant, exclusive, self-serving, money-grubbing, careerists—and they purchase their status by discrediting everybody else as 'amateurs'." Ehrenreich (1989) similarly finds the professions to have become more the self-serving monopolies of particular services than forces for social equality and human betterment. The elitist, nonegalitarian, and often manipulatory tendencies of such experts and their methodologies have been a major focus of conferences, intellectual debates, and media discussions (Kanigel 1988; Evetts *et al.* 2006). Not only are they accused of lacking solutions relevant to the diverse range of interests in society as a whole, they have been charged with using their professional authority and methods to buffer economic and political elites against challenges from below. Professional experts, in short, have been portrayed as perpetuating, if not creating, many of the social injustices plaguing modern Western societies (Wineman 1984; McNeil 1987; Illich 1989). Radical critics frequently use phrases like "tyranny of expertise" and "conspiracy against society" (Lieberman 1972; Illich 1989).

In the professional disciplines, such charges have, to be sure, generated a good deal of concern. Alternative or movement-oriented professionals have commonly spoke of a "crisis of the professions" (Withhorn 1984).

21

Critics typically attribute these failures to overly technical and hierarchal conceptions of theory and practice. In the professional schools, this political strife has often centered on perceived normative and epistemological limitations, giving rise to demands for social and political relevance, most commonly defined as the pursuit of value-oriented, humanistic, and critical approaches to theory and practice (Schoen 1983; Fischer and Forester 1993). This has laid the groundwork for slowly but gradually emerging alternative practices in the professions.

For most of the critics the problem can be attributed, in one way or another, to the narrow forms of technical specialization that characterize professional education and practice (Fischer 2003). Because of the growing specialization, professionals neither learn much about broader social and ethical implications of their occupations nor are they earnestly counseled to take them seriously. Education related to social equality, ethics, and human betterment, if it emerges at all, is itself typically compartmentalized as part of the curriculum and thus not seen as part of the central concerns of professional activities as a whole. As a kind of compulsory add-on, such instruction takes a backseat to other more immediate practical issues. Fallows (1989) found this basic neglect of social and ethical values to not only create social inefficiencies, but also to reproduce and stabilize inequalities among the various groups in society. One clear manifestation of this was witnessed during the deregulatory climate of the 1980s, when lawyers and doctors rejected proposals to offset basic inequalities. Lawyers objected to an American Bar Association reform proposal requiring them to offset basic inequalities by engaging in pro bono work for fixed numbers of hours with those poorly served or neglected by the profession. Physicians, during the same period, rejected requests that they stop referrals to medical facilities in which they hold financial interests (Brint 1994). For those still ascribing a social trust to professions a social trust, the professionals are "in danger of losing their soul" in what one writer described as a "race to the bottom" (Caplan 1993: A29)."

For this reason, scholars, social movement activists, and professional reformers have at various times called for the reconstruction of the professions. The challenge, as they have advanced it, is a return to social responsibility and public commitment. Too often, though, the approach has been in the form of a moral appeal, missing the underlying technical and structural features that impede such change. To better grasp the nature of these barriers we need to look more specifically at the origins of the idea of the professional as "social trustee" and its evolution.

From social responsibility to commerical practices

Professionalism, as an ideology and practice, has been advanced both in terms of technical skills and moral commitment. One the one hand, professions promise to engage in the competent exercise of skills based on complex, systematic knowledge obtained through formal training. On the other, they agree to be morally guided by an understanding of and commitment to socially accepted goals and the values upon which they rest. They also ask for the right to self-governance on the grounds that other groups are not qualified to judge either their knowledge and skills nor the exercise of their professional judgment. Professional activities, in short, are justified by the societal purposes to which they are put. The British historian R. H. Tawney (1921: 92) captured the thrust of this in these words: professional practitioners such as doctors "may grow rich; but the meaning of the profession, both for themselves and for the public, is not that they make money, but that they make health, or safety, or knowledge, or good government, or good law..."

This social commitment of the professions has its origins in an earlier sense of *noblesse oblige* assimilated from the English gentry, which was often resistant—if not hostile—to the profit-oriented mentality of the entrepreneurial classes. The emphasis was on moral character, cultivated judgment, and social trust (Rothblatt 1968). Although these ideals were to erode under the influence of free-market capitalism, the idea of the professional as a "social trustee" remained important into the early twentieth century (Brint 1994).

Stress on moral character and social virtue was clearly present in the early American colonies as well, largely a legacy of British professional practices. Character was closely identified with class standing and the professions were mainly practiced by gentlemen. A portrait of this gentleman is also found in de Tocqueville's (1969: 264–7) writings about America in the 1830s. Taking Daniel Webster to be a model of such public virtue, Tocqueville saw the lawyer as an important professional figure holding together a society otherwise tending toward social fragmentation.

At roughly the same time that Tocqueville would write about his observations, however, the social status of the professions was beginning to suffer serious setbacks (Sullivan 1995). During the period of Jacksonian democracy, the idea that professions spoke for—or even should speak for—the public good fell out of favor. Given the politics of the era, focused on the "common man," the legitimacy of the professions began to clash with the emerging values of both commercial entrepreneurship and populist understandings of democracy. Jacksonian politics unleashed a considerable amount of hostility toward the ideal of leadership based on professional knowledge and judgment. After Jackson's presidential election, public opinion even turned openly against professionalism and its emphasis on education and merit. Against this new sense of egalitarianism, supported by the both ordinary citizens and small business entrepreneurs, the professions became the symbols of privileged elites and thus a direct object of this politics. Instead of wealth and money-making, special privileges became the objects of hostility and educational credentials were taken to be a form of privilege. So virulent was the reaction that many states ended the practice of licensing the professions.

The political implications of the period were most obvious in the public service. They were captured in the famous slogan "to the victors go the spoils," which turned the civil service into a patronage system (van Riper 1958). In short, any citizen, it was argued, could do a government job and a constant turnover of political appointees worked to prevent an entrenched, privileged bureaucracy. Although "muckraking" journalists targeted this practice in their challenge to the political "boss system" that dominated urban government later in the century, they made little headway with their reform efforts until a disgruntled office seeker shot President James Garfield. The public shock accompanying the shooting opened the way and gave impetus to the modern system of civil service testing and appointment based on educations and merit.

During the same period, professions such as medicine and law were compelled to look for new organizational practices. The new model was to take a commercial form, or what has been called the "free professions" (Sullivan 1995). So successful had been the Jacksonians in identifying individual economic opportunity with democracy that when institutionalized credentials and professions began their comeback at the end of the century, their advocates would justify the reassertion in terms of their utility for national economic progress rather than social trusteeship. Whereas earlier professionals had been judged as genteel, even inclined to purism, this new stress on applied technical expertise in the name of economic efficiency found legitimacy in both American and British culture. It was especially the case in the pragmatic, problem-oriented society of the United States.

In contrast to social trustee professionalism, "expert professionalism" needed no sharp distinction from business enterprise, and it required less separation from the idea of offering services for profit. One aspect of the complex movement toward expert professionalism therefore involved a closer association between the major professions and business, along with the weakening of barriers to the pursuit of profit in competitive markets.

Professionalism in the progressive period: expertise as political ideology

Emphasizing technical expertise, the professions made a dramatic comeback in the latter part of the century, establishing themselves more and more on a national scale, especially in the United States. It is not that public responsibility or social trusteeship was dropped altogether, but it clearly took a backseat to an emphasis on technical expertise. By linking technical expertise to the impressive techno-industrial achievements of the time—from the spectacular constructions of modern engineering to the medical eradication of disease and the prolongation of life—the professions presented themselves as agents of the emerging industrial society (Wiebe 1967). Given that it was a period of considerable social chaos—resulting from vast immigration, and unregulated economic activity, the rapid emergence of the new and more monopolistic business corporation, and various social groups looking for protection against unregulated economic competition—the problematic societal consequences of the time led many to see the revitalization of technical expertise as a source of hope. In the context of an unruly, unregulated society, many social and political groups believed that the technical expertise of the professions could provide the basis for far-reaching societal reforms.

Indeed, professional advice and practices, particularly of a technical nature, were often at the forefront of the Progressive Movement's efforts to find solutions to the growing problems that accompanied the industrial era. Basic to this period of American politics, the movement sought to position its reform agenda between the new corporation and the state via technical knowledge and professional skills based on educational credentials. It advocated techniques that its members believed could be employed to make industry more technically efficient and at the same time the economy more socially just.

In conjunction with this acceptance of the new corporate form of economic activity, professionalization itself took on new organizational dimensions. More and more the professions shed their earlier free-standing occupational status and tied themselves to organizations and institutions, often themselves becoming more managerial. This reflected in no small measure the ascent of scientific management, which emerged as one of the hallmarks of the period. Influenced by the work of Frederick Winslow Taylor—the founder of scientific management and father of modern management studies more generally—efficiency became the reform gospel of the day (Hays 1964). Indeed, with assistance from movements such the Progressives, Taylorism spread throughout society. And as part of that phenomenon, the new organizational professionals often advanced themselves as experts in efficiency (Fischer 1990). Where many applied these techniques to private sector organizations, others in the new and emerging professions such as economics, social work, and public health applied their practices to public sector organizations. In the process, the rhetorical emphasis shifted from the man of knowledge and skill to the man who could apply the new techniques to get things done. It was, as Wiebe (1967) has argued, just the kind of orientation that the expanding techno-industrial order needed.

During this period, it is important to stress, the label of "profession" was extended beyond the traditional categories of medicine and law to new occupational groups. These new professions were more typically concerned with particular policy areas such as health, education, and social work. Described as the "weaker professions," they generally concerned themselves with activities carried out in public organizations. Because they combine professional knowledge with the organizational criteria of the agencies for which they worked, they are generally not as independent as the stronger professions of medicine and law. In time, though, the management of organizations, both public and private, was itself to be considered a professional activity (not to mention that more and more doctors and lawyers began to work for organizations).

Part of what facilitated the appearance of the new managerially oriented professions was the dramatic specialization to which the industrial division of labor gave rise. Tasks were increasingly defined in narrower, technical terms. Another part was the profound shift in the modern university, especially the American university, to accommodate this new understanding of the relation of knowledge to problem-solving (Bledstein 1976). Drawing eclectically on practices of British, French, and German universities, especially the later, the focus was on advancing scientific research and the training of expert personnel based on it. Whereas the earlier more traditional universities mainly tended to educate upper class students (with learning and the pursuit of knowledge being presented for its own sake), the emphasis in the newer institutions shifted increasingly to problem-oriented training and appealed to the newly emerging middle classes. As the professional disciplines featured this more job related course of study, the middle classes flocked to them, given the upward career potentials they offered.

In the course of this development, US universities began to establish a new model for professional schools based on a standardization of curricula. Especially important were the new schools for the organizational professions, such as business management, public administration, social work, and public health. With these educational developments the professional orientation moved to center stage by mid-century. As Sullivan (1995: 58) puts it, "the new middle class of educated 'knowledge workers' . . . was on the road to become a growing, confident, and successful sector of society, in particular more to the national system rather than local communities." In this later respect, professionals become primary actors in this twentieth-century story, serving as bridges between the local communities and the national system—that is, as chief agents through which cosmopolitan values and practices would penetrate local life (ibid.: 60).

In the process, civic social responsibility increasingly became defined as making the capitalist system more fair and just. Given that social and economic problems abounded in nearly every sphere of American society, this concern was scarcely dismissed as capitalist ideology. But it was technocratic expertise rather than social engagement per se that was to show the way.[3] The organization and guidance of capitalism was to be made more managerial—then referred to as the "managerial revolution"—with management itself joining the ranks of the professions. The major institutional step designed to bring about this new commitment was the emerging graduate business school. The new professional managers would learn to combine scientific techniques with a new corporate social responsibility to society.

But not all of the emphasis was on the industrial system. Other Progressives emphasized public responsibility by stressing the social uplift of the lower classes, particularly through education (Haber 1964). Although they are best known for their attacks on corrupt urban political machines and their uneducated immigrant supporters, they did not neglect the poor and down trodden. In addition to their new forms of technocratic governance, less than democratic in theory and practice, they sought to uplift the great unwashed by imbuing them with education. Often overlooked is the fact that the Progressive conception of public responsibility rested on a generally paternalistic understanding of service. In view of the class

---

[3] Technocratic expertise refers to an emphasis or reliance on technical knowledge as basis for decisionmaking and governance (Fischer 1990).

struggle between the upper and middle classes against the lower classes that underlaid Progressive politics, the reformers sought to inculcate the poor with the values of the educated classes.

One of the most famous of the projects dedicated to this was the Settlement House movement, which sought to bring the middle and working classes together both socially and culturally. Settlement house social workers organized a range of uplifting educational and cultural activities, but rhetoric aside, democracy per se as such was not one of them. It is not a point that went unnoticed. Jane Addams, the famous settlement house leader and ardent advocate of democracy, expressed concern about the paternalistic attitudes that were behind the activities of many settlement houses (Knight 2006).

Without denying the value of many of these efforts, as she made clear, one of the regrettable results was more to show the enterprising poor how to escape the slums rather than deal with the problems of their urban environments per se. In this sense, civic-oriented professionalism under the influence of the Progressives accommodated itself to the values of dominant social and political elites.

Addams's friend and fellow reformer, John Dewey, also shared these concerns. Looking beyond the technocratic reforms of the period, Dewey called for new participatory forms of democratic governance. Indeed, he was worried more generally that the newly emerging technological society posed a serious threat to the very future possibility of a democratic public. He asked how the public could deal with the social and organizational complexities presented by a highly differentiated, technologically-driven society? Could citizens be adequately informed in such a social system? Could they participate in policy decision-making so obviously dependent on the knowledge of experts? The emerging society, increasingly defined as a mass society governed by economic and political elites, offered less and less political space for the individual citizen in the policy process. Moreover, the newly developing communications technologies all too easily facilitated political demagoguery, as made clear by the rise of European fascism.

The answer for Dewey was to rethink professional expertise, in particular that of the social scientists, educators, and journalists. As a counter to these trends, he called on them to do more than provide information for public decision-making and problem-solving. Beyond their traditional tasks, these professionals should facilitate democratic deliberation and public learning. A democratic society, he argued, required a new cooperative division of labor between experts and citizens. On the technical front, experts would empirically identify basic social needs and problems, as well as alternative solutions to address them. On the political front, citizens would democratically establish an agenda for dealing with these issues. To integrate the two processes, Dewey called for improvements in the methods and conditions of debate, discussion, and persuasion. The experts would have a special role in such deliberation, but it would take a different form. Instead of only rendering judgments, they would analyze and interpret them for the public. If experts, acting as teachers and inter-preters, could decipher the technological world for citizens in ways that enabled them to make intelligent political judgments, the constitutional provisions designed to advance public over selfish interests could function as originally conceived.

The Progressive Movement died out after the First World War. But many of the ideas advanced by its advocates and the professionals to whom they had turned lived on and became important theoretical and political foundations of professionalism in subsequent decades. Among them, though, were neither Addams's emphasis on social commitment nor Dewey's call for participatory democracy. Instead the focus of the profes-sional became increasingly technical. By the end of the Second World War, as Brint (1994) has pointed out, the idea of the professions as a status category became more and more disconnected from functions perceived to be central to the public welfare and more exclusively connected to the idea of expert knowledge. And, in just this regard, one of the most influ-ential professional orientations today is that of the school of manage-ment, now prominently featured in the British and European academic landscape as well. Indeed, the phenomenon is global in nature; such schools, largely patterned after the American model, are to be found everywhere. Only in more recent times, in many ways thanks to the theorists of deliberative democracy, has Dewey's contribution been revit-alized, a point to which we return in later chapters.

Post-industrial information society: Professionalism as technostructure

The experts of the Roosevelt New Deal of the 1930s, the so-called "Brain Trust," played a major role in developing the welfare-regulatory system in the United States, a weaker form of that which was emerging in Britain as well (thanks to the Labor Government of that same period). Even more important during the 1940s was the role of scientists and other professionals in the execution of the Second World War. These developments, taken together, gave shape to a new techno-industrial society which the leading sociologists in the 1950s and 1960s would depict as governed primarily by the professions. The professions had emerged as the dominant social institution; they were now central to the new techno-industrial society.

During the postwar years, there was a marked turn toward technocratic thinking among professionals. Besides Bell's (1960) "end of ideology," Galbraith (1967) identified the "technostructure" of professional experts as increasingly guiding the corporation and the state. Price (1965) saw the rise of a "Scientific Estate" as posing worrisome political concerns for democratic governance, although on balance he was supportive of the development. Eulau (1977) spoke of the "skills revolution" giving rise to a "Consultative Commonwealth," in which professional expertise would serve as the "solvent" for the political and social divisions of the new order. As he put it, reliance on professionals brings new "norms and modes of conduct" that become "acknowledged components of individual and collective choice-making at the level of both policy and administration." These writers represent just a few of the theorists who have focused on the increasing importance of professional expertise in the Western postindustrial or information society.

Such ideas, moreover, did not just appear in the academic literature. They were also given expressions by leading politicians of the time. One of the most celebrated statements was a speech by President John Kennedy at Yale University. Kennedy argued that the tasks of government had transcended the more limited concerns of the traditional party orientations, namely liberalism and conservatism. As he put it, "the fact of the matter is most of the problems . . . that we now face are technical problems . . ." (Kennedy 1963). Another influential political writer at the time spoke of the "professionalization of reform" (Moynihan 1965). Indeed, this was the description applied to the President Johnson's "Great Society" of the 1960s, when policy professionals were generating and packaging the influential ideas that constituted the program of the Democratic Party.

If professionalism was celebrated during these years, its leading enthusiast was Talcott Parsons (1968), the dominant figure in sociology at the time. Parsons, as we already saw, spoke effusively of a "professional complex" guiding modern society. For him, the defining feature of the new postwar society was a shift from capitalism to professionalism. The latter, he argued, would work to alleviate the legitimacy problems confronting the economic corporation and the capitalist class. Toward this end, he sought to re-emphasize the moral component of professionalism, although in the service of a particular economic formation. Indeed, Parsons argued that managerial capitalism was converging with professionalism. Both, he wrote, accepted the central importance of technical efficiency within relatively well-defined spheres of authority and competence; both were increasingly governed by general principles based on impersonal rules. As such, business was largely adopting the practices of professionalism, which was serving to soften—others would say conceal—business's overriding commitment to profit. By assimilating business to the "collectivity-centeredness" of the professions, and the social responsibility that accompanied it, Parsons sought to provide a new legitimacy for the older established capitalist business class.

Parsons' conception of the professions' rigorous positivist science and codified knowledge was thus combined with a return moral character. Although his emphasis on moral character reads more like a normative prescription than an empirical description of professional practices, he saw the professional orientation giving rise to managerial social responsibility, a theme often intoned as well in the business literature of the time. Leading economics and business professors wrote extensively about the newly emerging corporation guided by socially responsible managers (Mason 1964). Parsons thus painted a picture of a new national elite drawn from a reoriented managerial business class, morally uplifted by and aligned with the professional classes generally. At the same time, the new class would take shape within a framework of concerns and commitments that broadly supported the imperatives of a managerially-oriented business society. While still bound by respect toward the established business class, the new professional-managerial class was portrayed as focused primarily on helping to expand the productivity of society rather than enhancing its own income. In short, the floundering legitimacy of the old business class was to be rejuvenated by uniting it with the knowledge and practices of the new class, that is by professionalizing it.

At best, though, this was a compromise between the newer claims of the professions and the more traditional ones of the old business elites. Gouldner (1979) described it as a backward looking compromise based on the assumption that the old class still had a future, and that its problem was one of legitimacy. Independent of the fate of the old class, Gouldner was correct to see Parson's theory as a professional ideology glossing over the professionals own self-seeking character as a status group with vested interests, thus ideologically romanticizing both the old and new classes. Moreover, Gouldner argued that Parsons ignored the tensions between the old and new classes and the ways in which the new class ideology of professionalism tacitly subverts old class legitimacy by grounding itself in a moral collective orientation, scientific knowledge and problem-solving skills. Missing was the profit-pursuing egoism of the old class.

By the late 1960s, however, the debate took another turn with the rise of the student movements across elite universities in the United States and Europe. While Parsons was busy lecturing on the stabilizing role of the university system in American society, the students at many of these very universities were taking over their administrative offices and demanding social change. Fundamental to their critique was the kind of narrow, career-oriented training offered by the professional schools. For many students, the critique represented an articulation of their own personal experiences and more than a few of them turned to social movements and other projects dedicated to rethinking the role of knowledge and the practices of professional expertise. In doing so, they emphasized the values of social equality and political democracy over the instrumental rationality and organizational imperatives of the techno-industrial system for which they were otherwise being trained to serve. It was an attitudinal shift that many of them brought into the professions themselves.

Activist professionals: Advocacy and deprofessionalization

In the latter part of the 1960s, and into the 1970s, there were an array of efforts on the part of activist professionals to work out alternative models of practice aimed more specifically at promoting social justice and democratic participation, particularly among the poor. Many of them were products of the social turmoil of the period, having been radicalized by the protest movements on university campuses. Those who entered one of the professions often brought their political concerns to the workplace, the result of which was a blossoming of activism within the various fields. While there were differing approaches to activism in the various professions, these efforts were particularly prominent in the fields of medicine, law, public health, urban planning, education, and social work. Many young professionals in these fields, affected by the social activism of the day—the civil rights movement, the anti-Vietnam War struggle, the woman's movement, and environmentalism—became political spokespersons for the poor and disadvantaged minority groups. In some cases medical doctors joined hospital picket lines, lawyers got themselves arrested, social workers helped unions organize disruptive strikes, and urban planners assisted radical community activists, all activities otherwise seen as unbecoming to the members of the professions.

Organizations such as Health/Pac, the Lawyers' Guild, Planners for Equal Opportunity, and the Planners Network challenged the standard models of professional practices, particularly the emphasis on personal detachment, social status, and financial gain. Basic, in this regard, was a critique of the narrow focus on technical knowledge, purported to be value-neutral. The professions were criticized as impediments to progressive social change. In response, various universities set up curricular activities that directly and indirectly supported and advanced these new orientations. Law Schools, for example, established urban legal clinics that offered students opportunities to gain experience working with the poor and underprivileged.

It was a period defined in part by the redefinition of services as rights, by demands for community participation, local control, and efforts to radically transform the delivery and outcomes of social and medical services (Hoffman 1989). A representative statement from a California health project asserted that "the responsibility of the health professional goes beyond the provision of health services to political action: to obtain and insure the right to adequate health care for all members of the society; to provide programmes which extend adequate health care; to recognize and oppose those aspects of society which prevent provision of adequate health care; to eliminate those conditions which destroy life and health" (cited in Hoffman 1989: 47). The free clinic movement was offered as the radical health alternative.

From within the ranks of the professions, both practitioners and academics attempted to bring about change by exhorting their colleagues to examine the ways their practices contributed to the inequalities of the larger social system of which they themselves were a part. Toward this end, they adopted an advocacy role. As Davidoff (1965) contended, the increasing movement toward advocacy planning in the name of poor people was an important advance in extending the planning process to include those previously unrepresented. They sought, as such, to incorporate the poor into the market of services by giving technical aid. Some argued for empowering the community by transferring professional knowledge to the citizens themselves. Beyond teaching people how to read maps, planners needed to help citizens "overcome the awe of professionalism, and develop the ability to question 'professional advice' and demand relevant explanations in place of technical language, and responsiveness from government agencies" (cited in Hoffman 1989: 83). Other pressed their professional establishments—in particular schools of professional education and national associations—to fulfill their stated commitments to service.

Beyond the radicalism of the period, these professional challenges were driven by postwar federal interventions in professional training, research, and service delivery that generated contradictions in the functions and practices of the professions. Of particular importance were the interventions triggered by the anti-poverty programs of the 1960s. Prior to this period, the professions were sometimes accused of class bias, racist practices, and self-interest. But the expansion of professional services as part of the welfare state required turning many of the victims of these practices into clients. In the process, confrontations with low-income and minority groups became difficult to avoid. In so far as unequal treatment was structurally built into professional practices, these new associations created external demands for change and, at the same time, dissent within professionals on the part of the newly minted activist professionals (Hoffman 1989).

In response to the War on Poverty many young doctors demanded better medical care and service for their patients. Their legal counterparts set up law clinics to help people fight for their rights, some of them working out a new "critical legal theory." Radicalized city planners sought to help the poor revitalize their ghetto neighborhoods with the assistance of federal monies such as those provided for by the Model Cities program. Teachers developed innovative programs to help disadvantaged urban children cope with the problems of the ghetto. Social workers explored new ways of dealing with urban crime and delinquency. And so on. Such efforts often involved a mix of alternative services, public demonstrations, and other direct political activities.

An important part of this orientation was an empowerment strategy that emphasized process as much as outcomes. Professionals were being criticized as bureaucratic actors working in agencies that served the dominant interests of an unequal society. Professionalism, in the process, came to be seen as part of a system of dominance and dependence; it was the culprit and deprofessionalization was seen to be the solution. In this view, the problem confronting the poor and minorities was a not lack of experts and services, but rather the dysfunctional, inhibiting power of the professional bureaucracies that were established to provide them. The alternative role of the activist was to mobilize these client communities by transferring expertise in ways that assisted them in taking control over their own affairs. Some spoke of democratizing service delivery.

Connected to this strategy was a radical critique of society designed to inform strategies for changing the economic and political requirements of a capitalist society. The activist solution was to create a political movement for system-wide change. In some cases, it involved workplace organizing; in others it involved creating an intellectual cadre that worked to demystify and politically educate workers and clients. Particularly important was an effort to make transparent the technocratic character of the knowledge claims advanced by traditional professional approaches. The technical knowledge base of the various professions was portrayed as ideological; its applications were described as supporting—wittingly or unwittingly—the existing political-economic system seen to be responsible for the problems in need of amelioration.

Arguing that the poor and disadvantaged needed better and more equitable services, the activists saw the issue to be more a matter of sociopolitical orientation than the mainstream emphasis on technical knowledge and practices per se. Viewing professional knowledge itself as part of the problem, as Hoffman (1989) explains, they depicted it as a constraint on their efforts to address the issues posed by inequality. The problem, they argued, was lodged in the institutional and societal arrangements that both defined and managed these problems. Not only did technical knowledge fail to address these structural issues, even worse, it served and supported them—namely, the institutions of the very system that was the problem. As they began to more directly engage in efforts to change the social system itself, they thus attacked the knowledge bases of their own professional associations, accusing their members at the same time of adopting an overly narrow and often self-serving view of the problems of their clients. They were, in short, roundly chastised for advancing their own professional interests over the needs of those they were supposed to be helping.

In taking this political stance, the activists increasingly adopted the role of client advocates and, in many cases, community organizers. This, however, proved to be more problematic for this new cadre of professionals than it first appeared. It wasn't so much that they had difficulties developing the critique, but rather that it generated unanticipated consequences. The effort to weaken or transform the professions, in short, proved to be self-limiting. The undermining of the image and quality of professional knowledge claims worked unexpectedly to weaken their own base of authority. They discovered that dismissing their specialized knowledge tended to undercut their own status and legitimacy with the communities they sought to assist. As it turned out, the communities wanted the technical knowledge and were less interested in having outside groups advocate their causes for them (Hoffman 1989).

This resulted in a precarious position that was to ultimately fail. On the one hand, members of the community started to view these professional activists as emerging political leaders seeking to intervene in struggles that belonged to the community. Unexpectedly, many local leaders argued that what they needed was the technical advice of the professional, rather than a new set of activists. They often defined the problem in terms of power and decision-making. In this view, the activists were seen as outsiders seeking to assume a political role that was unwanted. Community leaders wanted medical treatment and representation in the courtroom for local residences, but preferred that they themselves made their own social and political decisions. At the same time, they were being roundly denounced by their professional associations for criticizing the technical knowledge and practices of the field, the very things that otherwise would give them standing in the community. This left them adrift in a kind of no-man's land. Without the claim that they had important professional skills to bring to bear on community problem solving, and being rejected by professional associations, they lost their basis of legitimate authority. Without it, they were just another set of political activists seen to be competing with the communities own political activists.

Working within the system: Civic renewal, health, and environment

Activist professionalism, as such, died out. The reasons are various, but clearly an important one was the tensions between the communities and the activist professionals. Also important, the monies that made such activities possible began to dry up with the changing political climate beginning in the 1970s, a process that accelerated through the 1980s. As conservative governments assumed power, they quickly shut off these sources of funds and called for more traditional political and technocratic approaches to governance. This is not to say that there were no more alternative projects, but those who organized them tended to be less strident, seeking more moderately to draw lessons from the past in developing new alternatives. In the process, the focus of a new breed of civic activists also tended to shift away from advocacy and an emphasis on social equality to democratic participation and deliberation on the part of the citizens themselves.

36

While radical activists still exist in the professions, their activities are today a marginal endeavor in the larger picture. There are, however, a number of interrelated experiences that suggest that if or when another wave of such commitment comes back, it will be able to draw on a variety of collaborative experiences that could contribute to revitalizing a publicly oriented set of professional practices. Among the most important of these efforts have been the movements in civic renewal during the 1990, especially in community health, environmentalism, and journalism. As civically oriented journalists have developed the most elaborate, self-conscious theory and practice for public engagement, we take their activities separately in the next section.

The civic renewal movement has in large part emerged from citizens initiatives, although professional assistance has often facilitated their activities. This new relationship between citizens and experts has emerged from a more sober assessment of the earlier radical experiences of the 1960s and 1970s. Indeed, Sirianni and Friedland (2001) show this to be the result of a broadly gauged social learning process involving groups across the country based on the collection, interpretation, and assimilation of successes and failures. This social assessment and the political knowledge drawn from it, as they show, have given rise in various ways to a new civic oriented movement. Shedding much of the radical activism of the earlier period, the emphasis shifted to a more cautious but yet innovative strategy of building *within* the system. Absent is the more explicit emphasis on societal transformation; in its place the basic self-propagated values of the system are stressed, democracy in particular. Driven more by the middle classes than the poor and their leaders, social equity is still an issue but the focus has shifted more to citizen engagement. Participatory democracy is still the goal, but it is no longer *radical* participatory democracy. Now it is much more closely geared to the specific tasks of community-building. As such, the movement bases its legitimacy on its effort to fulfill the political system's own unfulfilled commitments to local self-governance. In this sense, its advantages are also its limitations. Without denigrating these efforts, they focus more on reforming liberal capitalist democracy rather than changing it in more fundamental ways, to which we return later in the book.[4]

---

[4] This does not always mean that these newer activists have a less critical view of capitalist democracy. Some would rather emphasize a different theory and strategy for achieving more fundamental changes. Rather than radically confronting the institutions, as they argue, they seek change through them.

The number of activities across the country, many sponsored by major nonprofit foundations, are too numerous to discuss in any systematic way. But it is important to take note of some of these innovations in community development, health, and environmental protection. In community development, the Community Development Corporations of the 1980s and 1990 built on lessons from the Federal Community Action and Model Cities programs of the 1960s, which emphasized "maximum feasible participation" and facilitated much of the advocacy professionalism in urban planning during that period. As Sirianni and Friedland explain (2001), it became clear in the 1970s and 1980s that the knowledge base for policy to promote the development of social capital and community problem-solving was poorly developed. Protest politics and radical community participation, in short, were not enough, a realization that led to a period of learning and capacity building. Although the federal government had withdrawn much of its money, the period saw many new collaborative efforts to rethink old strategies and to innovate new ones, thanks in significant part to philanthropic organizations that stepped in to supply resources. Just to mention a few of the kinds of new programs that emerged, John Kretzmann and John McKnight (1993) at Northwestern University developed an "assets–based approach" that offered a broad inventory of effective practices, along with an institute to assist communities in identifying their resources. Kenneth Reardon (1997), then at the University of Illinois, forged cooperative relationships between the planners at the university and community members in East St. Louis in what came to be a model for new forms of cooperative community development. Norman Krumholz, former director of the Cleveland Planning Commission and later president of the American Planning Association, developed and locally introduced an innovative model of "equity planning" based on trust building strategies among community groups, political officials, and agency planners (Krumholz and Clavel 1994). Many similar activities were supported by nonprofit foundations such as the Pew Charitable Trusts, particularly by the foundation's program for "Partners in Civic Change" (Sirianni and Friedland 2001).

Community health also experienced dramatic changes over the subsequent decades (Sardell 1988). Moving away from the medical activism of the 1960s, community groups and health networks generated a range of participatory innovations, organized around community health centers delivering medical care for the poor. Emerging from the Community Action Program of the 1960s, federally funded Health System Agencies promoted citizen participation in health planning in communities across the US. The Health Decisions movement in Oregon, for example, institutionalized civic deliberation about basic health values before the practice spread to other states; and the healthy communities movement, emphasized participation and self-help approaches in areas such as AIDS prevention, disability, woman's health, and independent living for the elderly (Sirianni and Friedland 2001). Although there are numerous differences among these programs, they have typically brought together community members and professionals to deliberate and plan health decisions. In one health community initiative, for instance, health practitioners identify and develop leaders from the community who can define their own problems, assume ownership of strategies, including coalition building, policy and media advocacy. According to one official programmatic statement, "In many ways the practitioner's function is to produce community organizers." It is "not to 'do', but to 'enable.'" Health professionals "serve as facilitators while the community does the work." As Sirianni and Friedland (2001: 170) sum up their investigation of these efforts, they involve "a health reform process that educates citizens . . . as well as health care professionals and nonprofessional employees who will collaborate in building healthy communities." These sustained public discussions help citizens learn about "the social determinants of health, the limits of medicine, and the deeper civic, cultural, and religious traditions and assets that can be mobilized through shared public work." It challenges them to move beyond a narrow consumer orientation to medical care.

In environmental protection "civic environmentalism" emerged as a project to bring together citizens and experts to monitor environmental matters at the community level (John 1994). Combined with the "environmental justice" movement, originated in black and minority communities, the success of such efforts convinced the US Environmental Protection Agency to establish an office of community liaison that sponsors similar projects across the country (Foreman 1998). In many of these projects citizens and professional experts work together to monitor particular levels of degradation, including watersheds, environmental habitats of diverse species, forest protection, and toxic wastes. Especially important in the case of toxic hazards has been the development and use of "popular epidemiology." In this approach citizens learn to do their own research in the areas in which they live. With the assistance of trained scientists, they design research strategies, collect data through a variety of methods, make the results known, and discuss them in public fora (Brown 1990).

We find in these illustrations a more system-oriented approach, working with the institutions rather than challenging them directly as was the case in the 1960s. Professionals and their skills are involved but they are usually not *the* driving force. These efforts emerge more typically from community groups, which seek to draw on professional skills as needed. In a sense, this corresponds to earlier community demands, although the transition was scarcely smooth. If local citizens were to learn to get more involved in the renewal of their own communities, a good deal of that has taken place. The professionals are now there as facilitators and educators assisting them along the way. But here again, this does not involve all professionals. It is mainly the work of a smaller number who recognize the need for social change and have committed themselves out of a sense of civic responsibility.

These three sketches scarcely exhaust the discussion of new civic activities involving professionals. To this list we can add the efforts on the part of lawyers and psychologists to develop alternative dispute resolution procedures, a restorative justice movement innovated by criminal justice professionals, deliberative consensus conferences and citizens juries designed by policy oriented social scientists, deliberative polling developed by political scientists, and the bioethics movement by applied ethicists (some of which we return to in following chapters). But most important for present purposes is public journalism, which has gone furthest to offer both a theory and practice for democratic professionalism. For this reason, we single out public or civic journalism (depending whose terminology one uses) for a somewhat more detailed discussion in the next section.

Public journalism and social responsibility: Facilitating citizen engagement and public deliberation

An especially important professional commitment to social responsibility in recent years has been the public or civic journalism movement (Sirianni and Friedland 2001; Haas 2007). Advanced by reform-oriented journalists, the movement represents one of the most impressive attempts by professionals to work cooperatively with citizens, in this case readers, listeners, and viewers. Beginning with a controversial set of experiments in the early 1990s, some of which were funded by the Pew and Kettering foundations, public journalism has been a part of the activities of many newspapers, radio, and television stations an effort to establish a more democratic relationship with their publics. Practiced by journalist in numerous parts of the US and in other places around the world, its practitioners have developed both a theory and set of practices aimed at facilitating citizen engagement and public deliberation (Schaffer and Miller 1995; Friedland and Nichols 2002).

In terms of theory, they advance the view that engagement should be part of the journalist's role in a democratic society (Rosen 2001). At its core is the belief that journalists have a responsibility to public life—a special obligation that extends beyond just reporting the factual news (Merritt 1998). Journalism and democracy are seen to function at best when the media offer more than a portrait of the dominant culture and the issues as its representatives define them. When citizens are encouraged and assisted to move beyond political consumers of the news, it is argued, they can become full-scale participants in political society (Public Journalist Network, http://pjnet.org). Journalism, in this view, has a strong impact on how citizens see themselves and their environment, which, in turn, significantly influences whether or not they engage in the kinds of civic life essential to a democratic society. Public journalists, in short, reject the idea that their readers are mere audience in political and social processes and seek to help them find ways to become active citizens. The press should transformatively engage their readers through spirited engagement of the civic issues that influence their own lives. As part of an effort to increase a community's social capital, readers and other community members are engaged as cooperative participants in the gathering and reporting of the news.

Newspapers and their journalists, as Perry (2003) writes, are thus situated "as activist participants in community life, rather than detached spectators." In the process, the newspaper or television becomes a forum for collaborative discussion and debate of community issues and problems, which sometimes take place as a town meeting in places like the community center or local library. Some see this public journalism partnership as an adversarial form of activism in which journalists drop their independence to put forth the specific interests of the community (Hoyt 1995). This is surely true in many cases, but the specific interests are in large part those expressed by the citizens with whom they engage.

Although many traditional journalists have accused public journalists of violating the established canons of objective reporting, they reply that their emphasis on lay participation and public involvement strengthens rather than weakens objectivity and fairness. They contend, in this regard, that the social trustee model of professionalism no longer works when journalists become pressured or driven by market forces. Where journalism becomes a business, largely the standard model today, journalists are compelled to trade the public interest for the narrower concerns of the media owners and the business community. Under such circumstances traditional understandings of objectivity and independence only prove to be a guise for bias. (Typically they point to the very narrow framing of political issues in US journalism, particularly in the so-called "horse-race" coverage of American electoral politics that often takes the form of public entertainment.) The movement, so argue public journalists, is an effort to extend the news and the discussion of it to include a wider range of social and political interests in an effort to reintroduce objectivity and fairness.

With regard to specific practices, public journalism begins with a process of "public listening" (Charity 1995). The approach is to listen to the issues and concerns on the minds of the community members with whom they are working. Carried out through collaborative discussions to elicit the problems confronting the community, what the issues and options are, and how people think they might be dealt with, these "community conversations" involve different journalists focusing on different issues. As a rule, the meeting times and lists of events are published in advance in an effort to help a large number of participants make plans for attending.

The aim of this practice is related to a second task of civic education (Dzur 2008). The goal here, as Charity (1995: 2) puts it, is "to make it as easy as possible for citizens to make intelligent decisions about public affairs and to get them carried out." Toward this end, public journalists also seek to move beyond the immediacy of the current news cycle and prepare longer stories that provide more depth and insight into the issues at hand. Here, as Dzur (2008: 159) writes, such journalists "are not responding to the immediate wants of their readers so much as what the journalist consider to be their readers' long-term interests as citizens." Both of these practices, listening and civic education, provide the substantive context for public deliberation.

Public deliberation, the most controversial aspect of this new journalistic role, is designed stimulate civic engagement. The basic task is to provide fora in which members of the community can deliberate and debate the problems and solutions identified during the public listening phase. In the process, the journalist serves as moderator and catalyst for the exchanges. One the one hand, the role of the moderator is to give citizens an unmediated form in which ordinary citizens can meet and talk about their own views in their own vernaculars. On the other, the role of catalyst is to stimulate informed discussions. As Rosen (1996: 55) writes, when public journalists convene community meetings they "are to act not merely as facilitators but as cultivators as of civic dialogue," which he defines as holding the participants "to a respectable standard of discourse." It should be "a dialogue that can bring together citizens across economic and social divisions in an effort to find and combine common interests."

For some, this worrisomely means that journalists can end up providing their readers and viewers with the news that they themselves think the citizen should know. A tension can arise here, as Dzur (2008: 243) points out, between the role of moderating a community forum and informing the participants about both the important issues and the ways they should talk about them. The moderator's role "assumes that citizens voices must be heard along with official and expert voices" while the catalyst role "assumes that these voices must be informed and trained." This later role can provide a fair amount of guidance, sometimes into the considerations of what is important and what is not. Dzur (2008: 160) thus sees the need for establishing "standards of public engagement to determine what projects are suitable for the organizational capacity of news firms and the role of the journalist in a democracy." Indeed, the establishment of such standards of engagement would seem to be a fundamental task for democratic professionalism generally. Public journalists have so far tended to avoid this issue, mainly arguing that their practices are still evolving and that it is too early in the experimental stages to nail down specific methods and procedures. The position is understandable, but it is a task that should begin to make its way onto the agenda.

At this point, it is fair to judge these methods and practices of public journalists as an exemplary illustration of a profession engaging its public more democratically. Nothing would seem to come closer to the kind of professional reorientation that Dewey called for in the early decades of the twentieth century, namely the professional as facilitator of public learning and democratic deliberation.[5] Beyond helping citizens to engage the issues, however, one further question remains. Some see the need to democratize the professions themselves. Speaking of "democratic professionalism," they seek to take the project further—indeed, a dramatic step further—by calling for the democratization of the practices through which professionals go about assisting their clients. Can professionals, for

[5] It should be noted that after the several major US news syndicates that gave public journalism it's major push discontinued their support, the practice is no longer as extensive in the country as it was. This, however, in ways undercuts the validity of the model and the theory on which is based.

example, democratize their own relationship to citizens and what would be the practical consequences? Should they do it? And if so, what would this involve? We turn to this question in the final section of the chapter.

Democratizing professional expertise?

When we speak of a new democratic role for the professions in a democratic society, how then should we understand the relationship? Are we talking mainly about a more elaborate effort on the part of professionals in helping citizens participate in the decisions that affect their lives? Or are we speaking even more fundamentally about democratizing professional expertise as well (Liberatore and Functowicz 2003)? More recently, in this regard, Dzur (2008) has called for a new "democratic professionalism."

This work shies away from calling for the democratization of the professions. It does so for a number of reasons related to the nature of the professions themselves. For one thing, if the professions were to contribute more directly to democratic participation, public deliberation in particular, this would only involve one aspect of what the professions do. Professions provide a wide range of services that have little to do with democracy, from diagnosing illnesses, assessing the durability of physical infrastructure, and advising clients in personal matters, and the like. Such activities do not require public participation and would not be, most would argue, the better for it. The term "democratic professionalism" thus seems inappropriate for professionalism generally. Others, of course, will argue that we don't live in a participatory society. This criticism, while valid, is less problematic, as the goal is to help bring about a more participatory society. Another argument, one with more traction, has to do with establishing a special relationship between the professions and democracy generally. Why, many will ask, should professionals have such a role in something that belongs to everyone?

While the democratization of the professions can sound attractive from the perspective of participatory democratic theory, it tends to redefine professional activities in terms of a theory rather removed from traditional understandings of professional functions. Given that many professional tasks do not lend themselves to democratic practices, Sullivan's (1995; 2004) concept of 'civic professionalism' would seem more appropriate. In his conceptualization, emphasis is placed on public responsibility than a specific understanding of democracy. As such, it is more geared to serving the public good than facilitating political participation per se. In this regard, it nicely resonates with the civic renewal movement. It includes democratic participation, but is not limited to it. As a public good, participation stands alone side of other public values, social justice in particular.

In the view adopted here, a strong democracy would not require participatory discussion of every issue. But it should include open deliberation about which decisions should be dealt with democratically and which need not. No decision would be taken for once and all. Every decision not to debate an issue could be reopened whenever those affected deem that to be appropriate. In significant part, the decision to deliberate or delegate would depend on the nature of the issue or problem itself. In some cases, traditional patterns of expertise may be fully consistent with the nature of particular forms of problem-solving. In other cases, problem-solving might be collaborative but not altogether democratic. Recognizing these aspects of problem-solving would seem to increase the chances that professionals might take an interest in more democratic approaches to dealing with their respective problems. Toward this end, democratic deliberation is understood here to be one—but only one—of the important practices—involved in a more general task of reconstructing the public responsibilities of the professions, which would also include such things as assisting the poor with health care, financial assistance, and legal services. In the case of many client-oriented practices, this would involve deliberative consultations, but not necessarily be democratic per se. In the public realm, it would be mainly restricted to those aspects of their respective professional practices that directly affect the public generally, matters affecting public policy. From this perspective, as an effort to facilitated democratic practices, expertise would be judged as politically legitimate when it supplied the full range of participant s clear and transparent advice open to discussion.[6]

Given that most professionals are not well-suited by either training or task orientations to carry out public deliberation, there is a need for a more specialized role for such public deliberative practices. In view of the importance of the objective for a democratic society, it makes little sense to focus the role on professions that actually have little time—and probably interest—in carrying it out. This would most likely insure the failure of such a project from the outset. For this reason, the approach follows

---

[6] To use Jasanoff's (2003: 160) words, expertise would be legitimate when carried out in a way "that makes clear its contingent, negotiated character," leaving "open the door to critical discussion."

Dewey's lead and seeks to establish a new professional role for the social scientist, including social-scientific specializations such as urban planning, public health, public administration, social work, education, and journalism, given their direct relation to public discourse. This would not rule out the possibility of other professions participating in this task. But when it comes to facilitating public deliberation, the professional practices of social-scientific groups seem to be more suited to the kinds of activities involved.

This is not to suggest that the social sciences have thus far had a particularly good record in facilitating democracy. Although better equipped to deal with this role than are doctors, lawyers, or architects, the mainstream social sciences have themselves not been that sympathetic to a strong conception of democracy. By and large, they have tended to support a more elitist form of democracy. It is important, in this regard, to be clear that the task is to create a new role. For this reason, the role needs to become a research topic unto itself. Such research has to begin with the fact that advanced Western countries such as the United States, Britain, France, or Germany are not as participatory as they might be; despite all of the rhetoric about democracy we still need to learn how deliberative democratic politics might or might not work. One emerging model for this would be the public policy mediator developed by urban planners. Although dispute mediation itself is not democratic public deliberation, given its narrower emphasis on conflicts of interest, the role of the mediation practitioners could be restructured to serve as a model for developing a broader professional practice of public democratic deliberation.[7]

Democratic political theory, particularly its contemporary emphasis on deliberative democracy, would provide one foundation for the development of this role. But so also would recent research and experimentation with deliberation, as well practical work in citizen participation. Coupled with the contributions of the social constructivist understanding of knowledge and the argumentative approach to policy analysis, these lines of investigation open considerable room for innovation. They constitute an interrelated set of experiences and findings for rethinking the public

---

[7] A conference sponsored by the urban studies program at MIT in 2005 explored the relationships between dispute resolution and deliberative democracy. Bringing together both dispute mediators and political theorists, the discussions largely demonstrated the distance between these two different concerns, one practical and the other theoretical. While some of the dispute mediation participants had hoped to display their methods as a contribution to deliberative democracy in action, the argument was rather roundly rejected by the political theorists who argued that a focus on interests and stakeholders was too narrow to constitute a genuine theory of public deliberation, let alone deliberative democracy.

dimensions of professional expertise. In the follow chapters, the discussion attempts to bring them together in a productive dialogue.

Conclusion

The chapter has examined the central role of the professions in modern society, along with the critique of contemporary practices. The critique, as we saw, focused on the failure of the professions to make good on their role as social trustees. In this regard, the discussion examined the evolution of the tensions between the professions' early nineteenth century promises of civic responsibility and their twentieth century turn to a commercial orientation emphasizing technical knowledge. The focus then turned to some of the primary alternative efforts to develop alternative practices. It outlined the radical alternatives to established professional practices in the 1960s, and 1970s, in particular the attempts on the part of young professionals to speak on the behalf of the poor and disadvantaged. It concluded with a discussion of the more reform-oriented collaborative approaches that followed in the in the 1980s and 1990s.

Throughout, the underlying question has been whether or not the primary professional associations can make good on their earlier promise of social responsibility. And if so, what might the methods and practices be that could support it? While we have bits and pieces that suggest an emerging outline of some of them, there is still no organized body of knowledge or commitment in the professions to address these issues. Much of what follows thus continues to pursue this question. Following the lead of Dewey's earlier commitment to both participatory democracy and the development of a more normative conception of the social and policy sciences, the focus is on one important aspect of such a project—namely, the challenge of assisting citizens to understand and deliberate public problems, both their own and those of the larger society a whole.

This book offers no program for civic professionalism per se; this is something that should better emerge in the context of practical experiences. But it does seek to address and workout various issues, particularly procedures and methods, that would be central to that effort. Toward this end, we turn next to a discussion of citizen participation, exploring both its potentials and limitations. After that, continuing this line of inquiry, Part I closes with an examination of the theory of deliberative democracy and practical deliberative projects such as citizen juries and consensus conferences.

2

Citizen Participation and Deliberative Governance: The Problems of Knowledge and Complexity

Citizen participation and public deliberation are today fashionable topics in both political theory and the practices of government. Public engagement has come to be a—some would say "the"—dominant topic in political theory and has emerged in the theory of governance as a "best practice." In the world of politics it is more or less *de rigour* for policymakers to at minimum pay lip service to the importance of participation. Indeed, so widespread is this emphasis that some writers have now begun to describe participation as a new bureaucratic instrument for political-administrative manipulation.

The primary focus in this chapter is on citizen participation in policy deliberation and the problems posed by knowledge, complexity, and the need for expertise. Citizen participation, of course, includes more than deliberation. It covers a broad range of activities such as voting, campaigning, signing petitions, lobbying, writing letters to newspapers, fund raising, grass roots mobilizing, marching in protest, going on strike, and even at times throwing stones at policemen. Among these activities, though, deliberation has something of a special status. It can be understood as the most basic normative rationale for participation (Bohman and Rehg 1997). Deliberation on the pressing issues of concern to those affected is a basic cornerstone of democratic government.

Because modern policy decisions are complex, many ask whether or not it is realistic to expect citizens to meaningfully participate in the deliberative process. It is a question made all the more salient by the the fact that the levels of participation in Western political democracies are only a thin veneer of what might be expected of such systems. What C. Wright Mills (1959: 5) said about the American citizens many years ago still sums it up today: they feel they are "living in a time of big decisions; they know they are not making any."

More recently, to describe the contemporary state of decline in public engagement in Britain and other Western nations Crouch (2004: 12) has coined the phrase "post-democracy" to describe a situation "when boredom, frustration, and disillusion have settled in . . . ; when powerful minority interests have become far more active than the mass of ordinary people in making the political system work for them; where political elites have learned to manage and manipulate popular demands; where people have to be persuaded to vote by top–down publicity campaigns." In his provocative view, we have begun "a move beyond the idea of rule by the people" to a challenge to "the idea of rule at all" (Crouch 2004: 13). The political world, now finding it more difficult to determine the views of the general citizenry, takes recourse to polling, marketing, and public relations techniques designed to manipulate public opinion. Such methods give political leaders the advantage of discerning the public's views without providing citizens with the possibility of taking charge of or controlling their own communicative responses.

These increasing levels of voter apathy and citizen distrust have led to what various writers have called a political crisis of representative democracy (Gaventa 2006). In face of this declining role of the citizen, participation and devolution of public responsibilities have come to be a standard part of the call for reform in the US, Britain and elsewhere. In an effort to sort out this situation, we need to begin with some basic questions. Perhaps the most fundamental—if not awkward—question upon which all others rest is this: Can citizens intelligently deliberate on complex matters of public policy? Is citizen participation meaningful in the face of complex issues that require a fair amount of expert input? If this question cannot be answered affirmatively, there is little need to address any of the other questions associated with participation and the various reform strategies designed to increase it. They would be, by consequence, rendered moot. Before more specifically addressing the problems posed by knowledge and deliberation, however, it is useful to briefly examine both the factors that lead to citizen participation in general as well as why it should be considered a good thing.

Citizen participation: Who and when?

The role of citizen participation, as a basic political value, is not always as straightforward as one might think. On the one hand, almost everybody is for participation; on the other, many are quite skeptical of its value in practice. In numerous ways, there would seem to be considerable reason for enthusiasm. According to research foundations like Freedom House, there has been an increase in new democracies around the world during the past fifty years. Freedom House's definition, for example, defines democracies as "political systems whose leaders are elected in competitive multi-party and multi-candidate processes in which opposition parties have a legitimate chance of attaining power or participating in power" in systems that have a universal franchise. By this definition, there were almost no democracies at the beginning of the twentieth century. But today, by these standards, around 120 of the more than 190 countries qualify as democratic governments, governing roughly 60 percent of the world's population. Moreover, the majority of them protect human rights and the rule of law enough to count as "liberal democracies."

But a closer look reveals that these figures are based on a very thin conception of democracy. Indeed, as Warren (2002) points out, these otherwise impressive results have been achieved in significant part by reducing the standards of what qualifies as a democracy. If we turn to the long-standing democratic norm that democracy requires citizens to have roughly equal opportunities to participate in the decisions that affect their own lives, the judgment has to be much less positive. Indeed, if we follow Barber (1984) and elevate the standard to at least include an occasional possibility of participating in such decisions, the judgment doesn't improve that much. In fact, none of the criteria he sets out for a participatory democracy in his oft-cited book, "Strong Democracy," are much in evidence in contemporary political systems. Such a theory, he writes, must be grounded in "a theory of talk, judgment, and public seeing" and would as such offer "alternatives to representation, simple voting, and the rule of bureaucrats and experts." It would also "deal concretely with the obstacles that modernity appears to place in the way of participation: namely, scale, technology, complexity, and the paradox of parochialism" (Barber 1984: 262).[1]

---

[1] Emphasizing "viability and practicality," Barber (1984: 262) argues that participatory institutions must first be "realistic and workable." They would "for all practical purposes . . . be a product[s] of actual political experience." As a theory of talk and judgment, a strong democracy would "complement and be compatible with the primary representative institutions of large-scale modern societies;" and would "directly address liberal anxieties over such

The reasons for this thinner evolution of democratic practices are complex, but the broad outlines are not difficult to identify. In significant part, the ideals of participatory democracy were pushed to the margins of mainstream democratic theory and ideology following the rise of Fascism, Stalinism, and the Cold War. As expressed by elite theorists of a realist persuasion, particularly Joseph Schumpeter, the understanding of democracy was redefined and limited to elections competitively pursued by elite groups. In this view, citizen participation is mainly limited to the periodic opportunity to vote. Although the Cold War is a concern of the past, as Warren points out, the same argument is now advanced to deal with the limitations of scale, complexity, functional differentiation, and pluralism.

The results of this particular understanding of democracy are easy to identify. They have been reflected in low levels of participation in Western democracies for some time now. The United States, which prides itself as the world's leading democracy, is the best example of this. Measured in terms of citizen engagement, the American political system leaves much to be desired (Putnam 2000; Skocpol 2003). Participation levels are low and a large percentage of citizens report that they have little or no contact with their political leaders; many say they are turned off by the process. And much of the same can be said of Britain, once considered to be a model of political interest and participation for the rest of the world (Almond and Verba 1963). But during recent decades there has been growing concern about declining levels of participation, especially among the young citizens (Qvortrup 2007). As citizen participation is the normative cornerstone of a democratic system, this is indeed cause for concern.

For purposes of illustration, we can get a rough portrait of this concern by looking at various studies of public participation in the United States. From these investigations we see that those who participate are only a very small tip of the iceberg. Speaking in approximate terms, only about 5–10 percent of the population as a whole today fully participates in political matters. This would include people who are professionally engaged in governmental activities, such as politicians and public servants. Another 15–25 percent follows politics attentively and are potentially mobilizable. Much of the effort in political campaigns is directed toward this group. The next 30–40 percent don't follow politics but can be interested at particular times, although mobilizing them is difficult. This group will

unitary propensities of participatory communities as irrationalism, prejudice, uniformity, and intolerance."

include a large number of non-voters. The remainder of the population is virtually never interested or involved in the political process in any form (Neuman 1986; Conway 2000). A large percentage of this group constitute something of a social underclass in American society.

The seriousness of this picture for a country that calls itself democratic has led to a considerable amount of concern in various quarters, including a good deal of empirical research into the question of why and when citizens participate (Verba, Schlozman, and Brady 2006). A survey of this research shows a number of more specific findings. For example, only about half of the citizenry in the United States participates in presidential elections (often explained by pointing to the inconvenient scheduling of election during workdays, difficulties in registering to vote, and a large number of elections). In Britain, by contrast, over 70 percent of the eligible public has voted in national elections in past decades, although there have been some declines in recent years. In Germany the figure is approximately 90 percent.

When it comes to joining organizations, only about half of the American citizenry belongs—in one way or another—to organized groups that take stands on political issues (Schlozman 2002). With regard to such non-electoral forms participation—working for political campaigns, making contact with officials, or participating with other community members on particular problems, and the like—participation in the US and other Western democratic systems is about the same. In any particular year, only about a third of the public in the United States has contact with a politician or public official at one level of government or another, and only about half this number devotes time to working in their community to solve a particular problem. Fewer that ten percent of the citizenry typically reports having campaigned for any candidate. Research also shows that citizens belonging to political organizations are typically inactive members, mainly paying dues to a central leadership. And less than five percent have attended a protest march to express their opinion on a pressing public issue.

Knowledge and complexity: Can citizens participate?

From the foregoing discussion we see that the vast majority is not politically involved. Although a democracy is supposed to offer its citizens opportunities to participate, most citizens are cut off from a meaningful role in ongoing political activities. It is a basic reality that many find worrisome. Such concern is certainly prominent among democratic political theorists. A closer look, however, shows that not all observers find this reality to be either surprising or necessarily problematic. More than a few take a more sanguine view of the given state of affairs.[2]

Those opposed to citizen participation, or the expansion of it, can be seen as part of a long tradition of politicians and political philosophers, mainly of a conservative persuasion, who question the wisdom of broad public engagement. Why, they ask, should we consult people who either have little knowledge of the issues or backward view on views (on issues such as the death penalty, sex education, or gun control, for example)? Indeed, reservations about democracy and citizen participation are as old as the topic itself; both Plato and Aristotle were opposed to the idea of democracy. Present-day concerns, though, can often be interpreted more specifically as variants of a technocratic perspective that dates back to the Enlightenment and the origins of social science and the modern professions. Democracy, in this regard, is a much more modern concept than most realize. In fact, until well into the first decades of the founding of American government, democracy remained something of a derogatory word. Although the point has long been swept under the carpet, the Founding Fathers were not supporters of democracy per se. For this reason, they established a Republic. Political sovereignty was anchored to the people, but they were ruled by their political representatives, whom at the outset they did not directly elect. It wasn't until much later that the word came into vogue, appearing more or less about the time of President Andrew Jackson and his political emphasis on the "common man" or "Jacksonian democracy," as it was known.

Given the low levels of participation, coupled with large numbers of people with limited levels of knowledge about public affairs, the realities posed by the complex nature of most of today's policy issues have led many to ask if it would not be better to rely on the more informed members of society. Is not, they ask, expert decision-making more likely to support the values of social justice (the liberal position) or efficiency (the conservative position)? In view of nationalistic, class, and racist attitudes found in segments of the general populace, are we not wiser to invest our trust in the knowledge elites?

---

[2] This view, however, is more difficult to survey. One important reason for this has to do with the ideologies surrounding participation. Publicly, one is supposed to support participation in a democratic society, and indeed, most discussions of politics are steeped in the language and iconography of democracy. Thus many who are opposed to more citizen participation are often reluctant to speak openly against it. This makes it somewhat difficult to get an accurate picture of the distribution of beliefs about participation and democracy.

Those opposed to participation typically argue that the elite politicians and professionals should govern in the interest of competence. The experts are the ones with the knowledge and skills needed to render the competent decisions required for effective social guidance. It is an argument typically buttressed with ample survey data indicating low levels of knowledge, interest, and participation on the part of the public.[3] For many, the public and its opinions emerge as something to worry about, if not fear. Sometimes the position is bolstered with the argument that there is already too much participation in Western political systems and that much of it is little more than a reflection of the public's limited, self-serving understanding of the complicated problems confronting the country.

The argument has in recent years received support from a number of prominent social and political theorists who have argued that the possibilities and benefits of participation are now seriously limited by technological and social complexity. Zolo (1992), Habermas (1996), and Offe (1996), for example, contend that complexity now virtually makes democracy and participation impossible in anything but a restricted form. The degree to which Western political systems are organized around functionally differentiated tasks carried out by different groups is seen to have created levels of fragmentation that now make it exceedingly difficult to bring decisions under the control of elected representatives, let alone the public more generally. Indeed, whereas earlier theorists pointed to the problem of technical complexity, others today see social and political complexity to be increasingly problematic.

Bobbio (1987), for example, has argued that the list of claims for democracy represents so many broken promises that a lowering of expectation is in order. Consider the failures. Popular sovereignty, defined as contact between individuals and a unified ruling body, is now as a rule an effect of conflict and cooperation among groups. Representation turns out to be about organized group interests rather than the opinions of individuals. Oligarchic power structures remain prominent features of democratic

---

[3] Daniel Yankelovich (1991: 9), leading pollster and thoughtful political observer, describes this view as part of the "Culture of Technical Control," which holds that "policy decisions depend on a high degree of specialized knowledge and skills", only possessed by experts. The public is basically apathetic to most issues, other than those "concerned largely with their own pocketbook interests." Where the citizens do hold views, they can be determined by experts through public opinion polls. With regard to issues where public understanding and support are mandatory, "they can be achieved through 'public education' where experts who are knowledgeable share some of their information with the voters." And that the media imparts to the public "the information and understanding it needs to develop responsible judgments on key issues facing nation."

societies and their institutions. There is thus little in big business corporations, or government bureaucracies that would qualify as democratic decision-making. And while democracies have held out the promise of educating the public for citizenship, most governments represent large numbers of citizens uninformed and uninterested in public matters. Such realist assumptions are advanced to support the need for accepting a less active form of democracy.

Others extend the argument against participation by portraying it as a leftist project imposed on a citizenry that would prefer to leave complex problems to their elected leaders (Hibbing and Theiss-Morse 2002; Posner 2003). American citizens are said to have little desire to participate in matters of public policy. Indeed, surveys and focus groups elicit views that suggest many see political argumentation and disagreement to represent a failure of the system. Deliberation, as such, is deemed potentially detrimental to effective policymaking.

This perspective is supported by the fact that most policy issues now become the terrain of policy communities, removed from public discussion. These "hidden hierarchies" have, in ways suggested by Foucault, substituted their expert discourses for those of ordinary political talk about the pressing policy issues of the times. With each area of modern life under the control of disciplinary expertise—welfare, crime, family, environment, schools, and so on—there is little that the citizen would seem to be able to offer. To be sure, the citizen can still express his or her view, but in a world dominated by a centralized state guided in large part by the views of administrative and policy experts, professional advisory committees, think tank specialists, governmental policy staffs, academic consultants and the like, they have less and less chance of being taken seriously. In face of this situation, deliberation based on public opinion moves from being considered a waste of time to being detrimental to the making of effective policy decisions.[4]

---

[4] From a historical perspective, it is worth noting here that the concept of public opinion has been fraught with contradictions. Coming into widespread usage in the eighteenth century, the term was advanced by Enlightenment thinkers as a way to challenge the entrenched authority of the aristocracy and church. However, after the French Revolution and the reign of terror to which it gave rise, public opinion came to be considered something of a "wild beast" to be feared. Ever since public opinion has carried both meanings. At the very same time that it is denigrated as an inferior, often irrational, form of knowledge grounded more in emotion than reason, the opinion of the sovereign citizenry in a democracy is romantically elevated to a virtue unto itself. Both of these contradictory views, as we see here, are alive and well today. In some contexts public opinion represents little more than ignorance; it others it treated as nearly sacred.

Understanding the citizen: Incompetence or disengagement?

The arguments for more participation are often as ideologically grounded as the case against participation. Leftists of various stripes have held out political participation as the alternative to elitism in it various forms, political or technocratic (Chomsky 1989; Morrison 1995). In the most radical versions of this view, much of expert discourse about public policy is seen to be little more than mystification. From this vantage point, so it is argued, there is little or no reason to believe that citizens cannot meaningfully participate in the deliberation of policy issues.

Careful analysis shows that the data about participation and non-participation is more complicated than it first appears. The first problem that arises concerns participation itself. How do we define it and by what criteria do we judge it to be successful? Certain procedural characteristics related to such an assessment are fairly clear. We can ask about the degree to which the discussion relationship—i.e., a relationship for talking and listening, asking and answering questions, suggesting and accepting courses of action—is governed by clear and fixed norms or rules. Are the rules governing who gets to speak fair and equally distributed? Is the discussion open? Is the deliberative agenda transparent to all participants, or are particular elements hidden and secretive? To what degree are all of the participants represented? Here the question also arises as to whether or not there is a difference between how the participants might be represented, as well as how they think they are represented.[5] The answers to these questions depend in significant part on the equality of the power relations in the deliberative setting.

Participation can also be judged in terms of three effects: instrumental, developmental, and intrinsic. Instrumental effects refer to participation designed to achieve particular goals or outcomes. People are seen to participate in order to achieve things that they cannot get through private efforts. Developmental effects refer to impacts that participation can have on human development, such as expanding the individual or group's education and power of thought, feeling and commitment, as well as ability to take action. People learn from experience how the social system and surrounding environments work, come to understand diversity and tolerance, and gain political skills that help them efficaciously contribute

---

[5] Citizens with democratically elected governments around the world question the ability of representative democracies to effectively serve the interests of their citizens. They hold widespread views that their political systems represent the interests of political and economic elites, especially the leaders of big business.

to social change. Intrinsic skills can be understood as the internal benefits of participation. Whereas developmental effects pertain to specific action-oriented skills, intrinsic benefits refer to the less tangible internal effects that result from participation, such as a sense of personal gratification, heightened self-worth and a stronger identification with one's community (Nagel 1987).

Further distinctions have to be made between political apathy, indifference and disaffection. What first appears to be apathy and indifference can turn out to be disenchantment with politics. A good deal of evidence shows that citizens who consider their political institutions to be corrupt, unreliable, or incompetent are unlikely to trust them. A typical reaction is the desire to have nothing to do with them or the political process associated with them. Even though this often leads to a withdrawal of participation, some have argued that this disaffection should be viewed as a reflection of an increasingly critical assessment of politics and government on the part of citizens. It is an argument supported by data that can be generalized over quite a range of countries. Norris (1999), for example has found a growing numbers of disenchanted citizens, or what she calls "critical citizens." She discovered support for democratic ideals to be high and thus citizens increasingly disillusioned with governments they find disappointing, unresponsive, and unaccountable. Along with Norris, writer such as Inglehart (1997) and Warren (2002) see this as a positive development that holds out potential support which may lead to democratic reforms.

A strong case can be made that the general citizenry, or at least a significant portion of it, is more capable of making informed, intelligent assessments about public issues than many conservative politicians, social scientists, and opinion researchers suggest. Indeed, the question of public ignorance proves to be much more complicated than is usually recognized. Part of the problem is the lumping together of a wide range of citizens under the category of "the public." Averaged together, opinion surveys can produce quite depressing portraits of the public's intellectual capabilities. We also need to recognize that most experts are themselves only members of the public when it comes to many areas of expertise other than their own. Given the complexity of many of these fields, an expert in one field rarely has expertise in others. The rocket scientist might be the contemporary symbol of high level expertise, but he or she is seldom qualified to perform medical surgery.

Then there is the fact that a lack of interest in politics is often mistaken for public ignorance. This misperception jumps over a more fundamental question: namely, whether the public generally is inherently incompetent to engage intelligently in political matters, or whether the low level of public activity only reflects the populous's limited opportunities to develop the interest and participatory skills required to engage meaningfully in public issues. What should we really expect from the public under the given political circumstances?

Extensive political and sociological research into why citizens do or do not participate offers a wealth of information on the subject. Such empirical investigation has sought to sort out the array of factors that help to explain why a citizen might or might not choose to take an active public role in the political process. Not surprisingly, we see that the reasons for participation correlate highly with availability of financial resources, civic skills, educational levels, party recruitment, and political orientation. That people with financial resources have the ability to influence the outcomes of political activity is well known, and the skewed distribution of incomes that leads to this distortion has received much attention. Civic skills refer to those organizational communications capabilities that make it easier to get involved and that enhance an individual's effectiveness as a participant. They are acquired through the life cycle—first during childhood at home, then in school, later during adulthood (on the job, at church, in nonpolitical organizations, as well as in politics). The degree to which particular citizens possess the necessary education and communicative skills correlates—as does money—much more highly with family background rather than innate intelligence. Social privilege, in short, plays a basic role in determining who does and doesn't participate in public affairs (Schlozman 2002).

Among those who do participate, an important catalyst is recruitment. Citizens who have the wherewithal and the desire to take part in politics are most likely to do so if they are asked to participate. Traditionally, political parties have played an important role in recruiting participation, but in more recent decades this role has faded with the rise of the media and other institutions in contemporary politics, this being especially the case in the United States. Today, people obtain their political information and cues much more from the mass media than from political parties. The problem here is that the media—particularly the electronic media–has turned more to the task of entertaining rather than informing and educating the public. This is also the case during elections, which are transformed into "horse races" among the candidates, instead of important events about pressing policy issues. In this respect, the media has also contributed to the decline of a democratic society.

Beyond political parties and the media, there are many institutions and groups that seek to mobilize citizens to participate. Here we learn that the nature and operation of these organized groups are also important determinants of the willingness to get involved. Research shows that most interest groups are not particularly good at promoting participation, as they tend to be run by a few people at the top. Most of the members are little more than a name on a mass mailing list.

Further, the recruitment of citizens is influenced by aspects of everyday life outside of the formal political sphere. Relatives, neighbours, friends, co-workers, fellow members of social organizations can have an influence on a citizen's decision to participate. But as Schlozman (2002) finds, "no matter whether the request comes in a mass mailing, through a phone call, or over the backyard fence, those who seek to get others involved choose as their targets people who would be likely to participate if asked." Therefore, "while the request may generate activities, those who are asked tend to have characteristics that make them inclined to take part." For most people, though, everyday life among friends and neighbours is an apolitical experience and has become more so as the political culture has increasingly denigrated politics and the public sphere (Eliasoph 1998; Putnam 2000). In the case of the US, for example, Americans are first and foremost socialized into the role of consumer rather than citizen. (And here, I think most would admit, Americans don't seem as ignorant or passive as they do in the public sphere, certainly an argument against the innate stupidity of the populous).

Most of this research focuses explicitly on *public* participation. But other research suggests that the focus is too narrow. The degree to which citizens participate may have more to do with the particular political context in which they find themselves. Whereas the relevant silence encountered in the public sphere is interpreted by many to reflect either lack of interest or ignorance, Eliasoph (1998) has shown that many more people often do discuss the political and policy issues but not on the center stage of the public sphere. Instead of engaging in the kind of public deliberation that political scientists and sociologists look for, citizens more often than not do it in less visible private contexts. That is, they do have opinions and discuss them with the friends and citizens with whom they are familiar, but avoid doing it interactively with other citizens, especially in public fora. The reasons for this would appear mainly to be related to the complex nature of the political psychologies that citizens develop in the face of social class differences, ethnic group relationships, and unequal power structures. Given the importance of this finding, we return later to a more careful examination of the way ordinary citizens often deliberately avoid public discussion of pressing political issues.

Learning political skills

Frequently overlooked or neglected is the fact that people have to learn how to be political. Some of what they need to learn is taught in school. For example, they generally get a rough outline of the history of democratic politics, the crucial events and actors, basic information the branches of government, political parties, the structure and timing of elections, perhaps also an account of the leading ideologies, and so on. But civic education is seldom presented as more than a secondary requirement. There is, moreover, little attention given to the kinds of civic skills necessary for citizen participation. This is not to deny the existence of a debating club, or an occasional civic event. These, however, are usually activities for the few already interested in such topics, not the broad body of the student population. For most students, schooling is a fairly passive phenomenon and the structure of the educational process does little to discourage this—teachers talk and students listen.

Political parties, movements, unions, and interest groups have also functioned as schools of a sort, teaching their members the ideas that the groups are organized to advance. Some might argue that this not a particularly good form of education, given ideological and other considerations. Whether these experiences are good or bad, they are enormously important for political life; the political identity of most people—particularly those engaged by politics—are influenced by membership and participation in these organizations. But many of these organizations offer few participatory opportunities to their members. Members pay dues but the elites at the top of the interest group organization will do their bidding for them.

Of course, political identities are also shaped by familial life: people with particular opinions marry people with similar views and raise children to whom they try, most often successfully, to pass on those opinions. Socialization in the family, however, is seldom participatory; parents generally only imbue their offspring with a particular ideological orientation, with little or no encouragement to question the basic beliefs. Those who come to question such views are usually influenced by ideas and beliefs encountered outside the family in various public settings or through the media. The contemporary media, beyond moralizing editorials pundits, rarely presents a critical perspective on contemporary affairs. The general offering usually hues a line close to official elite opinions. There is, more-over, little by way of an interactive component. The viewer is only part of a large and relatively passive audience.[6]

In response to those who fear public ignorance, one can just as easily point to the failure of the political system to socialize its citizens for an active role. Missing from Western political systems are well-developed political arrangements that provide citizens with multiple and varied participatory opportunities to deliberate basic political issues. In the case of the United States, for example, a Kettering Foundation (www.Kettering. org) study found that citizens are ready and willing to express this concern themselves (Harwood 1991). Extensive interviews across ten US cities registered that citizens are not only acutely aware of their remoteness to the political system, but are eager for constructive involvement in public life. They express resentment toward those who write them off as ignorant and apathetic and are angry about being "pushed out" of the process by party politicians and lobbyists. One citizen poignantly captured the feel-ing in these words: "I'm never aware of an opportunity to go somewhere and express my opinion and have someone hear what I have to say." In the words of one commentator, the study shows that "ordinary citizens seem to share the democratic theorists' concern that our democracy does not offer structures for citizen deliberation and involvement in public decisions" (Hudson 1995: 136).

While it is difficult to pinpoint the blame in such a complicated matter, one surely has to include the failure of political party systems to adequately represent all of their citizens. Especially problematic in the US has been the electoral laws and the two-party system. The traditional function of a party is to convey the public's opinions to the political decision-makers. But US parties have given up this role and serve mainly electoral functions; they have become little more than political labels behind which well-financed candidates organize their electoral bids. The parties' traditional role as communicator has been taken over by the public media. But the media, financed by commercial advertisers, fails as well. By mixing the selling of products with the task of informing the populous, the media emerges as a highly compromised instrument of elite/mass society.

To lament this disappointing state of affairs—widely acknowledged throughout the US and a growing number of other Western countries—is

---

[6] Some will point to possibilities offered by the newer forms of electronic communication, pointing in particular to blogs. But these remain largely individualist contributions without face-to-face interaction.

not necessarily to call for direct or radical democracy, as some seem to quickly assume. Too often the call for more participation is posed as a fundamental challenge to representative democracy. Such arguments misconstrue participation with direct or radical participatory democracy. One can easily acknowledge that citizens in a complex society cannot be—or are incapable of being—involved in all decisions at all times and still call for more participation, especially given the disturbingly low levels of citizen engagement in American society. To do so is not to entertain the kind of utopian fairy tale radical democrats are typically accused of promoting. Given the fact that only a small percentage of the public is actively engaged in politics, the effort to increase participation hardly need be considered extreme.

This work concedes straight away that even though direct democracy has a role to play in particular cases, it is not a tenable model for the society as a whole. We argue instead for a vigorous participatory democracy capable of supporting representative democracy. Given the elite/mass structure of politics today, representative politics as practiced becomes a hollow elitist conception of democracy. Plenty of political experience in the United States and other Western industrial nations attest to the pitfalls of such a system. Elite liberal representatives have their own interests and no matter how hard they might try to speak for the poor and the working classes, their advocacy typically remains an elite understanding of what these other groups believe and strive for. History shows, moreover, that a struggle for social justice unsustained by broad participatory support tends to be a short-lived activity.

If representative democracy is to have anything more than the patina of legitimacy, it has to be undergirded by a vibrant local system of citizen participation. Beyond simple platitudes about the need for increased voter participation, it requires structures and organizations that offer citizens opportunities to deliberate more directly in the decisions affecting their own lives. In so far as citizen participation is a touchstone of a democratic system, societies with such low participation rates need to be concerned about its democratic status. In contrast to those who perceive democracy to be destructive or counterproductive, others argue that it is time to explore the boundaries of the possible, the approach we take in chapters that follow.[7] The work proceeds from the belief that a great deal

---

[7] Mansbridge (2003: 177) interestingly points to what Arnold Kaufman referred to as the "paradox" of participatory democracy. Kaufman (1971), who introduced the concept and theory of "participatory democracy," emphasized its positive impacts on citizens. Exercising

more participation is both possible and necessary than presently exists in Western democratic systems and that, among other things, this means rethinking the relationship between experts and citizens. Significant moves in this direction have been the focus on two interrelated concepts, citizenship and new forms of "governance," to which we return in the following two sections.

Citizenship and participation

The promotion of citizenship has become an important topic in both political theory and the agendas of democratic governments over the past several decades (Kivisto and Faist 2007). The reasons for this are complex and varied (Heater 1999). In general, they have to do with changing patterns and expectations of governance. One of them involves an heightened political awareness of the cultural and ethnic differences within nations-states, closely related to international migrations. Some nations-states have sought to bridge these divisions by drawing on the notion of citizenship as a way to establish a new commonality among its peoples. Another has to do with globalization and the need to connect the global to the local levels of governance. This has led to a recognition of the need for a multi-layered understanding of citizenship and the need to address the political exclusions created by both the linkage of citizenship to the traditional nation-state and the increasing globalization of political institutions and civil society (Falk 1998).

Citizenship, as a theoretical and political question, now penetrates an astonishing array of disciplinary discussions. The range of literatures on citizenship extends from writings on political and legal rights, to civil society, democratic theory, participation and deliberation, political identity, multiple and global citizenship, human rights in foreign policy and development theory, feminist theory, the protection of minorities and the disabled, scientific and technological citizenship, among others. These sophisticated discussions can scarcely be more than introduced here as part of an array of theories that all converge on citizen participation.

political power, he argued, develops citizen's abilities to think and act politically. But he also saw a paradox associated with effective participation, namely that those citizens who have not experienced it may not yet have the capacity to engage in it. As Mansbridge (2003: 177) captures the predicament, "what they need is precisely what, because of their need, they cannot get."

Below we only focus on a few points, particularly as they relate to participation and expertise.

In political theory the major concern with citizenship is on rights and obligations, including the question of who is included and excluded as a member of the community (Dahl 1989). In liberal political thought citizenship is understood as a formal socio-legal status that entitles individuals to specific universalized rights enshrined by law. Offering each autonomous, self-interested individual the same political and legal rights is taken to promote equality by making an individual's economic and political power irrelevant to his or her claim on rights (Rawls 1971). In this view, freely autonomous citizens can choose to participate—or not participate—depending on the assessment of his or her own interests. As such, liberalism generally emphasizes representative rather than participatory government.

Communitarians, by contrast, take issue with the idea of a fully autonomous and independent individual. They see these same individuals as developing their sense of civic identity—and the rights and obligations that go with it—through social relationships with other members of the community. Here the individuals and the groups to which they belong can only realize their identity and interests through common deliberation over the public good, with individual liberty maximized by the pursuit of public over individual interests (Sandal 1998). The communitarians thus emphasize particular civic virtues, with tolerance, respect for others, and public service to one's own community being the most important.

The third theoretical contribution to the debate, civic republicanism, attempts to chart a course between liberalism and communitarianism. It incorporates the liberal notion of self-interested individuals but sets them within a communitarian framework of egalitarianism and community virtues. Its advocates argue that civic identity should be shaped by a common public culture rather than community values. Civic identity and belonging, they argue, should not be founded only on the individual's separate identities as members of different groups and communities. Citizen participation in public deliberation must instead be focused more on fairness among the multiplicity of different communities that constitute a complex modern society. Deliberation, as such, should take place at the level of governance upon which the major decisions shaping the society as a whole are made (Miller 1988)

Beyond political and legal theory, Mouffe (1992) argues that in real-world practices citizenship rights, rather than being established through formal political arrangements, are constructed and mediated within the multi-sited arenas of political struggles, including the global arena. In more recent years mass civic protests around the globe against the World Trade Organization's pursuit of neo-liberal economic policies, huge marches opposing the Iraq War, and ongoing demonstrations demanding attention to environmental degradation have been political struggles about citizenship rights and representation in undemocratic decision processes as much as they have been about the particular issues themselves. Citizenship is thus fundamentally about agency in the world of political confrontation. As Lister (1998: 228) has put it, citizenship claims represent "an expression of human agency in the political arena, broadly defined; citizenship as rights enables people to act as agents." In view of the central role of the individual's self-identity as a political citizen, these writers place the emphasis on the relationship between thought and action that enables citizenship.

Of particular importance, especially for the themes under consideration in this work, has been a focus on scientific and technological citizenship in science and technology studies (Frankenfeld 1992; Elm and Bertilsson 2003; Jasanoff 2004). As the boundaries between science and technological applications have become increasingly blurred, there have been a more and more conflicts of interest resulting in a decline of public trust, portending at times a "crisis of governance." In significant part, the concept of scientific citizenship is proposed to restore trust by bridging the gap between scientific expertise and the society that it exists to serve. It is seen as a major challenge for the future evolution of the contemporary "knowledge-based society" and the "distributed intelligence" upon which it rests (Joly 2005).

In view of the dramatic advances in science and technology at both the local and global levels of engagement, and the increasing role of the "scientific estate" as part the governmental process, the call for scientific and technological citizenship is in essence a call for a new social contract between the general citizenry and the scientific community. Given that many technological advances have political decisions built into them, and thus pre-ordain the course of future political possibilities, it is a call to work out a new understanding that bring citizens into closer contact with expert communities and the decision-making processes that direct their activities (Fischer 1990).

The possibility of a new conceptualization of scientific citizenship focuses in large part on questions of inclusion and exclusion. In view of the complex technical nature of many of the decisions at issue, the question is: who has the right to be included in the decision process and who should be excluded? As we shall see in Chapter 5, some scholars have labored to set out a scheme for answering such questions based on scientific competence and technically-related experiences. Others, by contrast, argue that the emphasis has to be place more on the normative assumptions involved in technical analysis and their larger social implications.

The ability to participate in the discussion of technical issues is a question of basic importance in a democratic society. What does it mean, in short, for the fate of democracy if political decisions are increasingly made by technocrats and their expert advisor committees? What does it mean for democratic practices if citizens, as cornerstones of democratic government, cannot competently participate in many of the most important political decisions? Efforts to answer this question have involved creating institutional mechanisms capable of building citizens and stakeholders into various stages of the research and development processes. As an effort to both improve democratic governance and technological innovation, they have led to experimentation with approaches to participatory technology assessment, consensus conferences, scenario workshops and the like, topics to which we turn in the next chapter.

Beyond an extensive theoretical literature, much more work needs to be done to determine the political effectiveness of this emphasis on citizenship. As Jones and Gaventa (2002: 28) write, "very little is known about the realities of how different people understand themselves as citizens, and the ways in which this impacts on the different dimensions of their lives." We know too little about how "rights language" is actually used "in situated struggles, by different individuals and groups, and to what effect."[8] In so far as the connections between people's senses of citizenship and participatory practices are basically dependent on both the specific political context and form of participation, as Mansbridge (1999) argues, the relationship is difficult to demonstrate and clearly requires closer examination.

One practical venue for further exploration of these linkages is the theory and practice of "governance" that emerged in the 1990s, which continues to be a strong theme in both political theory and governmental practices. As Jones and Gaventa (2002: 7) have put it, citizenship and governance have converged in ways that potentially open spaces that "meet in the concept of citizenship participation" (Jones and Gaventa 2002: 7). In this governance literature, an emphasis on citizenship has led to concerns about both the citizen's voice and greater citizen influence in

---

[8] Writer such as Schneider and Ingram (2006) have asked how particular public policies promote or do not promote citizenship. They point for the need, in this regard, for policies toward citizenship.

matters related to public accountability. It has contributed to renewed thinking about the relationship of the state to civil society, in particular the direct intervention of citizens, nongovernmental organizations (NGOs), and other civil society actors in the provision and monitoring of public services, as well as the accountability of the state and other responsible institutions more generally (Gaventa and Valderrama 1999). Here we can identify in governance something of the communitarian and civic republican emphasis on public engagement. As Cornwall and Gaventa (2002: 54) write, "when citizens perceive themselves as actors in governance, rather than passive beneficiaries of services and policy, they may be more able to assert their citizenship through actively seeking greater accountability, as a well as through participation in the shaping of policies that affect their lives." Given the importance of governance for the questions of citizen involvement, we turn to a more detailed discussion of it practices and implications.

New forms of citizen governance: Civil society and participatory politics

An influential effort to deal with the lack of opportunities to participate has been a shift in both theory and practice away from a focus on "government" to "governance" (Pierre 2000). This move away from traditional patterns of government has emerged in significant part to deal with the traditional state's inability to cope with a range of contemporary social and economic problems, including global problems that reach beyond established state boundaries. This "New Democratic Governance," as it is sometimes called, has largely evolved in non-electoral realms in response to the democratic deficit of representative democracy—which has created mounting difficulties—both politically and functionally—for engaging in the kinds of policy problem-solving that faces modern states. The capability of these political systems and their institutions are said to be "outstripped by the development of the societies in which they are embedded" (Warren 2008)[9] The new "decentered" and more "reflexive"

---

[9] Warren has succinctly delineated the state's problems this way: "Under the standard model of democratic self-rule...citizens elect representatives who then make policy on their behalf. They legislate goals and means, and then pass these broad directions to administrators, who then further develop and execute policy." These "linkages that establish democracy are...broken at almost every step: territorial electoral constituencies do not match issue constituencies, which are increasingly non-territorial. Electoral systems only roughly

forms of governance is the primary domain of the growing development of the citizen engagement initiatives that we have already point to. It has evolved to identify and explain new spaces for participatory decision-making and accompanying modes of citizen-solving problem that fill gaps created by the failure of traditional approaches (Sorensen and Torfing 2007). Promoting de-centered citizen engagement, governance is touted for being both a much more flexible and democratic way to deal with public problems.

At the outset of this development, the most important actors in the effort to innovate new forms of governance were mainly social movements; many of them worked to carve out new arenas for different forms of political engagement. Operating in the spaces between formal governmental structures and the citizenry, these efforts have emphasized civil society as a place for public deliberation and problem solving (LaForest and Phillips 2006). Civil society can, in this regard, be understood to constitute an intermediary social space between the government and the private citizens which enables citizens and their associations to engage in free, relatively egalitarian discussion with one another about matters of common interest and purpose, at times forging themselves into cohesive groups capable of undertaking political action. Basic to this turn to the civil sphere on the part of movements has often been an emphasis on new and participatory forms of "cultural politics," focusing in particular on the empowering politics of social meaning and identity.

For many of these movements in the US and Europe the goal has been to find new forms of *authentic* political engagement. Toward this end, they have succeeded in inventing a range of new participatory mechanisms that offer significant insights into questions that have long been ignored in traditional political analysis and in democratic theory, including efforts to bring together citizens and experts in new forms of cooperative activity. Promoting serious discussion about how citizens can participate in complex decision processes, this work has included the exploration of the role of local lay knowledge and the deeper impact of social and cultural factors on the design and facilitation of democratic discursive spaces. In the process, it has explored ways in which professional expertise might

---

reflect citizen preferences, and they do so in highly aggregated, information-poor ways. Legislatures have very low policymaking capacities, and so pass most decisions to executives and executive agencies, which are then often left to guess what constituents want. These problems are multiplied . . . by the influence of markets, corporatism, and bureaucratic power and inertia. The bureaucratic form of policy development and implementation has inherent limitations as well: rule-based hierarchy tends to be rigid and information poor."

restructure their traditional practices to include other modes of reason. Thanks to the accumulation of these activities, particularly prevalent in the areas of environmental politics and community development, a considerable number of experiences and practices in participatory governance are available for scrutiny.

Fundamental to the activities of many these citizen-oriented social movements has been the creation of alternative political cultures and the participatory institutions and practices that can sustain them. Movements concerned with the environment, feminism, disability, and development, among others, have provided social fora—even laboratories—for experimentation with new participatory cultures, including participatory approaches to science and expertise. Such experimentation, emphasizing empowerment and self-help strategies, is largely designed to counter the top–down bureaucratic tendencies that define contemporary political and organizational decision processes. It draws, as such, on a critical-theoretical understanding of empowerment. Whereas much of the contemporary literature on empowerment defines it as giving people power to make decisions over their own affairs, typically through participation, a critical perspective holds that genuine empowerment must address the material conditions that create dependency.[10]

Stressing the development of nonhierarchical cultures, the theorists of these movements have attempted to address a critical question: Is it possible to democratize—or at least make more democratic—the largely hierarchical, often authoritarian relationships among public administrators and policy experts on the one hand, and citizens on the other? Toward this end, the key target of such "movement intellectuals" has been the hierarchical superior-subordinate relationship that professionals maintain with their clients. In the academic sphere, these efforts have received theoretical and experimental support in various quarters, especially from social constructivism in science studies, taken up in later chapters.

---

[10] While there is no simple agreement on the meaning of empowerment, it generally denotes that a person feels able to move events in a desirable direction. People, as such, are given the power to make decisions over their own affairs. This is often approached through delegations of authority and participation. From the perspective of critical theory, however, empowerment efforts must reach deeper into the organizational structures and processes in which this participation occurs. Power, in this view, is seen to depend on location in a system of social relationships. Effort to empower people must thus be designed to counter existing power relations that result in domination of some groups over others. This involves "a process in which traditionally disenfranchised groups become aware of forces that oppress them and take action against them by changing the conditions in which they live and work (...) not merely [through] participation but often resistance to, and conflict with governance structures" (Hardy and Leiba-O'Sullivan 1998: 468–9).

Many of these movements stress "people's self-development," emphasizing the role of social identity, political recognition, and citizenship rights in the development of participatory approaches (Rahman 1995). Rather than merely speaking for poor or marginalized people's interests and concerns, they have sought to develop people's abilities to negotiate directly with official decision makers. Beyond institutionalizing new bodies of client or user groups, they have created new opportunities for dialogue. These have ranged from the introduction of and experimentation with citizen juries to innovative modes of "deliberative policy analysis," topics to which we return.

Whereas the cultural orientations of social movements have proven difficult to sustain over time, have they left important byproducts. One of them has been their impetus or influence on the emergence of the more progressively oriented NGOs. While NGOs are themselves principally civil society organizations, they have formed more pragmatic relationships with their governmental counterparts. Situating their activities in the institutional cracks of the traditional state, or what Hajer (2003) has termed the "institutional void," NGOs constitute new forms of social and political engagement typically associated with governance.

NGOs have been an important part of what Salamon (1993) has referred to as a "revolution" of civic sphere associations. Basic to this multiplication of citizen-oriented participatory spaces has been a different brand of social actors. In both the developed and developing countries, this has involved two important shifts. In ways similar to the activities of the civic renewal movement in the US, discussed in the previous chapter, the most prominent shift has been away from state-centered activities to "civil society organizations" that deliver services and offer various forms of support to economic and social development (Bevir 2006). These emergent organizational spaces have in some cases taken over traditional governmental activities to such a degree that some see them as having reconfigured parts of the public sector, supplanting states whose accountability has long been in question. The other often related shift in these civic society organizations, less prominent but every bit as interesting, has involved a transition from professionally dominated to more citizen- or client-based activities (Sirianni and Friedland 2001).

Of particular significance among these organizations has been their efforts to represent and serve the needs of marginalized or excluded groups. In some of these alternative spaces, excluded peoples—such as the poor, women, AIDS victims, and the disabled—have been able to create a collective presence that permits them to speak for themselves, the significance of which has been measured in terms of their affects on mainstream institutions and policies. In numerous instances these activities have given rise to a breed of "civic society professionals" devoted to offering assistance to such efforts. Often schooled in NGOs, such professionals—as government officials or independent consultants to parallel institutions—have played an essential role in the development and spread of participatory approaches to governance.

It should be noted here that others have started to take a less sanguine view of the role of NGOS. While much of the literature on these organizations (especially the earlier literature), has optimistically portrayed NGOs as a panacea for the ills plaguing the traditional state, a more critical perspective on these organizations has begun to emerge in recent years. As Mercer (2002: 7), puts it, "while some suggest NGOs can strengthen state and civil society, others argue that strengthening NGOs actually undermines democratic development." Abdelrahman (2004) and Ebrahim (2003), for example, argue that many NGOs in the developing world tend to end up replicating the top–down bureaucratic tendencies that they are supposed to be countering. In some ways, this should not be altogether surprising. For one thing, different NGOs emerge in different political environments and their structures and practices reflect that, sometimes necessarily so. Many of the NGOs working in authoritarian countries have chosen to put their emphasis on delivering services to people in serious need of help, which frequently requires working with the existing state bureaucracies. Often a focus on participation has put their very survival at risk in precarious political environments. Another part of the explanation surely has to do with a well-established pattern of organizational development, namely the "iron law of oligarchy." Over time, particularly as organizations get bigger and more complex, there is a well-documented tendency for them to become more centralized, professional, and top–down. This has also been the case for many social movements. Given the administrative requirements associated with organizations of all types—social movements and NGOs included—the question of how to avoid this does not lend itself to easy answers. But if there is one, it surely involves a new breed of participatory professionals.

While these cautions and reservations are important, they should not at the same time lead us to overlook or reject the important participatory innovations in governance. Indeed, as Warren (2008: 1) has interestingly asserted, this "governance-driven democratization" has evolved unexpectedly—even ironically—in and around the less likely realm of public policy and public administration than the traditional spheres of democratic politics, in particular electoral and party politics. Democratization, he avers, is now a project of policy issues and policy decision processes. Put pointedly, the agents of the process appear to be acting in those parts of the government—the administrative sector—traditionally viewed as the less democratic of the various arenas. As he has captured it, "who would have thought that public policy and policymaking—the province of experts—would move into the vanguard?"

Much of this work, moreover, is not difficult to find in new theories and practices of public administration. For example, this emphasis on a new kind of professional and more inclusive participatory practices has led Feldman and Khademian (2007) to reconceptualize the role of the public manager as that of creating "communities of participation." In their view, the challenge confronting those working in the public sector is to inter-actively combine knowledge and perspectives from three separate do-mains of knowing—the technical, political, and local/experiential domains. Bringing about more inclusive practices of governance involves inventing contexts in which the representatives of these forms of knowing can share their perspectives in the common pursuit of problem-solving.[11] Beyond merely identifying and disseminating information from these various ways of understanding and analyzing policy problems, such work involves "translating ideas" in ways that facilitate mutual under-standing among the participants and seeking to promote a synthesis of perspectives that helps to stimulate different ways of knowing relevant to the problems at hand (Wenger, McDermott, and Snyder 2002). This, in turn, involves what they call "relational work," designed to create "con-nections between people in ways that legitimize perspectives and create empathy for participants who represent different ways of understanding and addressing the problem" (Feldman and Khademian 2007: 306). It can be understood as designing and setting up a community of participation in which social learning can take place (Fischer 2000: 221–41; Roberts 1997).[12] In later chapters we take up a number of the epistemological issues involved in such translation and communication.

---

[11] Also see Denhardt and Denhardt (2007) calling for a new public service based on a more value-oriented, citizen-based facility role for public administrators; Barth (1996) on the facilitative role of the public administrator; and Miller and Fox (2006) for a more critical perspective emphasizing discourse in public administration. Some have also begun to speak of this facilitative role in terms of increasing "public value," although there is no firm agreement on the meaning of the term. See Stoker (2006) for a discussion of the concept.

[12] As Senator, Barack Obama spoke of communities of participation and the need for a more facilitative approach in these words: "People are hungry for community; they miss it. What if a politician were to see his job as that of an organizer, as part teacher and part advocate,

These participatory and deliberative practices have scarcely gone unnoticed. Indeed, governance has, albeit it a more bureaucratic form, received pushes from important governmental institutions, the European Union being the most important (Lebessis and Paterson 1999). Given the problematic distance of European citizens to both the European Union's Executive Council in Brussels and its Parliament in Strasbourg, reflected in the rejection of a proposed constitution by voters in France and the Netherlands, the Council issued a widely circulated White Paper on the need to promote civil society and citizen engagement through participatory governance. As an effort designed to involve citizens and their civil institutions more directly in the policy decision processes, especially at the regional and local levels, the White Paper and the substantial monies made available for governance research turned European "multi-level governance" into something between a good governance practice and a political buzzword. A reference to governance seemed to emerge as a requirement signaling political relevance in both funding institutions and public administrative agencies.

Such bureaucratic interest is not without its risk; participatory projects can easily be co-opted by powerful institutions for their own ends. The World Bank is seen by many as a case in point. Adopting participatory practices, the Bank has been accused of instrumentalizing participation to serve its own purposes. To the point, the World Bank has borrowed ideas from the participatory work of NGOs in developing countries to set up its own participation program in the 1990s. Having learned the relevance of local involvement and participation from many of its Third World investment failures, the Bank took an interest in the advantages offered by direct local contact with the communities it seeks to assist (World Bank 1994). Not only have senior bank staff members been directed to get to know a particular region better (through a week of immersion in one of its villages or slums), the bank has pioneered a technique called participatory poverty assessment designed "to enable the poor people to express their realities themselves" (Chambers 1997, p. xvi). It has been adapted from participatory research experiences in more than thirty countries around the world (Norton and Stephens 1995). But reports from the field suggest that such efforts have largely been employed to motivate local citizens to participate in preconceived programs. The design of the programs, as part of an empowerment strategy, has seldom been part of the process. The

one who does not sell voters short, but who educates them about the real choices before them"? He poses it as a new role for the publicly elected official (quoted in Lizza 2008: 49).

definitions and understandings of poverty and development are determined in advance by the Bank.

But this has come as no surprise to many practitioners in the field. A substantial amount of policy research has demonstrated the use of public participation for manipulative purposes. In developed as well as in developing countries it has often been introduced to simply mollify an otherwise politically problematic public (Rowe and Frewer 2004). Policymakers have recognized that failing to consult the public can easily lead to political resentment and thus resistance to the programs they seek to implement. In these cases, participation has largely been a token gesture designed only to increase public confidence in the policy process rather than genuinely seek out the opinions of the citizens for whom the policies were intended.

Beyond such tokenism, writers such as Foucault and Bourdieu have taken an even more critical stance toward these participatory projects. Rather than seeing participation merely as a practice gone astray, they identify its uses as symptomatic of the nature of political control in the modern state; it is designed to pacify the public in the interests of governing elites. For Foucault, such instrumentalization of participation is best described as a "political technology" used to manage decision processes and control projects in ways that constrain popular engagement and discipline citizens. Bourdieu (1977) speaks of it as an "officializing strategy" designed to domesticate public engagement, detracting attention away from other more empowering forms of political action. Similarly, Beder (1999: 169) has shown that the kinds of public participatory consultation that government agencies and corporations began using in the 1970s have largely become public relations exercises designed to manipulate public perceptions and opinion in response to public protests by local citizens. Drawing on research related to environmental issues in Australia, she illustrates the ways in which "PR tools for communicating risk, categorizing 'publics,' dealing with intractable opponents, and fostering trust are all utilised under the guise of public participation." Given the widespread manipulation of participatory techniques, Cooke and Kothari (2001) are led to describe participation as "the new ideology."

Given the consequences of these activities, both good and bad, participation has gained a place across the political spectrum as a central feature of good governance, both in the worlds of government and academia. Promoting decentralization, good governance practices have added an additional layer of local participatory institutions to an increasingly complex institutional landscape that in some cases has given rise to transfers of both resources and decision-making powers (Stoker 2000). Some countries, such as Brazil, India, Bolivia, have even passed national legislation mandating popular participation in local governance, including planning and budgeting. Of particular note has been the innovation of citizen-oriented participatory budgeting in Brazil, now practiced in various forms in a number of European countries as well.

Conclusion

We have investigated the problems of complexity and their implications for citizen participation. After examining reasons for the decline of participation, we explored how citizens gain political skills, the concept of citizenship, and participatory governance. Participatory governance practices, we saw, represent an attempt to develop intermediary spaces that readjust the boundaries between the state and its citizens and, as such, seek to establish new places in which the participants from both can engage each other in new ways (Cornwall 2002). These spaces are sometimes used for radical self-help activities outside of the state, but they have also had significant impacts on formal governmental institutions. Indeed, some of these deliberative innovations seek to colonize state power by transforming the interfaces between local citizens and higher levels of government (Fung and Wright 2003), a topic to which we return in Chapter 9.

The picture, though, has not been all positive. The experiences have ranged across the spectrum from very impressive to disastrous, which in turn has politicized the issue. This has led to various efforts to sort out the positive and negative elements contributing to such participatory projects: What is good and what is bad, what works and what does not.

While there is still much to learn about participation, what we do know offers justification for optimism, although only cautious optimism. Despite much of the rhetoric surrounding the discussion of participation, experiences with participatory governance demonstrate participation to be neither straightforward nor easy. A closer look shows that citizens can participate, but that participation has to be carefully organized, facilitated—even cultivated and nurtured. Such work rests, among other things, on difficult questions about what constitutes successful participation? Does it have to contribute instrumentally to a special goal or achievement to be counted as successful? Or is it enough for it to only contribute to the development of citizens' political competencies?

In view of the difficulties involved in designing and managing participatory processes, it comes as no surprise to learn that citizen participation
schemes rarely follow smooth pathways. Local people may themselves be
highly skeptical about the worth of investing their time and energy
in participatory activities. In some situations, participation will lack immediate relevance; it may carry more significance for outsiders than it does
for those in the relevant communities. Moreover, not everyone within the
communities will be able or motivated to participate. Even when there
is sufficient interest in participation there may be time barriers. And so on.
The point is this: Without concern for both the *viability* and *quality* of
participation, it is better to forego the effort. Citizen participation, in
short, is a complicated and uncertain business that needs to be carefully
thought out in advance (Fischer 2000).

We turn at this point to two other lines of investigation that have
emerged to support participation and, in various ways, theories of participatory governance. One is normative, namely the theory of deliberative
democracy in political and social theory; the other is empirical, the investigation of a range of deliberative experiments and practices that have
developed over the past two decades or so.

3

Citizens and Experts in Deliberative Democracy: From Theory to Experimentation

In contemporary political theory, citizen participation and deliberation, as already seen, have emerged as dominant themes. Since the early 1990s, talk about deliberation in democratic theory has become something of a growth industry. In the main, this deliberative orientation has emerged to counter the overly simplistic approach to individual deliberation that dominates most of the interest-based theories of political analysis, rational choice theory in particular. The emphasis in these approaches is on citizens rationally pursuing their own self-interests. They take citizens to know their own interests and preferences, which can thus be analytically treated as empirically given. Beyond the rhetorical value of appeals to the "public good" in political debate, there is in such theories little or no room for considering common interests, shared beliefs, or the need to deliberate with one's fellow citizens.

In sharp contrast, the work of deliberative democratic theory is designed to revitalize a more classical conception of democracy based on citizen participation, moral reason, and a return to the public interest. Toward this end, as Chambers (2003: 309) has put it, deliberation is understood to refer to "debate and discussion aimed at producing reasonable, well-informed opinion in which participants are willing to revise preferences in light of discussion, new information, and claims made by fellow participants."[1]

---

[1] Fearson (1998: 63) makes a distinction between deliberation and discussion. In his view, deliberation is a subset of discussion more generally. Whereas a discussion does not necessarily involve careful reason, deliberation is defined as "a discussion that involves the careful serious weighting of reasons for a proposition" or course of action. He suggests six reasons as to why citizens might discuss the issues before taking a collective decision: "(1) Reveal private

In the process of arguing their interests, participants are expected to offer reasons as to why they believe their positions to be in the legitimate interest of all other affected parties. The key contention put forward by its theorists, as Warren (2007: 272) explains, is that "deliberative approaches to collective decisions under conditions of conflict produce better decisions than those resulting from alternative means of conducting politics: coercion, traditional deference, or markets. The decisions resulting from deliberation are likely to be more legitimate, more reasonable, more informed, more effective, and more politically viable."

Deliberative theorists understand citizens in a very different way than do those who focus on interests. Without denying that citizens make many—perhaps even most—decisions to satisfy their own interests, they are also seen to be capable of moral reflection on their actions and, at times, willing to collaborate with fellow citizens in the achievement of common interests. Informed by a sense of the "good society," as well as a consideration of the interests of others, citizens are seen to reflect periodically on existing interests as well as to create new one. From this perspective, the task of governance involves designing democratic institutional arrangements that enhance the chances of full and equal engagement by citizens as they attempt to clarify, extend, and revise shared understandings and values in the course of collaborative problem-solving (Rosenberg 2003).

Deliberative democracy: Moral reason and the common good

The interest in deliberative democracy in political theory is anchored to a critique on individual rights that has long been the core component of liberal political theory, the dominant school of Anglo-American thought (Bohman and Rehg 1997). In this view, an overemphasis on individual rights—at the expense of social obligations—has led to the neglect of common moral issues. One reason has to do the with legalistic nature of individual rights. As rights are typically treated as matters for courts to decide, the moral questions associated with them are removed from the

information; (2) Lessen or overcome the impact of bounded rationality; (3) Force or encourage a particular mode of justifying demands or claims; (4) Help render the ultimate choice in the eyes of the group, so as to contribute to group solidarity or to improve the likely implementation of the decision; (5) Improve the moral or intellectual qualities of the participants; (6) Do the 'right thing,' independent of the consequences of discussion" (p. 45). To this list Elster (1998: 11) adds "to improve the moral and intellectual qualities of the participants."

larger public sphere of citizen discussion.[2] As Marcedo (1999: 3) puts it, "when moral controversies such as those over abortion, gay rights, affirmative action, and assisted suicide are routinely decided by the courts, critics charge that it is no wonder that the office of citizenship comes to seem of marginal importance." When citizens are denied the opportunity to grapple with important questions about right and wrong, equity and fairness, they "lose a vital part of the training in responsibility and self-control that citizenship should bring." If the citizen's role "in negotiation and consensus-building is by-passed, moral decisions may lack political balance and legitimacy."

Deliberative democratic theorists also often complain that the liberal emphasis on the authority of certain kinds of reason restricts the agenda of public discussion. Resting on an overly narrow conception of rationality, largely influenced by the dominance of scientific reason, what can count as legitimate political argumentation is problematically defined in advance. Often neglected are the distinctive viewpoints of groups at the margins of the dominant culture, in particular those who employ other modes of reason and expression. It is an argument basic to feminist critiques of the dominant neo-positivist epistemology, as well as much of the Third World literature on indigenous knowledge. Religious groups frequently add their voices to this critical chorus, charging that liberalism rests on the authority of a secular scientific rationality that discounts the concerns of religious citizens, unfairly restricting or silencing their voices in political debate. Deliberative democrats respond to many of these disparate sources of complaint by arguing for a more wide-open and inclusive model of democratic discourse.

For two of the leading theorists of deliberative democracy, Gutmann and Thompson (2004:7), it can be defined "as a form of government in which free and equal citizens (and their representatives), justify decisions in a process in which they give one another reasons that are mutually acceptable and generally accessible, with the aim of reaching conclusions that are binding in the present on all citizens but open to challenges in the future." At the core of this theory is a conviction that much of contemporary politics is made up of a broad swath of moral conflicts that should

---

[2] While one of the reasons put forward for deliberative democracy is the view that certain issues are not appropriately decided in the court room, others disagree. This view, in their opinion, neglects the fact that much of legal theory actually recognizes such problems. Indeed, it takes into account the fact that no one has answers to many of these problems and somebody has to decide. Some argue that the "courts are better suited for achieving principled resolution among contentious moral perspective in the public realm than are other political institutions" (Shapiro 2005: 31).

neither be relegated to the courts nor treated as problems to be resolved by mere interest group bargaining (1996, 2004). These moral conflicts, they argue, call upon citizens themselves to act as "reason givers" and "reason demanders." Political institutions and public practices should be arranged so as to encourage citizens to grapple with these moral conflicts on their own terms. They should, in short, develop and give reasoned arguments that can be publicly discussed and accepted by their fellow citizens. The acceptance of reasons, in this view, helps to build the motivations necessary to implement the political actions which citizens come to agree upon.

Attempting to reorient political theory from principles of rights to moral issues as they are disputed in the public realm, Gutmann and Thompson argue that a shared political culture functions better if citizens and their representatives are encouraged to engage in a wider discussion of moral values and their application to specific situations. Moral disagreement in politics, they recognize, is to be expected even under the best of conditions. Even when citizens are motivated to find fair terms of social cooperation, disagreement will still emerge from the fact that different people hold different and sometimes incompatible norms and values. Moreover, citizens have incomplete understandings of many problematic issues, as well as differing interpretations of the meanings and consequences of actions. Despite such barriers to agreement, however, deliberation is seen to contribute to the health of a democratic society. Not only does it encourage public-spiritedness, deliberation introduces citizens to considerations of the common good. In doing so, it helps to promote tolerant, mutually respectful decision-making which can, in turn, hold out—if not increase—the possibility of reaching better understandings and eventual agreement. By keeping open the channels of conversation and coordinated interaction, so the argument, mutual respect and understanding can also assist democracies in correcting the mistakes of the past decisions.

Deliberative citizens, in this view, must reason beyond their own narrow self-interest and consider what they would be able to justify to other citizens who reasonably disagree with their arguments. Such a deliberative orientation, as Gutmann and Thompson concede, does not address citizens who reject the goal of finding fair terms for public cooperation. Deliberation cannot influence those unwilling to advance their public claims in ways that acknowledge their fellow citizens. But by promoting a broader range of reasons exchanged by fellow citizens in the public realm, deliberation can nonetheless adjust for liberalism's overly narrow conception of reason, shaped in part by a scientific understanding of rationality.

Although Gutmann and Thompson reject the scientific/positivist understanding of moral reason, they do acknowledge that moral discussions have an empirical as well as a normative dimension. Here, however, they offer little by way of methodological insight. They only say that when we rely on empirical evidence we should honor relatively reliable methods of inquiry and eschew implausible assertions. It is illegitimate to appeal to "any authority whose conclusions are imperious, in principle as well as practice, to the standards of logical consistency to or reliable methods of inquiry that themselves be mutually *acceptable*". This is not altogether to reject or exclude other forms of knowledge, such as religion, but rather "any authority that is impervious from a variety of reasonable points of view." Beyond these generalities, however, their emphasis remains anchored to moral reason. On questions about empirical knowledge and the professional practices of expertise, as they present it, deliberative democratic theory is largely silent.

Deliberative democracy in critical perspective

Such theorizing on deliberative democracy has increasingly encountered sharp criticisms. Blaug (1999: 134), for example, has usefully pointed to the distance between the perspective of the deliberative theorist and the ordinary citizen. As he writes, "if deliberative theory is to be of real use, if it is to be a pragmatic and earthbound practice, it will need to address democracy not just as it appears in the elevated view of the political theorists, but also as it is actually encountered in the everyday world of ordinary people."[3] Democratic deliberation thus presents very different issues and problems from the point of view of the citizen participating in the realm of action. In this regard, it can better be understood as an experience rather

[3] As Wolin (1994: 14) puts it, few citizens are engaged in statecraft. "We do not face the problem of reforming an entire social order, or of ridding *all* discourses of exclusionary practices. We live firmly upon the earth, grubbing around in our work, our civic involvements, our religious affiliations, our familial and social groups and in our intermittent political activism. For the most part, it is in face-to-face discussion that ordinary people actually confront the problems of democracy. Here, more democracy means greater fairness and participation in the decisionmaking process of an actual group. All of the work put in by the theorist to make democracy real by giving it an institutional location is a matter of little interest to us as participants in an actual discourse. This is because in a real situation, the dimensions of 'where' simply does not arise. What we want is more democracy right here, right now" (Blaug 1999: 134–5).

than institutional procedures and practices. Democracy for citizens, as Wolin (1994: 14) has put it, is something that "breaks out." It is a social and political experience that happens to participants in the process of discussion and deliberation. Usually, it is characterized by a sense of immediacy and frequent emotional outbursts with no particular discursive form. Such "fugitive democracy" occurs for periods time—shorter or longer—sometimes even revolutionary in character—then it recedes and fades, often as such talk is subdued by the institutions that take it over.

From this perspective, the theory of deliberative democracy is unrealistic and utopian. First and foremost, in this respect, is its high level of abstraction. Consider, for instance, Cohen's (1996) much cited criteria for judging the legitimacy of deliberative democracy. Citizens need to be free of constraints; participants have to have equal chances to contribute to the deliberative exchanges; deliberative outcomes need to be based on reasons; and final consenses should be geared to the common good.[4] All are, to be sure, worthy principles of democratic deliberation. But they fall short of the political dynamics of the contentious, pluralist world in which citizens find themselves; they are important ideals but only ideals. There is, of course, no such thing as a totally free space for deliberation, the world we live in is highly unequal, conflict is as prevalent as consensus, and the mode of argumentation based on the giving of reasons would seem to leave out other important considerations. Based on a rational conception of argumentation, for example, it neglects the role of emotion in reason, although emotions are everywhere fundamental to political behavior. Reason, as we shall take up in Chapter 10, is seldom—if ever—divorced from emotional commitment.

While there is certainly a place for ideals in political theory, the degree to which an idealistic—some say utopian—theory of deliberative democracy has moved to the center of political theory has caused concern. Theorists such as Shapiro (2005) and Walzer (1999) worry that deliberative democracy pushes other important topics to the side, indeed topics that bear directly on its own viability. One of these concerns is the role of interests. While deliberative democracy has correctly challenged the liberal-theoretical understanding of individual interests, the theory seems to err too far in the other direction. Although deliberative democrats do not deny the central place of interests in politics, they fail in fact to place enough emphasis on the importance of this fundamental political consid-

---

[4] Habermas (2006), whose early work is the foundation of such theory, has recently further elaborated this claim by arguing that the very legitimizing core of democracy rests on the epistemics of rational reason. On the epistemics of democracy also see Estlund (2007).

eration. Given that many people are unwilling to discuss matters that might adversely affect their own interests, particularly if they are satisfied with the provision or protection of these interests, this necessarily poses problematic questions about the viability of the theory.[5]

Beyond a strategic refusal to deliberate on interests, there is no necessary reason to believe that citizens will come to agree. Even when they are willing to deliberate about issues relevant to their interests, their conflicting interests are at times irreconcilable (Shapiro 2005: 35–49). Indeed the very definition of an ethical dilemma in politics is a conflict between two or more value commitments that cannot be supported or carried out at the same time, if at all. Often there is no way to deal with this but to aggregate interests and vote—the position supported by the largest number of supporters wins. In addition to deliberation and voting, bargaining also plays a major role. Those with differences, irreconcilable or otherwise, can work out solutions that are essentially compromises between their diverging positions.[6] These measures fall far short of moral resolution, but they do provide a way to move forward.

A second related and equally important concern is the absence of power in deliberative democratic theory. People with power can and do use it to avoid situations that might not be to their advantage. There are many ways of doing this, ranging from simply refusing to participate, controlling the agenda of a political discussion to make sure that it is difficult to raise certain issues, or manipulating others to hold different views. Given the highly unequal distribution of power, especially reflected in the ability of money to stand in as a form of political expression, power in the form of wealth poses a fundamental threat to contemporary democracy. Some ask if we should even be talking about democracy under such existing circumstances of inequality, as it tends only to mask the underlying realities of a political world increasingly dominated by wealthy elites far removed from ordinary citizens.

Some accept deliberation but ask how extensive it should be. How open-ended should it be? Is it ever proper to impose limitations on democratic

[5] Bessette (1994: 144–6) contends that the more politicians are required to deal with policy issues in public settings, rather than behind closed doors, the less likely their decisions will be a product of deliberation.

[6] Deliberation, it is pointed out, is only one way to deal with problems, and in some cases not the best. Some institutional contexts may actually hinder deliberation (Thompson 1998). Moreover, bargaining and voting have long been basic political practices to deal with the fact that people often are unable to come to a workable agreement. There is seldom a form of deliberation that isn't combined with bargaining or voting in one way or another. Indeed, as Elster (1998: 7) argues, political decisionmaking processes usually involve a mix of these various forms, although none exist independently of some form of deliberative argumentation.

deliberation? Is popular deliberation about politics simply an end in itself, or does it lead to good political outcomes? If popular reflection on moral questions is valued as an end in itself, is such deliberation purchased at the cost of other political goods, such as social justice, the application of expertise, efficient solutions, and perhaps political stability? Some contend, in this respect, that deliberative democracy emphasizes procedures at the expense of substantive principles (Purcell 2008). What happens, they ask, when deliberation produces unjust outcomes? While Gutmann and Thompson (2004: 42) reply that "the substantive justice of a particular decision depends on establishing a just process," many of their critics ask which comes first. At the more practical level of real world politics, a good deal of evidence shows that there is nothing simple or straightforward about the connection between substance and process, a topic examined in Chapter 9.

Yet others challenge the assumption that citizens who follow logical rules of discourse can reach rational consensus through deliberation. Here two questions arise. One has to do with consensus. While there are surely occasions when the rules of discourse help to promote consensus, they ask if conflict and disagreement are not as much or more the outcome of deliberation in pluralistic political systems than consensus. For writers such as Young (1990) the emphasis is better placed on difference than consensus. Such theorists also see pluralism as bringing forth a wider range of perspectives, in particular those that tend to get suppressed in a political world of unequal opportunities and, at the same time, supplies a better check on the abuse of power. Indeed, it would be better to shift the goal of deliberative democracy from consensus to critical learning based on the communicative interactions of those who differ. Whereas consensus remains an elusive goal in complex pluralist societies, a precondition for reaching it is more often than not some form of learning among the participants. From a dialectical understanding of knowledge and learning, as we shall argue in Chapter 8, the deliberative confrontation across differences is one of the conditions for transformational learning.

Beyond logical rules, some pursue the issue further and question the assumption that citizens can or actually do follow rules of reasoned argumentation. And if so, do they follow the same rules. What, indeed, if citizens do not have the communicative competencies that would make deliberative democracy possible? Do they have the inherent capacities required to engage in logical argumentation with one another? Influenced by the seminal contributions of Rawls (1971) and Habermas (1987), most deliberative theorists take for granted that citizens can be logical and reasonable, at least under particular circumstances, which makes rational consensus possible. For Habermasians, this is governed by implicit understandings of ideal speech embedded in language and the very act of communication itself. They are seen to be self-reflective actors who not only identify and pursue interests, but also actively define and critically reflect on their own preferences—as well as those of others—in light of basic motives and values (Bohman 1996). Many deliberative democracy's harshest critics take this characterization of everyday actors to be unrealistic and, indeed, there is much in cognitive psychology that suggests the need to think more carefully about this set of assumptions (Fischer 2000: 242–62). Such research shows that people in fact exhibit different capacities to reason; often they are at different stages of development (Rosenberg 2003). Even when their capacities are well developed, their modes of reason can take different forms. These issues, as Young (2000) and others have argued, have largely gone unattended (Mansbridge 2003, 2007). For this reason, we take up the narrative form of knowing as well as the interplay between emotion and reason in Part III.

Questions about communicative competencies and different modes of reason also relate to the issue of knowledge and expertise. As already noted, Gutmann and Thompson's work fails to rigorously confront the role of knowledge and complexity. With regard to the relation of experts to citizens in such deliberative contexts, the assumptions about reason and competence are of critical importance. A great deal of what cognitive psychologists have learned about the interactions between professional experts and citizens points to conflicts between different ways of reasoning. Although such conflicts are typically attributed to the citizen's inability to understand the technical aspects of any complex issue, such a conclusion may only reflect the privileged position of expert knowledge in modern society. It does not necessarily mean that citizens are in unable to reason logically. Other research shows that citizens are frequently only exercising a different mode of reason in arriving at their conclusions, often more appropriate to the social situation, an issue that we take up in Chapter 5. Once the nontechnical forms of logic relevant to social action are recognized, particularly the intermixing of technical and normative considerations that confront the applied disciplines, we can open up and explore a range of new innovative approaches designed to bring together professionals and their citizen clients. One of the practices that has already made important steps in this direction is participatory research, addressed in Chapter 8.

These criticisms have led some to argue that the theory of deliberative democracy is simply too far removed from politics as we know it, and thus too distant from what we can realistically expect of citizens. An alternative would be to better situate deliberation in the context of existing realities. One the one hand, the democratic principles of the theory are not at issue; the theory can well serve as a counterfactual against which a range of deliberative practices can be judged. On the other, deliberation can be one of the various strategies of a democratic system, without attempting to redefine the system itself. In this respect, it is generally better suited for a range of smaller political and civic associations that a centralized polity. This would include local level community-oriented deliberations, deliberation in professional associations, civic associations, political parties, social service agencies, labor unions, public advisory bodies, and the like. In this view, deliberation more generally should be *one* of a variety of strategies for resolving difference, along side of interest aggregation, voting, bargaining, and court litigation.

We need, in short, a democratic theory in which deliberation has an important role to play but is not all of it. Part of that theory would be a more empirically informed approach to deliberative political practices. Toward this end, we would do well to follow Mansbridge's (1999) suggestion and focus on the broader deliberative system of a society. We could, in this way, attempt to find ways to connect a fuller range of discursive interactions—from everyday talk, media discussions, expert deliberations, courtroom argumentation, and citizen juries to parliamentary debate. With such a model we could work toward a theory of discourse, which includes power, interest group bargaining, and struggles in civil society that, at the same time, holds deliberative democracy out as a theoretical ideal against which actual practices could be measured (Dryzek 2000, 2001). Not only would it give us a way of examining "deliberation outbreaks, " to use Blaug's (1999) term, but also, following Parkinson (2006), to explore how the concept of the deliberative system can be used to connect the deliberation of small groups to the larger society. Insofar as competent citizens in civil society and others in the media reflect on and accept the outcomes of such deliberative activities, the linkage can contribute to the legitimacy of the deliberations of "minipublics" (to use Fung's term) for the larger society.

Conceding the highly theoretical nature of deliberative political theory, Chambers (2003) sees the need to move from a lofty theoretical endeavor to a "working theory" and points to experiments on deliberation, such as the Danish consensus conference, citizen juries in the US and Britain, and planning cells in Germany as the beginnings of a move in this direction. As things currently stand, however, there has been far too little communication between the theorists of deliberative democracy and empirical research on deliberation, the work of Fiskin (1996) being an important exception. Although deliberative democracy has surely served as an inspiration for many of those involved in deliberative experimentation, the theory has thus yet to offer many specifics on the kinds of institutional designs that can facilitate real-world practices. Given the importance of such an interaction, we turn next to deliberative research.

Deliberative research: Experiments and experiences

Deliberative research refers to a series of empirical investigations and practices that have emerged over the past several decades designed to explore the possibilities and potentials of citizen deliberation (Gastil and Levine 2005). An examination of the literature on citizen juries and other deliberative fora does not immediately suggest that it is a "working theory" for deliberative democracy. At the same time, though, it does speak to some of the basic issues and assumptions upon which deliberative democracy rests, in particular the assumption that citizens can participate meaningfully in decisions about complex social and technical issues. It offers, in this respect, useful insights that bear directly on the issues and problems raised by deliberative democracy. Of special importance for the present discussion is the way citizens reason in such matters and how their own deliberative processes relate to expertise and professional knowledge. Given the centrality of these questions for the work at hand, we shall examine these deliberative projects in that light. First, however, we begin with some general observations before turning more specifically to particular experimental projects.

Among the studies of citizen participation, knowledge and expertise, no case better illustrates such capabilities of ordinary citizens than that of the gay movement's struggle against the spread of AIDS. As gay AIDS activists have shown, citizens can not only learn a great deal about science, they can take charge of their own research experimentation when deemed necessary. During the height of the AIDS crisis, many lay groups in San Francisco and New York even started their own journals to report on personal experiments with potentially life-saving drugs that were prohibited by medical authorities. Epstein (1996) has documented the degree to which the boundaries between scientific "insiders" and lay "outsiders" crisscrossed in the struggles to find a cure for AIDS, or what he has called "credibility struggles." In addition to revealing how scientific "certainty is constructed or deconstructed," his investigations have shown non-scientists to have gained enough of a voice in the scientific world to have shaped to a remarkable extent National Health Institute-sponsored research.

Some have countered that the gay community is fairly middle class and thus tends to be better educated than a large segment of the public. But this criticism misses the point. It is true that members of the gay community tend to be better informed than many other citizens, but this is not the same as being a scientist or having scientific training. Moreover, they are generally well informed in the case of HIV because of it critical importance to them personally. Other experiences show that less formally educated citizens also become much more interested and involved when an issue directly affects their own situation. The crucial point is that, in contrast to those who downplay the possibility of such participation, the experience with HIV in the US illustrates that when necessary, many citizens are able to learn enough to play an important role in the relevant policy decisions.

The point has been further documented by an environmental educational project at the University of California, Berkeley, which addressed more generally citizens' abilities to deal rationally with questions of risk. It was found that many can learn and use enough science to understand and assess questions of technological risk for themselves (Wildavsky 1997). Such learning takes time and effort, but the capability is there. This kind of learning does not involve laboratory research but, as we shall see, it does not need to in matters related to policymaking, which involves not only comprehending research findings but, equally important, judging them in the light of values, norms, and goals.

Numerous other examples come from efforts to cite and operate hazardous facilities (Paelhke and Torgerson 1992; Rabe 1992). One study, for example, demonstrates the degree to which citizens were able to participate in sophisticated policy decisions concerning complex technical issues (Hill 1992). Once issues and questions were no longer posed in technical languages alien to the average citizen, comprehending and judging the basic elements of a policy argument about a complex technology was inherently no more complex than what the average citizen manages to accomplish in the successful running of a small business.

Most often such cases involve a cooperative relationship between citizens and experts. Rather than a matter of citizens merely going it alone, nearly all such cases reveal the involvement of a "citizen expert" of some sort.[7] For example, citizen struggles against the siting of toxic wastes typically involve the presence a professional expert who assists the community in answering its own questions on its own terms (Levine 1982). Sometimes members of the community themselves, such experts step forward to help communities grasp the significance of evolving developments, think through strategies, and even directly confront a community's opponents (Edelstein 1988). Such participatory consultation, in the process, serves to both broaden citizens' access to the information produced by scientists and to systematize their own "local knowledge." The most politically progressive example of such participatory consultation in the United States has taken the form of "popular" or "lay epidemiology" in political struggles about environmental justice, particularly as they have pertained to the impact of toxic chemicals on the health of local citizens (Novotny 1994).

Deliberative experiments

A numerous civic activists and scholars in the US and Northern Europe have developed projects and procedures for bringing citizens's preferences to bear on public policy (Gastil and Levine 2005; Fishkin 1996; Bohman 1996). All of these fora seek to elicit citizen views on complex economic, and social issues that bear directly on policy decisions. In general, they involve two different types of citizen participants, one being partisan stakeholders and the other non-partisan lay citizens. Such research has ranged from investigations of traditional citizen surveys and public meetings to innovative techniques such as deliberative polling, televoting, focus groups, national issue conventions, study circles on to more sophisticated scenario workshops, citizen juries, planning cells, consensus conferences, citizens' assemblies, and public budgeting (Crosby 1995; Joss and Durant 1995; Fishkin 1996; Lindeman 1997; Andersen and Jaeger 1999; Gastil and Levine 2005; Hendriks 2005; Rowe and Frewer 2005;).[8] In the most participatory of these methods, the expert role is limited to supplying information that citizens find necessary; experts only answer

---

[7] The point is applicable across cultures. Tze-Luen Lin of the National Taiwan University explains that researchers in Taiwan have found such expert involvement in nearly all of the many cases they have observed.

[8] According to the National Coalition for Dialogue and Democracy, some thirty deliberative techniques have been developed and employed. Others put the number as high as fifty such procedures.

questions that citizens put to them. Although little known to citizens and politicians, not to mention academics, these experiences offer important insights as to how to bring citizens closer to public decisions processes. Especially significant, they have shown that citizens are capable of much more involvement in thinking about and assessing technical questions than is conventionally presumed.

These efforts have been developed in part as a response to the fact that the dominant technique for learning what citizens think—the traditional public opinion survey—generally supplies its participants with very few avenues for expressing themselves (Schlozman 2002). Most problematic, standard polling techniques offer citizens little or no opportunity to reflect on the questions put to them, especially with regard to those questions that involve unfamiliar or uncomfortable ideas. Such techniques cede agenda control to the survey designers, who assume they not only know the right questions to ask, but how to interpret the citizens' responses. In addition to structuring the agenda for the discussion, designers determine which facts and arguments the participants should respond to.

This deliberative research has thus focused in particular on efforts to extend the role of citizens in setting the agenda for such inquiries. Concerned with what Fishkin (1996) describes as "considered judgment," such work seeks to understand the processes citizens engage in to arrive at informed, responsible public preferences. Toward this end, research has followed two particular lines of investigation, poll-oriented and group-oriented deliberation. On one end of the spectrum are those experiments that have tried to improve on polling techniques themselves, by developing methods of "deliberative polling" that give citizens more of an opportunity to express their opinions on their own terms.[9] One of the most

---

[9] The American Talk Issues Foundation (1994), for example, has used telephone interviews to mitigate the problems of polls by giving respondents more time and resources to assist them in thinking about their answers. This method is based on the idea that if policy choices are clearly worded, basic textual information provided, and key arguments on both sides clearly presented, people can often come to considered judgments in a few minutes. Such deliberative telephone polls attempt to mirror more closely public opinion through large samples (1,000–1,500) of respondents. The approach is clearly an advance, but it still remains subject to the main criticism against polls—the designers play too great a role in the process. Another method is the televote. In this approach, participants are solicited by random digit dialing, receive an informational brochure with basic background information, varied expert opinions, and policy alternatives. Not only are they encouraged to take as much time as they need to read the materials, they also discuss them with other people before casting their "votes." Some televotes have been conducted in conjunction with "Electronic Town Meetings" that allow larger numbers to participate. The main criticism of the televote is that, like any forced-choice survey technique, it elevates to the designers control over the agenda of questions and language in which the responses must be given.

interesting efforts is Fishkin's National Issues Convention, which seeks to combine deliberative polling and small group deliberations (1996; Fishkin and Farrar 2005). This approach has involved gathering 450 citizens from around the country to meet for four days of discussion on crucial national issues. Participants assembled in small groups to talk about their positions, listened to experts and presidential candidates, and have an opportunity to ask questions of those witnesses.

Another technique is the focus group. It offers a way to bring together a smaller number of citizens (usually between six and ten participants) to discuss specific topics. Developed first as a marketing research technique designed to elicit consumer attitudes about new products, this approach has also been widely used to probe public policy issues. Permitting the investigator to interact with citizens in a more natural setting than the standard one-on-one interview, it can rapidly generate useful information and at relatively low cost. The sample size can also be extended by increasing the number of groups. A moderator guides the participants through a deliberation that probes attitudes about proposed policies or services. The exchanges are loosely structured, and the facilitator encourages the free flow of opinions and ideas (Marshall and Rossman 1999). The agenda of questions to be discussed, however, is typically determined by those in search of the information. Some have criticized the focus group as having the potential for groupthink, but other argue that such pressure to conform can be controlled by a trained and experienced facilitator.

Citizen jury

The citizen jury or panel permits a much higher degree of unstructured citizen involvement. Providing citizens with an opportunity to deliberate in considerable detail among themselves (usually for three days) before coming to judgment or decision on questions they are charged to answer, they hear expert discussions, pose their own questions to the experts, and deliberate the matter among themselves (Crosby and Nethercut 2005).[10]

---

[10] The forerunner of the citizen jury, and still a classic example of efforts in this direction, is the work of the Berger Inquiry Commission (Berger 1977, 1985; LaForest and Phillips 2006) in the 1970s in Canada. In this case, a prominent high-level judge was appointed to assess the environmental impact of an oil pipeline designed to run through the traditional lands of native northern Americans. For this purpose, he organized a series of deliberative fora that brought together members of the local indigenous communities, industry representatives, government and political officials. Heralded in many quarters as a major contribution to participatory deliberation and decisionmaking, the reports of the Inquiry Commission were instrumental in halting a project widely viewed as portending social and environmental

The basic concept of the citizen panel was developed in Northern Europe and the United States before spreading to a range of countries around the world (National Research Council 1996). One of the more elaborate formulations of the method has been developed by Pieter Dienel of the University of Wuppertal in Germany. Dienel's concept of *Plannungszelle* (planning cell), later described at times as *Buergergutachten* (citizens' assessment), involves bringing together assemblies of twelve to twenty four randomly selected citizens for three to five days to discuss among themselves a particular question or issue (Dienal 1992: 10; Hendriks 2005).

Exempted from their regular work obligations, the participants in a typical *Plannungszelle* are asked to spend a period to time discussing their preferences for one of three or four policy options. The panel is assisted by a moderator who helps the citizens keep the deliberation moving, often with minimal intervention. The management of planning cell dynamics, as such, involves little attention to preparatory exercises, such as group-building empowerment exercises. Such facilitatory activities are often viewed as potentially manipulative (Hendriks 2005). In Dienel's view, citizens best learn to deliberate by working together on the tasks at hand.

The panelists, as such, have considerable discretion to determine both their own discussion agenda and procedural rules pertaining to schedule and moderation (e.g., time limits on individual and group exchanges). The moderator arranges for experts to be available during the deliberation to help clarify questions of fact with panelists being encouraged to actively interrogate the answers of the experts. Because these panelists have considerable time to hear expert testimony and to ask questions, they can learn much more about an issue than is the case in other deliberative fora, such as deliberative telephone polling or televoting.

At the end of their deliberation, a report on the panel's findings and conclusions is prepared. Conflicts among panelists are generally resolved through the principle of majority vote, although minority views can be reported. The report is then sent to a range of public decision-making bodies concerned with the topic and media outlets agreed to by the participants at the outset.

The main criticisms of citizens panels are that these issues concern narrowly defined local problems (e.g., how to reorganize public transportation routes); that the discussions among the participants are closed to

disaster for these distant native American communities of northwestern Canada. In many ways the grandfather of the citizen jury, the Berger Inquiry supplied the beginnings of a publicly oriented mode of participatory inquiry.

outsiders; and that the report is at times written with the assistance of the group moderator of the project. Many of these problems are corrected in the Danish consensus conference, the most sophisticated of the panel or jury methods.

Consensus conference

Whereas most methods for citizen deliberation have dealt with issues at the local level, the Danish Consensus Conference is institutionalized at the national level and addresses broad social and economic questions. In general, the consensus conference differs from the citizen jury in a number of respects. One is that the participants are given no specific charge to answer; for a given topic they decide for themselves which questions they want to answer. Another is that the citizens more actively cross-examine the expert. The deliberations also tend to run somewhat longer than in the citizen jury (more commonly five days rather than three). And further, where most forms of citizen panels operate behind closed doors, the Danish consensus conference is more open to the public as a whole. Indeed, one of its primary purposes is to inform and stimulate broad public debate on the given topic.

The consensus conference, developed by the Danish Board of Technology, has emerged as the most elaborate of the citizen-oriented deliberative procedures. Inspired in the 1980s by the now defunct US Office of Technology Assessment (OTA), the Board of Technology sought a new and innovative way to get around the divisive conflicts associated with environmentally risky technologies such as nuclear power. The idea was to find a way to make good on the OTA's original mission of integrating expertise with a wide range of social, economic, and political perspectives (Joss and Durant 1995). Toward this end, the Board developed a model for a "citizen's tribunal" designed to stimulate broad social debate on issues relevant to the parliamentary level of policymaking. In an effort to bring lay voices into technological and environmental inquiries, the Board sought to move beyond the use of narrow expert advisory reports to parliament by taking issues directly to the public. In compliance with the long standing Danish political tradition of "people's enlightenment," which stresses the relationship between democracy and a well-educated citizenry, the Board developed a framework that bridges the gap between scientific experts, politicians, and the citizenry (Kluver 1995). As a highly innovative contribution to the facilitation of democratic practices, the consensus conference has provided a model for giving citizens discursive influence in the policy process. Not only has it been widely credited with invigorating contemporary democratic practices, it has built understanding and trust among citizens and experts as well.[11]

The formal goals of the consensus conference are twofold: to provide members of parliament and other decisionmakers with the information resulting from the conference; and to stimulate public discussion through media coverage of both the conference and the follow-up debates. First implemented in 1987, conferences have dealt with issues such as energy policy, air pollution, sustainable agriculture, food irradiation, risky chemicals in the environment, the future of private transport, gene therapy, and the cloning of animals.

A consensus conference is organized and administered by a steering committee appointed by the Board of Technology. Typically, it involves bringing together between ten and twenty-five citizens charged with the task of assessing a socially sensitive topic of science and technology. The lay participants are usually selected from written replies to advertisements announced in national newspapers and radio broadcasts. Interested citizens, excluding those who are experts on the particular theme, apply by sending a short written statement explaining why they would like to participate in the inquiry process. The statements are evaluated by the steering committee to determine if a candidate is sufficiently dedicated to fully participate in the conference process. Citizens are asked to participate as unpaid volunteers, but the Board offers compensation for any loss of income that might occur as a result of the involvement.

From the choosing of a topic to the final public discussions after the formal conference proceedings, the process typically runs several months with the participants meeting on a number of weekends. The conference itself typically runs for five days. Central to the inquiry process

---

[11] Since the outset of the Danish experience, consensus conferences have spread to Austria, Holland, Britain, New Zealand, Norway, Switzerland, Japan, and Taiwan, among others. A preliminary pilot project dealing with the topic of telecommunications was also conducted in Boston in 1997 by the Loka Institute and another one in North Carolina employed the internet. No country has more energetically pursued the consensus conference than Taiwan, which has established an elaborate network of academics, community colleges, civic organizations, and government agencies energetically involved in promoting the consensus conference (as well as citizen juries and deliberative polling). It is seen as part of an important effort to extend democratic learning and skills in the country's continuing efforts to development of its democratic form of government (Chen and Deng 2007). I am especially thankful to Professors Dung-Sheng Chen, Wen-Ling Tu, Tze-Luen Lin, Yen-Wen Peng, and Alan Li for taking the time to explain these elaborate developments to me while teaching and lecturing at Taiwan's Shih Hsrin University, the National Taiwan University and Tamking University in May of 2008.

is a facilitator who works to assist the lay panel in the completion of its tasks. Working closely with the panel, he or she guides the process through an organized set of rules and procedures. In addition to organizing the preparatory informational and deliberative processes, he or she chairs the actual conference itself. Somewhat like a judge in a jury trial, the facilitator maintains the focus of the experts on the lay panel's questions during the conference and assists panelists in finding the most direct answers to their questions. Compared with the planning cell, consensus conference facilitators tend to be much more involved in assisting the participants with the allocated assignments.

Following their selection, the lay participants are assembled for informal meetings on the topic. At the first meeting, the steering committee outlines the topic for the participants in general terms and informs them that they may define their approach to the topic in whatever way they see fit. Not only can they frame their own questions, they can seek the kinds of information they find necessary to answer them. At the same time, panelists are supplied with extensive reading materials by the steering committee and given a substantial interval of time to study the materials at home.

After reading the materials, the panelists are asked to develop a list of questions pertinent to the inquiry. The steering committee uses the participants' lists of questions to assemble additional information for the panelists and to identify an interdisciplinary group of technological and scientific experts to make presentations to the citizen panel. During a subsequent informational meeting, the citizens review new materials and further refine their list of questions, dropping some as well as adding new ones. In some cases, a hearing is also organized for parties interested in the selected subject. Such groups—e.g., individuals or companies with extensive knowledge, influence and/or dependence on the field, research institutions, research committees, traditional interests groups, and grass roots organizations—are provided with an opportunity to contribute information to the deliberative process. At this point, the official conference begins, typically lasting three to five days. After each presentation, the members of the lay group put questions to the experts and cross-examine them. In some cases, representatives from relevant interest groups are present and can also be questioned. Within given time limits, citizens in the audience are also invited to make statements or ask questions. On the second day, the citizen panel more actively cross-examines the experts. Again, at specific points, the public and interested parties are themselves encouraged to ask questions.

At the end of this process, typically on the third day of the meeting, the citizen panel retires to deliberate on the exchanges. With the assistance of a secretary provided by the steering committee, the group prepares a report (fifteen to thirty pages in average length) that considers all of the issues that bear on the topic and their recommendations. Beyond scientific and technical considerations, it addresses the spectrum of economic, social, ethical, and legal aspects associated with the topic. After completing the report, the citizen group publicly presents its conclusions. Normally this occurs in a highly visible public setting in the presence of the media, a variety of experts, and members of the general public. Subsequently, copies of the report are distributed to members of parliament, scientists, special interest groups, and the public. Consensus conference reports often complement formal expert assessments as part of larger technology assessment project.

Of particular interest here is the impact participating in a consensus conference can have on citizens. Research shows lay panels to have both an increased knowledge of the subject under discussion and a new confidence in their ability to deal with complex policy issues generally (Joss 1995; Gastil and Weiser 2002; Delli Caprini et al. 2004). Moreover, participants tend to describe the consensus conference experience as having had a stimulating impact on their personal lives. Joss describes them as saying that the experience gave them a new interest in a variety of issues that they had generally thought were beyond their intellectual reach. More than a few participants explained that they discovered that they could in fact understand and discuss scientific and technical issues, and having learned this, became actively involved in such discussions in a range of formats after the consensus.[12]

Of special importance with regard to understanding citizens's capacities have been the innovative "Citizens' Assemblies" on electoral reform held in British Columbia and Ontario, whose recommendations were put to public referenda. Research on assemblies (which draws on the experiences of citizen juries and consensus conferences) shows the intellectual and deliberative capacities of the ordinary citizens to have been impressively high, as documented in an important volume by Warren and Pearce (2008). Indeed, Blaise, Carter, and Fownier (2008)

---

[12] In considering the extension of these practices to other social contexts it is important to recognize the middle class nature of Danish society generally, as well as the country's long tradition of "people's enlightenment."

found that these citizens not only made good, reasoned choices, but that they did at least as well as the experts on the topic.

Citizen inquiry as deliberative practice

Finally, one should also take note of various deliberative practices that have emerged to deal with a key aspect of citizen deliberation, namely how to get the information required for meaningful deliberation. In most of the projects surveyed above, educational materials of various sorts are supplied to citizens by the facilitators or experts. But this need not be the entire story. The other possibility is that the citizens go after the information themselves (Stilgoe *et al.* 2006: 55–66). In this case, the process of citizen participation evolves to an even more sophisticated level of involvement in the inquiry process. It is important, in this regard, to explore the kinds of participatory research and collaborative inquiry that have emerged to bring citizens together in pursuit of answers to their own questions. Toward this end, we introduce this practice in the context of the discussion of deliberative experiments, dealing with several of the approaches in more detail in the last three chapters.

Even though the practices of citizen inquiry are closely related to the kinds of deliberative experiments discussed above, they have largely been treated by different sets of scholars generally understanding themselves to be involved in different, even unrelated projects. Neither the scholars of deliberative democracy nor deliberative research have drawn citizen or lay inquiry into their spheres of discussion. At the same time, the supporters of participatory citizen inquiry have largely been concerned with less theoretical issues related to practical projects, in particular in fields such as environmental and development planning.

It is thus necessary to briefly take into consideration a range of impressive efforts in which citizens, often in conjunction with experts, have developed techniques for conducting their own empirical inquiry, typically in local settings. While we will deal with several of them in more detail in a later part of the book, it is important to posit the place of deliberative-related practices such as participatory research, action research, popular epidemiology, citizen study circles, participatory resource mapping, and collaborative planning in the broad spectrum of citizen engagement (Fischer 2000). Some of these activities have been organized and facilitated by community-based research programs and sciences shops at local universities. Such programs have often helped local community members research particular problems by offering technical guidance and assistance in various forms.[13]

Although such citizen inquiry is not always entirely local in nature, most of it is. Especially significant in this work, for this reason, has been the concept of "local knowledge." It has emerged as both an empirical and normative knowledge related to a particular local context. Typically, it is understood as an important element of problem-solving that is unavailable to traditional expertise. On the one hand, it involves the information that only the residents in the area in question have access to, in large part because of their more intimate knowledge of the area. But it includes as well a better awareness of local understandings of issues and problems, as well as the norms upon which it rests. Such research, in which local citizens collect the data themselves, sometimes through door-to door surveys, interviews, or empirical measurements of various variables can, as we will see in Chapter 9, function in conjunction with citizen-oriented deliberative projects.

In some cases, citizens have developed and carried out these activities on their own, particularly in struggles against obstinate authorities, either professional or political-bureaucratic. More typically, however, they have engaged in such activities with the assistance of professionals who have taken it upon themselves to help local citizens develop and carry out a research strategy. Often professional experts have helped them as well to organize and present the data for wider public consideration. Sometimes, this has included the development of action plans as well. Not only do these endeavors show that citizens are capable of much more rigorous

---

[13] The "science shop" was developed in by Dutch universities in the 1970s (www.science-shops.org; Sclove 1995). A network of public-oriented science shops were established to respond to the concerns of community groups, public interest organizations, and trade unions about social, environmental, and technological issues. Local citizens can bring their questions to science shops for assistance. Staffed by faculty and students, these research shops sometimes do the research for community members; sometimes they do it cooperatively. Science shops have now spread throughout Europe and are receiving support from the European Union (Jorgensen, Hall, and Hall 2004). The US has no science shops, as such, although the US National Science Foundation offered to support similar activities through its Science for Citizens Program in the late 1970s. But the program was abruptly terminated in the Reagan years. Across the US there are, however, a variety of projects that carry out similar projects. Community-Based Research programs at a number of universities often conduct such activities, in particular helping citizens and professional experts carry out together local research and related planning projects. One of the best examples has been the collaborative partnership established between the University of Illinois and residents of neighboring East St. Louis. The university's planning faculty, students and local residents worked for ten years as "co-planners" to establish a Community Development Corporation which increased public and private investment, produced sustainable housing, and assisted a chemical company add scrubbers to its smokestack, and more (Reardon *et al.* 1993; Reardon 2003).

intellectual work than generally assumed by the conventional wisdom, they represent an extraordinary example of citizen engagement in action. Later in the book we return for a more careful analysis of several of these activities.

Problematizing participation

While the deliberative innovations that we've surveyed here provide a considerable amount of information about citizen participation and the fora that can facilitate it, there remains the need to sort out the different types of participation and their purposes (Rosenberg 2007). Among the things we do know is that people tend to participate in deliberative projects for several different reasons. Research shows that many participate because they want to learn. Others say they want to have an impact on public decisions (Gavelin and Wilson 2007). And some people simply like to meet and socialize with other people. Typically, citizen participants appear to do it for more than one of these reasons, if not all of them.

With regard to the fora themselves, participation raises basic questions related to legitimacy (who do the participants represent?), deliberative capacity (how high is the quality of the communicative interactions?), and impacts (do they affect policy decisions?)[14] Here much of the evidence is only suggestive. It tends to indicate that partisan oriented stakeholder participants tend to be more impact-oriented, although they can encounter problems of legitimacy as representatives of narrower group interests rather than the larger public interest. Although some believe that stakeholders have more impact on policy outcomes, the evidence appears to be mixed. At the same time, nonpartisan groups tend to demonstrate higher degrees of deliberative capacity, especially in terms of the range of issues they discuss (Hendriks, Dryzek, and Hunold 2007). They tend to focus more on common rather than specialized interests.

In all cases, there is substantial evidence that such participatory fora enrich public understanding and discussion. In this regard, it represents a substantial step beyond asking citizens with limited information and understanding of the issues to make one-off comments about what they think the impacts of policies or projects might be. Such engagement is

[14] For a very important effort to assess these questions, especially questions of political representation and the deliberative capacilities of citizens, see the assessment of innovative "Citizens' Assemblies" on electoral reform in British Columbia and Ontario, whose recommendations were put to public referenda (Warren and Pearse 2008).

seen to hold out the possibility of moving policy deliberation away from narrowly construed technical models of discourse—informed by methods such as cost-benefit analysis and risk assessment—by confronting the conventional thinking and underlying assumptions upon which it rests. Challenging the status quo, it brings to the fore a richer public conversation about the social visions, political purposes, and programmatic ends that shape policy decisions, as well holds decision-makers accountable for them.

Of special importance, we have learned from these fora that citizens can in fact participate, but that it seldom just happens. Group deliberation has to be organized and facilitated—even cultivated and nurtured. Missing, moreover, is a set of agreed upon criteria for determining what constitutes success and failure (Rowe and Frewer 2005). This has led Cornwall and Jewkes (1995) to suggest the need to *problematize* participation in an effort to learn what is good and what is bad, what works and what does not. From this perspective, a concern for the *quality* of participation is essential. If not taken into consideration, such efforts will almost surely fail, and the failure only offers the critics of participation ammunitions to suggest the foolishness of the commitment. It is thus important that such projects be well-thought out and carefully guided to avoid such failure.

Before advocating or entering into a participatory project, we need to recognize that citizen participation schemes rarely follow smooth pathways. Working with local citizens is far from easy. Moreover, local people may themselves be highly skeptical as to whether it is worth investing their time and energy in participation. In some situations, participation can also lack local relevance. Other experiences, especially those in Third World developing countries, show that community participation can carry more significance for outsiders—for example, NGOs and academic researchers—than it does for the poor in those areas. Within communities, not everyone will be able to participate, nor will everyone be motivated to be involved. Even if there is interest, there may be time barriers. And so on.

What is needed is more careful research into what citizens can in fact do, what kinds of institutional designs will help them do that, and in which kinds of policy domains such activities are appropriate.[15] In this regard, the kinds of deliberative research presented in the latter part of this chapter makes a good start. Particularly important is further exploration into the question of when citizens should and should not participate. To say

[15] In recent years a number of theorists have begun to focus more rigorously on questions of institutional design. For an very helpful discussions see Fung (2003) and Warren (2007).

that citizens are capable of participating is different from saying that they should always participate. There is no shortage of evidence to indicate that participation for its own sake can be misguided. Experience shows that citizens will agree that participation is highly useful in some cases and not in others. Although participation may help us with a variety of intractable problems, it can also waste a good deal of time and lead nowhere in complex technical issues. Much of the writing about deliberative democracy aside, deliberative experimentation shows participation to be a complicated and uncertain business that needs to be carefully thought out in advance.

Part of the problem of determining what works and what doesn't work has to do with difficulties inherent to the evaluation of such projects. There is often little agreement on what constitutes genuine public participation (Rowe and Frewer 2004). For some, it is counted as participation if people are simply asked to express their opinions, regardless of how the information is used (Rowe and Frewer 2000). At the opposite end of the spectrum, others argue that true participation has to lead to citizen empowerment. From an empirical perspective, this raises problems for the empirical operationalization of participation. The inability to say with precision what constitutes effective or successful participation poses serious problems for meaningful measurement. This has led others such as Joss to accept more informal, subjective assessments based on people's reports of their own experiences. It is a position consistent with contemporary qualitative understandings of inquiry that challenge the validity, even possibility of meaningful empirical analysis in such cases (Yanow 2000; Fischer 2003). Although one can amass a considerable amount of information about participation based on qualitative assessments, this is typically unacceptable to empiricists. While writers such as Webler (1999) have importantly stressed the need for a systematic agenda for research on public participation, the construction of such an agenda will ultimately turn on the outcome of these deeper epistemological issues.

Conclusion

We began by examining the political theory of deliberative democracy. As we saw, this theoretical work has generated an interesting and insightful discussion about the role of citizen deliberation, including the ways it might alleviate a destructive overemphasis on individual self-interest and rights. It is held out as a way to revitalize debate about the broader public interest or common good. But, as we also saw, the theory's critics have portrayed it as theoretically abstract, far removed from the real world of power and politics. In response, some of the defenders of deliberative democracy have presented it as a counterfactual theory designed to generate, if not guide, the search for new deliberative mechanisms that might be introduced in contemporary political settings. This suggested the possibility of posing research on the development of such deliberative arrangements as something of a working theory for deliberative democracy.

The subsequent discussion focused on ways that deliberative research can inform deliberative democracy, short of providing a working theory per se. Beyond the possibility of these practical connections, it can also serve in another, perhaps even more important way, to support the theory of deliberative democracy. Often, as we saw, deliberative theorists are accused of being rather idealistic, if not utopian. They are often asked to explain on what empirical grounds they take citizens to be interested in or capable of such deliberative participation. Here deliberative projects of the sort surveyed above supply something more than an alternative based on normative ideals. As Dewey (1927) argued, political reformers can justifiably base their "oughts" on activities that have already emerged.[16] The consensus conference and citizen jury can supply deliberative theorists with just such a way to ground their "ought" with an "is." It might not satisfy all parties, but it does bring the project out the realm of utopia.

While there is still much to learn about participation, the forgoing discussion of deliberative experiments also shows that we know enough to justify a degree of optimism, even if only cautious optimism. The next step needs to be a more detailed examination of what works, what doesn't, and why? As experiences with new forms of participatory deliberation show them to be neither straightforward nor easy, we need a rigorous research agenda designed to sort out the settings and practices that lead to successful participation. When should participation be introduced and when is it best to proceed by other means?

Although it is not the focus here, the research agenda needs to also take up questions concerning the level and scope of deliberation. The innovations described here generally involve small groups, typically at the local level. To what extend can deliberative practices be extended to the society as a whole? Can deliberation be introduced on a grander scale in a large country with mass public? Earlier Arendt (1972) suggested a "council

---

[16] Dewey draws his position from the ethical tenets of the philosophical theory scientific naturalism.

system" of governance that featured graduated debates starting with small numbers. More recently others have sought to elaborate similar ideas. Tirtanadi (2006), for example, has suggested the formation of "standing policy councils" made up of random samplings of the citizens. Somewhat similarly, Leib (2004) has proposed a popular deliberative branch; and Ackerman and Fishkin (2004) have suggested a "national deliberation day" to take place before general elections.

Another issue has to be epistemological in nature. Of particular importance is the need for a better understanding of the citizen's relation to expert knowledge (and the other way around). It is a question that rests not only on the need for practical experimentation, but also on complicated questions about the nature of knowledge or "knowledges." Here we can find some assistance from the social constructivist understanding of knowledge, which gives us a better understanding of the social-normative and technical-empirical sides of this question. By sorting out these considerations, we can begin to develop a theory for guiding the interactions between experts and lay citizens. It is to this issue that this work is largely addressed. In Part II, we thus turn to social constructivism, the role of the deliberative practitioner, and what Collins and Evans have called a "contributory theory of expertise."

Part II

Situating the Technical in the Social: Implications for Policy Deliberation

4

Deliberative-Analytic Policy Inquiry: Postempiricist Practices

The opening chapter pointed to John Dewey's call for the democratic facilitation of public deliberation. His move in this direction was shaped by two interrelated concerns. For one, he was disturbed by the effort on the part of American political scientists such as Merriam to redefine the basic principles of democracy (Westbrook 1991). "Democratic realism," as Merriam and his colleagues called it, held that democracy should be less understood as a polity of involved citizens that a system of responsible elites, as American democracy appeared to be evolving (or what later was called "democratic elitism"). Advanced as well by the famous journalist and political theorist, Lippman (1922), the view was seen to be supported by new "objective" scientific facts emerging from psychological research. The evidence, they argued, led unavoidably to scepticism about meaningful citizen participation, especially in face of the emerging technological society. In Dewey's view, this position closed off the gap between an existing reality and a more ideal state of democratic politics.[1] Not only did he believe in the presence of a high degree of practical intelligence—albeit dormant—in the public at large, he also argued that such unexpected talent could be released through more direct participation. But for this intelligence to emerge the citizenry would need a local community as its deliberative arena.

Dewey, at the same time, fully recognized the challenge posed by the newly emerging technological society. Indeed, he worried that social and

[1] Dewey's objection to democratic realism involved several interrelated lines of argument. Even if the mass citizenry was as intellectually disappointing as charged, citizens would possess too many demands and too much political power to permit the more knowledgeable elites to rule. Furthermore, experts could not make policy that was genuinely public. Without participatory interaction among citizens and policymakers there would be no reflection on common interest and needs. It was, as such, an argument against professional policymaking.

technical complexity posed a serious barrier to the kind of direct citizen participation that he was calling for. To redress this, Dewey envisioned a new role for the professional expert, namely that of facilitator of democratic deliberation. He saw it as a role to be performed by the newly emerging social science professions, along with a place for social scientifically oriented journalists and educators. The task was not just to provide technical information for problem-solving, but to combine it with a new function of facilitating public deliberation and learning. Toward this end, he called for a cooperative division of labor between experts and citizens and an improvement in the conditions and methods of debate that would bring them together. This would require a central role on the part of professional experts, but it would take a new form. Rather than only rendering judgments, they would analyze and interpret for the public. If experts, acting as interpreters and educators, could decipher the social and technical complexities of the modern world for citizens, they would have better chances of making informed political judgments.

Similarly, following Dewey's lead, Lasswell saw the need for the facilitation of democracy and advanced his concept of a "policy sciences of democracy" as a contribution to that end. But Lasswell never fully made good on this normative commitment, in part because of his interest in the development of the empirical "behavioral revolution" and scientific relativism in the social sciences (Brecht 1959: 242–9).[2] In this regard, he joined with others working out a conception of the social science advisor that can be interpreted as a mediator between elite government decisionmakers and the broader mass public, particularly with the assistance of the newly developing methods of survey research (Fischer 1990). It was, in fact, more a contribution to what was later to be called "democratic elitism" than participatory democracy.[3] And this can also be said of the form of policy analysis to emerge. It evolved in large part as a public administration

---

[2] A closer reading of Lasswell reveals him to be different things at different times. Although he recognized the importance of norms and values in the shaping and application of knowledge, he was also an ardent contributor to the empirical "behavioral" orientation that was to shape political science over following decades (Brecht 1959: 242–9). While some of his writings leave his orientation ambiguous, Lasswell supported an effort to develop an empirical, value-neutral conception of political science. In fact, it is only later that others such as Torgerson (2006) have recognized and emphasized the finer contextual aspects that at other times accompanied Lasswell's work. Part of the problem, no doubt given the understandings in political science at the time, is that his rigorous empirical-analytical contributions came to overshadow his other emphasis on normative context.

[3] Lasswell, it should be noted, had been a former student of Merriam and was influenced by both his scientific and political thinking, including democratic realism. This included an interest in the implications of psychology for political behavior, a topic which Lasswell explored in considerable detail.

reform strategy that has focused on the kinds of narrower instrumental questions that confront administrative decisionmakers, which in turn supports a more top–down elitist conception of political decision-making. It evolved in large part as a public administration reform strategy—technocratic in many ways—that has focused on the kinds of narrow instrumental questions that seldom raise more fundamental issues about governance.

Part of the reason that the call for a policy science of democracy failed to materialize, then, has had to do with the concept of knowledge on which it has rested. Despite his important contributions to our understanding of knowledge, especially its uses in society, Lasswell still held onto an empirical understanding of science. But like Dewey, he did recognize that science could not answer the value-oriented political questions that arose in public deliberation. Moreover, the promotion of a mode of policy inquiry aimed at facilitating democracy was clearly a progressive position. Neither Dewey nor Lassell, however, had at the time the benefit of a more modern-day constructivist understanding of social-scientific inquiry.

Today, however, we can see the task differently. From the perspective of a constructivist social-epistemological orientation, the goal can be reformulated. If policy analysis is to help democratize public deliberation, the next step is to open up the empirical/normative divide in ways that can facilitate a closer and more meaningful deliberation among citizens and experts. Up to this point, efforts to introduce deliberative interactions between them have subtly and not so subtly privileged professional expertise. Such knowledge, first, presents itself as value-neutral, when in fact it has incorporated normative assumptions. This side of the discussion is thus taken to stand on its own. Only those with the proper training and experience can meaningfully enter this domain. This gives the public the impression that there is little to talk about from the technical side of the divide, a perspective which experts seldom discourage. What is more, the expert seldom shows the citizen where the interactive points for deliberation are to be found. The same pattern is found in citizen juries designed to bring them closer together. The citizens take testimony from experts, even cross-examine them, but the two spheres are kept separate. In such a process, scientists often present their findings—intentionally or unintentionally—in an intimidating language that gives citizens the sense that they can't discuss the issues. The product comes across as a closed package. The end effect is that the process works—subtly and not so subtly—to privilege expert knowledge, thus maintaining a barrier to a fuller form of democratization.

On the other side of the divide, we confront a situation in which there are no rigorous procedures or standards for judging normative arguments.

This is partly because such arguments are seen to be fuzzy by comparison. But even more importantly, it is because we have neglected this side of the interaction. In so far as the dominant ideology, neo-positivism, has long held such discussion to rest on irrational foundations, there has been little effort to work out rules that govern such exchanges. What then appears as a lack of rigor has led many to conclude that the social side of the divide is soft or mushy. Moreover, involved with conflicting perspectives, it strikes many as a hopeless morass. This has meant that despite efforts to bring in the citizens, the attempt has often faltered on the epistemological divide. Most people think that the idea would be nice, but don't really see it within the realm of the possible (Carolan 2006).

The goal, then, is to seek ways to open up the empirical/normative divide that can facilitate a closer and more meaningful deliberation among citizens and experts. This would hold out the possibility of moving beyond Dewey's division of labor between experts and citizens by elucidating the ways in which the objects under investigation are themselves a composite of empirical and normative factors (Latour 2005). As we have seen, there has been a growing recognition of the need to take citizens more seriously, including incorporating their local knowledge. But much of this work has tended to swing too far in the other direction, seemingly implying that "street science" can and should take the dominant role (Coburn 2005). Despite the impressive cases of citizen inquiry, experts in most cases still need to play a leading role. But their practices have to be transformed to facilitate that role, a point most often born out by the cases themselves. There are relatively few instances in which citizens have proceeded successfully without some sort of assistance and support from experts who emerged to help them along the way. Toward this end, they need to learn to better understand citizens' modes of thinking and deliberation, as well as when deliberative inquiry is useful and when it is not. Citizens have a good deal of information but much of it remains tacit, fragmented, and disconnected. To be useful, it has to be organized. Professional experts need methods and practices that can help them to do this. Although we still have much to learn about how such a deliberative-analytic process would work, a range of experiences offer a beginning for thinking about new ways to present policy problems in practical experiments such as citizen juries and consensus conferences.

This challenge is no less important today than it was back when Dewey first raised it. The disturbing decline of public involvement today, as we saw in Chapter 2, has led many to look for new modes and practices to support or revitalize citizen deliberation. Important initiatives in this direction, as we have seen, are deliberative polls, citizen juries, consensus conferences, and scenario workshops, all designed to bring citizen opinion to the fore. To this, as we have seen, one can add as well the very active intellectual support offered by political theories of deliberative democracy.

Along the same lines, others have sought new models of governance designed to better connect policy decision-making with an active citizenry. This shift from "government" to "the idea of "governance" and "governance networks" captures the need for a more interactive, less vertical system of policy decision-making (Rhodes 1996, 2007). This is generally understood as developing the middle levels of democratic deliberation. Moreover, Hajer and Wagenaar have suggested that the model require a form of "deliberative policy analysis" to support the more participatory dimensions of network governance. Elsewhere I have suggested that this might take the form of participatory inquiry drawing on a combination of methods and practices borrowed from Paulo Freire's pedagogical theories and the methods of action research, a topic we take up in Chapter 8.

All of these important efforts can be seen as moves following paths laid out by Dewey. The requirements of a deliberative participatory democracy, however, suggest the need to open up the process more fully. But this is not an easy matter. The possibility of bringing experts and citizens into closer interaction is controversial and depends in various ways on what one means by expertise and knowledge. The possibilities of rethinking this relationship improve, we argue here, with a turn to the social constructivist perspective on knowledge. In this view, we see the normative and empirical fused together in ways that require a closer interaction between experts and citizens. Toward this end, we need to explore the constructivist conception of knowledge.

Beyond empiricism: The social constructivist alternative

The postempiricist social constructivist alternative emerges from an intersection of developments in the natural sciences, the history and sociology of science, and contemporary cultural studies (Jasanoff *et al.* 2001). It constitutes a complicated and multi-dimensional perspective that is not easy to summarize. With that caveat, however, the essential findings and their implications can be presented in outline form.

Most fundamentally, social constructivism reveals the intricate interplay among social and technical concerns in scientific research which cannot be strictly separated, as prescribed by standard methodological principles. Sociologist and historians of science have not only demonstrated that what we take to be knowledge is socially conditioned, but also how other historical periods have defined knowledge in quite different ways. Such conclusions help to make clear that neopositivist epistemology, as a product of a specific socio-historical context, is not necessarily relevant to all other contexts. It should *not* be taken, as has been the case, as the universal model for scientific practice as a whole (Callon 1995).

A closer look shows the methodological components of empirical inquiry—from hypothesis formation and observation through data analysis and explanation—to be grounded in the theoretical assumptions of the sociocultural practices through which they are developed (Rouse 1988; 1996). Although the point is especially important for the social sciences, it is in principle and practice valid for the natural sciences as well. From this perspective, science must first and foremost be analyzed as a form of human activity. In addition to being a matter of rigorously applying reliable methods, the pursuit of scientific questions is also seen to be influenced by social perceptions, beliefs, and motivation of members of the scientific community. Taken together, these historical and sociological findings about science have shaped an alternative perspective referred to as "social constructivism."

Basic to this view is an acknowledgement that "reality," as we typically think of it, is a social construction (Berger and Luckmann 1966). Although there are disagreements as to exactly what this should be taken to mean, it generally refers to the basic understanding that scientific work is better understood as an active mix of discovery and construction of reality, rather than a straightforward uncovering of a given reality awaiting to be revealed. As such, social constructivism starts from the recognition that facts are normatively grounded. Rather than maintaining the methodological fiction of a fact–value separation, social constructivism more typically refers to "normative facts" and thus the need for an interpretive orientation in all scientific research.

An interpretivist orientation understands social reality and the empirical observations of it only to exist in terms of a mental construct for thinking about them. These mental constructs are grounded in values that shape our perceptions of reality. such, the research findings are not a report of that which is "out there," as positivism would have it, but rather part of a process that creates that version of reality. Knowledge in the social world, then, "is a human construction never certifiable as ultimately true but problematic and ever changing" (Guba 1990: 26). In this view, theory and knowledge can never be fully probed. Not only is there no genuinely value-free knowledge, there can be no definitive criteria for choosing between theoretical orientations.

Knowledge, or what we call knowledge at any particular point in time, is obtained in the social constructivist view through a dialectical process of interpretation (Guba and Lincoln 1989). Dialectical logic understands knowledge to be a result of a confrontation among differing interpretations, the outcome of which can be a constructive synthesis leading to a new intersubjective perspective. Knowledge, in this understanding, is the product of a confrontation between competing, conflicting perspectives. A dialectic approach thus seeks out and emphases the importance of differences rather than prematurely stressing consensus. Furthermore, in this view, consensus is arrived at through a new understanding that emerges from the clash of opinions rather than a simple agreement on specific facts. It typically involves a new way of seeing things, with learning understood to be the result of confrontation with different points of view.

Unlike the positivist conception of knowledge, such consensus does not rest on a reality independent of those who shape and share it. In so far as the possibility of further confrontations with differing points of view always remains open, the construction of a consensus is never fully finished or complete. There can be progress in the production of consensus, but such knowledge can never be proved in the standard sense of the term. The process by which the production of such a consensus is shaped becomes the special interest of social constructivist investigation.

The scientific community, as a social structure, can be understood in many ways to be as much like a sociopolitical process as it is a disinterested body of in the pursuit of truth for its own sake. In the process, as Kuhn (1962) and others have shown, deviance and novelty are often suppressed in attempts to uphold the views of the authoritative gatekeepers of knowledge. Social and political factors are always found to impinge on the practices of science and play an important part in determining what the scientific community counts as certified scientific knowledge. In short, the status of data and theories is rarely established by definitive findings as to their "truth," but rather through a consensus that certain data and/or theories are useful to the largest number of practitioners who are entitled to participate in the decision process. In the process, access to scientific knowledge can be highly restricted. And often what is considered good science may have been decided by those who offer the resources for the scientific research (Fischer 2000: 89–108).

From such investigations we see the degree to which the application of scientific methods to particular problems involves social and practical judgment. None of this means that science, whether physical or social, should not be taken seriously. Or that one should not perform empirical tests. But it does mean that whatever constitutes scientific truth at any particular time has to be understood as more than the product of empirically confirmed experiments and tests. Such truths are better described as scientific *interpretations* or *beliefs* based on an amalgam of technical and social judgments. To be sure, technical judgments are more decisive in some cases than in others, but social considerations are always involved (with the mix between the two empirically determined case by case). Shaped by more than the idealistic "pursuit of truth," scientific claims thus have to be understood as the relative product of a community of practitioners who establish the evidential criteria and guide the processes through which truth claims are decided. The communities that render these judgments, as sociological and historical analysis demonstrates, constitute hierarchies of practitioners organized around their own status claims, interests and internal power structures (Kuhn 1962).

Such research also helps us understand that scientific communities are not the only groups capable of making judgments about the same reality. Alternative groups grounded in other forms of rationality can offer relevant judgments about the same phenomena. Historically, the determination of whose rationality prevails has been decided by those wielding the most influence or power. Invariably these decisions have been subject to future challenges and new findings have always played an important role in the process. Their role, however, has generally been mediated by changing beliefs. In contrast to the standard story, new findings alone have seldom been decisive. The progress of knowledge, in short, is not a linear process driven by the better experiment.

Given this sociology of scientific practices, postempiricism focuses on science's *account* of reality rather than on reality itself. This is not to say that there are no real and separate objects of inquiry independent of the scientific investigators. It is the conceptual vocabularies social actors use to know and represent the objects or their properties rather than the objects per se that become focus of such investigation. Scientific accounts are generated by observers with different types of educational training, ideational frameworks, research experiences, perceptual capacities, and the like. The objective is to understand how these varying cognitive elements discursively interact to shape that which comes to be called knowledge. Postempiricism's interpretation of the scientific process is, in this regard, founded on a "coherence" theory of reality that emphasizes the temporally bounded and finite character of knowledge (Brown 1977; Stockman 1983).

In contrast to the positivist correspondence theory, which takes scientific concepts to be the direct referents of reality, coherence theory confronts the indeterminedness of empirical propositions. Describing a world that is richer and more complex than the empiricist theories constructed to explain it, coherence theory strives to incorporate the multiplicity of theoretical perspectives and explanations that bear on a particular event or phenomenon. In Toulmin's (1983: 113) words, postempiricist coherence theory brings to bare "the range and scope of interpretive standpoints that have won a place." Alongside quantitative analysis, the postempiricist orientation includes the historical, comparative, phenomenological, and ethical perspectives. Quantitative empirical research, in the process, loses its privileged claim among modes of inquiry. While it remains an important component of theory construction, it no longer offers the crucial test.

Here we can recognize what groups of experienced social scientists actually do to obtain a consensus. Based on their own disciplinary training and theoretical orientations, coupled with their accumulated wisdom, they explore and thoroughly probe a question or issue until they arrive at a sense that they have satisfactorily, if not fully, explored the topic from all of the relevant angles. From these perspectives they ask if it is the right question? Was the inquiry appropriately organized? Do the data speak to the conclusions? Can one imagine other possible interpretations? Is the problem better explained from different theoretical perspectives? And the like. One can witness this in various fora where a body of research is presented and discussed. This art of such probing can easily be seen, for example, in an academic colloquium among peers, the deliberation of a dissertation on the part of the faculty, or in a workshop devoted to a particular research problem or topic. The abstract description of the exercise can sound rather mundane, but the actual experience of the process is typically highly stimulating, even exciting. When it happens, all present can attest to its occurrence. Indeed, as the essence of the scientific endeavor, it is often encountered as something of a heightened intellectual experience.

Knowledge in this postempiricist perspective is better understood as consensually "accepted belief" than as demonstration or proof (Paller

1989). In what is taken to be an evolving conversation, such beliefs are shaped through an interpretive forging of theoretical assumptions, analytical criteria, and empirical tests discursively warranted by scholarly communities (Lauden 1977). With an essential difference, this description is not altogether inconsistent with the neoempiricist understanding of the process. Rather than understanding these beliefs as the empirical outcomes of reliable tests, the postempiricist by contrast sees them as the product of a chain of interpretive judgments, both social and technical, arrived at by researchers in particular times and places (Bernstein 1983). In this view, social scientific theories can be understood as assemblages of theoretical presuppositions, empirical data, research strategies, interpretive judgments, and social practices (Deleuze and Guatarri 1987). One of the primary strengths of a theory, in this respect, is its ability to establish discursive connections and contrive equivalences between otherwise disparate elements, as well as incorporating new components.

Given the multi-methodological nature of this orientation, the principles of postempiricism cannot be as firmly fixed as those of neopositivism. But such inquiry does not lack rigor. In many ways, the approach opens the way to a more complex, sophisticated form of rigor. Instead of narrowly concentrating on the rules and procedures of research design and statistical analysis, the postempiricist approach engages a wider range of methodological criteria, both qualitative and quantitative. It recognizes that a methodology which defines knowledge and rationality in terms of technique, be it logical deduction or empirical falsification, is simply too narrow to embrace the multiple forms of reason involved in scientific practices. The interpretive judgments that are characteristic of each phase of a scientific inquiry, as well as the cumulative weighing of evidence and argument, are too rich and various to be captured by the rules of inductive or deductive logic (Scriven 1987). Formal logic, in short, is too confining for a methodology that needs to combine quantitative and qualitative orientations. Some postempiricists have sought a new methodological configuration through an informal deliberative framework of practical reason.

Practical argumentation: Reason in normative context

The development of a postempiricist alternative starts with the recognition that the formal models of deductive and inductive reason misrepresent both the scientific and the practical modes of reason. The models of both inductive and deductive reason, as Scriven (1987) has demonstrated, provide inadequate and largely misleading accounts of both academic and practical reasoning. The reason of the physician, judge or historian, for instance, are incomplete and more appropriately conceptualized as forms of Aristotle's concept of *"phronesis"* and the informal logic of practical reason with its own rules and procedures. Such practical reason connects theory to practice and action (Fisher 1989; Flyvbjerg 2000: 55–65).

Informal practical logic, designed to probe both the imprecision and incompleteness of existing knowledge, reconceptualizes our understanding of evidence and verification, both of which have been mistreated by formal logics (Scriven 1987). Challenging science's emphasis on generalizations, informal logic probes the argument-as-given rather than attempting to fit or reconstruct it into the confining frameworks of deduction and induction. As such, it emphasizes an assessment of the problem in its particular context, seeking to determine which approaches are most relevant to the inquiry at hand. By expanding the scope of reasoned argumentation, the informal discursive logic of practical reason offers a framework for developing a multi-methodological perspective.

Basic to practical reason is the recognition that the arguments relevant to different problems depend on the nature of those issues: What is reasonable in jurisprudence or clinical medicine is judged in terms different from what is "logical" in geometrical theory or physics (Toulmin 1990). Fundamental to such judgment is a sensitivity to the contextual circumstances of a problem or issue. The reason of practical discourse, as *phronesis*, differentiates among the world of theory, the mastery of techniques, and the experiential knowledge required to put techniques to good use in concrete cases. It supplies, as we will see, a conception of reason that is better suited to the forms of rationality exhibited in real-world policy deliberation, inherently concerned with the connections of knowledge to concrete cases. Practical reason, as we shall see, supplies a framework for examining and testing the logical components of a policy argument.

Concerned with the systematic study of the rational processes related to human reason about action, practical reason deals with cases in which decisions have to be taken among various action alternatives. Practical reason, as a theory of argumentation, holds that a decision depends on the person making it, and that formal rules of decision-making cannot be abstracted from these people and their actions into formal systems of demonstration modelled on deductive logic. "Reasoning" refers here to convincing or dissuading adversaries; it involves coming to agreement with others about the legitimacy of a decision. In this regard, theorists such as Toulmin (1958) and Perelman (1984) identify legal reasoning as the exemplifying case of practical reason. An analysis of judicial reasoning, based on probable premises rather than fixed proposition, is shown to provide important insights into the process of practical deliberation. Legal procedures, including the arguments of lawyers, the pronouncements of judges, and legislative decisions regarding the formation of laws, all represent forms of practical reasoning.

Practical deliberation, as such, operates between the logic of demonstration and theories of motivation and action. Not only does it include an empirical assessment of the situation in question, but it also takes into account the actor's motives for an action. Motives that have successfully undergone the test of argumentation can count as "good reasons." Whereas positivist theories of behaviour downplay or deny the importance of the reasons people give for their actions, practical reasoning takes them seriously. An argument as to whether position X or position Y should be accepted and used as the basis for an action is assessed on the merits of the evidence in the case, rather than as a mere acting out of the psychological or sociological forces that are behind the discussion.

Practical arguments are, in this respect, propositions that strive to determine if particular acts are good and should be performed. Practical reasoning takes into consideration, however, the conditions and circumstances under which actors in real life accept the relevant action-oriented norms as meaningful and commit themselves to them personally. In pursuing a judgment on which action should be taken, a practical argument starts with the norms to which the participants in the controversy are committed and seeks, by means of argument, to ground the decision on them. Practical reasoning thus requires normative commitments. Such normative commitments are never lasting or universal; all that is required in practical reasoning is that they be recognized by the audience—larger or smaller—to whom the argument is addressed at the specific time it takes place. In contrast to the timelessness that is fundamental to deductive reasoning, context and the notion of temporality is essential to practical reasoning.

Deliberation is thus basic to deciding among the interpretations of subject matters and activities. This applies to empirical as well as normative inquiry. Whereas a mathematical or logical proof is either true or false, practical arguments are only more or less convincing, more or less plausible to the audiences to which they are addressed. In addition, there is no unique way to construct a practical argument: data and evidence can be selected in a wide variety of ways from the available information, and there is no one method of analysis or of ordering values.

More specifically, practical argumentation differs from formal demonstration in three important respects. Whereas formal demonstration is possible only within a formalized system of axioms and rules of inference, practical argumentation begins from opinions, contestable viewpoints, and values rather than axioms. It uses logical inference but is not limited to deductive systems of formal statements. Second, a formal demonstration is designed to persuade those who have the requisite technical knowledge, while practical argumentation always aims to gain acceptance of the broader audience to which the claims are presented. And third, practical deliberation does not seek to achieve purely intellectual agreement but rather to present acceptable reasons for choices relevant to action (including, for instance, a disposition to act at an appropriate moment).

This emphasis on the kinds of practical discourse in which both citizens and politicians engage is an important step toward a better understanding of how we might think about Dewey's call for the facilitation of public deliberation, particularly the task of breaking down a rigid division of labor between expert and citizen contributions. As a next step, we can turn to the application of this postempiricist perspective and practical reason to the field of public policy analysis, a field of inquiry closely connected to public deliberation.

Postempiricist policy analysis: Argumentation and practical deliberation

This postempiricist perspective has been carried into the field of policy analysis and planning by a range of scholars (Dryzek 1990; Hajer 1995; Gottweis 1995; Healey 2006; Innes 1998; Forester 1999; Yanow 2000; Fischer 2003). The object of the critique and reconstruction has been the positivist or so-called "rationality project (Stone 2002). In this view, rationalistic policy analysis is not only methodologically misguided, but serves as well as an ideology that masks political and bureaucratic interests. The argument is supported by the fact that the standard approach has failed to contribute to the kinds problem-solving that it has promised from the outset. Neither have the social sciences generally produced anything vaguely resembling a causal, predictive science of society, nor has the policy analysis sub-field been able to provide indisputably effective solutions to pressing economic and social problems (Lindblom 1990).

This does not mean that policy research has had no impact on public issues. Postempiricist policy scholars argue rather that the field has misunderstood the nature of its contribution. While policy analysis has delivered few solid—i.e. unchallengeable—answers or solutions to public problems, it has contributed significantly to the political process of public deliberation. Although deliberation is generally recognized to be important to effective policy development, the field's continuing reliance on neo-empiricist methods has done more to hinder than facilitate deliberative processes. From the postempiricist perspective, conventional approaches have impeded policy analysis's ability to more directly do what it can do well, namely improve the quality of policy argumentation in public deliberation. Or, in the context of the present discussion, the field has done little to take up the kind of public deliberative challenge that Dewey called for, which Lasswell later echoed in his call for a "policy sciences of democracy." It is the task to which the "argumentative turn" has sought to return.

The argumentative turn is in significant part an effort to revive and strengthen this deliberative function of policy analysis by setting it out on its own epistemological footing. It has developed as an effort to both understand the nature of the problem and to find new and more relevant ways of dealing with policy deliberation and advice-giving. Anchored to an alternative epistemological orientation that understands knowledge to be the product of interaction—including conflict—among competing interpretations of a policy problem, it brings empirical and normative inquiry together in a deliberative framework. At the same time, it is seen to provide a better description of what real-world analysts and policy-makers actually do when they examine a particular problem, namely bring together the relevant considerations and deliberate about both their relationships to one another and their resultant implications for action.

Drawing on social constructivism, postempiricists employ interpretive and discursive methods to show that politics and policy are grounded in subjective factors and, in the process, demonstrate that the "objective" findings reported by rational techniques are as often as not the product of deeper, less visible, social and political presuppositions. For these analysts, the social construction of 'facts' and their subjective interpretations are the stuff of policy politics. Towards this end, they emphasize the role of subjective presuppositions and assumptions in directing our perceptual processes in pre-shaping what are otherwise generally taken to be strictly empirical factors.

Rejecting the pretence of objective, natural scientific policy analysis, the postempiricist policy analyst is attuned to the theoretical constitution of facticity, directing inquiry toward aspects of policymaking that are obscured or overlooked by the "myth of the given." By reconsidering questions neglected by the prevailing models of policy research, a theoretically informed policy analysis strives to identify the grounds for contentions that arise from the theoretical assumptions, conceptual orientations, rhetorical approaches, methodological commitments, and various disciplinary practices closely intertwined in policy disputes (Hawkesworth 1988). As such, the focus is on the discursive social constructions of the political actors, policy institutions, and analysts, in particular their use of language, rhetorical argument, discourse, and stories in framing both policy questions. It demonstrates the ways normative presuppositions operate below the surface to structure basic policy definitions and understandings. Such research shows how our understanding of the social world is framed through the discourses of the actors themselves, rather than fixed in nature (Gottweis 1998).

Given this contestable nature of empirical assertions, this means that postempiricist analysts have to understand and accept the need to explicate the multitude of dimensions inherent to deliberation and debate relevant to most policy issues. Analysts need to probe the presuppositions that discursively structure social perceptions, organize factual information and, in the process, deem events as normal, natural and expected. Focusing on the theoretical and normative assumptions that underlie competing discourses, definitions, contestable findings, questionable explanations, and contentious arguments, they have to apprehend the ways in which such assumptions shape actors' understandings of policy alternatives, and thus influence the range of choice-limiting decisions. In the process, policy inquiry can facilitate rather than supplant informed political choice.

Such a discursive perspective does not, however, ignore the role of politics and power. In so far as the web of presupposed assumptions underlying political and social propositions are reflections of particular social arrangements, they are themselves influenced by power and politics. To this end, it recognizes that much of what is important in political struggle is about establishing definitions and assigning meaning to social problems (Gusfield 1981; Edelman 1988; Best 2007). The attempt to separate out meaning and values thus removes the very heart of politics from social and policy research. In a quest for value-neutral generalizations,

121

neopositivist/empiricist social science detaches itself from the social contexts that give their research findings meaning.

From this perspective, what we identify as knowledge in the policy world is the outcome of a negotiation between those with expert knowledge and the actors in the everyday world, in particular those with political power. For this reason, the process of knowing cannot be understood as the exclusive jurisdiction of the expert. It means that the policy analyst must know what social actors believe reality to be. They need to know the competing meanings that people employ; as Innes (1990: 32) puts it, "such meanings are essential 'data' for any analysis." Proper policy investigation thus requires the policy researcher to deeply involve him- or herself in the normative understandings and social processes of everyday life.

This constructivist view helps us see that it is often the deeper social and cultural factors in policy debates, rather than the "facts" of the arguments, that play a decisive role in citizens' assessments of the competing positions. By drawing attention to the sociocultural contexts that underlay the citizen-expert relationship, the constructivist approach demonstrates how citizens interpret the "objective" assessments of professional experts with the help of their own cultural experiences and the social dependencies inherent to them. Given that these sociocultural meanings are inaccessible to the neopositivist's empirical methods, such inquiry often tends to underestimate the degree to which lay citizens are ambivalent or alienated toward professional experts and their policy institutions.

In an effort to combine expert and lay judgments postempiricists like Flyvbjerg (2000) have turned to "phronesis" to connect theory to practice and action. Phronesis, as we saw, distinguishes contextually between the realm of theory, the mastery of methods, and the experiential knowledge required to put techniques to work in concrete cases. Countering social science's emphasis on generalizations, the practical logic of phronesis is oriented to the argument itself rather than an attempt to fit it into the confining frameworks of induction or deduction. Toward this end, it stresses an assessment of problems in their particular contexts, seeking to determine which approaches are most relevant to the questions at hand. By expanding the scope of reasoned argumentation, the discursive logic of practical reason offers a framework for developing a multi-methodological perspective.

Policy analysis, as phronesis, can be better defined as a "craft" than as a science in the positivist understanding of the term. In this view, we can best account for the ways professional policy analysts employ knowledge and skills acquired more through imitation, experience, and practice than formal methodological training. The task of the policy analysis depends, as Majone (1989: 43–4) puts it, "more on 'knowing how' than 'knowing that'." Rather than a purely logical activity, following the social constructivist perspective, such policy-analytic work is a social process. The repertoire of craft knowledge and skills exercised by the analyst constitutes procedures, conventions, and judgements that combine social, institutional, and personal factors. In deciding "whether specific data is of acceptable quality," explains Majone, the policy analyst "applies standards that derive from his own experience but also reflect the professional norms of teachers and colleagues, as well as culturally and institutionally determined criteria of adequacy." Much of the experimental knowledge on which such judgments rest is often as tacit as it is explicit, a topic further examined in Chapter 8.

Successful practice, as in the case of traditional crafts, depends on a highly personal knowledge of tools, materials, and tasks on the part of the craftsperson. Rather than dealing with materials such as stone or wood, the policy analyst qua craftsperson, works with technical tools, data, concepts, and theories to structure evidence and arguments that support particular conclusions (Majone 1989). How analysts put these components together is based on the analysts' knowledge and experience, both explicit and tacit.

From this craft perspective we thus learn that the job of the policy analyst is guided by all sorts of informal judgements and inferences involving the various dimensions of a particular problem. Although the basic principles and precepts of the craft can never be fully spelled out, especially those that constitute a form of tacit knowledge based on experience, the good craftsman can generally determine good from bad work (Majone 1989: 66). In order to properly understand and appreciate these craft-oriented aspects of policy analysis and to be able to competently judge the quality of the end product, the analyst needs to learn how to explicate and explore the microstructures of a policy argument. In Majone's words, "such detailed examination would have only academic interest if it were possible to assess the quality of a policy analysis simply by comparing its conclusion with policy outcomes." But complexity and uncertainty make it necessary to supplement outcome-oriented criteria with process criteria that pertain to social considerations. In the final analysis, as Majone (1989: 67) argues, a policy analysis has to be judged by tests of its appropriateness "to the nature, context, and characteristic pitfalls of the problem."

In this perspective, the focus shifts to the policy argument and its features. Majone (1989: 63), in this regard, suggests that the structure of a policy argument can be understood as a complex blend of factual statements, interpretations, opinion, and evaluation. The function of the argument itself is to provide the links that connect the relevant data and information to the conclusions of an analysis. Majone's analysis of the features of a policy argument is an important contribution to the development of argumentative policy analysis, but it does not yet clarify the normative dimensions that intervene between findings and conclusions. The task here involves establishing interconnections among the empirical data, normative assumptions that structure our understandings of the social world, the interpretive judgements involved in the data-collection process, the particular circumstances of a situational context (in which the findings are generated or the prescriptions applied), and the specific conclusions. The scientific acceptability of the conclusions depends ultimately on the full range of interconnections, not just the empirical findings. While neo-positivists see their approach as more rigorous and therefore superior to less empirical, less deductive methods, this model of policy argumentation actually makes the task more demanding and complex (McClosky 1994; Fischer 1995). Not only does it encompass the logic of empirical falsification, it includes the equally sophisticated normative questions within which it operates. The researcher still collects the data, but now has to situate or include them in the interpretive framework that gives them meaning. No longer is it possible to contend that such normative investigations can be ignored, as if they somehow relate to another field of inquiry. This involves a multi-methodological framework for integrating these component parts. In *Evaluating Public Policy* (1995), I have outlined such a framework based on insights drawn from Toulmin (1958) and Taylor (1961). In this model, based on the informal logic of practical reason, empirical finding are normatively explored in an interrelated set of normative contexts (from local and societal to ideological), each with their own logical requirements.[4]

---

[4] For an elaboration see Fischer (1995). Essentially, the practical logic of policy deliberation works on two fundamental levels. The first is concerned with a program, its participants, and the specific problem situation to which the program is applied. The second is focuses on the more abstract level of the societal system within which the programmatic action takes place. A policy assessment, in this regard, must always look in both directions, one micro, the other macro. To take an example, a policy to introduce a multicultural educational curriculum at a particular university should not only specify the specific courses to be offered, but would also have to address the larger requirements of a pluralist societal system, such as the need for a set of common values capable of holding the system together.

Policy analysis, as deliberative craft, thus seeks to bring a wider range of contextually sensitive empirical and normative criteria to bear on the argument under investigation. As Hawkesworth (1988) explains, the reasons provided in support of alternatives organize evidence, marshal data, apply explanatory criteria, address multiple levels of argumentation, and employ various strategies of presentation. But the reasons given to support one theory over another seldom, if ever, offer definitive proof of the validity of a competing alternative. Through the processes of deliberation and debate, a consensus emerges among particular researchers concerning what will be taken as valid explanation. Although the choice is sustained by factual and normative reasons that can be articulated and advanced as support for the inadequacy of alternative interpretations, it is the practical judgment of the community of researchers and not the data themselves that establishes the accepted explanation. Such practical judgments, rather than supposed reliance on proof, provide the mechanism for not only identifying the incompetent charlatan but for investigating the more subtle errors in our sophisticated approximations of reality. To be sure, the informal logic of practical reason cannot guarantee the eternal verity of particular conclusions, but the social rationality of the process is far from haphazard or illogical.

Perhaps most important, practical reason supplies us with a way of probing the much neglected contextual dependence of most forms of argumentation (Scriven 1987). Bringing together the full range of cognitive strategies employed in such inquiry, it judges both the application and the results of such methods in terms of the contexts to which they are applied. Recognizing social context to be a theoretical construct, as well as the under-determination of our available knowledge, practical deliberation probes the competing understandings of a particular problem and the range of methods appropriate to investigating them. Framing the analysis around the underlying presuppositions, postempiricist analysis seeks to anticipate and draw out the multiple interpretations that bear on the explanation of social and political propositions.

From this perspective, the role of the postempiricist expert is that of an interpretive mediator operating between the available analytical frameworks of social science and competing local perspectives. In the process, a set of criteria is consensually derived from the confrontation of views (Innes 1990). Such criteria are used to organize a dialectical exchange that can be likened to a conversation in which the understandings of both the policy analyst and the citizens are extended through discursive interactions (Dryzek 1982). Thus, exchanges among policy experts, citizens, and policymakers are restructured as a conversation with multiple voices.

The task, as Hawkesworth (1988: 192) puts it, is to enlarge the range of political possibilities through a greater "awareness of the dimensions of contestation, and hence, the range of choice," although the judgment of the analyst can never substitute for the choices of the political community. Postempiricism, as such supports a participatory practice of democracy. "By encouraging policymakers and citizens to engage in rational deliberation upon the options confronting the political community," as Hawkesworth (1988: 193) writes, postempiricist analysis "can contribute to an understanding of politics which entails collective decision-making about a determinate way of life."

The argumentative turn also emphasizes the *productive capacities* of deliberation—namely, its ability to generate ways of thinking and seeing that open new possibilities for problem-solving and action. Or in Habermas's (1987) language, its focuses on "communicative power." Well-designed argumentative processes are seen to facilitate communicative competencies and thus citizen learning, which draws attention to the democratic potential of policy analysis. It thus extends Lasswell's earlier call for a "policy sciences of democracy."

Deliberative policy inquiry as dialectical argumentation: From theory to methods

From the kind of work outlined above, we can begin to construct more practically new ways of thinking about and designing alternative argumentation-oriented inquiry systems for policy deliberation and decision-making.[5] The starting point for such a system is the adoption of a dialectical understanding of inquiry and the recognition that the most fundamental aspect of inquiry is the identification of ways of seeing (Guba and Lincoln 1989; Guba 1990; Fischer 2003). While the technical aspects of problem solving still have an important role to play in policy formulation and evaluation, even more significant from the perspective of dialectical argumentation is the way in which the actors see a particular problem and thus shape the issue agenda. In the contemporary methodological

---

[5] Much of the deliberative or communicative approach can be grounded in Mill's (1959: 108) argument about the necessity of testing ideas against each other. As he put it, human beings are "capable of rectifying [their] mistakes by discussion and experience...There must be discussion, to show how experience is to be interpreted."

vernacular, this is discussed in terms of problem framing. The process of framing is the basis for not only identifying the problem, but also for defining it. In this sense, the processes of framing predetermine the direction and nature of the technical analysis that might follow. From the argumentative perspective, then, inquiry has the broader function of enlightenment as opposed to the narrower problem-solving orientation traditionally associated with policy science.

The insight is not altogether new to the field of policy studies. Although working in a different context, Carol Weiss (1972, 1990) advanced the "enlightenment function" as the goal for policy analysis in an earlier critique of traditional policy analysis methods. In an effort to explain the failure of policy decision-makers readily to adopt the analyses of policy analysis, she argued that the contribution of much of the work was misunderstood. While it did not offer unquestioned policy solutions, namely the conventional goal of the discipline, it did supply enlightening perspectives to the relevant decisionmakers. And in many ways, this contribution to the broader processes of deliberation and argument counts as much or more than the narrower focus on achieving administrative goals. This important insight makes clear that the limitations of rigorous scientific policy research in no way renders the enterprise useless. Although Weiss did not draw it out per se, her emphasis on enlightenment also implied alternative ways of seeing a problem, potentially introducing a phenomenological understanding of social and political reality. Based on this and other similar insights, postempiricist policy analysis shifts the focus to the processes of policy argumentation. How does argumentation work? And how can it be better informed?

Once we stress different ways of seeing as the essential contribution of the enlightenment function, it becomes easier to recognize the dialectic role of conflict over empirical consensus in postempiricist inquiry. It is not that consensus is unimportant, but rather that it tends to operate more *within* normative frameworks than it works to open them up. This in term facilitates the technical orientation that continues to dominate policy analysis. From the dialectical perspective, it is the clash of ideas that leads people to a deeper and potentially more enduring consensus, although the path to such consensus is generally longer and more time consuming. But such argumentative conflict takes the inquirers beyond an easy consensus based on conventional ways of viewing things, typically embedded in a given set of power relations and their discursive constructs.

A dialectical/argumentative approach, then, begins with the normative rather than the empirical task. Instead of fitting the norms and values into the empirical framework, the task is to test empirical findings within normative frameworks. In this view, normative-based analysis can be facilitated by an organized deliberation among competing normative positions. Designed to both identify potential conflicts and create consensus, the model emphasizes the interactive and productive role of communication in cognitive processes. Unlike the more abstract or academic modes of reason removed from the real world, the power of critical judgment depends on potential agreement with others. In fact, such judgment depends on, even anticipates, communication with others.

In such a scheme, policy analysts and decision-makers each take on the assignment of preparing arguments for and against particular policy positions. In the process, they spell out their positions in the deliberation and leave the task of taking apart the arguments of those on the opposing side, including the alternative empirical evidence used to support them. Such policy argumentation begins with the realization that policy analysts and decisionmakers do not have solid answers to the questions to be deliberated or even unambiguous methods for obtaining the answers. They seek to organize the established data and fit it into the normative frameworks that underline and support their own arguments. Each then confronts the other with counter proposals, comparing the underlying assumptions and findings being used, both normative and empirical. The grounds or criteria for accepting or rejecting a proposal are the same grounds for accepting or rejecting a counterproposal and must be based on precisely the same data. The goal is to synthesize the competing positions into a meaningful perspective capable of generating a workable consensus. The problem posed by the absence of appropriate evaluative criteria can be mitigated by designing rational procedures to govern the formal communication between the various points of view that bear on the decision-making process. Toward this end, some have suggested that legal courtroom procedures can offer insights into the development of rules for governing such discursive policy deliberations (MacRae 1976).

The argumentative model reverses the analytical process from the standard task of fitting qualitative data about norms and values into an empirical model through quantification to the process of judging the empirical data against normative frameworks. The central locus of the judgmental process is thus expanded from the expert community to include the inquirers of the practical world of action. In this model, each participant would cite not only what he or she take to be the relevant causal relationships, but also the norms, values, and circumstances to support or justify a particular decision. The final outcome of evaluative inquiry is determined by the giving of reasons and the assessment of practical arguments rather than technical demonstration and verification. As in interpretive explanation generally, the valid interpretation is the one that survives the widest range of criticisms and objections. Such interpretive evaluations, as practical arguments, connect policy options and situations by illuminating the features of those situations that provide grounds for policy decisions.

In this scheme, the formalized deliberation is itself seen as the most instructive part of the analytical process. The technique is designed to clarify the underlying goals and norms that give shape to competing positions, and enables qualitative judgment to be exercised in as unhampered a way as possible. The free exercise of normative judgment, released from the restrictions of the formal policy model, increases the chance of developing a synthesis of normative perspectives that can provide a legitimate and acceptable basis for decisions and actions based on the strongest possible argument. Even if analysts cannot agree, the argumentative approach provides a procedure for probing the normative implications of recommendations and for indicating potentially consensual conclusions that can offer productive ways to move forward. In the process, it also makes clear the basic points of dissensus that stand in the path of agreement.

Similarly emphasizing argumentation, Turnbull (2006) has suggested that policy analysts should rethink the Lasswellian problem orientation and adopt a conception of questioning. Drawing on the philosophical perspective of Michel Meyer and his philosophy of "problematology," Turnbull retains the problem focus but reframes it through an interpretative conception of the relationship between question and answer. From this basis, he attempts to re-emphasize the political dimension of policymaking, in which rhetoric—rather than science or pure rationalism—is the operative logic.

A principal advantage of this argumentative approach is that it better informs the policy decision-making process than does traditional empirical policy analysis. In particular, it more closely corresponds to the way real-world policy deliberation actually works. In politics, politicians and policy decision-makers advance proposals about what to do based on normative arguments. Empirical questions seldom drive the process in politics and policy. They come into play, to be sure. But they mainly do so when there are reasons to doubt factual aspects of the argument.

And here again there have been policy-relevant moves in this direction, mainly emerging in organization theory. The path-breaking but now mainly neglected work of C. West Churchman (1971) and his colleagues on dialectical inquiry systems for managerial decision-making is based on a dialectic understanding of deliberation. Unfortunately, this important line of theoretical work has became lost in the return to traditional decision-practices in more conservative times, such as rational choice theory and "evidence-based policymaking." A similar methodological strategy is also found in work by George (1972) and Porter (1980) dealing with the task of organizing expertise advice in policy areas such as national security and economic policymaking at the presidential level. The assumption underlying what George calls "multiple advocacy" is that a competition of ideas and viewpoints, rather than reliance on analyses and recommendations from advisors who share the perspectives of the policymakers, is the best method for developing security policy. As such, multiple advocacy is described as a process of debate and persuasion designed to expose the policymaker systematically to competing arguments made by the advocates themselves. Through the efforts of an "honest broker," his approach attempts to ensure that all interested parties are genuinely represented in the adversarial process, and that the debate is structured and balanced.

These argumentative approaches represent important steps toward the development of a dynamic methodology designed to facilitate complex dialectical exploration of facts and values, empirical and normative inquiry, throughout the policy decision process (Mitroff 1971). At minimum, the work of these theorists goes considerable distance toward removing the ideological mask that has often shrouded policy analysis and the resultant expertise drawn from it. Like any step forward, however, it only brings us to the next set of hurdles. One of them has to do with the scope of participation. Can it be extended to a larger number of participants?

While this question relates first to larger questions of democratic legitimacy, it also raises a methodological issue. As Tannen (1998) has argued in her book on the development of an "argument culture," especially as it has emerged in the United States and Britain, there is a risk in argumentative processes that involve a limited number of participants of giving rise to an unproductive adversarial environment in which both sides become entrenched in their own positions and talk past each other, often in increasingly aggressive ways that make it even more difficult to come to agreements. This is particularly the case when the exchanges take the form of a two-party debate in which one side wins and the other loses. She thus points to the need to engage a larger number of perspectives in an effort both to avoid such counterproductive standoffs and to bring out the wider range of insights embedded in the various perspectives.

With regard to such potential blockages, we can take the primary political-procedural critieria—as opposed to technical or instrumental criteria—for judging the outcomes of participatory deliberations to be the protection the communicative structure, namely the task of preserving and improving the capacity of make future decisions. The best political decision, Diesing has argued, should be the one that avoids complete identification with a particular point of view. From a political perspective, in his words, "the best available proposal should never be accepted just because it is best; it should be deferred, objected to, and discussed until all major opposition disappears" (Diesing 1962: 203–4). Although decisions based on comprom-ise are usually less than acceptable in nonpolitical decisions—matters re-lated say to economic or social policy—they are the essence of wisdom in political judgments. Only decisions that have eliminated major opposition can contribute to the harmony of the decision structure and thus the group's capacity to make future decisions. Given that such decisions involve the widest range of viewpoints, the process constitutes the basic form of demo-cratic enlargement. Toward this end, Diesing (1967: 196) has suggested four general criteria for judging the effect of a political decision on the commu-nicative structure: the ability of the decision to reconcile conflicting factors that block a decision; its the ability to increase toleration among various groups with differing view; its ability to establish an equilibrium among opposing forces in a destructive struggle; and its ability to reject, repress, or exclude the threatening factors from the decision problem.

Although Churchman and his followers focus rather narrowly on managerial decision-making, this understanding of a decision-making structure would not need to be confined to the interactions between organizational policymakers and policy analysts. Ideally, it could be extended to the range of differing interests and political viewpoints drawn from the policy environment. Importantly, it is a consideration taken up by a major scientific organization in the United States, the National Research Council, an arm of the US Academy of Science.

Extending deliberation: Citizens and stakeholders

Over the past decade or more there has been an increasing recognition of the need for deliberative interaction with the broader public in policy-analytic inquiry. An important sign of the extent of this development has been the National Research Council's call for an "analytic-deliberative" method for bringing together a wider range of stakeholders. Although the Council focuses on policy issues related to science, technology, and the environment, its proposals are broadly applicable to policy analysis more generally. Specifically, the Council has taken the position that coping with technological and environmental risks requires "a *broad understanding* of the relevant losses, harms, or consequences to the interested and affected parties, including what the affected parties believe the risks to be in particular situations" (National Research Council 1996). It thus becomes necessary to find ways to incorporate the perspectives of these groups into the processes of policy analysis and decision-making.

Toward this end, organizations are counseled to make special efforts to ensure that the interested and affected parties find reasonable the basic analytic assumptions about risk-generating processes and the methods of risk estimation. Although recognized to be often time-consuming and cumbersome, at least in the near term, the Council argues that it is wiser "to err on the side of too-broad rather than too-narrow participation." Organizations are advised "to seriously assess the need for involvement of the spectrum of interested and affected parties at each step, with a presumption in favor of involvement."

The methodological challenge is described as the need to develop "an analytic-deliberative method" capable of bringing together citizens and experts. Such a deliberative method is required to guide a participatory process capable of "broadly formulating the decision problem, guiding analysis to improve decision participants' understanding, seeking the meaning of analytic findings and uncertainties, and improving the ability of interested and affected parties to participate effectively in the risk decision process" (National Research Council 1996). The process must have an appropriately diverse range of participation representing the spectrum of interested and affected parties, of decisionmakers, and of specialists in risk analysis at each stage of the process. Most important is the need for participation in the early stages of problem formulation.

In this view, analysis and deliberation are presented as complementary approaches to gaining knowledge about the world, forming understanding on the basis of knowledge, and reaching agreement among participants. Whereas analysis "uses rigorous, replicable methods, evaluated under the agreed protocols of an expert community," deliberation is a process "in which participants discuss, ponder, exchange observations and views, reflect and attempt to persuade each other" (3–4). Deliberation, moreover, just doesn't come at the end. It is important at each step of the process that informs decisions, from deciding which problems to analyze to how to describe scientific uncertainty and negotiate disagreement. Such structured deliberation contributes to sound analysis by adding knowledge and perspectives that improve understanding and contributes to the acceptability of problem characterization by addressing potentially sensitive procedural concerns. As the Council puts it, "deliberation frames analysis, analysis informs deliberation, and the process benefits from the feed back from the two."

For organizing such a deliberative process, the Council takes the additional step of advocating that organizations reach out with technical assistance to unorganized groups or those inexperienced in matters of risk analysis and regulatory policy. As the Council puts it, "if some parties that are unorganized, inexperienced in regulatory policy, or unfamiliar with [the] related science are particularly at risk... it is worthwhile for responsible organizations to arrange for technical assistance to be provided to them from sources that they trust." In this regard, the Council suggests that experts must at times assume the role of facilitators.

Such deliberation cannot, to be sure, be expected to end all controversy. It does not guarantee that policy decisionmakers will attend to the results of such deliberation, prevent disappointed participants from attempting to delay or walk away from the outcomes. Controversies, in this view, are seen as constructive in helping to identify weak points from which scientific expertise can benefit rather than merely as impediments in the path of expert decision-making. Not only do controversies encourage in-depth analysis to identify and explicate the social implications of a policy solution, they can also surface partly conflicting assessments of programs and policies that can then be further articulated and consolidated in the course of a controversy. In this view, the proper function of a controversy is the identification and evaluation of potential problems, that is, as an informal complement to conventional methods of policy analysis.

Examined against the Council's earlier technocratic beginnings in risk analysis and management, this newer emphasis on public-oriented deliberation can only be judged as an impressive advance. Although technocratic practices still remain dominant, the fact that many of the contemporary methods in technology policy analysis and risk assessment were initially influenced by the Council itself holds out hope for change, even if it only comes slowly and reluctantly. The acknowledgement of the centrality of participation and deliberation by this prestigious body should not be underestimated. In this regard, the shift of the Council from its earlier technocratic perspective to an analytic-deliberative model is important documentation of a move toward an argumentative approach to public policy.

But, again, the step forward brings us to the next issue. From a post-empiricist perspective based on the findings of social constructivism, the question turns more specifically to the divide between empirical and normative deliberation. Must analytic work and normative deliberation remain separate, complementary processes? The challenge of postempiricism is to bring them into closer interaction with one another.

Participatory inquiry: A postempiricist challenge

The "analytic-deliberative" approach advanced by the National Research Council remains attached to conventional notions about science, in particular the epistemic division between the empirical and the normative inquiry. In this respect, it reflects Dewey's call for interaction between experts and citizens but maintains a division of labor between them. The postempiricist perspective seeks to move beyond this divide by opening up to critical scrutiny the practices of science itself. Of essential importance here is the fact that the normative elements lodged in the construction of empirical policy research rest on interpretive judgments and need to be made accessible for examination and discussion. Recognizing that the social meanings underlying policy research are always interpreted in a particular sociopolitical context—whether the context of an expert community, a particular social group, or society more generally—a fully developed postempiricist deliberative approach focuses on the ways such research and its findings are themselves built upon normative social assumptions that, in turn, have implications for political decision-making. That is, they are embedded in the very understandings of the objects and relationships that policy science investigates. Indeed, the very construction of the empirical object to be measured is sometimes at stake.

For this reason, empirical policy science cannot exist independently of normative constructions. While introducing deliberation as a complement to the analytic process is an important advance over a narrow technical orientation, from the postempiricist perspective it can only be understood as a platform from which the next step can be taken. Beyond a complementary approach, deliberation has to be moved into the analytical processes as well. Beyond understanding empirical and normative inquiry as separate activities that can potentially inform one another, they need to be seen as a continuous process of inquiry along a deliberative spectrum ranging from the technical to the normative. As deliberation and interpretative judgment occur in both empirical and normative research, they need to be approached as two dimensions along a continuum.

It is important to concede that postempiricist policy inquiry enters here relatively uncharted territories. From a range of practical experiments, such as consensus conferences and citizen juries, it is evident that citizens are more capable of participating in deliberative processes than generally recognized. But questions about the extent of participation, as well as when and where it might be appropriate, pose complicated questions and thus need to assume a central place on the research agenda. Particularly challenging is the question of the *degree* to which citizens can actually engage in the analytic aspects of inquiry. Various research projects demonstrate that they can participate in at least parts of it, but where should we draw the line (Wildavsky 1997)? Reconceptualizing empirical and normative inquiry along an interpretive continuum offers an approach for pursuing the answers to these questions. In the chapter that follows it is proposed that such investigation be taken up as a component of a new research specialization called "policy epistemic" (Fischer 2000).

Conclusion

This chapter started with Dewey's call for social scientists to facilitate public deliberation. It began by showing that policy analysis and the expertise drawn from it have emerged in just the sort of techno-bureaucratic context that Dewey worried about. Much of what is taught and practiced today supports a technocratic, apolitical understanding of policy issues. The task is largely understood as offering useful information—mainly of a technical-analytic/empirical nature—to public decision-making, in particular administrative decisionmakers. The given configuration of politics is taken for granted, with policy issues treated as matters to be solved through program development and administrative implementation. Questions about the deeper social and political roots of why something came to be considered a problem, normative assumptions, or why a problem is framed in a particular way as opposed to another, are seldom taken up as part of the analysis. The public, for the most part, doesn't come into the picture. If asked, the policy analysts typically say that that is the job of the politician. They are only providing technical information as an input for decision-makers.

Toward this end, the discussion suggested the need to move beyond an epistemic division between experts and citizens based on a separation of empirical and normative inquiry. We also noted that such a division of labor is still a prominent feature of contemporary fora like citizen juries, where the experts do their part, with the citizens mainly listening. The move beyond such a division, it was argued, is made possible by turning to the new understandings of science and politics made possible by the social constructivist perspective on inquiry. From this view, we come to recognize that science itself has values and norms embedded in its formulation and that the recognition of this makes it possible to bring experts and citizens into closer interaction. It is not that the citizens make the calculations but they should be in a position to discuss the normative aspects upon which the empirical information rests. This would be a joint endeavor that brings both groups together. As such, it could lead to greater understanding and improve the decision-making processes.

Toward this end, the chapter called for a line of work devoted to learning more about the processes of deliberation, the ways in which arguments are communicated, and how to better design procedures that facilitate such exchanges, a topic to which we return in later chapters. As a step in this direction, we turn next to one of the basic questions underlying communicative interactions involving complex technical-laden decisions: Who should be entitled to participate and when?

5

Technical Knowledge in Public Deliberation: Toward a Constructivist Theory of Contributory Expertise

One of the oldest questions in political theory is the relation of science to politics, expertise to democratic participation. Indeed, it is one of the central concerns that Plato and Aristotle raised against Athenian democracy. For them, democracy was a dangerous system in that it permitted the less intelligent to rule over the more intelligent. This led Plato to argue for rule by the "philosopher king."

Today the question is still not only relevant, it is in most ways even more pressing, given the complexity of modern society. In an earlier section concerned with participatory inquiry, it was argued that we need to exam more carefully what citizens can and cannot do (Fischer 2000). In the view there, participation was seen to be a valuable tool for decision-making, but it needs to be disconnected from the ideology associated with it (progressive liberals typically calling for more; conservatives for less). Toward this end, we not only need to examine more carefully what citizens can actually do, but also identify the circumstances under which this can happen.

One of the most prominent efforts to deal with this question in recent times has been that of Collins and Evans (2002, 2007).[1] Writing from the perspective of the discipline of STS (Science, Technology and Society), they lament the development of postmodern challenges to science, especially those that would seem to relegate science to the status of ideology and elevate the citizen to the level of expert. This work, they argue, is an unfortunate by-product of the social constructivist phase in the social

---

[1] Collins and Evans's article (2002) on the Third Wave is the most downloaded essay to have ever been published by *Social Studies of Science*, one of the prestigious journals in the field of science, technology, and society (STS).

studies of science over the past three decades, which they refer to as "Wave Two" (replacing the earlier "Wave One" perspective that naively celebrated science as the pure pursuit of truth for itself). Although their criticisms of Wave Two seem exaggerated, there have indeed been those in postmodern cultural studies who have taken this position. Collins and Evans would sometimes give the impression that these arguments have gained much more influence than they have, and have thus created a potentially worrisome, if not dangerous, situation for society in general. For them, this is *the* critical issue of our time. To deal with it we need a new "Third Wave" of science studies that focuses on developing a "normative theory of expertise" which can guide us in understanding how we should employ and relate expertise to lay citizens and democratic politics.

Their work represents an interesting effort to theorize about expertise and it has succeeded in creating a heated reaction from those who call for more democratic citizen participation.[2] Many suspect that a more technocratic, elitist understanding of decision-making lurks behind Collins and Evans's concern. They vehemently reject this charge, but their answer is not entirely convincing. The reason, I will argue below, has to do with the way that they misunderstand science's relationship to democratic politics.

This chapter takes seriously their concern about losing the technical contribution to public policymaking, but examines it from the point of policy and policy studies rather than STS. Several of their critics have argued that STS scholars should pay more attention to the emerging work on expertise in the field of policy studies (Rip 2003). I shall argue here that politics and policy indeed offers a different perspective that does help to inform this question. Drawing on this approach, I try to work out a more compelling understanding of the relationship of scientific expertise to democratic decision-making, as well as what Collins and Evans advance as a "theory of contributory expertise." But it is first necessary to begin with the work of Collins and Evans: What do they actually say?

Legitimating technical decisions: The problem of extension

The basic question that Collins and Evans (2002) raise is this: "Should the political legitimacy of technical decisions in the public domain be

[2] See, for example, the heated exchanges in a subsequent issue of *Social Studies of Science*, featuring leading theorists in the field, including Jasanoff (2003a, 2005), Rip (2003), and Wynne (2003).

maximized by referring them to the widest democratic processes, or should such decisions be based on the expert advice?" By technical decision-making they mean decision-making at those points where science and technology intersect with the political domain because the issues are of visible relevance to the public . . . " For example, how should we decide questions concerning nuclear power or coal-fired power stations, whether to vote for a politician who opposes the Kyoto agreement, or support research related to human cloning? The argument is not that the public has nothing to say about these matters, but rather "how to make good decisions in the right way." Toward this end, their position is about "the value of scientists and technologists' knowledge and experience as compared with others' knowledge and experience." The question is, how far should it be extended in technical decision-making in the public realm?

The dominant trend in the social studies of science over the past decades has been to replace epistemological questions with social questions. The problem with this approach, they argue, is that it has led to a relativism that has undercut the pursuit of "scientific truth". In fairness to Collins and Evans, they are not to be counted among the intellectual reactionaries who have generated the "science wars" of the late 1990s, such as Sokol (1996) or Gross and Levitt (1997). They accept the major contribution of the social studies of science of the past three decades, in particular the view that we can no longer simply accept the claim that we should trust scientist because they have special access to "truth." Building on this, their question takes an additional step: "If it is no longer clear that scientists and technologists have special access to the truth, why should their advice be specially valued?" This poses the question in a different way. Expertise may not be what it is thought to be, but most people think that only the fool would not want some expert advice in technical matters. For Collins and Evans, this is now the most pressing problem confronting both policy decisionmakers and the field of science studies. Specifically, as they put it, "technical decision-making in the public domain is where the pigeons of much recent social science are coming home to roost."

The problem with expertise, in their view, is caught in a tension between the "Problem of Legitimacy" and the "Problem of Extension." As they write, "though science studies has revolved the Problem of Legitimacy by showing that the basis of technical decision-making can and should be widened beyond the core of certified experts, it has failed to solve the Problem of Extension: How far should participation in technical decision-making extend? The constructivist sociology of science, in short, "has shown that there is more to scientific and technical expertise than is encompassed in the work of formally accredited scientists and techno-logists, but it has not told us how much more." The problem, then, that they set for themselves "is how to find a clear rationale for the expansion of expertise." In other literatures the question would also involve how to include the local knowledge of the citizen.

From social constructivism in science studies we now know that it is necessary to draw on extra-scientific factors to bring about the closure of scientific and technical debates—scientific method, experiments, ob-servations, and theories are not enough. In this work, science became reconceptualized as a social activity, with attention being directed to how scientific knowledge is used in social institutions such as schools, courts, policymaking agencies, and public deliberations. These investiga-tions focus on the question of how expertise has emerged, how it is socially constructed, and how it gets taken up by various institutions (Stilgoe 2004; Fuller 2006). For Collins and Evans this has led to an inability to distinguish between experts and non-experts. If the similarities of different types of knowledge have been emphasized, what then are the differences? After two decades of deconstruction, they argue, it is now time to "reconstruct" the concept of expertise. The task is how to accept the relativist contribution of social constructivism while at the same time finding a special rationale for science and technology—that is, to accept that science and technology are much more ordinary than we once thought, but still unique and special.

The reconstruction of expert knowledge has to begin with identification of the role of the expert as both an analyst's category as well as an actor's category, concepts which in turn will permit the development of prescrip-tive as well as descriptive statements about the role of expertise in the public realm. Much of social constructivism has preferred to wait until after the fact to see whose claims have become convincing and acceptable in the course social and political interaction. In this view, only down-stream can we come to see who gets defined as expert, actor, or analyst. The problem here, according to Collins and Evans, is that such an ap-proach misses an important aspect of public issues, namely that decisions have to be made according to a timetable established within the political sphere, not the scientific or technical sphere. Because the pace of politics is faster than the pace of scientific consensus formation, decisions have to be made before the scientific dust has settled. They put it this way: "Political decisionmakers are... continually forced to define classes of expertise before... the judgments of history have been made... [They are] defining classes of experts actors in the political sphere; they are making history rather than reflecting on it." In this sense, they clearly adopt the policymakers situation and seek to assist him or her with a prescriptive theory.

Whereas social constructivism has largely dealt with how scientific consensus is shaped and formed, Collins and Evans want to add the question of how we can make decisions based on scientific knowledge before there is an absolute scientific consensus. Where the constructivist question has involved an element of relativism, something in addition to relativism is required for answering this second question. One way to get at this, they argue, is to look at the way science is granted legitimacy in the political, legal, or other spheres. In fact, much existing writing in science studies which deals with science in the public domain has approached the problem this way. But what they are trying to understand and explain is why science *should* be granted legitimacy because of the kind of knowledge it is. That is, what makes it special. In a sense, it is a return to the earlier Mertonian question, but in the light of later research.

Collins and Evans approach this problem by building categories of expertise. They begin by examining the "esoteric" or hard sciences, which they do for two reasons: they are most familiar with them and they are the traditional "hard case" starting point for more general studies of science. The approach is "to work outward from [our] esoteric starting point in a coherent manner, ending up with the public-domain sciences which are our target." They thus begin with what they call the "core set" of scientists, defined as being made up of those scientists deeply engaged in experimentation or theoretical argumentation that is directly applicable to a scientific debate. A core set, which can be small, is the more solidaristic group of scientists which appears after a controversy has for practical purposes settled down. In the hard sciences—the laboratory sciences—only members of the core set of scientists can "legitimately contribute to the formation of the consensus, and develop the science thereafter" (or what Kuhn called the resultant "normal science"). It is not always easy to define the boundaries of a core set because disputes within core sets often involve the "boundary work of trying to define people in or out—that is defining them as legitimate or illegitimate commentators." But if one looks at a scientific controversy such as the detection of gravitational waves, it is fairly easy for Western scientific society to identify them.

At this point, they introduce a theoretical innovation that permits them to extend the category in a way that deals with their major concern about Second Wave social constructivism—namely the question of other contributors, including laypersons. What distinguishes the core set, they argue, is not credentials per se. It is relevant "experience." The core set compromises those who have actually done relevant experiments, or who have developed or worked with theories relevant to the issue in question. The core specialist position, apart from the possession of the necessary scientific and technical equipment, arises from their long experience and integration into the specialized social group of which such expertise is the collective property. Core-set members do not by definition possess *extra* formal qualifications, and they have not undergone appropriate periods of formal training beyond what they needed to qualify as certified scientists in the first place. It is not more certification that qualifies them for membership of the core; it is the informal criteria of relevant experience. Beyond the core there are non-specialists in the scientific community. These members can understand the issues but they have knowledge that is based on digested sources such as scientific journals, the scientific media, and the broadcast media, and conversations with colleagues. Their knowledge does not include the richness of a dispute and its potential for being re-opened which comes from the lived history of the core set.

The aim is to approach the develop a theory of who should and should not contribute to decision-making by virtue of their expertise. Toward this end, they argue that the "rights" to participate in decision-making based on expertise should be understood one way, while rights accruing to other stakeholders who have no any special technical expertise, must be understood another way. Stakeholders rights are not denied, but they play a different role from the rights emerging from expertise. In this view, political rights make nearly no contribution to technical decision-making, being almost entirely superceded by top–down expertise.

In this scheme, then, specialist experts with rights to participate in technical decisions—whether credentialed or not—possess what they call "contributory expertise." They can offer propositional knowledge and are able to adjudicate between competing knowledge-claims and to determine the content of knowledge. They are separated, in this respect, from non-specialists, whether certified or not. But because they also define expertise in terms of experience rather than in terms of truth per se, people need not have certification to be able to make contributions. This permits the possibility of non-specialist scientists, scientific project managers, and even citizen laypersons, where their experience is relevant. This is a useful theoretical contribution.

Underlying this scheme, as they clearly state, is a preference for a way of life that gives special value to scientific reasoning in answering propositional questions. They thus seek to work out what is special about systematic scientific inquiry, in face of the relativist challenges. Toward this end, they want to treat expertise as a category that is *sui generis*, that is separable from its politics and its attributions. Expertise, they acknowledge, does not provide certainty; it is not like truth. One of the paradoxes of expertise, in fact, is that we might need to consult it even when the likelihood of it producing correct knowledge is almost zero.

With regard to the separation of science and politics, they concede that science can be invested with politics, and that expertise does not operate in an exalted realm. Since expertise itself contributes to the framing of technological decisions, policy solutions can be pre-empted by scientistic framings. But this, in their view, does not mean that we don't need or can't have a theory to resolve what they call the problem of extension, namely how to establish boundaries and order between different kinds of contributions to expertise. That is, who should be considered an expert and who has no expertise in particular questions?

The underlying concern of the proposed Third Wave is to determine how to decide about expertise in "real-time policymaking." Collins and Evans, toward this end, want to contribute to the "policy turn" in science studies, identified with figures such as Jasanoff, Wynne, and Rip. Although they acknowledge that they "are a couple of novices knocking on the door of this already flourishing programme" of policy-oriented research, they want to add to it "a new scheme for the reconception of expert knowledge as something special." The many "thoughtfully executed policy researches, gratefully received by governments thrown into panic by the demise of public deference to science and technology, needs to be underpinned by a prescriptive theory of knowledge." In the absence of such a theory, "the twin dangers are that science becomes synonymous with politics or that there is a backlash that takes us all the way back to the earlier theories of Wave One" (that overemphasize science as a value-neutral, pure pursuit of truth). Independent of "where one stands on these issue," they argue, it is their hope that their proposed "way of looking at expertise . . . will prove useful."

Technology policymaking in the public realm: Confronting the epistemological gap

Up to this point, Collins and Evans do indeed make a useful contribution to our understanding of technical decision-making. Helping to clarify the relationship of core-set scientists to other potential contributors, in particular laypersons, is an important step toward a more refined understanding of the technical aspects of expertise. One is tempted, though, to suggest that they might be explaining this to the wrong audience. The paper is written as if to clarify this for wrong-headed social constructivists, in particular those who have gone over the relativist edge. But they are more likely to find a positive reception among many social constructivists than they are in the scientific community. Few members of the scientific community have shown interest in expanding their understanding of contributory expertise. In all but the most enlightened quarters, the idea that lay persons might have something to say is regularly rejected.

The task, then, is to start with the "hard" core set of technical experts and extend the theoretical line out to other contributory experts with the public domain sciences as their target. So posed, the approach is innovative, but the task itself is not new. It possesses more than a family resemblance to that which technocratic theorists have set for themselves since they can first be identified in the literature of the social and policy sciences. Their conceptual innovation is to be found in their attempt to establish a theoretical framework for understanding the extension of contributory expertise to a wider range of participants.

If, however, Collins and Evans's underlying concern is the "demise of public deference" for science and technology, this cannot be redressed through a contributory theory of technical expertise per se. The legitimacy problems of science and technology are lodged in the neglect of a more fundamental epistemological problem that underlies the public's concerns, albeit largely unarticulated and latent as such. Whereas Collins and Evans want to solve the problem by extending technical expertise to the decision-making problem, there is in fact no linear bridge which connects the hard sciences to the public domain sciences.[3] There is, in short, no epistemological road over which expertise can directly travel from one domain to the other. For those in the policy sciences attuned to epistemological issues, this is generally no surprise. It is what they have discovered over the past three decades (roughly paralleling the work on social constructivism). Indeed, for them, this might be *the* lesson of the policy sciences. This, however, is not to say that all have learned it, as in

[3] The constructivist approach has generally focused on the boundaries between experts and citizens with regard to empirical knowledge. The approach here extends the constructivist position by focusing on the justification of the norms and standards against which empirical claims are made. That is, it includes lay knowledge but also examines the acceptance of the normative, practical arguments upon which expert and lay judgments are made.

the case of social constructivism with regard to the science. In Britain, for example, the current concept of "evidence-based" policymaking underscores the point. Although a growing number of scholars have begun to understand its limitations, those who support it would openly accept the work of Collins and Evans as a contribution to evidence-based policymaking.

To examine this more carefully, we need first to deal with what appears to be a confusion related to their use of the term "technical decision-making." They seem to ambiguously use this term in two ways. The first concerns "technical decision-making" inside the expert communities, that is, decision-making concerned about technical objects or phenomena themselves. If the concept is so defined, Collins and Evans are on solid ground. But a problem arises when they subtly assume this concept to be synonymous with the question of technical decision-making in the public domain. In the public realm the crucial questions are generally not about the technical findings. Rather they are about political policymaking, which raises a different set of concerns. Technical—or better technological—policymaking in the public realm is not the same as technical decision-making as identified by Collins and Evans. In the domain of public policy the issue is seldom about the technical characteristics of the phenomenon per se. Fundamentally, it is about the relations of technical phenomenon to society. It is the normative question of what should be done. The fact that a technology can be built or implemented is not in the normative world of the public domain a reason to do it. And if it is to be done, the facts of how to build it seldom tell us how it should be implemented.

It is here that the problem of public deference to science and technology raises its head. Rather than a lack of respect for science, it is more fundamentally the consequence of an inappropriate overextension of scientific rationality in a realm governed by a different logic. Having dealt with the question of decisions about the technical object, and who can participate in making them, Collins and Evans shift to the public realm, suggesting that they have supplied a prescriptive framework for the policymakers. But what they have done, like a long line of technocratic theorists preceding them, is to have exported the logic of technical expertise into the sociopolitical realm of the public which is more fundamentally governed by a logic of its own. Decision-making in the public domain extends to a different line of questions. While the move by Collins and Evans's is subtle and difficult at times to recognize, it is the source of much of the confusion their work has generated. From their writings, one has to conclude that

Collins and Evans either miss or neglect this alternative form of practical reason (Richardson 2002; Fischer 2003). Moreover, they make matters worse when criticized; in face of criticism they tend to retreat and argue that they are only trying to develop a normative contributory theory of technical expertise. Let us look at this public dimension more carefully.

The classical defining question of the public domain is that of "what to do," which goals and values to pursue. It is a question typically ignored, left unanswered, or suppressed in an era dominated by technology. More specifically in the present context, the question is whether or not we want the technology. This concern operates independently of propositional knowledge—or knowledge of any sort—about the technology. The normative question here is basically about the way of life and the impact of the technology on it (Ferkiss 1969; Beck 1985; Winner 1989). Nobody *needs* cell phones, computers, or GM foods to have a good life. In the case of computers, for example, they have for many people—despite all of the promises to make us smarter and to provide more leisure—only sped up their lives, with questionable impacts on the quality of their lives. We have lived without these technologies and can continue to do so. Indeed, the question is still very much with us, even if marginalized by the ideologies of technology.

Philosophers of technology have long called attention to this question of social choice. But Collins and Evans, like technologists more generally, simply ignored it with the argument that they prefer to live in a "Western technological culture." So stated, they have little or nothing to say to someone who doesn't accept this choice. In this regard, what they have actually done is develop a normative theory of technical decision-making for a particular kind of society. Wittingly or unwittingly, the work, in this sense, is ideological.

This means that Collins and Evans, despite their protestations, become part of the problem for those who oppose the unreflected adoption of these technologies. For those raising this concern, the question is quite different. Rather than a critical need for a theory of contributory expertise in technical decision-making, the task concerns the relationship of technologies to society. Beyond expressing their allegiance to Western technological society, Collins and Evans show no interest in this question. They are simply dismissive. This is one of the major reasons for the strong reaction that their work has confronted.

But even here we can stay with the commitment to Western technological culture and show that it doesn't altogether answer the question. The culture can mean numerous things. One is that the projects of the scientists and engineers have priority. This is the idea that science and technology, based on the pursuit and application of truth, are basic to human progress; they are essential to our well-being. Little or nothing should hinder the development and implementation of new technologies. It is the idea to which Collins and Evans subscribe. Western technological culture, however, could also mean a culture that accepts the positive advantages of scientific technologies but still considers their place in democratic society, where citizens would ask whether they want to implement certain technologies and, if so, how. Despite their denials, the fact that Collins and Evans skirt this issue gives their work its technocratic First Wave implications. It a considerable source of resistance to their Third Wave normative theory of expertise. Moreover, their objections to the critique suggests that they do not understand what the opposition to science is about. Much of the postmodern anti-science protest in society is in fact about the indiscriminate application of science and technology, rather than an entirely irrational response to it. In fact, as we shall see, it can be interpreted as closer to rationality—more broadly understood—than the position Collins and Evans take.[4]

Beyond what might strike some an academic issue for the political philosopher, the problem pertains directly to the activities of science itself. What we have learned from the constructivist contribution to science studies is that the problem manifests itself in the very scientific and technological framing of social issues. This defining and framing of the problem to be researched often implicitly rests on a particular understanding of a way of life, as opposed to other competing views. The new biological science of genetic engineering, for example, involves much more than mere representations of an existing reality (Hacking 1991; Wynne 2003). Such bio-technological science is itself an intervention into society that shapes the very direction of its future development. The kinds of unpredictable consequences that it sets into motion reach beyond our prevailing scientific knowledge, and thus, elicit legitimate questions from ordinary citizens about the social and political goals creating them.

Through the process of framing the issues to be investigated, science predetermines the answers to these otherwise reasonable questions from the public. Science treats these questions as either settled or unimportant. This neglect is often the source of much apprehension—and even

---

[4] There are, of course, populist know-nothings, but in so far as their issues concern a way of life, they have to be dealt with on a political rather than a technical basis. Collins and Evans are themselves only putting forward their own preference for a technological culture and must be responded to on the same basis.

rejection—of science by ordinary citizens. Although citizens frequently are themselves unable to fully articulate their concerns, they often sense that something is missing, something remains to be discussed. Scientists, including Collins and Evans, fail to recognize that the meanings or framings that the public attaches to an issue is never entirely fixed and undisputable, and not infrequently opened for further consideration, before the kinds of propositional questions about risk and benefits that they emphasize emerge as relevant concerns of public actors. In this respect, Collins and Evans's argument is not much different from that of scientists who treat the core meanings embedded in scientific research as objective and thus given. It is what Wynne (2003) identifies as the tacit "cultural politics of science." They perpetuate, in the process, the assumption that public issues are science-centered in terms of their meaning, and in doing so, delete the very sociopolitical contexts which permit us to understand what is going on in the public domain, in particular with regard to the public resistance toward science and technology. Focusing on who can contribute to technical decision-making, they miss the point that the political tension is about the social meaning of the technical and its societal implications. As scientific framings include some people while excluding others, this raises the problem of legitimacy of these decisions. It remains unresolved in their work.

The Third Wave fails to see that the public domain issues are about what Wynne (2003) calls "the democratic cultivation and negotiation of public meanings through the conduits and interwoven textures of public experiences, knowledge, and interactions, in essentially open-ended historical form." Thus public decisions require an extension of participants, but it is an extension to include a normative discussion of the social meanings of particular projects and their broader implications for society. More than a set of apolitical, fragmented, ahistorical, "decisionist" understanding of technology policymaking based on expert knowledge, we need a more relational vision of technology and society. We need to understand technology as part of the societal context in which it is embedded.

Thus, while public opposition to science and technology is defined as either a misunderstanding of or willful rejection of science, it is in fact more generally generated by a broad and growing public alienation created by the responsible techno-managerial institutions that impose social meaning, including the widespread view that the issues are matters of risk and safety properly defined by science itself (or as Beck has explained the public concern, those who are the culprits are also those who preside over the court). In this respect, Collins and Evans are not the first to misunderstand the nature and causes of the legitimacy crisis of science; they join a long list.

Recognizing these omitted issues—questions of how definitions of public issues are established and maintained, the way some things become salient and others deleted from collective action—brings the importance of social framing into focus. But Collins and Evans, even though their own efforts fail to hit the target, are still not wrong about the need for a prescriptive theory of technology policymaking. They are correct when they say that social constructivism has not sufficiently addressed this issue. A theory to correct this deficiency, however, needs to take a very different, more genuinely normative form than the one they set out.

The public's turn to normative reason also has a more pragmatic dimension related to public decision-making, to which we turn in the next section. In line with social constructivist studies, Collins and Evans seek to acknowledge what they call "extra scientific judgments;" indeed, they assign them to a special category they call "discrimination." Regrettably, as we see below, they fail to draw out the social and political consequences of the concept.

Extra-scientific judgments: Discrimination as sociocultural reason

Collins and Evans introduce the concept of discrimination to acknowledge that there can be nonscientific reasons for questioning—even rejecting—scientific or technical findings. But they relegate the concept to a secondary status, serving as something of a corrective to misguided judgments in the technical realm. As presented, the concept fails to capture the centrality of the phenomenon it seeks to incorporate, namely that once technology enters the public realm of normative judgment, it unapologetically takes a seat along side of technical reason. Discrimination, as they develop it, involves the ability of social actors to make judgments about knowledge claims based on something other than their scientific knowledge. Judgments of this sort, as they recognize, can be made on the basis of actors' contextual or experiential knowledge. Such factors "as the personal demeanor of the expert," they assert, "might be the crucial inputs to these adjustments, rather as one might judge a politician." They illustrate the point by offering a number of questions that can relevantly be brought to bear:

"Does the author of a view come from within the right social networks, and has he or she the appropriate experience to make their claim credible?"

"Does the author of a claim seem to have integrity?'

"Is the author of a claim known to have made unreliable claims in the past?"

"Are there are also secondary features of a claim itself that can be judged with only minimal scientific understanding?"

"Is a claim internally consistent or inconsistent, or consistent with other claims made by the same person?"

"Does the claim seem so self-serving as to give concern?"

Although these questions emphasize what can be called nontechnical "social knowledge, Collins and Evans fail to acknowledge or recognize the significance of this for the development of a normative theory of expertise. In their work, the concept is more narrowly honed along technical lines. "To make the notion of discrimination do any work," as they write, "it is once more necessary to distinguish between specialists and the population as a whole." They elaborate the point in these words: "Most members of a society, just by being members of that society, are able to discriminate between what counts as science and what counts as non-science." This involves, for example, "the ubiquitous judgment on which we rely when we dismiss astrology and the likes as potential contributors to the scientific element in technical decision-making." The members of society, by and large, "have sufficient judgment to know that the social and cognitive networks of, say, astrologers do not overlap with the social and cognitive networks of hard scientists with relevant experience."

On what basis can such discriminations be made? "This kind of discriminatory ability, as they put it, "comes with participatory expertise in the matter of living in society!" That is, discriminatory knowledge on the part of nonspecialist members of society is interpreted as a form of technical awareness—generally low-level but sufficient awareness—derived from having lived in a scientifically and technologically based social system (perhaps having also taken some high school courses in basic science). It is the kind of general information that one gleans by virtue of being a member of such a society and having gained relevant experiences along the way. And this is not wrong. But the interpretation rests on the view that laypersons have, in short, enough sense to defer to the scientists.

What they fail to see is that discrimination is not a weak form of technical judgment that in some cases can serve as a corrective, but rather based on a different from of reason. As I have argued elsewhere, it rests on a form of "sociocultural reason" (or "cultural" for short) that relates to but serves a different purpose than technical reason. Indeed, it has a different logic and rationality of its own. Whereas technical reason emphasizes scientific method, logical consistency, empirical outcomes, and generalizability of findings, cultural reason is geared to social process. Where the former emphasizes expert judgments and depersonalized calculations, the latter emphasizes social knowledge gained from experience—personal and otherwise—derived from being a member of the society. Drawing heavily on traditional social and peer groups—family, church groups, labor unions, political associations, etc.—cultural reason takes unanticipated consequences to be fully relevant to near-term decision-making and trusts process over predicted outcomes. Beyond statistical probabilities and risk-benefit ratios, it places emphasis on the circumstances under which the judgment was made, identified and publicized, the standing or place of the individual in his or her community who announces it, and the social values of the community as a whole. That is, the very sorts of things that Collins and Evans identify as the questions of discrimination. Cultural reason can, in this respect, be understood as a form of rationality inherent to the social-life world. It is concerned with the impacts, intrusions, or implications of a particular event or phenomenon on the social relations that constitute that world.

The role of cultural reason in technical decisions is clearly evident in matters related to risk and uncertainty, considerations almost always evident in technology policymaking. When citizens have reasons to suspect that a risk assessment is superficial or false, as studies show, they turn to their own cultural logic and examine the results in terms of previous social experiences (Plough and Krimsky 1987). Turning from the empirical studies, they ask questions like: What are our previous experiences with these people? Is there reason to believe we can trust them? Why are they telling us this? Such questions are even more evident when crucial technological decisions are made by distant, anonymous, and hierarchical organizations. Citizens want to know how conclusions were reached, whose interests are at stake, if the process reflects a hidden agenda, who is responsible, what protection do they have if something goes wrong, and so on? If they believe the project engineers and managers either don't know what they are talking about, or are willing to lie or dissemble to serve the purposes of their company, citizens will obviously reject the risk assessment statistics put forth by the company. For example, if they have experiences that suggest they should be highly distrustful of particular company representatives or plant managers, such information will tend to override the data itself.

151

Questions of trust and anxiety are often associated with the kinds of technological decisions for which Collins and Evans would like to develop a normative theory of expertise. First and foremost, consider the central importance of scientific and technological interventions in modern life. Such interventions are basic to every aspect of society—from the food we eat, the way we work, how we communicate with one another, our modes of mobility, how we understand our bodily functions, among others. Moreover, these interventions occur with increasing speeds that allow us little time to examine or discuss their implications for the lives we live. Indeed, they often seem to take on a life of their own. In the process, people lose the feeling that they control their own lives, as the activities of getting on become an adaptation to one new technology after the other—i.e. we scarcely learn how to use the computer and we suddenly have the internet and digital phones—all of which speed up everyday life. For some people this might be an exciting, adventuresome new life, especially for educated young people. Often they know no other world. For others, it creates a growing source of anxiety, mixed in part with a feeling of alienation. Because the evidence that we—or at least most of us—live better because of these technologies is not always so clear, the result for many is a sense of distrust and a temptation to resist, the resultant tensions being directed at the experts who plan and manage disruptions. This is not to say that technological change is all bad. More-over, many people are simply adverse to change. But technological change does also have it negative sides, which serve to confirm and support such anxieties. The environmental degradation resulting from fast-paced technologically driven economic development is everywhere to seen. Many people lose their jobs to new technologies, and so on. Indeed, these are standard themes of contemporary anti-technology movements, both global and local. And they are basic to the politization of science and technology over the past three decades, the very phenomenon that Collins and Evans want to limit, if not circumvent.

Behind this broader social response to technology is yet another—more specific—reason for the turn to cultural reason and its forms of extra-scientific discriminatory judgment related to science itself. Over the same thirty years we have gained a new understanding of the nature of science and technology, one that often supports the doubts of everyday citizens. Much of this is in fact owed to the Second Wave of science studies. Such work shows that science never reaches "truth" per se. At best, it can only *strive* for truth in an uncertain world in which knowledge is ever in need of qualification and revision. In one important way, this should not be surprising. The basis of the scientific method is uncertainty and change; science works with findings that are are overturned by new research discoveries. In this sense, science is only the consensus of the scientific community at any particular time. The problem, however, arises from the official depiction of the science advanced in public, namely a lofty endeavor devoted to truth. This understanding is, in fact, what normatively grounds the privileged position given to the scientific community in matters related to science and technology policymaking. But the increasing awareness of the distinction between the pursuit of truth and the possession of truth has played an important part in the politicization of science, the very problem that Collins and Evans want to circumvent or supplant. The realization that there is always need for a skeptical attitude about knowledge at any point in time affords science's critics the opportunity to legitimately—even when self-servingly—question particular findings and the projects based on them—i.e. it can always be done in the name of methodological rigor.[5] In face of the politicization of science and technology, Collins and Evans want to establish a basis for deciding who can rightly judge the results in the face of uncertainty. For them the answer is those in possession of technical *experience*. And in many cases this is a valid argument. But given the inevitable mix of empirical uncertainty, coupled with social and other normative considerations, technical experience is scarcely a firm category. Indeed, with the concept of discrimination they themselves note the need for extra-scientific judgments. Where, then, does one draw this line? If they mean the extra-scientific judgments of technical experts, this does not fill the bill. In the social realm, technical experts are only citizens like everyone else; they have no privileged status.

To this we also need to add the problem of self-interest. Whereas science was accepted in earlier periods as a distinterested pursuit of truth, it is today also seen by many—not altogether wrongly—as an interested group advancing its own status, both materially and socially. This results in various ways from the central role conferred on it in politics and policy, both wittingly and unwittingly. It is a role evolving from two interrelated directions, one related to an emphasis on scientific decision-making and the other science's need for public monies to support its research

---

[5] The science about global warming is perhaps the best contemporary example of this politics of methodology played out to challenge particular findings. The critics of global warming science have persistently argued that the findings related to the human impact on climate change have not been proven, which is technically correct. But it is also the case that there will never be proof of this contention in this sense of the word "proven."

project, mega-projects in particular. In the course of these processes, science has emerged itself as an interested community and, like any other interest group, possesses its own motives and intentions which can be examined and called into question. Under these circumstances, as the history and sociology of science have persuasively shown, it is not enough to simply consider the scientific findings at face value. The motives and intentions of particular scientists become part of the equation, as the concept of discrimination partially recognizes. For example, as science has become more and more dependent on public largess for its research projects, the scientific community's advice about funding projects is intricately bound up with the advance of the community's own interests. Beck (1985), as already noted, has likened this to putting the bank robber in charge of the criminal investigation.

Competing interest groups in science and technology policy thus struggle over competing interpretations of the findings. The question of how to define a particular problem is often as problematic as the question of what to do about it, with each side employing its data and interpretations to suit its own interests and purposes. For the public the process poses a difficult problem. How can citizens judge between these competing empirical analyses? If two experts stand before an audience of citizens and argue over the empirical reliability of a given set of statistics, what basis do citizens have for discriminately judging the competing empirical claims? In this situation, citizens are forced to rely as well on an extra scientific assessment of the factors surrounding a decision. And not without good reason. In the absence of empirical agreement, there is every reason to believe that interested parties will strongly assert themselves, advocating the findings that best suit their interests. In such cases, at least in the immediate situation, there is little science can do to help citizens discriminate between such claims.

One can, of course, call for more research, which is how most in the technical community respond. To be sure, more research and informed judgment might reduce the levels of uncertainty associated with technically oriented policy decisions. But the crucial point is that it cannot reduce it all together, or at least not often. There is, in short, little guarantee that further research will bring either certainty or timely results in a particular conflict. Recognizing the problem, Collins and Evans seek to privilege the "best judgment" of the technical experts. But this ignores the need for sociocultural reason, a realm in which technical experts have no privileged role. Their theoretical effort thus misses the problem to which cultural reason and the problem of discrimination is addressed. This later concern is not to be answered with greater scientific clarification per se, but through answers to normative questions about uncertainty in the social system and the way of life more generally. Whereas Collins and Evans take this to mean a call for a different society, and thus reject it as irrelevant, significant numbers of people are worried that the society they live in and accept is not working the way its leaders tell them it does. For this reason, any attempt to rule out normative judgments can only miss the crucial part of the problem. Indeed, given the fact that decisions have to be made (what Collins and Evans take to be the essence of policy science) in the face of such uncertainty, people have to rely on other sources of social knowledge in order to discriminatively exercise good judgment. From the perspective of cultural reason, to act otherwise would itself be *irrational*.

There cannot be, for these reasons, a normative theory of expertise that establishes as final arbiter of public decisions those who have the ability and experience to speak about the technical components of the particular policy issue. When it comes to technology policy in the public domain, we see that discrimination is much more than a secondary category to deal with awkward problems. The challenge ahead then is not just more science, but rather how to better understand the interrelationships between technical and cultural reason, that is, how to relate science to norms, and values in a more comprehensive mode of reason. What we need is a theory that necessarily includes both technical-scientific and normative-political considerations, but it cannot set out a fixed set of substantive criteria for making the judgments. There can be substantive criteria, but they have to be established through *non apriori* procedural processes.

Interrelating technical and cultural reason: Practical discourse as public epistemology

When deliberation occurs in public decision-making, as we saw earlier, technical and social criteria confront each other without a common metric. In these exchanges it is not only a question of which group has the best answer to the problem, but rather also a question of purpose and goals. For what purpose *is* and *should* the most effective solution be put. A technical analysis does not in and of itself carry the answer to this question.

Once we recognize this, we confront the long-standing epistemological problem of the relation of the empirical to the normative—or facts to values—and enter the realm of practical discourse. While Collins and

Evans would include "extra-scientific" dimensions of technical decisions, they do not appreciate that this category of criteria involves a fundamental shift in epistemology in the realm of public discourse, namely to practical discourse, concerned with the question of "what *ought* to be done." Such discourse is about practical matters. While lacking the formal rigor of technical reason, it offers a solution to the problem by incorporating technical information into a normative framework. Whereas technical decision-making per se rests on values that it takes for granted—that is, they are not singled out as part of the analytical assessment—practical decisions are fully open to a consideration of the normative implications of technical findings for the social world. Moreover, while it does not focus on the analytics of technical reason, it does provide for raising questions of both their credibility and acceptability.

Basically the normative questions that define practical discourse operate in the pragmatic intersection between technical and cultural reason (Fischer 1995; 2003). Where technical reason focuses on the measure of causal relations or outcomes in terms of particular criteria or standards, taken as given, the normative line of cultural reason is essentially the pursuit of the justification for the use of those standards. Beyond the "decisionism" of technical decision-making, the larger framework of practical discourse submits the sociocultural decision criteria—or warrant—to three interrelated normative assessments. One concerns the relevance of the impact of the technical decision on the particular social context which it affects. In matters related to technology and environment this discourse is readily apparent in conflicts over NIMBY. Local residents can be saying yes to nuclear power, but not in their location for particular reason (e.g. an areas's vulnerability to hurricanes). The answer to this question will turn on the normative persuasiveness of the contextual arguments, but admit to empirical information (e.g. a geographical analysis), or what might more commonly be called "the facts of the situation."

Practical discourse also directs the deliberation to the impact of the technology on the larger societal system. Should the societal system return to nuclear power because of global warming? Or does nuclear power pose too many safety threats in the face of terrorism? Here the answers would relate to the specific economic and social functions of the political economy. Does nuclear power make a functional contribution to the existing arrangements as they work? The answer will depend on an interaction of normative priorities, including conflicts from competing sectors of the society (such as education or business), and different empirical understandings of how the social system actually works (the subject of the empirical social sciences).

But as industrial and political elites know, to their chagrin, this latter question poses yet another one: do we accept this societal system? Namely, should we accept the values, or operational definitions of the values, that underlay the existing system. In matters related to technology, this question is best known in terms of the green critique of society. Radical greens call for a basic normative reorientation of modern society (e.g. from urban-industrial society to more traditional decentralized regions). While these arguments may strike many as unworkable and thus irrelevant, they are legitimate social questions. Moreover, at times they can even be the harbingers of fundamental long-term change. Although this level of practical discourse raises questions related to the highest levels of philosophical and ideological thought, it need not operate independently of empirical knowledge, as the "naturalist" school of philosophy has long demonstrated. While empirical information cannot settle such questions, a great deal of empirical information can be brought to bear on such ideological deliberation (e.g. competing views over human nature and their respective implications for the good society).

Practical discourse is not governed by calculation but rather by "informal logic." It focuses as much on asking questions as it does answering them. Serving as a direction finder, it seeks to identify what we know and what we need to find out. Its conclusions rest on consensus and there is no guarantee that it will be reached. There is little here that is hard or fixed as there is in technical decision-making. Positive outcomes in practical discourse depend on reasonable people. Short of that we need to understand the relations of such practical discourse to social change. It does not have a direct influence on power but can work its way toward change, a process that we need to better understand.

Although the challenge is more difficult in the public realm, as many technocrats have regretted, there is no avoiding it in an open, democratic society. Where in the realm of technical decision-making the effort can be to focus on a core-set of experts, in the public realm there is no way to formally limit participation. The public realm includes the widest possible range of participants and discussion can only under limited circumstances be narrowed to particular segments of society.

These are the kinds of questions that actually emerged in the Second Wave, particularly as they pertain to science policy studies, and they are the questions that Collins and Evans would like to avoid by focusing on the technical core, expanded to include those with contributory expertise.

Although they take offence at the suggestion, this is basic the long-standing technocratic strategy. Perhaps the difference is they have dressed it up in sophisticated clothing and give it an appeal by relating it to an important theoretical question, which in the process seems to cover over these normative questions.

At this point we can ask how we might actually guide or facilitate a deliberative process that focuses on the interaction of these two different modes of reason? In the next section, we consider the practices of translation and facilitation of public deliberation.

From technical translation to public facilitation

Public deliberation involves many more groups with a much wider range of opinions than does technical deliberation, often conflictual opinions that do not sit easily next to one another. While Collins and Evans make clear how technical decision-making might best be guided, cultural reason turns our attention to the social meanings and assumptions underlying specific public statements and claims. Indeed, these meanings and assumptions often play as large a role as the statements themselves in clarifying the discursive ground that makes meaningful public deliberation possible. Collins and Evans come close to recognizing this; they identify the need for "translation." For different groups to talk to each other, they argue, the non-empirical function of translation is often necessary. Toward this end, people with the special ability to take on the position of the "other" and to alternate between different social worlds in order to translate across them are needed. Such translation, they explain, involves the sort of skills possessed by "the journalist, the teacher, the novelist, the playwright, and so forth, skills notoriously hard to explain—as qualitative sociologists know all too well."

But again they pull up short from what is otherwise a useful direction. Despite the fact that they speak of "social worlds," they limit their discussion of translation to communication among different technical groups with different levels of knowledge and interest. Their effort, in fact, is to linearly extend the logic technical decision-making into the public realm, as if that is the primary problem confronting technology policy. While technical communities surely constitute a specialized segment of the social world, they are at best only a limited part of it. Indeed, the members of a technical community themselves are as well members of the larger social world, from where they draw their own attitudes and opinions.

The successful translator, as they define him or her, requires what they call "interactional expertise." By interactional expertise they mean the ability to have enough information about the various groups to be able to explain the concepts of one community to another. In particular, they speak of the need to be able to understand enough about the relevant technical processes to succeed in communicating them to other actors, short of being able to carry out the research. The task, as defined, is important and surely relevant to technical decision-making. But in the public realm the task has to include more than the requisite technical understanding. Here the focus is on social relevance and the meanings *assigned* to particular technical objects and artefacts. The role of translator thus centers around the ability of speak to different social and political groups in their own "social languages." In this respect, the task is much more complicated than Collins and Evans recognize.

Moreover, from the perspective of the public sphere, the role can best be understood as something more than a clarification of concepts. In public debate, it would involve the active facilitation of public learning. Rather than providing technical interpretations designed to resolve political questions, the function of the translator is that of a facilitator. He or she assists the participants—both citizens and experts—in examining the technical information in terms of their own interests and values. It can be understood as translating technical conclusions into the social contexts of the various relevant or interested groups.

To conceptualize this role we need to move beyond a technical theory of knowledge to a postempiricist, interpretive understanding of communication and argumentation. For this task the central focus shifts to socially shared beliefs and an examination of the way they are intersubjectively "constitutive" of the social reality into which the technology is introduced. Analytically, this involves a critical assessment of the assumptions that organize and intepret the various ways of knowing and the knowledge that results from them. In this process, the translator must actively employ his or her own subjectivity to understand the views of others—citizens, politicians, decisionmakers, stakeholders, and others. More than just an alternative epistemological orientation, it provides a realistic description of the actual relationships between citizens and experts. In this sense, it is embedded in the empirical realities of such exchanges.

Grounded in particular social contexts, this interpretive function requires the professional to involve him- or herself in the modes of thought and learning of everyday life, including the local knowledge and understandings of the ordinary citizen. Knowledge is, in this way, recognized to be more than a set of relationships among selected data and variables isolated or abstracted from their social context. To be meaningful for the public world of decision and action, such variables have to be interpreted in the situational contexts to which they apply. Knowledge and reasoning, in this view, are recognized as taking many forms, from empirical analysis to expressive statements in words, sounds and pictures (Healey 2006: 29). Of particular importance is the narrative form of the story; in everyday life it is the primary means of giving meaning to complex phenomenon.

In such inquiries citizens and experts form what might be described as an interpretive community that involves bringing together professional knowledge and lived experience. Through mutual discourse they seek a persuasive understanding of the issues under investigation. This occurs through a transformation of individual beliefs, including social values. In this process the inquirer, as part of a community, is an agent in the social context rather than an isolated, passive observer. Means and ends are inseparably linked together in such a discursive process; and, importantly, those who participate need to accept the practical and moral responsibilities for their decisions and their consequences.

The postempiricist facilitator of technology policy deliberation also accepts the task of working to develop arenas and fora in which knowledge can be debated and interpreted in relation to the relevant policy issues. Contemporary examples of such fora would include such deliberative experiments as citizen juries, consensus conferences, and deliberative polls. Whereas the goal in the technical community is to find the one best solution to a problem, the facilitation of a public deliberative forum has a broader function. The process in the latter is not only to arrive at a workable decision, but also to find the workable decision that holds the decision-making participants together. In this regard, the effective political decision is the one that preserves or even improves the capacity to make future decisions. Here the goal is never to simply accept the "best solution" in terms of cost and effectiveness, but rather to deliberate about the decision in ways that can eliminate or reduce all major opposition to a particular decision. As such, the final judgment should, to the degree possible, avoid complete identification with any particular proposal or point of view. As Diesing (1962: 203–4) has put it, "the best available proposal should never be accepted just because it is best; it should be deferred, objected to, and discussed until all major opposition disappears." Although decisions based on compromise are generally less than acceptable in non-political technical decisions, they can represent the essence of wisdom in political judgments. Only political decisions that have eliminated major opposition—regardless of efficacy—contribute to the preservation and improvement of decision structure integration.

In guiding a public deliberative process, then, a facilitator's major goal is to try to reconcile or harmonize conflicting factors that block decision-making; to increase the tolerance between various groups and their respective beliefs and values; to facilitate an equilibrium between opposing forces in a destructive struggle with one another; and to reject, repress or otherwise exclude the threatening factors from the particular decision problem. In the public world, of course, the deliberative participants can only rarely arrive at fully harmonious, conflict free decisions. In the interest of minimizing resistance to the implementation of the decisions, the goal is to work to increase understanding among the participants in ways that help to reduce conflict and generate cooperative behavior in the face of differences.

Policy epistemics for the public realm: Extending the theory of contributory expertise

We turn in this final section to policy science itself. Collins and Evans want to contribute to the "policy turn," defined as the ability to bring knowledge and expertise to bear on the public decision process. But, as seen, they have failed to take account of the epistemological disjunction separating the scientific reason of the technical commmunity and the practical reason of the public sphere. Following this line of argument, it is necessary to outline a very different agenda for policy science than the more traditional—postempiricists would say "outmoded"—orientation to which they appeal. Perhaps the best way to approach the task at hand is to present it as a reformulation—or extension—of their own effort to develop a theory of contributory expertise, the difference being the need to extend it to the practical logic of public policy decision-making itself. In this respect, the problem can be understood as the need for a normative theory of policy expertise applicable to the public realm. Rather than simply trying to extend the technical into the public, with the technocratic implications that would go with it, the task would still be to move technical knowledge into the public realm but in a way that situates it in a broader contributory theory of practical deliberation.

In this task the focus shifts more centrally from technical knowledge and experience to the epistemic translation of social meanings and the facilitation of collaborative decision-making. This would give rise to a new

161

and underlying specialization in the field that might best be called "policy epistemics" (Fischer 2000).[6] Such a perspective would emerge from the postempiricist work in policy analysis, especially as it has been influenced by the social constructivism of the Second Wave in science studies (Fischer and Forester 1993; Forester 1999; Yanow 2000; Fischer 2003; Hajer and Wagenaar 2003; Healey 2006). From this literature, as well as the foregoing discussion, we can see that a fully developed policy science requires a multi-disciplinary perspective. This involves a multi-methodological framework that extends across the empirical and the normative, the quantitative and qualitative inquiry. Its focus would be on bridging the epistemological gap separating these two realm of inquiry.

In Collins and Evans's terms, this extension of expertise into the public realm of practical discourse can be understood in terms of both sociocultural experience and techno-analytic knowledge, both contributory and non-scientific. The turn to practical discourse, as we saw, offers a framework suitable for integrating these empirical and normative orientations, clarifying the logic that connects them and working out problems of translation. Such translation problems would be facilitated by making clear the ways in which technical information is normatively situated in the local contextual, societal, and ideological contexts in which public policies are embedded (Fischer 1995). As such, practical discourse helps us to better understand and develop guidelines for deliberative contributions.

Given its emphasis on ordinary language, practical discourse is well suited for including the public judgments brought to bear on the normative implications of the different policy choices, including those of lay citizens. Beyond contributing to the legitimation of public policy, citizens can supply particular facts about the situational context that are needed for effective decision-making. Indeed, the need for such citizen/expert interaction has led others to focus on participatory or collaborative inquiry (Laird 1993; deLeon 1997). Such approaches promote a dialectical interaction between the theoretical knowledge of the expert and the sociocultural knowledge of the lay citizen.

In addition to lay knowledge, both empirical and sociocultural, such a contributory theory to practical reason would include information and

[6] Several decades earlier the concept of "knowledge utilization" was advanced, along a journal by that title, to explore to deal with the failure to of technical knowledge to translate into useable knowledge. Although it largely took an empirical rather than a constructivist approach to the problem, the focus identified many of the same problems. It emerged, however, as the interest of a particular group of scholars rather that a disciplinary specialization.

beliefs about societal functions, such as how particular institutions work, the legal rules that normatively govern these institutions and their functions, as well as knowledge about basic normative preferences related to different ways of life. This later information would not only include knowledge about the existing normative foundations of the societal system—both explicit and implicit norms and values—but also views about how the system might or should change. While a normative theory of public contributions cannot privilege any particular group as final arbiter in public disputes, it can help to make clear how specific contributions might relate to some questions and not others. It could tell us when and how we might want to turn to various segments of the society—local citizens, legal experts, political and economic leaders, philosophers, and the like—for particular kinds of information and points of view. While all of these perspectives would have to compete in the deliberative processes of the public sphere, such a "meta theory" could help to make sure that the right kinds of questions were being asked, where to seek the answers to particular questions, who to include at specific points in the discourse, and the like. Policy epistemics could, for example, examine and help us better understand when citizens have something in particular to offer and when deliberation might best focus on professional judgments, a concern basic to Collins and Evans's Third Wave of theorizing.

Such investigation, as the public counterpart of the Collins and Evans's theory of technical expertise, can similarly contribute to our understanding of who can best participate in public decisions and under what circumstances. In the process, policy professionals have to learn to appreciate that policy science, as an applied research methodology, is always addressed to the world of action and, as such, necessarily situated within a practical/normative discourse. Rather than understanding normative discourse as an inferior form of reason (turned to in face of a general ability to deal with the intellectual rigors of technical analysis, or to deal with problems of empirical uncertainty), the policy science community needs to come to grips with the fact their research questions not only emerge from the world of action, but that the acceptability of their findings must as well ultimately be judged by normative standards in the public realm. That is, epistemologically speaking, their technical proposals of necessity have to be judged within the societal context to which they apply. Social context, both local and societal, has to be understood as part of the knowledge essential to the evaluation. This involves a different kind of logic and deliberation. Many of—if not most—scientists fail to see this because of their continuing attachment to the technical component of a larger, more comprehensive assessment (Fischer 2003). Policy experts have an essential contribution to make, but so do others adhering to different modes of reason, including citizens.

Policy epistemics, as such, would focus on what Yankelovich (1991) has referred to as citizens' "public judgment." As opposed to uninformed public opinion, he uses public judgment to capture the ways in which citizens can struggle with a political or policy issue, reflect on it own their own terms, and form an opinion they are ready to stand up for. Public judgment, or practical reason in the terminology employed here, is understood as a form of knowledge that rests on cognitive knowledge, but also involves its interaction with normative, emotional, and moral questions. Given practical knowledge's reliance on a diversity of perspectives, it is similar to Arendt's (1972) concept of "political judgment," which rested on her theory of "representative thinking" (involving the exploration how others see the same issue). She took it to be the most essential element of political judgment. The task of policy epistemics, as proposed here, refers in important ways to the same effort to increase the citizens'-capacities and opportunities to improve the quality of their own public judgments.

A theory of policy epistemics would thus formally address the ways people communicate across differences, the flow and transformation of ideas across borders of different fields, how different professionals groups and local communities see and inquire differently, and the ways in which differences become disputes (Willard 1996). Bourdieu (1993) speaks of examining the structure of a discursive field. This field shapes and constrains the argumentative positions that actors can take. It is reproduced in subsequent exchanges, but can sometimes be altered by events and interactions. This would involve focusing on how controversies and arguments shape the various networks and communities that deal with policy issues, technology policy in the case at hand. Specifically, this would mean focusing on "policy communities" and "issue networks" (for example, technology experts, the network of social scientists, policy analysts, journalists, politicians, administrative practitioners, and involved citizens who offer contributory expertise to an ongoing discourse about policy matters in a particular substantive areas (i.e. nuclear power, medicine and health, transportation, etc.). The goal would be to study the ways in which the members of these communities share background assumptions about the particular problem area, their ideas about the relations of particular scientific findings to decision-making, the role—if any—of citizen involvement, how they respond to criticism and opposition from outside their communities, and more.

Whereas traditional policy analysis has focused on advancing and assessing technical solutions, policy epistemics would investigate the way interpretive judgments work in the production and distribution of knowledge. Drawing on the contributions of the Second Wave and its emphasis on social contructivism, this work would concentrate on the movements and uses of information, the social assumptions embedded in research designs, the specific relationships of different types of information to decision-making, the different ways arguments move across different disciplines and discourses, the translation of knowledges from one community to another, and the interrelationships between discourses and institutions. Most important, it would involve innovating methods needed for coordinating multiple discourses in and across institutions.

Uncovering the epistemic dynamics of technical controversies in the public sphere would allow for a more enlightened understanding of what is at stake in a particular dispute, making possible a sophisticated evaluation of the various viewpoints and merits of different policy options. In doing so, the differing, often tacitly held, contextual perspectives and values could be juxtaposed, the viewpoints and demands of experts, special interests groups and the wider public directly compared, and the dynamics among the participants could be scrutinized. This would by no means side-line or even exclude scientific assessment; it would only situate it within the framework of a more comprehensive evaluation.

The areas from which we have already learned the most about these interactions are the fields of environmental and technical policy and risk analysis, in particular from Second Wave research. Although grappling with the reliability of knowledge claims and the credibility of advocates is common to all fields, the problem is especially chronic in these technically laden areas of public policy. That failures in technology policymaking can often be attributable to simplistic technocratic understandings of these relationships is clearly seen in the case of hazardous technologies and the politics of Nimby. It is just to these kinds of cultural rationalities underlying citizens' understandings and responses to expert advice that policy epistemics would turn our attention. Not only would it help to make clear why citizens are at times hesitant to accept the authority of the experts, but how that knowledge gets translated and processed in the citizen's interpretive community. Such knowledge would help us better understand the ways in which the various players react to the scientific uncertainties that plague such policy areas. It also offers the possibility of finding ways around political standoffs such as Nimby. While policy epistemics might not offer us policy solutions, at minimum it could show us ways to "keep the conversation going" (Rorty 1979).

In this view, an epistemic approach would help to connect technology and its assessment more directly to the public controversies that it seeks to inform. In terms of methodologies and their uses, it would make available to decisionmakers a more in-depth and transparent characterization of the nature of public controversies than either conventional assessment methods or media debate can offer. For the purpose of policy deliberation, policy analysis would not only constructively open up the full complexity of such public controversies, but would also feed its results back into the evolving controversy. In the process, it would contribute to informed public discussion and facilitate the closure of debate.

Included in such analysis would also be the ways in which such analytic tools as technology assessment are themselves influenced by the processes of public discussion and controversy. Indeed, such methods have been introduced by a polity in significant part as a political response to technological controversies. Important, for this reason, is the recognition that the mode of deliberation, decision-making, and conflict resolution in politics is not as different from the processes of scientific deliberation as the scientific community would have us believe. In fact, science and its expert communities are themselves social communities with an internal politics.

Conclusion

Technocracy is an old theme in the social science literature and the substantial interest in the recent work of Collins and Evans show that it is still alive, even if in a much more sophisticated form. This work has saluted Collins and Evans for their effort to rescue technical expertise from the charlatans of postmodern cultural studies. But it has also taken them to task for failing to recognize the epistemological challenge involved in relating technical expertise to public deliberation and normative decision-making. Although their interest in turning to the policy sciences for assistance is noteworthy, they have neglected to systematically examine this literature. A more detailed reading of the policy literature, particularly the postempiricist policy contributions over the past two decades, underscores the epistemological gulf between technical and public decision-making—namely, that there is no technical bridge that can connect the two. For this reason, the essay has attempted to clarify the problem and set out a new avenue that can interconnect them. The logic of practical discourse, as we saw, is not only inherent to public deliberation, but is capable of logically incorporating both empirical and normative analysis at the level of epistemology. As it stands, the analysis offered here is only a pathway, leaving much to be worked out. But finding the way is surely an important step, especially if one has already headed in the wrong direction.

Beyond technical expertise, it is also significant to note that the field of policy studies more generally has neglected this epistemic translation involved in policymaking. Indeed, this concern has been an important factor in the rise of the proposed perspective. The lack of attention to this dimension, it is important to emphasize, has occurred at considerable cost. Many of the important failures to implement technologies can be directly attributable to the kinds of communicative misunderstandings that have resulted from this neglect. It also occurs at a time when the need for deliberation between experts and citizens about a large range of public problems, social as well as technical, is ever more pressing. Moreover, it happens at time when spaces for debating the place of science and technology in society are squeezed ever thinner (Beck 1995; Jasanoff 2005). Policy epistemics, for this reason, can be posed as a major challenge involved in developing a more socially relevant Third Wave mode of professional practice.

6

Public Policy as Social Construct: Multiple Meanings in Sustainable Development

In the previous chapter we saw the way in which Collins and Evans have failed to grasp the social epistemology of the public realm.[1] In particular, they have failed to take into account how competing social meanings are attached to technological objects and how they can later become problematic assumptions in public decisions about technologies. It is, in fact, an epistemological error regularly committed by those still subscribing to the largely dominant technocratic approach to policy-making, including the contemporary emphasis on "evidence-based policymaking." It is thus important to gain a better understanding of the ways in which social meanings both infuse and interconnect the technical and social spheres. Toward this end, the foregoing discussion suggested the need for a more systematic examination of the epistemics of the policy deliberation. We set the stage for this exploration in Part III with a more detailed illustration of the socially constructed nature of public policy, focusing in particular on the role of social assumptions in policy decision-making. For this purpose, we turn to the interplay of multiple social meanings in the discursive struggle to politically define and shape the theoretical assumptions and practices of sustainable development, an environmental policy orientation inherently socio-technical in nature.

---

[1] Social epistemology refers to the investigation of the social dimensions of knowledge and and the socio-institutional and political processes that influence and shape its production. See *Social Epistemology: A Journal of Knowledge, Culture and Policy.*

Policy Assumptions: Social meaning and multiple realities

The exploration of policy assumptions is first and foremost about the meanings that we attach to actions and events. In the social world, humans understand their environment through the social meanings they assign to the elements that constitute it. Whereas physical objects have no intrinsic meanings, humans linguistically construct their social world as sets of meaningful relationships, both institutional and interpersonal. Human experience, from this phenomenological perspective, is embedded in spheres of non-material social, personal, and cultural meaning.

People, to be sure, do not construct and reconstruct their social worlds as they please. Most of the time members of society live in a social world constructed around previously given meanings that they take for granted. As a result of their socialization, this world of meanings generally comes to them more or less as an extant, fixed reality. Many of the ideas and social understandings upon which their world was constructed are so deeply embedded in the societal institutions and practices that they are difficult to recognize or identify. Typically, they are buried in everyday practices and treated as part of the nature of things. Indeed, for many, these ideas and beliefs take on the impression in the language of the everyday world as being natural. Even when people do have an appreciation of the social construction of these ideas and understandings, the original meanings of their forefathers may not be directly accessible to them. While these ideational constructions were usually appropriate at that time, they may no longer be relevant or right for a new generation and its social circumstances. Under such circumstance they can become problematic and subject to dispute.

While most people are first and foremost products of their social environment, they also can be agents affecting the world in which they live. One of the primary features of the politics of social change is the calling of particular meanings into question. Social movements involved in issues such as civil rights, women's liberation, or environmental protection have organized their struggles around calling attention to underlying social assumptions and their less obvious implications for contemporary life. Today, for example, women are no longer "ladies" or "girls." More than just different words for citizens of the same gender, these words identify different sets of social relationships. Anyone who fails to take notice of this runs the risk of getting quickly redressed.

This understanding of social reality is profoundly important for the way we approach the study of social inquiry, including public policy.

Dependent on social meaning—derived from goals, motives, intentions, purposes, and values—the analysis of social action has more in common with history and literature than with physical science. Rather than seeking proofs through formal logic and empirical experimentation, the investigation of social action requires the use of discursive constructs—metaphors in particular—to organize and connect different experiences based on perceived similarities. The meaning of a social experience is assessed in terms of its position in the larger patterns of which it is a part, be it a situation, a social system, or an ideology.

The failure of social scientists, including Collins and Evans, to connect or relate empirical findings to the social understandings of those under investigation is very much related to the disputes which have arisen. In their case, they take the understandings associated with technological society and its practice as clear and given; for them they are beyond challenge. By embracing the meanings of this dominant world, and thus treating their propositions as if they were based on unquestioned views, they in effect assign to them the sociocultural understandings of the political and economic elites of technological society. In doing so, they fail to recognized that much of the politics associated with technological controversies—of the kind that they wish to bring to an end—represents challenges to these understandings advanced by subordinates groups. This failure to translate and discuss empirical findings in the wider context of social meanings germane to the full play of politics underlies the charge of social irrelevance that has often plagued social science, including the social studies of science and technology. If the subtle pretence that empirical findings speak for themselves has managed to endure in much of academic social science, it can more quickly become a problem in an applied field of inquiry such as policy analysis, where the explicit goal is to facilitate real-world decision processes. Policy processes are entirely interwoven with dominant and competing systems of social meaning.

Policy meaning: Intepreting assumptions

The investigation of politics, and thus the making of public policy, is about politicians, interest groups, and citizens who hold multiple and changing meanings about the political actions and events that transpire in the world in which they operate. Indeed, the creation and recreation of meaning is a crucial dimension in the political manoeuvre for advantage—whether it be about the construction of beliefs about events, policies, problems, or political leaders. Such meanings, typically reflected in the assumptions we hold about the world and how it works, are basic to the mobilization of support for particular actions. And the same, of course, holds true for efforts to immobilize the political opposition.

The potency of political language does not stem merely from its description of the world as empiricists have maintained. Rather, it comes from its construction and reconstruction of the world—its interpretations of past experiences, its evocation of the unobservable aspects in the present, and constructions of possibilities and expectations for the future. These features make language a powerful constitutive force within politics. And, as such, the ability to use it effectively is an essential resource in the politics of policymaking.

Such constructions are worked out and in significant part conveyed through symbols. Created through language and communicative interaction, symbols signify the meanings of particular events and offer standards for judging what is good and bad. Edelman (1977, 1988), for example, illustrates how words such as 'welfare' generate images that cause people to reject the claims of groups in need of social assistance. Because the interests of different groups give rise to diverging meanings, as Edelman (1988: 15) put it, national security is understood differently by each of the parties concerned with it (e.g., the various branches of the arms forces, the General Dynamics Corporation, that firm's workers, the Women's International Leagues for Peace and Freedom, and potential draftees). In this sense, a problem is the result of negotiations among groups with competing definitions. This can, of course, be understood as interest group politics, but it differs from the standard approach that sees each group pursuing its own interest in a particular context. Here groups have different interests, but they also define and understand the problems and interests differently.

What is more, the reasons political actors generally offer for their policy objectives are rationalizations designed to persuade particular audiences. Various theorists have shown the way different actors employ particular words in defending policy positions or marginalizing their opponents. Competing political actors speak and write as if their language is a transparent lens through particular events and objects might be observed. But while purporting to be honest, rational, clear, and informative, such actors typically use language that is often one-sided, illogical, or patronizing. It is common for such speech to be filled with false metaphors, misleading analogies, and obscure ambiguities. Ideological arguments, as Edelman has demonstrated, are generally advanced through a "dramaturgy of objective description," which masks the performative function of political language (Edelman 1998: 15). In the name of such description, the acceptability of the policy argument ultimately depends on how effectively it succeeds in rationalizing a situation to its intended audience.

Basic to the policy process, then, is a struggle over social and political symbols invoked by competing actors (Maynard-Moody and Kelly 1993: 71). Indeed, the symbolic categories into which different problems and solutions are placed will ultimately determine the policy initiatives to be undertaken. On this view, the competing actors in the policy process, including professional policy communities, operate in a web of independent associations fused together through shared symbols. Such groups envision policy ideas that relate to particular conceptions of the "good society" as they struggle for common as well as personal interests (Stone 2002). The constructivist approach to public policy, for this reason, rejects the idea that individual interests are simply given. From this perspective, the analyst needs to interpretively account for how citizens get their images of the world in which they live, how they are socially constructed, and the ways these images shape individual interests and policy preferences.

Policy, as such, is a social construct rather than a self-defining phenomenon. As a sociopolitical agreement on a course of action or (inaction) designed to resolve or mitigate a problem, a policy is a created discursively. From a constructivist perspective, the political agreement upon which a policy rests refers to an understanding based on a set of normative and empirical beliefs embedded in narrative story-line. As such, there can be no inherently unique decisions, institutions, or actors constituting a public policy that are only to be identified, uncovered, and explained (Heclo 1972). Public policy is, in this regard, an analytical category with a substantive content that cannot simply be empirically researched; more fundamentally, it has to be interpreted. Hence our understanding of a policy and its outcomes cannot be separated from the ideas, theories, and criteria by which the policy is analysed and described (Majone 1989: 147).

The standard "production model" of policy, emphasizing efficiency and effectiveness, fails to capture the nature of the process (Stone 2002). The essence of policymaking, as Stone emphasizes, is the struggle over ideas and their meanings. Recognizing that shared meanings motivate people to action, as well as forge individual strivings into collective understandings, ideas are the medium of exchange in policymaking. They constitute a mode of influence as powerful, some would even say more powerful, than money, votes, or guns. In this view, policymaking is regularly a discursive struggle over the assumptions that shape problem definitions, the boundaries of the categories used to explicate them, the evaluative criteria for their assessment, and the meanings of the ideals that guide particular actions.

Viewed in this way, each policy-related idea is a normative argument—or rather a set of interrelated arguments—favouring different ways of looking at the world. The task of the policy analyst must then include an examination of the multiple understandings of what otherwise appears to be a single concept, in particular how these understandings are created, and how they are manipulated as part of policymaking strategies. Uncovering the hidden arguments embedded in each policy concept, Stone (2002) explains, can illuminate and even at times resolve the political conflicts that would otherwise only appear to be on the surface of the issue.

More than an instrumental strategy for public intervention, a policy must also be conceptualized and interpreted as a symbolic entity, the meaning of which is determined by its relationship to the particular situation, social system, and ideological framework of which it is a part (Fischer 1995). As Yanow (2000) puts it, policies are neither symbolic nor substantive. They are both at once. Even purely instrumental intentions are communicated and perceived through symbolic means (Yanow 2000: 12). The creation and implementation of a policy is about the creation of symbols, with programme names, organizations and rituals, even the design and decor of buildings being part of the process. In this formulation, notions of cause and effect need not disappear, as critics of interpretive analysis often argue, but the focus on such relationships does not take precedence over interpretive analysis.

Much of the best constructivist research has to do with determining how something comes to be considered a policy problem. In the constructionist view, the problems which governments seek to resolve are not just considered to have an 'objective' base in the economy or material structure of the society, but are also constructed in the realm of public and private discourse. As Edelman explains (1988: 12), such problems come into discourse, and therefore into existence as reinforcements of ideologies," not because they simply exist or are essential for social well-being.

Given these subjective—and thus less observable—dimensions of policy, it is difficult to justify the dominant "rational" modes technical analysis. On those rare occasions when social well-being is not closely linked to value differences and objectives are comparatively non-controversial, the standard technical approach to policy analysis—adjusting efficient means to political ends—may suffice. In the real world of policy politics, though, the majority of the situations involve much more than the logic of effective means to achieve social goals. Moreover, means and ends are often inherently connected in such ways that make it difficult to see which is which. Is, for example, the death penalty a means to a necessary end, or it is an evil end unto itself? It depends on whom you ask.

Despite the emphasis placed on discovering the objective facts pertinent to a controversy, policy decisions thus turn as often as not on the meanings that the issues generate. Indeed, it is precisely that events are assigned different meanings by different groups that makes them politically controversial. Even when groups can come to an agreement on disputed facts, the question of what these facts *mean* to those in the situation is still open. A question such as whether drug addiction originates from the social inadequacies of the drug addicts themselves or is the product of particular social pathologies of life in poor neighborhoods does not lend itself to unambiguous empirical answers.

To be sure, political news coverage and politicians' speeches about policy issues lead people to believe that policies are about factual problems and technical solutions, or at least that they should be. But the political construction of policy problems attaches them, both explicitly and implicitly, to normative symbols of right or wrong, good and bad. Contemporary conservatives, for example, often search for and insist on policy solutions that fit their ideological emphasis on free market-oriented solutions, regardless of the characteristics of the particular problem. Independently of any demonstrated effectiveness in eliminating a problem, a solution that emphasizes a greater role for government will be opposed as leading to the wrong kind of society. It is in this sense that a solution often goes out looking for a problem to solve.

Rather than taking the actions and assertions of politicians and policymakers as straightforward statements of intent, accounts of policy problems and issues need to examine and include the varying presuppositions about the meaning of social and political events. While factual information is not to be neglected, policy actions need to first and foremost be seen as resting on interpretations that reflect and sustain particular beliefs and ideologies. To be sure, empirical data and information play a role in policymaking, but their meaning is determined by how they fit into the particular arguments of a social context and the ideological framework brought to bear on it. Whereas the policy analyst can investigate the empirical dimensions of a problem and inform the political players of their findings, these research findings cannot be confused with an explanation of policy politics. The meaning of the 'facts' to the political actors is determined by political discourses and the meanings they assign to them can never be divorced from the political struggle—often that is what they are about. The social problems that enter the policy process are thus social constructions built on an intermingling of empirical findings with social meanings and ideological orientations. To understand how a particular condition becomes constructed as a problem, the range of social constructions in the discourses and texts about it need to be explored in the situational context from which they are observed.

By naming a policy one way rather than another, diverse and contradictory responses to a spectrum of political interests can be either revealed or hidden. Because an emphasis on policy differences and inconsistencies can generate unwanted political conflicts, policy names are often designed to reassure or assuage citizens and politicians. To offer an example from an otherwise highly techno-scientific issue, politicians speak of nuclear weapons as "peace-keepers" rather than deadly missiles.

Finally, it is important to recognize that ambiguous meanings often have important political functions. Seeking to satisfy different interest groups at the same time, government policies frequently comprise a sequence of ambiguous claims and actions that contain logical inconsistencies. Given the would-be irrationality of the process, policy scientists—technocratic analysts in particular—have devoted a good deal of energy to developing strategies for circumventing this inconvenient aspect of political reality. What they have generally missed, however, is the degree to which ambiguity enables conflicting groups to find ways to live with their differences. By helping to bring together citizens with varying policy preferences, ambiguous meanings often facilitates cooperation and compromise. Enabling politicians to blur or hide problematic implications of controversial decisions, ambiguity can assist in sidestepping barriers that otherwise block consensus-building. People who benefit from the same policy but for different reasons can more easily find ways to agree.

Furthermore, policies designed to deal with social problems are important determinants of which actors will have the authority and power to deal with the issues they raise. As Baumgartner and Jones (1983) point out, when a policy is presented as dealing with a technical problem, professional experts will tend to dominate the decision process. It is point clearly reflected in Collins and Evan's conception of technical problems in the public realm. But when the political, ethical, or social dimensions of a problem are seen to be the primary characteristics, a much larger group of participants usually becomes actively involved. The point is evident in the arguments of those who have taken issue with their call for a Third Wave; objecting to technocratic expertise, they call for public deliberation.

In the remainder of this chapter we turn to environmental policy to provide a more specific illustration of the role of policy meanings. We focus here on the way in which social and political meanings have initiated and influenced the development of a high profile policy agenda, namely the pursuit of sustainable development. Given that the professions of planning and policy science have largely developed a technical understanding of environmental crisis, the inherently socio-technical nature of sustainable development lends itself to a comparison of conventional and constructivist approaches. What follows by way of comparison is unabashedly offered in the form of a critique, largely as it has been developed and advanced by critical environmental theorists. Toward this end, we need to begin with the critique of technocratic reason seen to be at the root of conventional environmental policymaking.

Decontextualized knowledge: Technocratic policy science and the environment

The policy sciences, as we have seen, have largely developed as a product of neo-positivist epistemology. The technical rationalism of this mode of thought gives rise to a technocratic form of consciousness quite different from other worldviews and cultural orientations (Fischer 1990, 1995). Basic to its rationalistic worldview has been a fairly ambitious, if not arrogant, epistemological assumption—namely that the positivist method is the only valid means of obtaining "true knowledge." Still today such knowledge is seen to supply the only solid basis for solutions to many of our economic and social problems, in particular environmental problems. It is seen to facilitate the rational design of social and ecological systems in ways that enable us to better produce and manage, if not altogether eliminate, the persistent conflicts and crises that now plague them.

More specifically, this worldview gives shape to an abstract, technical formulation of society and its ecological problems. Conceptualized in technical terms, ecological problems are freed from the cultural, psychological, and linguistic contexts that give them social meaning. Breaking off connections to tradition and "ordinary knowledge" through the power of its unique abstract language, this rationalist form of thought creates an illusion of cultural and historical transcendence which, in turn, sustains a sense of political, cultural, and moral neutrality. In pursuit of the most efficient problem-solving strategies, typically expressed in the precise but abstract models of mathematics, experts appear to objectively transcend partisan environmental interests and the politics of meaning to which they give rise. Their technical methodologies and modes of decision-making are said to strive for value neutrality, if they are not in fact "value free."

This technical—"value-neutral"—understanding of environmental action is manifested through an administrative conceptualization of problem solving and policy formation. Basic to managerial strategy, the objective is to move as many environmental problems as possible into the realm of administrative decision-making, where they can be structured and accessed in technical terms. Such problems are thus interpreted as issues in need of improved administrative design and technical decision-making; their solutions are to be found through the application of managerial techniques, including environmental planning and policy analysis. A conviction fundamental to contemporary techno-managerial strategy, it has come in environmental policymaking to be identified with the managerial understanding of "ecological modernization."

Most fundamentally, such technocratic thinking fails to identify the distinction between two basic modes of reason, one technical and the other sociocultural. Each of these forms of reason pertains to different and autonomous realms of human activity. Whereas the sphere of economic production is governed by technical criteria such as efficiency, the world of everyday social life (including family, culture religions, and politics) is negotiated through social meaning and normative reason. Although each sphere is intertwined with the other, analytically they must be conceptualized as separate spheres governed by different modes of reason. Technocratic thought, however, fails to recognize these distinctions and has inappropriately applied its technical criteria to the society as whole. Such technical reason, through its unquestioned belief in technological and material progress, obscures an underlying epistemological concatenation of the two separate realms of human activity. Planners and managers blur distinctions between the worlds of economic production and social interaction, thus making it difficult for many to distinguish between the priorities of the economic system and the values and goals of the social realm. It is not that people should necessarily reject modern-day economic and technological progress, as some radical environmentalists have argued, but rather that they should establish their own meaningful relationships to it through processes of intersubjective discourse (Habermas 1973). This failure to examine the fundamental questions of value and social meaning posed by technological progress and the environmental crisis to which it has given rise presents a deep seated paradox: as technologically based affluence increases in advanced industrial societies, so does the sense of both meaningless social drift and environmental insecurity among the citizens who benefit from the material output.

Inherent to this strategy is a subtle, and sometimes not so subtle, form of authoritarianism. Once the idea that we can empirically calculate and administratively design "the right way" to accomplish our environmental goals is accepted, there is little reason to engage in the exploration of other views. The "rational" person is the one who agrees to submit to the technical and administrative knowledge derived through the proper application of expert methodologies. The authority of the expert, in this view, should take precedence over the democratic exchange of opinions draw from the everyday world of ordinary reason. In the process, questions of meaning are taken for granted; they do not come into question.

Underlying the hubris of this position is an anthropocentric understanding of the world. "Technocratic man," in this perspective, has managed to construe humankind's unique powers of the mind as legitimation for his own rapacious appropriation of the physical world. Nature, in short, is tamed and subordinated to serve man's own economic needs. Emphasizing the mechanistic character of the physical laws governing nature, this worldview takes nature's creator to be something of an engineer. Organized according to the laws of nature, human as well as physical nature, the environment is seen as posing a constellation of "problems" that can best be technically and administratively engineered by experts. This, in fact, has led some to foresee a kind of environmental technocracy (Ophuls 1977). In this view, such questions will be turned to an enlightened environmental elite capable of making the tough decisions based on the technical facts of the situation (Bahro 1987). Collins and Evans, one might assume, would concur.

Sustainable development as social construct: Socio-cultural assumptions and the politics of meaning

The repercussions of this technocratic mentality and its methods, as environmentalists point out, are especially striking in today's ecological crisis. What began several hundred years ago as the techno-industrial exploitation of nature's resources for unlimited industrial progress today constitutes a serious degradation of the ecosystem. Although substantial amounts of research and development monies are being poured into the search for technological solutions, much of this misses the point. By and large, the approach is governed by the same kind of technocratic thinking that gave rise to the problem in the first place. Rather than looking for new relationships between technology, nature, and society (emphasizing conservation and a more efficient planning and control of economic growth), experts move forward on the premise that future technologies and better managerial practices will themselves get us out of our present fix. Ignoring the need for a new "existential balance" among productive technologies, nature, and human purpose, the technocratic response to the ecological crisis is described by many of its opponents as a paradigmatic example of metaphysical crisis.

It is not that technical considerations are irrelevant to the ecological question, but rather that the need to attend to the ways in which ecological degradation is more fundamentally a sociocultural problem is even more important. Toward this end, as environmentalists have argued, we need to better understand how the technical dimensions of ecology are interwoven with complex social, intellectual, and institutional realities that create the ecological problem. Rather than simply accepting the utilitarian criteria of economists and planners—standards that neglect basic questions concerning the nature of social needs and the extant patterns of consumption, as well as the art of reflecting on them—environmentalists insist on meaningful discussions about needs, social values, and human purpose. Instead of substituting such discussion with techniques of risk and liability assessment, normative deliberation about the more basic sociocultural aspects of sustainability has to take place. The task is thus to find a sustainable balance between the technical and the social. Specifically, technical objects and analyses have to be examined in the social contexts that supply them with meaning.

The challenge is readily apparent in the struggle to define and shape the concept of environmental sustainability. Sustainable development, as initially advanced, is an inherently normative concept aimed at redressing the ecological imbalances among industrial development, environment degradation, human health, and the social relations underlying them. Through the concept of intergenerational equity, sustainable development depends on answers to a host of profoundly important questions— normative questions—about the responsibility of present societies and their communities to the future, the relation of the rich to the poor, the distribution of the costs involved in environmental clean up, questions

179

about the relative merits of relying on markets or states, the relation of individual freedoms to the collective good, as the well as questions about our appropriate relationship to other species.

Since the positing of sustainability as the over-arching environmental goal, however, environmental planners and policy agencies have steadily mis-translated the concept into a technical strategy for programmatic reform of existing socio-economic relationships. It is an approach often called "ecological modernization" (emphasizing technology, cost-benefit analysis, and market strategies), a strategy designed to technically guide and manage the future of advanced industrial society.[2] Toward this end, universities now train sustainable development experts to think in terms of calculating and planning the "carrying capacities" of regional and local ecosystems through the efficient application of such "ecoknowledge."

In the textbook, all of this might sound good. But in the real world of environmental politics, the assumptions—both technical and social— upon which the strategy is built are estimable. Most obvious is the fact that our knowledge is nowhere sophisticated enough to reveal the limits of nature, thus permitting us to exploit resources safely up to that limit. As environmentalists point out, we are only barely beginning to develop the capability to measure accurately and predict the phenomenon of climate change. The idea that such environmental change can literally be monitored and managed with the kinds of precision suggested by many economists and planners, it is argued, is more a scientific ideology than a certainty within our reach, especially not within the critical time frame posed by global warming.

Building social consensus: Deliberating the assumptions

Because science cannot answer the critical questions with any certainty, both the nature and implications of such complex environmental issues, they remain open to interpretation. In such situations, even technical knowledge is open to interpretation and thus easily translated into political disagreement. Each party to the dispute can use this interpretative ambiguity to argue the case according to their own needs and interests. Those who support action to stem the growth of greenhouse gases can point to the amassing evidence. Those who oppose the costs of such interventions can stress that it has in no final way been proven. In such

[2] On ecological modernization, see Young (2000) and York and Rose (2003).

cases, science actually intensifies rather than mitigates environmental politics. Instead of solving the problem, it only becomes another sort of political ammunition interests groups and their counter-experts fire at one another.

Beyond this inability to provide widely accepted scientific predictions, the technocratic approach poses a subtler, but much more politically significant concern related to the very definition of environmental problems. In order to frame an environmental problem, technically it is necessary to hold constant the basic structures and processes of society. This is typically achieved by assuming people's common interests in dealing with environmental efforts. While this might seem to encourage unified environmental action, it tends to conceal the economic assumptions, social choices, and risks that in fact block such action. By treating existing social and political structures as fixed, such models serve to draw attention away from the competing interests and understandings of differentiated social groups and nations, especially those among the rich and the poor, that are basic to grasping the causes of the problem, let alone the complicated political task of shaping acceptable solutions. Such inattention to national and localized political economies almost ensures that scientists, both natural and social, will continue to be fail to anticipate emerging conflicts and thus lead to false predictions. By setting the problem outside the context of social conflict, the "neutral and objective" pretences of scientific and technological solutions further work to block effective political consensus-building. Once the problem is analytically abstracted from the political realm, citizens and their governments tend to be separated from the environmental consequences of their actions; it obscures their need to assume responsibility for the outcomes. By treating environmental degradation as the negative *effect* of the social and economic activities that characterize our daily lives instead of everyday life as the cause of the degradation, scientists can concentrate on finding "technical fixes" to mitigate problematic side effects. Such solutions, of course, merely focus on pollution at the "end-of-the pipe," rather than the more challenging task of reinventing production processes to eliminate the need for the pipe. As such, they cover over the need to examine how pollution is more fundamentally a sociocultural problem related to the industrial way of life and the social assumptions that supply it with meaning.

Many fear an effort to open the door to a broader political examination of the underlying social assumptions of the environmental problem. Indeed, this is one of the key concerns that attracts people to the technocratic approach. For them, the technical problem is weighty enough;

attaching it to a whole host of conflictual questions about the competing ways of life—issues and assumptions about the social distribution of wealth, political participation, corporate control, government regulation, etc.—is only to court political gridlock (Bast *et al.* 1994). Without necessarily denying the pressing nature of these social and economic problems, so the argument, the urgency of the environmental problem should exempt it from such considerations.

This position, however, fails to confront the socio-technical foundations of the environmental problem. Which is another way to say there is no escape from dealing with the underlying social assumptions; environmental politics ultimately turns on them. In this regard, the challenge poses two problems. One is the scientific task of building analytical models capable of including the dynamic effects of social as well as natural systems and how each influences the other. Basic here is the need to learn how to link models of endangered ecosystems with the human actions and sociopolitical processes that foster and sustain them. Especially important is discovering how to interconnect the multi-levels of government, local, national, and global. Such research involves figuring out how to account for the fact that regions have a certain autonomy in terms of the larger systems of which they are apart, as well as the fact that bioregions and social systems often do not coincide in space and time.

But even more important for present purposes is the second challenge concerning the policy implications drawn from such models. That is, how do we move from an analytical understanding of the environment to the political task of forging a policy consensus around a particular model of the problem? In so far as each conceptual model of the environmental problem portends a particular impact on the sociopolitical world, the affected groups invariably seek to fend for their own interests. Given that these issues raise complicated problems related to burden-sharing, especially between the haves and have-nots, it is inevitable that each negatively affected group will do more than merely examine the technical data. Straight away, they zero in on the social assumptions that differentiate their ways of life. If the assumptions are disputed, the analysis is little more than a useless exercise.[3]

The question, then, is how do we take action in face of both scientific uncertainties, relative socioeconomic inequalities, and competing social assumptions? The answer is found in political coalition-building. Beyond technical analysis, environmental solutions have little value unless they

---

[3] The history of the relations between rich countries of the north hemisphere and the poor countries in the southern half since the first Earth Summit in Stockholm in 1972 has been a story of disagreement about social and political assumptions (Leis and Viola 1995).

can generate the political consensus necessary to adopt and implement them. For this reason, there is no choice but to open the environmental debate to a wider discussion of the economic and social assumptions upon which it rests. Viewed in this way, the problem has to be turned upside down. Before technical analysis can play a meaningful role there need to be basic understandings about who gets what, when, and how. Toward this end, citizens and the larger public need to be brought into the policy deliberations (Irwin 1995; Fischer 2000).

Given the nature of the social and political conflicts that accompany environmental deliberation, this is a formidable assignment. It means the development of a more participatory form of democratic decision-making than generally practiced in contemporary Western societies. It requires innovating new mechanisms for bringing together scientific expertise and democratic political deliberation. Required is a new epistemological understanding of these interactions. As argued earlier, this involves replacing the scientific framework with a multi-dimensional postempiricist perspective that recognizes the place of both empirical and normative modes of reason (Fischer 1995, 2003).

The co-production of environmental knowledge: Implications for collaborative inquiry

From the constructivist understanding of scientific activity we have learned the ways in which knowledge is co-produced by science and society. Co-production, as Jasanoff (2004) explains, focuses on the ways in which the world is known and meaningfully represented. The natural world and society are together inseparable dimensions of the world in which we choose to inhabit. Knowledge in its various forms—and material embodiments—is at the same time a product of the social activities that constitute a particular form of life. That is, society is an organized embodiment of knowledge; science, in turn, works with the support of societal institutions. Formal knowledge and the technologies derived from science, as Jasanoff (2004: 2) puts it, are both embedded "in social practices, identities, norms, discourses, and institutes—in short, in all the building blocks of what we term the social." The approach, as such, emphasizes the social cognitive understandings, meanings, and commitments fundamental to science while underscoring as well its epistemic and material foundations.

Co-production, as a postempiricist interpretive process, is central to a proper understanding of environmental science (Forsyth 2007). Most fundamental, it shows the ways in which the objects of environmental study are constructed and shaped by social understandings, particularly as reflected in language and discourse. For an easy example, notice how the meaning of environmental terms ranging from bad weather, climate change, or global warming can all refer to the same phenomena but lead to quite different social understandings and thus policy implications.

Similarly, Latour (1993, 1987) has argued that such combinations of technical findings and social framings give rise to socio-natural entities that he calls "hybrid" objects. Hybrids are common or ordinary objects that have the appearance of being real, unitary, and uncontroversial. In practice, however, they reflect diverse sets of historical framings and social experiences specific to particular actors and societal formations. The term, as such, refers to the social factors, both historical and contemporary, that have contributed to and shaped what is referred as reality. Hybridization is employed to help reveal the temporal processes through which social-natural objects or "quasi-objects" get bound together through sociopolitical discourses. It shows, for example, the ways in which a Western society's understanding of nature is a social construction resulting from a merging of a range of scientific findings, diverse experiences, and social norms. For this reason, efforts to create clear-cut rational explanatory devices for determining the causal relations between nature and society necessarily fail. Beyond empirical measurement, we have to look at the processes of "translation" through which networks between natural and social objects permit us to identify the way people experience nature.

From this co-productive perspective facts in both the physical and the social worlds thus depend to varying degrees upon underlying assumptions and meanings that define their objects and events. What is taken to be an established fact is in effect the decision of a particular community of inquirers who work within a particular set of theoretical presuppositions. Customarily, of course, we simply accept a particular view of the world; the presuppositions that undergird it are taken-for-granted and seldom come into question. Not only does science take its questions from the social understandings of society of which it is a part, scientific claims are the relative products of a community of practitioners who establish the evidential criteria and guide the research processes through which truth claims are decided. The communities that render these opinions, as social bodies, constitute hierarchies of practitioners organized in significant part around their own internal power structures, interests, and status claims that are part of society more generally (Kuhn 1962).

A second interpretive consideration of particular relevance to environmental protection is that of uncertainty. In matters of risk, the degree to which science can answer and resolve the complex questions about risk is uncertain, even limited (Ravetz 1999; Novotny 2003). Not only is the evidence often soft, there are simply too many factors contributing to the uncertainty of scientific explanations. This does not render science useless, but it does mean that its judgments have to understood as important considerations rather than as definitive answers. Those engaged in the decision-making process always need to weight the various social and pragmatic considerations against the technical uncertainties. What is the best thing to do under the circumstances? Should we accept synthetic biology and support its efforts to invent new life forms? Is it moral and ethical to tinker with nature in this way? What if it leads to the manipulation of species, human and animal? How about the possibility of creating dangerous organisms that medical and governmental bodies are unable to bring under control? In short, do the potential scientific and medical benefits out weight the risks, often unknown? These sorts of judgments require a multi-disciplinary deliberative perspective. Decisions under such circumstances are best reached by discussing things from different points of view, both scientific and normative. We need, in short, to consider the range of competing perspectives that can legitimately judge the normative implications of the different choices and assess them against the goals and values of the communities at issue. Scientific communities, for this reason, are only one of the bodies capable of making judgments about reality. Other groups grounded in different forms of rationality can also make relevant judgments about the same phenomena. At specific points, as the social studies of science and co-production have shown, this also includes lay people with relevant social and empirical experiences (Sillitoe 2007). Not only do citizens often possess particular facts of the situation that are needed by the decisionmakers, their legitimation and motivation are frequently essential for the effective implementation of environmental policies and regulations.

This integration of empirical and normative inquiry requires a framework of practical reason that organizes and guides such deliberation. Such a framework includes technical information but places it within the situational, societal, and ideological contexts in which public policies are embedded (Fischer 1995). In addition to incorporating norms and values, such an approach can also go considerable distance toward overcoming a knee-jerk resistance to science on the part of some citizens. To this end, the task is to set up a dialectical exchange between the theoretical knowledge of the expert and the sociocultural reason of ordinary citizens, including lay knowledge relevant to the decision. The challenge has led to a focus on participatory or collaborative inquiry of the type we examined in chapters 3 and 4 and to which we again return in chapters 9 and 10.

Finally, this constructivist, co-production understanding of scientific inquiry also helps us to better comprehend the nature of a process that has long created consternation among students of politics—namely, why citizens often fail to use the information that they often have at their disposal (Kuklinski 2007)? Research about public opinion typically concludes that citizens don't have much information about the relevant policy issues of the day and that when they do, they fail to take it into account. The assessment in this chapter shows this judgment to be misleading, even though not altogether wrong. It is indeed the case that citizens often appear indifferent to empirical evidence, or at least particular facts and findings. More specifically, citizens prove to be selective with the uses of information; when it doesn't fit into their own interests and ideologies, they often suppress or ignore it. But this is more than ignorance or irrationality, as it is generally portrayed. Such judgments fail to recognize that policy information is judged as well against the assumptions that it supports. As such, the cognitive behaviour of the citizen is more that a simple lack of use, an indifference to knowledge. Given that politics is about supporting or changing a particular state of affairs, people in politics use different frames of reference to determine the relevance and thus applicability of particular pieces of information. Fundamentally, they are less interested in proving something—one way or another—than following a course of action grounded in their belief systems. In this sense, it is true that they can ignore fact and findings for ideological reasons, but not because they are irrational. Valid information about a policy orientation that one doesn't want will be slighted or ignored. An assessment of its use can only be determined by examining the information against particular normative assumptions and standards. It is a point missed when opinion researchers simply focus on the use of facts, without looking at the way they are judged by competing belief systems.

Conclusion

This chapter examined the ways in which policies rest on social understandings, in particular meanings that are often embedded in their underlying assumptions and thus less apparent. As a response to Collins and Evans's failure to understand how technical knowledge is co-constructed in particular social contexts, the discussion examined the ways assumptions and ideologies, as well as the motivations and intentions associated with them, determine how people orient themselves to empirical findings of policy-relevant research. Technical information, to be sure, plays an important role in the evaluation of policy goals and objectives; it is essential information for the assessment of the causal and strategic relationships related to the instrumental achievement of objectives. But, as we have seen, policies are first and foremost judged in the social world of politics in terms of how they resonate with the assumptions and meanings that organize and structure the competing political beliefs and ideologies. The chapter then turned to the case of sustainable development to offer an illustration of the co-production of social meanings in the discursive struggle to define and shape the policy assumptions and practices of environmental reform.

In the next chapter we further explore the role of meaning through an examination of the narrative form of knowing. Narrative story lines, as we shall see, are the primary vehicles for the discursive organization and communication of social meaning. As such, they serve as important vehicles of sociopolitical understanding and thus policy learning.

Part III

Policy Epistemics for Deliberative Empowerment: Storylines, Learning, and Passionate Reason

7

Policy Advice as Storyline: Narrative Knowledge and Expert Practices

Both science and liberal political theory have sought to root out all forms of knowing based on subjective modes of thought. Liberalism has itself often been at odds with scientific positivism, buts its emphasis on deliberative democracy stresses rational deliberation and the giving of valid reasons as the proper basis for decision-making. Although deliberative democracy recognizes the presence of subjective factors in politics, including emotional passion, this reality is often indirectly discussed with more objective-sounding terms such as "commitment" and "motivation." Reasoned argumentation is given priority over uninformed beliefs and emotional expression. For some, the goal is to reduce or constrain unreflected belief, subjective opinion, and emotional commitment; for others the task is to submit them to deliberative argumentation. Rather than the impossible task of rooting out all subjectivity, it should be tamed and managed through deliberation.

Science, for its part, has steadily railed against forms of inquiry that involve subjective ways of knowing, from everyday commonsense to literary and historical modes of thought. Basic to the positivist mission has always been the goal of reducing subjectivity, in particular social beliefs and emotional passion. Non-scientific subjectively based forms of knowing are seen to involve mere opinion influenced by interest and emotion; they thus remove deliberation from the realm of rationality. In this chapter we turn to one of the primary objects of this aversion to the subjective, narrative storytelling. Narrative storytelling, unlike the giving of rational reasons, is designed not just to persuade people intellectually but emotionally as well. In large part, the power of a story results from an emotional appeal to particular values and is highly influenced by the tellers communicative abilities rather than just the reasonableness of the factual claims (Ryfe 2003: 165–7).

The view conventionally supported by scientific expertise and liberal democratic philosophy has become increasingly problematic.[1] Over the past decades, for one thing, we have come to see the degree to which science itself is infused with normative, subjective judgments. For another, we have also increasingly recognized the ways in which other forms of knowledge are basic to human ways of knowing and communicating, in particular the narrative or storytelling mode of communication. Indeed, we have come to understand that scientific knowledge typically takes its meaning and importance in the social realm according to how it fits into dominant or competing narratives. It is a social reality with special import for building on or elaborating the kinds of "translation" tasks between experts and the public to which Collins and Evans importantly call attention. As we saw in that discussion, there is no direct epistemological bridge between the technical and public realms, one being governed by the formal logic of science and the other practical reason. Which is not to say that knowledge does not move from one realm to the other. Instead, it is to recognize that ordinary actors—citizens and politicians—largely connect the two spheres through a narrative form of understanding. Interested in the meaning of such knowledge for social action rather than the technical validity of the knowledge per se—the assignment of members of the scientific community—ordinary actors fit it into their narrative understandings of society and politics. They test it against their narrative interpretations of social purposes, political intentions, underlying motivations, and basic value orientations.

When we examine communication in the everyday realm of politics and policymaking, we find people largely explaining things by telling stories. This is not to say that policies are simply storylines; they are presented more formally as rules and regulations. But the rules and regulations rest on narrative explanations. They reflect particular narrative stories about how the society works, how it should work, and what sorts of measures are needed to make it work that way. When policy-analytical findings are presented as advice for action—i.e. how actors should orient themselves to the findings, what lessons they should draw from them, etc.—the advice can only be understood in relation to a particular story (or storyline) about a situation, one located in a temporal and societal context.

---

[1] For a discussion of the tensions and contradictions between the liberal state and its reliance on expertise, along with a proposal for a rapprochement between the two, see Turner's (2006) essay on expert power and liberal political theory.

Generally, these stories are not immediately evident but they can be explicated and examined.[2]

We also do not imply here that arguments disappear. Rather it is to recognize that arguments typically deal with pieces of the larger patterns drawn out by a narrative. Is this factual statement in the story correct, can we rely on this or that contention? This means that translation in the public realm is more about fitting data into particular explanatory narratives than it is about clarifying and validating technical information. The latter is part of the assignment but it is only part of the job. Moreover, when people demand such clarification, they will often receive competing judgments from different segments of the scientific community, sometimes itself influenced by conflicting social narratives. Some scientists will, for example, side with industry's version of the story, while others will support the opposition movement's counter version (a process that will typically involve technical arguments based on the uncertainties of the findings). To get a better understanding of how narration works and its role in policy decision-making we turn first to the narrative itself—what is it and how does it work?

Narrative understanding: Social meaning and intentionality

An interest in narrative forms of knowing is relatively recent in the social sciences, although the narrative is scarcely new to the social realm. Indeed, the narrative form—or storytelling—is the domain of the spoken exchange in everyday interaction (Riessman 1993). Through narration individuals relate their experiences to one another; it is how they make meaning in their lives. It has been said that we virtually exist because we tell the story of our existence.

The contemporary focus on storytelling and narrative analysis owes much to the focus on language in poststructural and postmodern theories, particularly in literature and the humanities (Czarniawska 1997: 11–29; 1998). The emphasis of these approaches on narrative and discourse has played a vital part in the epistemological challenge to the dominant empiricist orientation. At the cultural level, this work has focused on the ways narratives serve to give cohesion to shared beliefs and the

[2] The term "storyline" is used somewhat differently by different writers. We take it here to refer to connecting thread that runs through a narrative. In this regard, it can largely be used interchangeably with "plot." In the context of policy studies, Hajer (1995: 56) defines a storyline as a "narrative that allows actors to draw upon various discursive categories to give meaning to specific social and specific phenomenon."

transmission of basic values. At the individual or group level, it emphasizes how people tell narratives about their own lives that enable them to understand both who they are and where they are headed (or in the language of sociology, to realize their agency). It comes then as no surprise that the growing literature on identity politics relies heavily on narrative storytelling (Mottier 1999). Given that the narrative is the cognitive form through which people convey what they think, feel, and understand about one another, in writing as well as speech, we can easily wonder why it has taken the social sciences so long to acknowledge the importance of this form, long essential to literature and history (Andrews 2007).

Stories, by their nature, are inherently joint social productions. All of the elements of a story—plot, structure, meaning, resolution, and so forth—are created by people conversing and arguing with others. It is through the act of storytelling that individuals understand the goals and values of their social groups and communities, internalize social conventions, understand who they are vis-à-vis other members of groups, and how to empathize with one another (Frank 2002). It is a process that begins in childhood and extends throughout a person's life. In the course of socialization, children learn early how to interpret and understand narrative stories, a process that continues into adulthood through an unending set of lived experiences.

Connecting actions and events into understandable patterns, the narrative is a cognitive scheme. Bruner (1986) describes the narrative form as one of the two means of knowing and explaining. Like the scientific mode of knowing, the narrative has its own distinctive ways of ordering experience and constructing reality. Instead of focusing on empirically based causal connections between events, the narrative form orders experience in terms of social purposes, human values, and the intentions and motivations of the participants. Narratives, as such, also provide an invitation to moral reason. In addressing the question of what ought to be done, as MacIntyre (2003) has clarified, a person can only explain his answer by first telling the story of which one is a part.

As an interpretively based qualitative mode of analysis, narration possesses its own operating principles and criteria for judging a well-formed narrative explanation. Whereas the scientific mode strives to identify stable, reproducible patterns of actions that can be explained without reference to purposes and intentions, the special subject matter of the narrative form is the "vicissitudes of human intention." In addition to social stability, the narrative is especially geared to the intentional goals and motivational understandings of the actors and the ways changing goals and intentions causally contribute to social change. It seeks to comprehend, convey, and assess the direction and purpose of human affairs—who is pushing matters in the particular direction and why? Events and actions are interpreted, understood, and discussed through the lens of competing storylines.

The narrative story thus adds an essential dimension to the explanation of social action. Resting on the interpretive process of *Verstehen*, or empathetic understanding, it points our attention to the role of subjective intentions, motives, opinion, and normative judgments as causal or quasi-causal forces that need to be taken into consideration when we move from the technical to public realm. As the work of historians makes clear, intentions contribute to making things happen and, as such, are inherent to the description and explanation of the causal mechanisms underlying political and social phenomena (Lin 1998).

While the direct observation of motivations is difficult, if at all possible, they are generally elucidated through texts and documents. Statements in texts, both written and spoken, are judged both on their own terms and against the observable actions of those who made them. Historians and journalists are in fact expected to assess the motives of great political leaders by interpreting their behaviours against written texts, spoken words, and their actions in particular contexts. There is always room for reinterpretation and debate about such assessments; interpretation is a good part of what a discipline like history is about. And the same is true in real-world political and social action.

The primary feature that distinguishes the "epistemic fingerprint" of the narrative from that of the logical-analytic mode of science, social or otherwise, is its stress on the temporal and spatial context of action. Emphasis on the context of action contrasts sharply with the scientific explanation which treats the written text as a self-referential world closed to the reader. Meaning and truth in such explanation are found in the accuracy of the observational statements and the logical soundness of the deductions that lead to the conclusion. Semantic meaning is to be found *inside* the text itself. For narrative contextual analysis, on the other hand, the semantic content of stories *resides* outside the sentence (Schiffrin 1994; Schiffrin *et al.* 2001). Rather than fixed and determined, meaning for the narrative is located in the readers' commonsense references to shared experience. The meaning of the story is, in short, determined by the social context in which it is interpreted. Social context furnishes the particular details that constitute the stuff of which social meaning is made. "Details, particular and familiar," as Tannen (1989: 136, 1985), "enable speakers and hearers to create images" and "it is in large part through the creation of a shared world of images that ideas are communicated and understanding is achieved." Whereas the social sciences have largely neglected or marginalized this contextual aspect of their subject matter, history, as a rigorous form of storytelling, always focuses on context. For the historian, as well as the novelist, the explanatory details are in the context (Kaplan 1986, 1993).

Storytelling thus expands epistemology beyond the narrow confines of observational statements and logical proof to a qualitative examination of the ways individuals are embedded in the wider social contexts of situation and society (Sarbin 1986). Furthermore, social action has to be located in time and space. This presupposes multiple agents in an ongoing texture of elaborated events, with each being influenced by preceding episodes and influencing following ones. It is the chronology of events located in place and time that captures the change in the structure of social situations and in the positions occupied by intentional actors oriented towards each other in the world, emotionally as well as cognitively. As Giovannoli (2000: 7) has put it, "actors have opposite positions, as if functioning on a stage as protagonists and antagonists, as they enter relations of love, hate, agreement, or disagreement." The protagonists' "feelings, thoughts, and actions can only be understood as emerging from their relationships with antagonists, who are co-constructing reality in often unpredictable ways." Giovannoli, in this respect, points to another central characteristic of the narrative form, namely that it is the carrier of the emotional expression. It is not that emotion doesn't accompany arguments; rather to explain those emotions the speaker has to turn to the narrative form. As we shall see in Chapter 10, the elements of emotional experience are tied together in a narrative structure (Goldie 2000).

This interpretation of subjective intentions is especially evident in political understanding. To offer an example, consider President Bush's war in Iraq. During the Bush years in the United States, the majority of the American citizens either passionately liked or disliked the president, with particular facts often playing only a minor role in their judgments about his political course of action. They essentially adhered to political narratives to explain the motives of the other side.[3] Events such as the

---

[3] The relation of factual information to political narratives is demonstrated, albeit troublesomely, by in the vituperative character of political debate in the United States. With less and less middle ground between conservatives and liberals, factual information frequently takes a back seat to the narrative. Often politicians literally say—or act as if—they don't care about

military surge in Iraq in 2007 have thus been judged as much or more in terms of an assessment of Bush's motives as its implications for the violent struggle in Iraq. Was the surge just the president's strategy to extend the war beyond his own time in office, and thus embroil his successors in a misbegotten war that he was unable to bring under control? Was it really related to the proclaimed possibility of winning the war? Or perhaps both? Without addressing the motives presented by the competing narratives, one cannot understand the domestic political struggle over the Iraq war. Political motives, moreover, will be one of the central questions involved in the historian's narrative assessment of the US's role in that country.

Typically structured sequentially with a beginning, middle, and an end, the narrative thus tells us about a state of affairs, an intervening event or action, and the resulting consequences. As a mode of thought, it furnishes communication with the particular details out of which social meaning is constructed. It is through storytelling that people access social positions in their communities, understand the goals and values of different social groups, and internalized social conventions. Narrative stories do this by imposing a coherent interpretation on the whirl of events and acts that surround us. Threading these sequential components together through storylines, narratives place social phenomena in the larger patterns that attribute social and political meaning to them. In the process, the storyline is at the same time an invitation to moral reasoning.

But how do we know if a narrative or its analysis is good or bad? If the ability to enhance a body of knowledge through the application of a set of accepted theoretical approaches and techniques represents the essence of a scholarly discipline, when does a narrative explanation merit acceptance? How does one know if it is credible?

evidence or research findings; they are only taken seriously to the degree that they comfortably fit into their narrative stories and the ideological orientations that underlay them. In a situation in which the goal is to protect or shore up one's narrative, political and policy deliberation becomes a limited, if not pointless, activity. Failure to recognize this interplay between normative storylines and empirical investigation undercuts the kinds of communication required to deal with pressing problems, leading to political frustration and consternation. In politics, factual information is important but not just for itself. As demonstrated in contemporary US politics, information attracts attention according to how it fits into or impacts on competing stories.

Storylines and narrative credibility: The analytics of good reasons

There are two basic approaches for assessing the validity or credibility of a narrative. One concerns the internal structure of the narrative story-line and the other the basic validity of its empirical and normative elements (Fisher 1989). The internal structural approach to the quality of a narrative explores the rigour of the logical coherence running through the parts of the story. In this regard, an assessment of narrative truth involves the internal connection among the basic elements of narra-tive—agent, act, scene, agency, and purpose. According to the basic rules of storytelling, some underlying consistency must be present among the holistic elements of a story. In Burke's (1945, 1950) classic statement, this means offering answers to five interrelated questions. What was done (act)? When or where was it done (scene)? Who did it (agent)? How he or she did it (agency)? And why (purpose)? Fisher (1989) calls the way in which the various elements—such as facts, values, internal coherence, and metaphors—systematically come together "narrative rationality."

Narrative rationality, in short, refers to whether or not the story 'hangs together'. Not unlike the task of the literary scholar, determining whether the narrative coheres involves determining the probability that the com-ponents of the narrative structure are credibly linked together. Do they have material or substantive coherence with other stories told in related discourses? Are the kinds of behaviours exhibited by the characters in the story—both the narrators and the actors—relatively familiar, reliable, or predictable?

As McCloskey (1990: 63) explains, the analyst must examine the 'apt-ness or rightness' of the narrative's dominant metaphor, commonly understood in social science as a model (a model being a metaphor elab-orated with details). Rather than examining a metaphor's prepositional truth, the analyst must ask whether the metaphor fits the story (Brown 1977). As a way of talking, does it stay on the subject or lead off into non-productive sidetracks? Can it reveal new insights that otherwise would not have been apparent?

The second approach investigates the substantive context of the narra-tive, focusing on the specific components of the story. Do they constitute accurate assertions about social reality and thus are good reasons for belief and action? Facts, in this respect, serve as constraints on the story. As McCloskey (1990: 83) succinctly puts it, "the fish in the fisherman's story was either a lake bass or a sunfish, and that's that." Determining which, of course, is the task of the empirical inquirer. Specific questions about a particular narrative can also be organized as social-scientific hypotheses and tested empirically. Similarly, basic normative propositions can be probed for agreement or credibility through the methods of normative discourse. In this approach, the narrative credibility becomes a matter of giving "good reasons."

As Fisher explains, the giving of good reasons includes but goes beyond the truthfulness of the empirical facts. Governed by the informal logic of good reasons, it involves applying "criterial" questions that can locate and weigh both the empirical information and the value judgments presented in—or engendered by—the story. In this sense, it includes formal logic, but also goes beyond it. Good reasons are conceived as those elements that "provide warrants for accepting or adhering to the advice" fostered by rhetorical communication (Fisher 1989: 107). A reason is considered good if it can meet the tests of fact, relevance, consequence, consistency, and transcendental values. The ability of a narrative to satisfy the tests of these criteria supplies it with both its meaning and its persuasiveness.

Finally, basic to all narratives is the question of character. "Whether a story is believable," explains Fisher (1989: 47) "depends on the reliability of characters, both as narrators and as actors." Such determinations are made by interpretations of values reflected in the character's decisions and actions. Character, as such, can be understood as a repertoire of tendencies to act. If such "tendencies contradict one another, change significantly, or alter in 'strange ways,' the result is a questioning of character." In life, as in literature and history, we expect our fellow citizens to conduct themselves characteristically. In the absence of "this predictability, there is no trust, no community, no rational human orders." Applying this criterion is an inquiry into motivation. As Fisher (1989: 47) puts it, "its importance in deciding whether to accept a message cannot be overestimated." Determining an actor's "motives is prerequisite to trust, and trust is the foundation of belief." For this reason, belief is not just a matter of what is said, but also of who is saying it. Some things may be empirically true, but certain people do not have the legitimacy or standing to make the claims.[4]

---

[4] The narrative paradigm, it should also be noted, does not neglect the roles of influence, power, ideology, manipulatory distortions, and irrational passion, as some have argued. On the contrary, as Fisher (1989) explains, narrative analysis fully recognizes that authoritarian forces can manipulate communicative practices. Acknowledging the distorting influences of such power, it recognizes that action always occurs in the context of competing stories about social and political phenomena, including the presence of the stories of the less powerful. If, as Fisher maintains, power and ideology were the only important explanatory dimensions of

Of particular interest to the policy inquirer is the role of formal-analytic discourses in the assessment of narrative fidelity. One of the key tasks of an informal logic is to classify and clarify different types of discourses and the purposes to which they are put. Toward this end, it is also useful to more closely compare the interaction of informal or ordinary narrative discourse with scientific and normative discourses, which take the form of arguments. Indeed, for the postempiricist policy analyst this is a crucial epistemic task. It is important not only for understanding how the real-world narratives of politics and policy bring analytical methods into play, but also for establishing narrative discourse analysis in the policy curriculum. Without a clear statement of the narrative's relationship to what we normally identify as policy argumentation and analysis, narrative analysis will only struggle to gain something more than marginal status in the disciplines. We thus need to be able to show both how these analytical perspectives relate to each other and, equally important, what difference it makes.

The starting point for such an analysis is the recognition that arguments and narratives are different modes of thought with different purposes and logical structures. Whereas a narrative ties together the sequences of a story through the device of a plot (as storyline), an argument is structured around premises designed to logically lead to conclusions. From the narrative we learn what happened and what it means. Based on these features, especially the end of the story, one can employ argumentation to persuade a listener(s) that they should orient themselves in one way or another to a particular situation. Whereas the narrative orientation of the everyday social world is oriented to belief, opinion, and common sense, formal discourses emphasize either scientifically tested knowledge about what "is" the case or critical normative deliberation about what "ought" to be the case (Habermas 1973). Normative argumentation, in short, seeks to persuade the listeners that something should be done. That is, a particular action should or should not take place, that an event should be interpreted in one way rather than another, and so on. Put simply, narratives are primarily designed to deal with an "is" (i.e. what is the situation, or what happened?), although they can include a moral, typically treated as a given. When it comes to making the case for an "ought" we offer arguments.

communicative practices, decisions and action would only be a question of whose domination should we submit to. But, as he puts it, "some stories are more truthful and humane than others," which can be sorted out through the discursive logic of good reasons. Indeed, in the politics of a democratic society the struggle for power is in significant part played out over time through arguments about the "best story."

This is not to overlook the fact that narratives are often constructed in ways that rest—implicitly or explicitly—on arguments. Frequently people construct stories in the hope that the storyline will itself facilitate or encourage the making—or acceptance—of a particular argument. Sometimes this occurs without the narrator fully recognizing the way he or she has intentionally designed the narrative. Such narratives can be intentionally or unintentionally structured to help or encourage a listener to arrive at a particular conclusion themselves. But this is a communicative strategy that should not be confused with the formal function of the narrative. The job of giving policy advice, then, is not just to offer a storyline. It is rather to translate a narrative storyline into an argument, or to tease out the argument implicitly embedded in the story. This is important to recognize, as different people construct different arguments out of the same narrative, despite the fact that a given storyteller had something in particular in mind.

In communicative interactions people can stop narratives to ask for or question information presented in the story. In these cases people will turn to empirical explanation, either of an informal or formal mode, to explore or test the validity of a "truth" statement that becomes the subject of dispute. Informal explanations may depend on what people have heard from others and they merely pass it along as truth. But in other cases, particularly in more serious discussions, people can and do turn to the findings of formally organized scientific communities that concentrate on this or that problem, physical or social, working constantly on the measurement of particular phenomena, the detection of new causal factors, and the like. In other instances people making arguments can be asked to explain how they justify a particular point. Here they may well stop and offer a story in explanation of why someone should believe the particular point.

In normal communicative interaction, basic validity claims usually do not come into question. Indeed, storytelling is typically facilitated by the fact that people share a wide range of commonly accepted assumptions that seldom have to be called into question. The majority of the citizens in Western nations do not, for example, question the values upon which a free enterprise economy is founded. Such consensus makes it possible to get on with talking about particular matters of business: who owns this, what is the price of that, and so on. These can be identified as underlying assumptions and interpretations—that is, as part of the "background consensus" that is behind every narrative exchange (Habermas 1973). This consensus involves underlying beliefs and norms that are more or less uncritically accepted by the speakers. It is nothing less than the existence of these *background* beliefs that makes the communication possible.

Discussions arise, of course, in which one or more of the background beliefs or assumptions become problematic in a fundamental way. Indeed, most political conflict concerned with social change pertains to controversies over such background assumptions. Arising within a framework of opinions and norms, these sorts of questions and controversies are generally difficult, if not impossible, to deal with in ways that simply yield to a request for more information, as if this might be enough to clear up a particular misunderstanding. To eliminate a disturbance in the background consensus, either by restoring the original consensus or by establishing a new one, a specific form of problem-solving appropriate to the validity claim in question must be initiated. That is, a "truth" or "legitimacy claim" has to be redeemed discursively through the logics of empirical or normative discourse. Only by entering into a normative discourse that has the sole purpose of judging the justification of a problematic norm, or an empirical discourse designed to get at the validity of a truth claim, can the disturbance or blockage be resolved.

As a break in ordinary narrative interaction, the communicative turn to discourse requires that judgments about certain states of affairs or norms be treated as hypothetical and subjected to systematic argumentation motivated only by the desire to achieve a rationally grounded consensus that terminates in intersubjective understanding, shared knowledge, and mutual trust. Such agreement is obtained through the "force of the better argument," governed by the logical properties of discourse. There are no fixed decision procedures or methodologies that differentiate a rational from a non-rational consensus. Nor is there any guarantee that such a process will end in consensus. What is important here is the adherence to the accepted criteria of a rational judgment. In the absence of consensus, differences of opinion are always subject to further argumentation and reflection through extended empirical and normative discourses.

Citizens and politicians seldom themselves turn to formal discourses to solve their disagreements about competing narratives, although this need not be ruled out. More typical is a turn to the existing bodies of knowledge in search of answers. In the absence of such knowledge, experts can be commissioned to supply it, a relatively common practice on the part of politicians and government officials. If a question is pressing enough, it will emerge of its own accord as a scientific question in the relevant expert communities. Science, after all, takes its problems from the society of which it is itself a part. Broad policy controversies such as global warming can, in this respect, be understood as public narratives that continually await the latest findings of the scientific community. Similarly, local questions such as what is causing the children of a neighbourhood to suffer from leukaemia can at times lead dissatisfied citizens to seek out their own facts, as experiences with citizen-oriented participatory research such as popular epidemiology have illustrated.

Finally, another aspect of the relation of narration to argumentation should be mentioned as well. Storytelling, as Schiffrin (1985, 1990) has found, may be crucial to initiating and sustaining both rational argument and public deliberation. Rigorous rational argument, she argues, frequently operates in a competitive, even aggressive, fashion. It is pursued through verbal combat with each party trying to undercut the position of the other side. Indeed, this point is often part of the feminist critique of rationality, namely that it follow the masculine competitive orientation more than it does the feminine emphasis on social integration and consensus. In her examination of "naturally occurring conversational arguments," Schiffrin (1990) discovered storytelling to lay the groundwork for and open the way to rational deliberation. People who tell stories seem not to try to undermine one another. Instead, they use narrative stories to justify their claims to credibility through appeal to general values or common experiences. "By inviting others to share a common understanding based in experience rather than reason," narratively oriented speakers seek to establish a collective identity with other members in the discussion. It is an attempt to establish stronger bonds with the other discussants, which in turn can motivate commitments to the ensuing social bond. She argues, moreover, that narration can facilitate such intersubjective bonds much more easily that the kinds of rigorous giving of reasons basic to formal argumentation. Others have also noted that narration, in the process, involves a "relational approach" to reasoning that privileges participation, consensus, equality, and community over competitive argumentation with the goal of winning (Sullivan and Goldzweig 1995).

Policy narratives

Over the past decade, the narrative mode of explanation has begun to receive increasing attention in public policy studies (Schram and Neisser 1997; Stone 2002; Lejano 2006). As this work makes clear, reliance on policy narratives is evident in even the most casual examination of policy discussions, whether in everyday interactions or official fora. The focus on policy stories has largely centered on the investigation of the issue-oriented narratives told by the various political and policy actors, using such analysis to clarify and elucidate policy positions and, when possible, even to mediate across them (Yanow 2000: 8). In much of this work, as Orsini and Scala (2006: 116) put it, "story telling is viewed from the perspective of a strategic actor, be it a pressure group or government agency, seeking to influence or shape the policy agenda with their 'version' of events." The goal is to increase the number of voices and thus perspectives in the policy process.

One approach to policy stories is to identify the problem situation and the need for policymakers to resolve it as the beginning of the story, with the middle part introducing the action or event that constitutes a policy intervention. The end of the story is then the consequences of a policy outcome, predicted or measured. Through the construction and interpretation of such narrative sequences, policymakers seek to weave their way through the uncertainty and unpredictability of politics and public administration. Some, such as Roe (1994) and van Eeten (2006) have sought to develop "meta-narratives" that bridge the differences and conflicts between competing policy stories in an effort to forge a new consensus.

Schram and Neisser (1997) take a different approach. They illustrate the ways that public policies are themselves understood as narratives, although they typically mask their narrative meanings. Whereas policies are generally treated in terms of rules and regulations pertaining to effective performance, they also more fundamentally narrate "our relations (between citizens, between citizens and the state, between states, etc.) in politically selective ways." Regardless of whether "stories are about foreign enemies . . . global environmental change, . . . welfare dependency, or the story of the state of race relations, the politics of public policymaking is played out in terms of stories that mediate how public problems are comprehended" (Schram and Neisser 1997: 2). Other work shows as well how policy can supply citizens with the social sense—positive or negative—of engagement in mutual ventures with the fellow members of their community. Schneider and Ingram (2006) have shown, in this regard, how policy designs have particular stories about the ongoing social understandings of their target populations built into them. These social constructions are built around images, stereotypes, and beliefs that narratively confer identities on people and connect them to social groups that are recipient candidates of beneficial or punitive policies. For them, the task is to penetrate and reveal what they see as "near-hegemonic" constructions of reality that often hinder democratic policy analysis and the politics of social change. Howlett and Rayner (2006) warn, in this regard, against a positivist approach to narratives. Stories, as such, are not just there waiting for a political scientists or sociologist to endow them with meaning; they are rather interpretively constructed and reconstructed by those who tell and hear them (Frank 2002: 13).[5]

Stone (2002) shows that policy controversies often turn on the underlying storyline rather that the apparent facts typically presented by the policy analyst. Critical of social science's efforts to avoid or downplay this dimension of policy analysis, she makes clear the reliance on policy narratives in even the most casual examination of policy discussions, whether in everyday or official form. Citizens, politicians and policy analysts alike tell causal stories to convey the nature, character, and origins of policy problems (Forester 1999). It is not, as we have seen, that the facts don't play a role; rather it is that they are embedded—explicitly or implicitly—in narrative accounts. What frequently seems to be a conflict over details, as she explains, is in actuality a disagreement about the more basic story.[6]

Stone's research on stories identifies two primary types of policy narratives. One focuses on decline or crisis, the other on human helplessness and the need for social control (Stone 1989). In the first type of story things are seen to have gotten worse, with empirical data usually cited to make the case. Typical examples would be the loss of valuable forests or a level of human poverty that is taking on crisis proportions. In the second type of story, what had previously seemed to be a matter of fate or accident is now portrayed as the result of human actions and in need of change through political or policy action. An example would be the rise or spread of unemployment. Whereas it might have been believed that some people were simply destined to be members of the underclass, or that there were and always will be poor people, the story now portrays unemployment as a consequence of the failure of the political-economic system to provide a sufficient number of jobs and points to the ways in which it can be ameliorated.

---

[5] Frank (2002: 13) writes that "in disenchanted times, when the only consensus is that there are no grand narratives with sufficient charismatic force to elicit mass belief, people begin with their own stories and proceed [according to] how these stories are accepted or criticized by their peers."

[6] For an interesting analysis of the relation of policy narratives to policy argumentation and discourse coalitions, in particular the "politics of narratives, "see Radaelli (1999).

Employing literary and rhetorical devices for symbolic representation, policy stories are tools of political persuasion. As strategies for depicting problems and interests, discursive devices such as synechdoches (which represent a whole by one of its parts) or metaphors (which make implied comparisons) are pervasive throughout policy stories. Such linguistic constructions are designed and introduced to convince an audience of the necessity of a political or policy action; they help to identify both the responsible culprits and the virtuous saviours capable of leading us to high ground.

On the surface of the matter, such rhetorical devices would only appear to make comparisons between seemingly different things. But, as Stone (1988: 118) writes, they do more than just make comparisons; in more subtle ways they usually imply a whole story and prescription for action. She offers the example of describing something as "fragmented." Although the word appears at first only to offer a description, against a narrative backdrop of a concern with order and efficiency, the word "fragmentation," without anyone even saying so, is usually also a call for reorganization.

It is common in politics to portray political opponents as engaging only in "rhetoric"; that is, concealing the real story, they offer a version of events constructed to promote their own interests and concerns. Missing from this view, however, is the recognition that all politics operates this way. Symbolic representation, in short, is basic to political argumentation (Edelman 1971, 1977). "Symbolic devices," as Stone writes (1988: 122–3), can be "especially persuasive and emotionally compelling because their storyline is hidden and their sheer poetry is often stunning." Frequently "a metaphor is so much a part of our cultural way of saying things that it slips right by us."

An important feature of symbols is their potential ambiguity. Symbols often typically mean two (or more) things at the same time: "equal opportunity in education can mean giving everybody tuition vouchers for the same dollar amount," or it can mean "providing extra resources for those with special needs" (Stone 1988: 123). Different people can thus understand symbols differently, especially when used in different social contexts.[7]

---

[7] For the empiricist conception of science, of course, this is problematic. The interpretation of events, social as well as physical, has to remain clear and constant for the work of the empiricist. To be replicable over time by different investigators, the objects of investigation require fixed categories. By contrast, symbolic ambiguity in art is generally taken to be a source of depth and richness. "Symbols," as Stone (1988: 123) points out, "call forth individual imagination, wish, and experience, and draw the observer into the work of art as an active

The argument can be taken even deeper into the heart of empiricist territory. Emphasizing "hard numbers," conventional social science, as we have seen, has ignored these rhetorical aspects of politics and policy. Typically, public policy problems are defined in significant part by the numbers assigned to them. But numbers, as Stone shows, are themselves symbols and, more than a little ironically, often function in ways similar to metaphors. To count something, as she (Stone 2002: 165) explains, is to categorize it, and, in doing so, we select a "feature of something, assert a likeness on the basis of that characteristic, and ignore all the other features." As with metaphors, counting requires categories that emphasize "some feature instead of others and excluding things that might be similar in important ways but do not share that feature." Based on such selections counting can be a political act. Which items fit into a particular statistical category? Which things are included in the category and which are left out? Such categorization thus sets boundaries in the form of criteria and rules that determine whether or not something belongs (Stone 1988: 128). In this way, a deliberate decision to include or exclude particular items is or can be a political act, either explicitly or explicitly.[8]

Policy scenarios as storylines

The relation of science to narratives is now more than an issue of theoretical interest. In the meantime, scientific advisory groups as important as the International Panel on Climate Change (IPCC) and the European Environmental Agency have come to recognize the importance of making their findings not only more accessible to citizens and policymakers, but also more meaningful to them. Toward this end, in year 2000 the European Commission initiated a series of scenario studies to examine the development of Europe up to 2010. The idea, as Professor Joseph Alcoma of the Centre for Environmental Systems Research at University of Kassel in Germany explains, was to develop a way to reflect upon future developments that would affect the Commission's thinking about policies that would guide a range of unfolding social and cultural trends, especially given their qualitative dimensions. The stated objective of these scenarios was "to stimulate debate inside and outside the Commission on the future

participant." In this sense, politics is more like art than science. For this reason, Stone (2002: 157) argues, "a type of policy analysis that does not make room for the centrality of ambiguity in politics can be of little use in the real world."

[8] See Hacking (1991) for a critical discussion on the role of statistics.

of European integration, and to develop a tool to put the Union's policies and strategies into perspective" in ways that would facilitate appropriate policy changes. Included among these "policy scenarios" was a study focused on the implications and consequences of adopting the US model of market competition and corporate organization. Another zeroed in on the advantages and disadvantages of a Europe that emphasized local and regional communities rather than centralized governmental institutions. And yet another explored the values of social equality and ecological consciousness in European development.

Of particular interest is the work of a group of environmental experts commissioned by the European Environmental Agency to develop a set of guidelines based in large part on their experiences in developing the 2010 scenarios, particularly as they pertained to ecological issues. Specifically, they developed procedural guidelines for translating scientific findings into narrative scenarios. Spelled out as the "Story-and-Simulation Approach" (SAS) to scenario development, the emphasis is placed on policy-oriented scenarios as "storylines."

Borrowing the concept of scenarios from performance theatre, where scenarios refers to the sequential elements of a stage production or screen-play, the idea was first adopted in the realm of politics and policy by strategic planners after the Second World War as a way to approach the analysis of war games. Among such analysts, scenarios commonly refer to a sequence of emerging events or an account of a projected course of action or events. They are, in this respect, like the plot of a story. Applied to environmental issues, storyline scenarios are fashioned to serve as a bridge between science and policy. As a qualitative tool, they can be an effective device for summarizing and synthesizing scientific knowledge that can be used in policy development. The method helps policymakers grasp the interplay of different aspects and connections of an environmental problem, and in particular to frame the issue in terms of time and space. As shaped by Alcoma and other European environmental experts, the SAS approach describes possible futures in words and visual symbols rather than numerical estimates. Quantitative information, however, still has an important role to play, with empirical data and findings being fitted into competing narratives. Although these scenarios include diagrams and tables, they are laid out as textual storylines. An important advantage is their ability to be used to represent the views of different stakeholders and experts at the same time. Compared with the dry numbers of scientific tables or complicated graphics, a well-written storyline is seen to more easily communicate practical understanding about future societal configurations and their social and political implications. (See also www.millenniumassessment.org).

More specifically, the primary goal of a narrative storyline is to highlight the main features of an action, event, or development, and the forces driving them. In the process, storylines portray step-wise changes in the future of society and its environment from competing perspectives (based on different social and economic assumptions, models, and data). Scenario development begins with the establishment of a team responsible for the creative inputs. The team first works to ensure a representation of a wide range of views, especially among stakeholders, policymakers, and scientific experts. It then sets out the basic scenario goals, and establishes the baselines dates (or time periods over which the storyline extends). Working with the relevant parties, through intensive discussion among different actors involved in the exercise, the team seeks to create a qualitative "draft story" that goes through various iterations, based on commentary, both social and empirical. Such commentary and deliberation can occur through both public meetings and the internet. The fitting in of new social perspectives and quantitative information, often depending on processes of deliberation and compromise, further elaborates the driving forces that the evolving storyline sews together.

This work, in short, constitutes an interesting and useful application of narrative storylines to bridge the world of science and policy; it is in all ways an improvement over a flat presentation of tables and numbers that typically organize a policy report. Illustrating the ways in which empirical findings fit into different storylines, as well as how different implications can be drawn from different scenarios, it clearly shows how quantitative and qualitative inquiry can be brought together to deal rigorously with complex problems and the issues they pose.

Stressing qualitative rigor, however, it is interesting to note that the report at times seems to offer somewhat of a conventional scientific understanding of what that means. One could say, in this regard, that the storylines they offer as illustrations tend to be relatively "bloodless." They emerge as object-like statements focused on consequences detached from social context. Unlike a narrative story in literature or everyday life, they display no social meanings. They convey neither a sense of commitment nor the kind of emotional sentiment that otherwise surrounds the debates of their storylines. In the case of these storylines, the readers have to bring their own social meanings to them, as has always been the case with the presentation of empirical findings. Fashioned in ways that downplay anything that might appear subjective, they are presented in a "scientifically" neutral manner and, as such, tend to hide or obscure their real function, namely to orient and motivate different citizens and policy-makers to adopt ways of seeing the respective problem. One might even say these position-less scenarios are to a degree "scientized" for use in technically-oriented environmental agencies. One has, in fact, the impression that these scientists are aware of having moved into controversial territories (especially for natural scientists) and don't want to ruffle their colleagues too much for fear of turning them away from an approach that has otherwise proven useful. This may be the most that such environmental scientists think they can do in a *public* policy-analytic context, and given the institutional structures in which they work, perhaps it is. In any case, an underlying anxiety about the broader receptivity of qualitative inquiry in the wider scientific community is to a degree evident. In the face of anticipated skepticism, the presentation proceeds cautiously.

Such caution makes clear that we still need a better understanding of the cognitive and empathetic processes at work in narrative storylines. In particular, we need to have a better grasp of how narratives do in fact conjure up and convey subjective responses, still the long-term enemy of positivist science, and how they play out in public deliberation. This need not be as epistemologically problematic as many scientists think, a point we turn to in subsequent sections. Towards this end, we take a first step in the concluding section of this chapter. We do it by introducing the concept of validity as understood in qualitative analysis.

Narrative validity as credibility

When empirical analysts speak of their confidence in the "truth" of a finding they refer to "validity." Within the prevailing empiricist research paradigm, "truth value" is objectively defined in terms of "internal validity," described as the isomorphic relationship between a set of data and the phenomenon those data are believed to represent. In a narrative world of multiple realities, however, the concept of an objective assessment of an isomorphism loses any rigorous meaning that neo-positivism assigns to it. More relevant is the compatibility of the constructed realities that exist in the minds of the inquiry's respondents with those that are attributed to them. This relationship is best termed "credibility" or "trustworthiness" (Mishler 1990).

The credibility of a story can be established with the individuals and groups who have supplied data for an inquiry (Bozeman 1986: 528). It is assessed by determining whether the narrative description developed through inquiry in a particular setting "rings true" for those persons who are members of that setting. Because these persons operate with different constructions of reality, and the emotional commitments that they have attached to them, a credible outcome is one that adequately represents both the areas in which these realities converge and the points on which they diverge.[9] Following Erlandson *et al.* (1993: 30), the credibility of a narrative can be said to "have the effect on its readers of a mosaic image; often imprecise in terms of defining boundaries and specific relationships but very rich in providing depth of meaning and richness of understanding."

Important here is also the fact that unstable and conflicting interpretations of narrative meaning may be attributed not only to error but also to "reality shifts." Thus, the investigator's quest is not for invariability but for "trackable variance," that is, variability that can be ascribed to particular sources (error, reality shifts, better insights, and so on). Consistency is conceived in terms of "dependability," a concept that embraces both the stability implied by reliability and the trackability required by explainable changes. Qualitative theorists have developed a series of strategies for accomplishing this (see, for example, Lincoln and Guba 1985; Yanow 2000; Yanow and Schwartz-Shea 2006). One procedure for doing this is the "dependability audit."

Today the question is not so much about the importance of the role of the subjective in social action; rather, the disagreements are over how to do deal with it methodologically. In particular, the issue is about the relation of the subjective to the empirical. While empiricist sociologists and political scientists have tried in the past to find ways to ignore or sidestep the subjective dimension—that is, to establish explanations that can stand independently of social meanings, or to treat meanings as manifestations of objective phenomenon—their stance today tends to concede and accept the relevance of subjective data but, at the same time, to subordinate it to—or situate it in—the larger empirical project.[10]

---

[9] Interpretive analysts recognize that the understandings that people hold of events is not necessarily correct, but they also realize that these views—independently of their truth value—influence their actions and thus are real in their consequences.

[10] The willingness of leading scholars such as King, Koehane, and Verba (1994) to concede ground to qualitative approaches has been the source of renewed interest and discussion. Given that quantitative social scientists have long denied or denigrated the validity of qualitative methods, qualitative researchers have had some reason for optimism. But it can be only a qualified optimism. These scholars have sought mainly to incorporate these methods on terms amenable to the logic of empiricist research (Buethe 2002). That is, qualitative research has to be designed and conducted in such a way as to render its results empirically testable.

For postempiricists, as we have seen here, the task is just the opposite, namely, to situate the empirical in the interpretive framework.

Conclusion

We saw in earlier chapters that the social translation of expertise in the public realm involves fitting policy advice into narratives that give them social and political meaning. We also examined more carefully the ways in which public policy is constructed around and embedded in a web of social meanings. Based on the implications of those discussions, we turned in this chapter to a more specific look at the vehicle that carries such meanings, the narrative form of explanation.

After taking note of the aversion to subjective forms of knowing on the part of both science and liberal political theory, the discussion examined the way the normative form furnishes intersubjective communication with the particular details out of which meaning and perspective are derived. As we saw, it is through storytelling that people understand the goals and values of different social groups, access social positions in their communities, and internalized social conventions. Narrative storylines do this by imposing a coherent interpretation on the whirl of events and actions that surround the members of society. Threading these sequential components together through storylines, narratives place social phenomena in the larger patterns that attribute social and political meaning to them.

Whereas the scientific mode of inquiry looks for stable empirically based causal connections betweens events and phenomena, the narrative scheme was seen to include empirical information but emphasizes its relationship to social purposes, intentions, and motivations. Shaped by the contexts of time and location that envelop actors and events, narrative inquiry is thus better suited than empirical analysis to render

---

Indeed, affirming their basic commitment to neo-positivism, they argue that the linkage has to be established through the logic of empirical science, which they describe as the single unified logic of inference (King, Koehane, and Verba 1994: 3). In short, other logics of inference do not lead to real knowledge. The primary goal of qualitative inquiry, however, is not to draw out empirically testable hypotheses for empirical researchers; rather, it is examine the narrative understandings of the actors. While qualitative research can indeed serve as a corrective or a corroborative perspective for the mainstream project and its problems, the approach offered by these scholars misunderstands and mistreats qualitative research. More than just another way of collecting data, such interpretation rests on an altogether different epistemological understanding of social reality and its construction. In short, this attempt to neo-positivize qualitative research fails to resolve the problem it has set out to solve.

an understanding of social change. As storytelling, it is seen to expand our conception of knowledge beyond the narrow confines of observational statements and logical proof to include an understanding of the ways people are located in the wider social contexts of situation and society.

The chapter also showed narrative understanding to have its own methods for judging stories as good and bad. Toward this end, the discussion presented Fisher's informal logic of narrative rationality, which turns on narrative probability and narrative fidelity. This was followed by a more specific examination of the role of policy narratives and storytelling through the contributions of Schram, Neisser, and Stone, as well as a practical policy application of narrative scenarios and their storylines. The chapter concluded with a discussion of the qualitative approach to narrative credibility.

Along the way, we have noted that social meanings are often taken-for-granted and thus not easily recognized by those who rely on them. They are in this respect, often tacit in nature. We thus turn in the next chapter to the nature of tacit assumptions in the construction of both facts and meanings, and an examination of the role of tacit knowing in critical learning in the deliberative process.

8

Transformative Learning Through Deliberation: Social Assumptions and the Tacit Dimension*

As seen in earlier chapters, we have learned a good deal about participatory deliberation, especially from consensus conferences, scenario workshops, public mediation, and the like. These efforts have provided practical experiences that have helped us better understand the interaction between citizens and experts—both how citizens relate to expert knowledge and how professional experts respond to the thinking of everyday citizens. But it is also important to note that most of these deliberative approaches have been geared to conflicts that revolve around established interests. That is, they deal with the existing configuration of interests and their surrounding power arrangements as they emerge in particular disputes. They are, as such, problem-oriented. This is not to say that the introduction of deliberative strategies to solve problems, or that the insights we have gained from these experiences, cannot be useful. In fact, while some have become disappointed with these deliberative methods, the critique has often been misdirected. It is not that deliberative approaches fail per se, but rather that the problem-solving orientation fails to take into account the fact that the problems to which they are addressed often have much deeper roots. So designed, deliberation cannot untangle the problems they set out to "solve." Such strategies typically attempt to avoid more fundamental questions, seeking to narrow rather than broaden the scope of the deliberative negotiations. The underlying sources of the conflict they seek to resolve are often not put on the table. In short,

* Co-authored by Alan Mandell, Professor of Adult Learning and Mentoring, State University of New York, Empire State College.

they constitute topics that the established interest groups are unwilling to discuss. They are excluded from the conversation.

In this sense, only what are deemed to be politically acceptable topics are available for discussion. Thus, discussions about restructuring basic social and political power relationships or redistributing resources are typically not options. The practices of policy mediation, for example, can only work out solutions that people are willing to accept within an existing sociopolitical consensus. Of course, for strategic reasons, at times this can work. Certain problems need solutions at a particular moment and people find it in their interest to solve them. In this regard, participants often understand the need to compromise in such matters. Yet, even when such decisions are made, they are often relatively unstable and time-bound.

So what then can we say about the use of deliberative strategies to deal with such problems? One point is of particular importance: that the process itself generally results in "learning." That is, even when it might not solve the immediate problems at hand, engagement in the process typically facilitates certain kinds of learning—strategic and otherwise. One of the significant discoveries, the importance of which is often overlooked or neglected, is that "citizen learning" contributes to personal self-transformation, which can, in turn, lead to new social engagements (Warren 2002).[1] A typical response of consensus conference participants, for example, is that they didn't think at the outset that they would be able to deal with the relevant policy issues: that the issues were either just too complex or that they were "not smart enough" to take on such significant topics. However, based on the opportunity and the experience that such deliberative practices offer, participants report that they became more motivated citizens and often began to participate regularly in local meetings and other venues of civic problem-solving. Put in simple terms, as a result of their participation, their sense of themselves as actors and as learners changed. That is, through the experience of deliberation, they engaged in a process of transformative learning.

No doubt, then, such shifts in personal and social perception are not something that should be treated as insignificant outcomes. In a

---

[1] As Warren (2002: 12) has written, "Without the experience of argument and challenge within the democratic public spheres, individuals will have little sense for what relates them to, and distinguishes them from, others; and this deprives them of an essential condition of self-development." By elevating "one's wants, needs, and desires to the level of consciousness and by formulating them in speech, one increases one's sense of identity and autonomy— aside from any advantages that might accrue from the substantive outcomes of collective decisions."

democracy, the availability of myriad chances to interact and participate is vital to the system. How can a political system rightfully call itself democratic if it *does not* provide its citizens with opportunities to engage in deliberative activities? Such activities are the training ground for the development of political skills, in particular deliberative skills, essential for citizen participation. Through these experiences, citizens learn to grapple with information, listen to others, articulate ideas, organize evidence, judge arguments, and compromise with peers. Gaining practice in such essential citizen-skills is at the heart of learning democracy.

At the same time, though, we need a more sophisticated understanding of the kinds of epistemological awareness and reflexivity that animate those engaged in such deliberations, especially as they step beyond problem-solving based on a narrow politics of interests. It is to this consideration that we turn in the discussion that follows.

Postempiricism and social meaning: The normative construction of interests

For the postempiricist scholar, the challenge of transformative learning turns on our understanding of "interests." Whereas mainstream approaches take "interests" as givens and work within the framework of existing interests as articulated by the participants themselves, the postempiricist recognizes interests to be socially constructed. Put another way, rather than taking preferences as originating with citizens themselves (i.e. that we always know our own interests and thus consider them to be relatively fixed), the constructivist view recognizes interests to be the products of a complex process of socialization that begins in childhood and extends into various stages of personal and social development. Indeed, always operating at both the conscious and unconscious levels, socialization inculcates young people with basic value-orientations and beliefs that become deeply rooted in their lives—that shape their ways of seeing, interpreting, and judging social experiences.[2]

---

[2] In part, these orientations are directly and indirectly supplied by formative experiences in a particular family, neighborhood, social class, race, and gender, and by what becomes an accumulation of daily confrontations with reality. Some, for example, grow up with a basic sense that life is hard, if not short and brutish. More often than not, they tend to lean toward more conservative orientations that will emphasis law and discipline. Others will lean in the opposite direction, finding life to be a relatively fulfilling and nurturing experience. They will more characteristically support more liberal positions that call for expanding the opportunities of individuals to develop their own capacities unencumbered by constrains of

As we recognize the deeply entrenched nature of these value orientations, we should not overlook that the fact that they do remain social constructions based on particular, often limited, sets of social experiences. That is, people are tied to them because they reflect their own encounters with social reality—their own socially constructed narratives and self-understandings. They do not reflect the whole of reality. In this respect, the goal of critical discourse is to help us recognize the constructed nature of what we take for granted and thus to open it up and re-examine it using new information and new angles of interpretation. Such critical discourse, of course, does not often occur. One reason is that people often lack the experience of grappling with and trying to make sense of this process; another is that our attachments to a worldview are deeply embedded in our emotional lives; and yet another is that society generally discourages exactly this kind of questioning. More typically, education focuses on instrumental forms of learning relevant to problem-solving behaviors and instrumental actions within the given sets of social understandings that undergird a particular society.

But a social or political theory that simply accepts these arrangements as givens—or as part of an empirically neutral description of reality—comes up short. In essential moments in the evolution of society, groups of citizens *do* question these socially constructed understandings and *do* struggle to change them. All of this is an essential part of the process of social change. A social science that ignores the less visible—if not at times hidden—nature of this process can only present an artificial picture and assessment of society. Moreover, such a social science provides a static explanation, which wittingly or unwittingly, serves to support the existing configuration of interests.

Understanding social reality to be a human construction, the postempiricist then turns attention away from a one-sided focus on the empirically measurable to emphasize the discursive processes and circumstantial contexts that shape the social construction of the meanings upon which thought and action are based. Such an analysis has to begin with the recognition that many of an adult's social meanings are culturally determined understandings acquired in early life and solidified through experience, which continue in important ways to determine how we experience the world. These tacitly—even in part unconsciously—held meanings provide the perspectives and schema through which each of us construe

---

disciplinary regimentation. Importantly, sometimes, such basic patterns of socialization can manifest themselves in political orientations that can become so firmly fixed that they can approximate the kinds of unmovable positions that mainstream theory takes as given.

experience, which otherwise is encountered as incoherent, even chaotic. Working through the basic processes of perception and cognition, such taken for granted meanings intentionally and unintentionally render as real and true the interpretations upon which social actors assess their situations and develop courses of action. At work here is a complex process involving the projection of internalized concepts and models onto particular segments of experience to make them understandable. For us to truly understand how people grasp the world and why they take particular things for granted, we have to attempt to dissect a multi-layered personal/social/historical context.

For the social constructivist, the basic concern revolves around the fact that human interpretations are fallible and often are predicated upon assumptions that may or may not be reliable. Moreover, people generally tend to accept and integrate experiences that comfortably fit their frames of reference and downplay, ignore, or outright negate those that do not. Critically examining both the content and justification for our interpretations, the special task of postempiricist inquiry is to understand how the frames of reference we use guide our awareness, influence our feelings, and shape our actions. Such clarification is the first step in a critical approach to social learning.

Attuned to the social-theoretical constitution of both normative and factual information, postempiricist policy inquiry focuses on the ways that conventional policy analysis is based on unquestioned meanings. As we saw in the previous chapter, scholars such as Schram (1993), Schneider and Ingram (2006) have provided important illustrations of how social meanings function as policy presuppositions. Public policy, as they have shown, does more than provide for material benefits or penalties. It also carries and transmits messages about the very populations to which it is addressed. The ability to make clear and discerning interpretations of policy meanings advanced by different groups, as well as to understand the elements through which these meanings are transmitted, allows the policy analyst to assist in identifying the underlying sources of policy conflict and to reformulate issues in ways that can move the dispute towards an acceptable and constructive resolution. That is, by examining the taken-for-granted assumptions that underlie citizens' everyday understandings and behaviors in problematic situations, the analyst can help us better reflect on the conflicting frames inherent in policy controversies, permitting us a clearer comprehension of the relationships among hidden premises and commonly accepted conclusions. As we have seen, by identifying such assumptions and the images associated with them, the postempiricist approach seeks to uncover the grounds for controversies and contentions that emerge from latent theoretical assumptions, rhetorical devices, conceptual ambiguities, as well as problematic methodological practices closely related to policy disputes. As such, specific attention must focus on the discursive constructions of the political actors, the social meanings that underlie them, the ways narratives frame policy issues, and the processes and practices of argumentation. Such an approach strives to show the ways presuppositions operate beneath the surface to shape and structure policy definitions and the meanings that support them. In the process, it also seeks to understand how theoretical and normative assumptions shape actors' understandings of any "problem" to which they are trying to respond. As we saw, postempiricist policy inquiry does not reject empirical research, but rather seeks to integrate it with normative constructivist inquiry.[3]

Social assumptions: The tacit dimension

The postempiricist task thus explores the less visible—often hidden—assumptions behind the social construction of the objects and statements it studies. But how do we go about studying that which is "hidden"? Indeed, this remains a topic in need of further research. But a starting point can be found in Michael Polanyi's work on tacit knowledge. In his seminal book, *Personal Knowledge*, Polanyi (1958) sought to explain how all knowledge rests on a deeper body of tacit knowledge that is not immediately available to either the researcher or the reader, yet deeply influences how that knowledge is shaped.

Polanyi's work on tacit knowledge grew out of his experiences in and observations of the physical sciences, although his conceptualization of such knowledge is no less relevant to the social and policy sciences or to the layperson's knowledge. In keeping with the spirit and direction of postempiricism more generally (a movement that in fascinating ways his

---

[3] It calls for a deeper understanding of what we are doing when we engage in such inquiry. Whereas technical or instrumental problem-solving (involving the manipulation of objects, physical or human) follows the logic of hypothesis testing and deductive logic basic to science, understanding the communication of meanings involves a "metaphorical abductive" model of analysis. Replacing hypothesis testing, it moves from the concrete to the abstract rather than from the abstract to the concrete. In such communication, we try to understand what someone else means "abductively" by drawing upon our experience to make sense of theirs. Where deduction deals with what "must be" and induction concerns what actually "is," as Hanson explains, abduction explains what "may be" (Mezirow 1991: 85).

work presaged), Polanyi described in detail how the investigatory behavior of physical scientists in pursuit of the so-called objective world does not correspond to the *official* epistemological principles of science.[4] Because of "personal elements," scientists can never in any formal sense be objectively detached. Indeed, for him, this very *lack* of detachment was basic to discovery and progress in the sciences. It was this position that he intricately worked out in *Personal Knowledge*, his lengthy and careful analysis of how we come to perceive, know, and understand the meaning of things.

What Polanyi recognized is that various traditions and conventions that influence and sometimes directly guide the social interactions inherent in any scientific inquiry are not immediately available to us. Toward this end, he identified a process of "tacit knowing" that is logically prior to the explicit form of knowing identified by objectivist epistemologies. Such tacit knowledge, he theorized, implicitly entered into the process of observation (both everyday and scientific), through the observer's very acts of perception, which rely on a gestalt of past experiences. This tacit knowledge, as a repertoire of understandings and beliefs that support any pursuit of knowledge, is the very fulcrum from which otherwise objective knowledge acquires both its possibility and significance. As such, cognitive knowing begins in the realm of the tacit—in the implicit—before becoming explicit. In view of these hidden influences, as Polanyi explains it, we always know more than we can say.[5]

For Polanyi, no intelligence can operate independently of assumptions and all inquirers work in like-minded "fiduciary communities," which supply them with a shared vision of the nature of things, including a common cultural heritage, intellectual interests, and a specific idiom of

---

[4] Specifically, Polanyi's "post-critical philosophy" focused on the inexactnesses involved in scientific work and how the scientific community always interpretively mediates abstract principles. Basing his observations and arguments in significant part on a reflective understanding of his own experience as a research chemist, as well as those of colleagues, Polanyi argued that the personal beliefs and commitments held by individual researchers actually enabled them to pursue their projects in particular ways.

[5] Polanyi identifies and then intricately explores an idea that is still difficult for many to accept or even grasp. It is one that fundamentally challenges the neo-empiricist understanding of the very possibility of a complete statement of each component involved in the creation of knowledge. Such full acknowledgement, Polanyi argued, is necessary for intersubjectively reproducing and thus testing the validity of empirical statements. But this, as he saw, is not as straightforward as it sounds. Recognizing that social interactions are based on intellectual traditions and that their conventions are central to any process of inquiry, Polanyi further understood that largely tacit social dimensions operating behind the scenes are involved in both the development of hypotheses and the assessment of the outcomes of the research designed to test them. In short, one's "loyalty" to this tacit level influences the ways investigators decide what is valid and what is not. The failure to take these tacit factors into account in any explanation of cognition, Polanyi (1974: 219) argued, will, at crucial points, lead to false accounts.

communication. It is upon this community and its tacit assumptions that we depend in our attempt to understand the world in which we live. And it necessarily follows that we have trouble understanding those from different intellectual traditions, even at times misunderstanding them altogether.

Given the times in which Polanyi (1958, 1966) developed his theory of tacit knowledge, his work represents an astonishing epistemological advance.[6] As noted earlier, his emphasis on social interaction and established conventions is truly a forerunner to a postempiricist, constructionist theory of the scientific community and its process of inquiry. Indeed, examining the role of tacit knowledge remains an ongoing challenge to those attempting to further elaborate a constructionist perspective. Thus, since his time, the social studies of science have deepened the perspective in one significant way that very much bears on the question at hand. This has to do with an analysis of the dynamics of the social interactions inherent in any scientific inquiry, and even more importantly, with the question of the origins of the tacit assumptions that underlie scientific work.

Tacit knowledge, as Polanyi theorized, is based on past experiences. It is tethered to bodily and communal social life. Focusing rather narrowly on the influence of the social conventions of scientific practice, however, Polanyi failed to fully work out the social implications of these origins. In contrast, the postmodern perspective demonstrates that these social dimensions reach deeply into society itself. In this view, the scientist is him- or herself rooted not just in the conventions of any particular scientific community (whether of chemists or policy scientists), but in the society as well. That is, the very practices of scientific inquiry must be situated within a particular social-historical context. On the one hand, we have learned that science has meant different things at different times, though this point need not be inconsistent with Polanyi's concept of knowledge being "shaped by convention" (1974: 16). Such an historical vantage point would only need to be developed and elaborated. Second, and more important for the present discussion, we have learned more about the ways that *particular* understandings of society permeate scientific practices themselves.

This deeper understanding of tacit knowledge contains the rudimentary elements of a social theory, one that includes the recognition and need to offer a critique of human nature, basic value configurations and their

---

[6] Polanyi's understanding of this tacit dimension was well ahead of its time and, as such, was not well received by scientists and philosophers, as reflected in the scholarly reviews of *Personal Knowledge* (see Earle 1959 and Brodbeck 1960).

implications for social arrangements, and fundamental notions about how change can come about. Here the work of feminist scholars provides an excellent example of attention to this deeper level of the "tacit dimension" and its effects upon the organization of society, including science.[7] For these theorists, by equating "detachment" with objectivity and uncritically elevating an ahistorical notion of rationality to the pinnacle of scientific thought, inquiry misses the ways in which subjects, knowledge, and power are interconnected, and how gender politics enters the making of knowledge at various points.[8]

Once we recognize this deeper societal influence, we can also appreciate how a scientists' own deeper layer of taken-for-granted social views and attitudes, especially as manifested in more latent tacit knowledge, influences their work. At the tacit level, such latent knowing operates more as tendencies, impressions, temperaments, or impulses that lead people to lean both cognitively and normatively in one direction or the other. Moreover, if such underlying knowledge orientations influence the natural scientist's work, it is much more influential in the development of social theory itself, where it is always difficult to separate empirical from normative considerations, and ideologies from explanations.

In Polanyi's own "post-critical epistemology," a proposal needs to be assessed within the traditions in which it is tacitly grounded. And as such, it need not be accepted by anyone holding a different set of assumptions, neither tacit nor explicit.[9] In fact, his own post-critical account of

[7] That is, feminist work on epistemology introduced two decades ago by such authors as Fox Keller (1985), Ruddick (1989), Gilligan (1993), and Chodorow (1994), shows us to the ways in which what Bordo (1987) describes as the "Cartesian masculinization of thought" has penetrated our ways of knowing. See, for example, the essays contained in Alcoff, L. and Potter, E. (eds.) (1993). *Feminist Epistemologies*.

[8] Fascinatingly, this kind of orientation, which emphasises the presence of "epistemic negotiations" and pushes us to pinpoint the specific ways in which beliefs and discoveries of all kinds are always made within "an interactive dialogic community" actually builds on attention to the influence of "basic beliefs" and "convictions" that Polanyi's descriptions announce. However, while Polanyi uses his insight to argue in general and ahistorical terms for our "liberation from objectivism," the feminists and others have gone beyond the mere acknowledgment of the "tacit dimension" to disclose its specific, socially and historically constructed nature and its possible limitations and systematic distortions.

[9] Polanyi's theory of tacit knowledge was influenced by the work of Gestalt psychologists. This work involved recognizing that we see objects by supplying forms or patterns in terms of which the various bits and pieces of our perceptual field gain meaning. It became clear from that experimental work that we do not perceive objects by inferring them from their given parts, nor by a process of induction from experience, inasmuch as we frequently see objects as complete even when some parts actually are not present. That is, in the very act of perception we seem to be completing the appearance, even if this means supplying the missing parts, without noticing that we do so. It sometimes requires a special effort for us to notice perceptually that some of the essential parts are, indeed, missing, even after the fact of their absence has been established in our minds beyond any doubt.

knowledge would mean that any scientist is responsible for publicly articulating these assumptions in the process of advocating his or her position.[10]

Tacit knowledge and learning in the professions

While the discussion of tacit knowledge might sound rather removed from the concrete practices of the professions, the topic has been taken up by a number of scholars in fields as diverse as medicine, law, management, and education. Drawing directly on Polanyi's concept of tacit knowledge, these researchers have sought to understand the ways in which important aspects of professional knowledge and skills are not captured and taught in either textbooks or in the classroom. Tacit knowledge, as they understand it, refers to nonverbal, unarticulated dimensions of professional knowledge that are mainly acquired through direct practical experience in real-world environments. Whereas most professional education involves verbally transmitting explicit forms of so-called objective knowledge—justified beliefs about facts and concepts—tacit knowledge largely operates on the intuitive level and, as such, is not readily verbalized or directly described in writing. As such, tacit knowledge has to mainly be inferred by observing the behavior of those who possess it. It is uncovered by identifying action-oriented assumptions, social biases, ways of looking at things, particularly as they manifest themselves in situational contexts. In effect, professional education demands a distinctive kind of learning in which the "tacit" plays a central part.

The role of tacit knowledge in the professions has long been reflected in the need for apprenticeships and on-the-job training, which emphasize the implicit learning obtained from "learning by doing." Thus, for example, physicians have long recognized such knowledge as the distinction between

---

[10] Despite their good beginning, however, Polanyi thought these Gestalt psychologists were mistaken in looking for mechanical or neurological explanations of this process. For him, in doing so, they failed to explain important psychological possibilities related to the central notion around which their discoveries revolved. What they missed, in his view, were the ways in which we perform an action in the very process of perception. This action involves a tacit integration of sensations and feelings into a perceived object that gives meaning to these sensations and feelings, which they had not previously possessed. In Polyani's view, this action introduces *the intention* involved in the quest for knowledge that is left out by objectivist accounts. Only by including intention, he argued, can we account for the way people use their senses to make judgments. Drawing on the experimental work of other psychologists, Polanyi took perception to be an intentional action in which we make tacit use of cues of which we are only aware of in a subsidiary fashion. That is, general notions that we have formed on the basis of past experiences enter tacitly and as further specification of what already has become part of our perceptual field via the operation of our visual mechanism.

the "science" and the "art" of medicine. Whereas the science of medicine in clinical practice is about correlating and applying axiomatic principles to the symptoms at hand, the art of medicine is practiced at the bedside. Bedside knowledge, as such, is intuitive, holistic, and experiential in nature. It is informed by a repertoire of meaningful practices internalized by the physician over time. From this understanding, then, students of the professions can only grasp the subtler dimensions of their respective fields by observing and working with seasoned practitioners. But more recent work has sought to bring this less visible knowledge more clearly into view by approaching tacit knowledge more empirically (Reber 1989). Some, such as Sternberg, have even sought to examine its acquisition through laboratory studies, developing ways to measure complex patterns of tacit or "subsidiary" knowledge in experimental contexts (Sternberg *et al.* 1995).[11]

This kind of work has led researchers such as Sternberg and Horvath (1999) to ask how we how we can learn more about the patterns of tacit knowing garnered in the early work experiences of professional practitioners themselves. For example, is it possible to uncover and use subtypes of such implicit knowledge to improve organizational performance? How can we develop proxies for such knowledge that can help young practitioners more quickly obtain such expertise? The challenge, as Horvath (1999, p. ix) presents it, is to obtain "a more differentiated understanding of the broad range of phenomena that have come to be grouped under the umbrella term of tacit knowledge."

Much of the value of this knowledge is found in its relationship to more formal knowledge structures. Such research shows that it often comes into

---

[11] In the field of organization and management, as Horvath (1999, p. ix) writes, a good deal of research has emerged to show that "much of the value-adding knowledge that resides within organizations is tacit" and that "new and powerful applications in the area of knowledge management ... are likely to require deeper understandings of tacit knowledge as a psychological and social and phenomenon." So too, Nelson and Winter (1982) have employed Polanyi's concept to develop a knowledge-based theory of business enterprise. Similarly, Argyris (1990) has identified tacit forms of "unspoken knowledge" essential to effective organizational learning performance. Still others have shown how tacit knowing can be embedded in ways of doing things in the workplace that can affect the kinds of innovation needed for successful competitive behavior (Kogut and Zander 1992). Nonaka and Takeuchi (1995), for example, have developed a model of organizational learning in so-called "knowledge-creating companies" that includes the role of tacit knowledge. Drawing on Polanyi, they understand the learning process as alternating between the explicit and the implicit. That is, in addition to the standard understanding of the codification and dissemination of explicit knowledge, for them tacit knowledge can also be made explicit through a process of "externalization" and codified in manuals, later to be reflected in new products and practices. In addition, workers can "internalize" this shared tacit knowledge through an ongoing process of socialization. This process is at the core of their SECI model (socialization, externalization, combination, and internalization).

play when theoretical knowledge has to be applied to ambiguous situational circumstances, especially when the theoretical knowledge is incomplete. Patel, Arocha, and Kaufman (1999) illustrate this by focusing on the cognitive processes that underlie the medical expertise of the diagnostician. In their view, the tacit forms of knowledge drawn from practical experience are fundamentally different in character from the knowledge found in medical textbooks. But, at the same time, the effective use of tacit forms of knowing depends in important ways on what they call "well-formed biomedical knowledge structures" (Patel *et al.* 1999: 79). Inexperienced diagnosticians base their judgments on these explicit knowledge structures, but over a period of time become more and more attuned to less obvious patterns of evidence and outcomes that reoccur in practice. As they become sensitive to such patterns, they begin to drift away from a reliance on explicit knowledge and reason more tacitly. In this regard, as expert diagnosticians examine complex real-world clinical situations, they also come to rely on their grasp of the social and political context of medical practice, e.g. as it is shaped by the institutions in which they work. Such knowledge and the "reasoning strategies" that flow from it permit the expert to respond adaptively to changes and constraints in the work environment.

Especially interesting for present purposes is the work on tacit knowledge in education. Given that the more conventional focus here is on deliberative learning, we need to understand the ways that learning is influenced by less visible dimensions of beliefs and knowledge. What researchers have seen in their inquiries into the influences of tacit knowledge on the learning process is that teachers and students typically hold a latent theory of how one best goes about learning. That is, most teachers use a working-theory of the learning process that is typically not visible. Torff refers to this as "folk pedagogy." Others have referred to it as a "hidden curriculum" that frames daily teaching and learning practices and, indeed the very workings of classrooms, schools, and entire educational systems.

In Torff's (1999: 196) conception, "folk pedagogy"—a set of "commonsense ideas about teaching and learning"—predisposes teachers "to think and teach in particular ways, some of which are inconsistent with the concepts and practices characteristic of expert teaching." Moreover, research finds that these tacit ideas tend to persist despite participation in training programs that might offer different notions about so-called "good" teaching. Becoming an expert teacher then is not simply a matter of gaining new knowledge, nor developing a repertoire of acceptable techniques, nor of replacing inadequate preconceptions with "better" ones—all in a straightforward manner. Rather, specific efforts need to be made to directly counter these uncritically held pedagogical beliefs, this underlying set of tacit understandings about teaching and learning, principally by encouraging prospective teachers to engage in activities that facilitate relevant forms of cognitive change. Seen within this context, prospective teachers would have to be encouraged to confront the scope and influence of their tacit conceptions of education and to experience instructional ideas and methods (ways of literally re-imagining the teaching and learning process) that fall outside their taken-for-granted—their implicit understandings.[12]

This folk epistemology, it is important to note, is of particular interest to the work at hand, as such a folk conception in large part mirrors a simplified version of the positivist understanding of knowledge and how to go about getting it, or what Freire called the "banking" theory of learning (to which we return below). From this view, knowledge consists of factual information stored in people's heads or in the tools people employ, such as books and computers. This information is thought to represent objective reality; it reflects "the way things are" in the world. Such objective information is "out there" to be known (or not known) by individuals. Learners, in this respect, often employ what they take to be a commonsense epistemology in which they see knowledge as a simple collection of many true statements that arise unproblematically (and directly) from sensory experiences and inferences.

Yet, as described above, there is a growing body of evidence, which shows that what can be understood as fundamental epistemological views—basic frames through which we see and understand the world—are learned in our earliest years and persist throughout adulthood. The power of such passionate emotional attachments to our ways of perceiving things accounts for much of our failure to distinguish between theories and beliefs, and alerts us of the need to recognize the importance of evidence as a means of providing justification for our ideas. In all, uncritical fidelity to folk epistemologies yields a rather thin and ultimately

---

[12] Such research further shows that people employ intuitive conceptions of learning that exert a powerful force on the kind of thinking they do in all sorts of situations inside and outside the classroom. Such intuitive conceptions are typically held apart from view and often take the form of assumptions on which patterns of thought are predicated. Intuitive conceptions also are sometimes (but not always) oversimplified, misleading or inaccurate. Finally, intuitive conceptions persist despite efforts to improve or replace them. As described here, this is especially the case with epistemological assumptions that inform the basic ways in which we define and address any issue.

distorted view of knowledge as a body of objectively held facts, the veracity of which is determined with little regard to supporting evidence.

Recapturing the critical perspective: Tacit knowledge and second-order knowledge in policy and learning

The topic of "learning" is not new to the professions. In fact, over the last twenty years, it has become something of a growth industry. In public policy theory and research, for example, emphasis has been placed on the ability of policymakers to make choices based on reflective examination of specific experiences rather than exclusively relying on pressure from institutional routines or electoral outcomes. Responding to different or changing social and institutional contexts, these practitioners are understood to be "learning" as they work with and implement policies or change future policy strategies accordingly. Public officials and politicians, in this view, adjust their actions by learning from experience. Towards this end, Heclo (1972) calls for an approach emphasizing knowledge acquisition and utilization that would produce better explanations and understandings of policy outcomes than the dominant theories.

A very influential contribution along these lines has been the "advocacy coalition framework" put forth by Sabatier (1988). In this model of policy dynamics, emphasis is placed on learning in policy subsystems. A central feature of the model turns on the ways members of different policy coalitions, organized around different policy beliefs, can learn from the technical research and debates in policy communities. As such, this orientation stresses the importance of the role of policy ideas and analysis in the policy process. Sharing knowledge, beliefs, and values, the members of policy advocacy coalitions differentiate themselves from their competitors along cognitive lines. With regard to learning, the model focuses in particular on technical considerations advanced through expert discourse. While the core beliefs of policy communities do not easily change, argues Sabatier, policy learning can affect the more technical, instrumental aspects of policy politics.

But this model, like most of the work in policy studies, relies on its own "folk pedagogical" understanding of learning—that is, one vested in the taken-for-granted "folk" ways of the given society. It is an orientation that is largely technocratic and positivist in nature, corresponding, as noted above, to what Freire (1973: 59) described as the "banking theory of education." In this view, education "becomes an act of depositing." The learners "are the depositories and the teacher is the depositor."[13] It is this pedagogical orientation with its architecture of subjects and objects that has explicitly and implicitly shaped much thinking in the policy sciences tradition. It is widely reflected in the emphasis on and understanding of public sector intelligence-gathering and in the construction of data banks (emphasizing information storage and retrieval), now greatly facilitated by the infatuation with new computer technologies, the Internet, and a preoccupation with instrumental problem-solving.

To be sure, some have sought to develop a more sophisticated understanding of knowledge in policy analysis, but such work largely remains on the edge of the discipline. Given that policy analysis is often an organizational tool, much of the theorizing has turned to an extensive literature on organizational learning. In organizational theory, for example, there is a considerable body of work dealing with how managers learn from practical experiences and apply such new knowledge to improve organizational performance. From this perspective, a so-called "learning organization" is characterized as an *adaptive* organization, i.e., an organization that is able to sense changes in signals from its environment (both internal and external) and adapt accordingly. This kind of organizational learning actively creates, captures, transfers, and mobilizes knowledge to enable it to shift within a constantly changing environment.[14]

While it is beyond the scope of this discussion to examine or even introduce all of the theories of organizational learning, one can easily establish that much of this work has been based on rather limited definitions of learning and to the largely technically oriented outcomes to

---

[13] Rather than communicating per se, "the teacher issues communiqués" and makes "deposits," which students patiently receive, memorize and repeat. As Freire put it, "knowledge is a gift bestowed by those who consider themselves knowledgeable upon those whom they consider to know nothing" (1973: 58).

[14] The key aspect of organizational learning is the interaction that takes place among individual participants. One important feature of such organizations are formal programs in which experienced organizational members "mentor" their younger employees (i.e., one needs to learn the tricks of the trade, to be guided by a more senior employee, who has significant experiential learning to share). There are many methods for locating and gathering this knowledge and experience, such as publications, activity reports, interviews, and presentations. But beyond the actual gathering is the organizing of this knowledge in ways that people can find and store it, such as developing multiple structures to facilitate searches regardless of the user's perspective (e.g. who, what, when, where, why, and how). The key aspect of such organizational learning is the interaction that takes place among individuals engaged in the pursuit of efficiency and effectiveness. But organizational learning is more than the sum of individual learning; the learning organization wants to actively promote, facilitate, and reward collective learning. Geared to achieving organizational goals, such learning is necessarily oriented to imbuing workers with "the ways" of the organization, that is, with myriad opportunities to internalize the rules, attitudes, and behaviors—both implicit and explicit—of the specific culture of work.

which they give rise. But not all of it. The organizational psychologist, Chris Argyris and his long-time associate Donald Schön are examples of theorists who have gone beyond a narrow understanding of the instrumental and acknowledged spheres of learning that are richer and more complex. Their work offers a useful glimpse of some of the best aspects of this work, along with an important critique of its limitations.

Synoptically stated, Argyris and Schön (1996) have distinguished between "single-loop" and "double-loop" forms of learning. The former involves learning in which individuals, groups or organizations modify their actions according to the differences between expected and obtained outcomes. In double-loop learning, on the other hand, these same learners question the values, assumptions and policies that led to the actions in the first place. If they are able to view and modify those taken-for-granted assumptions (which are often tacit in nature), then double-loop learning—as a form of learning about single-loop learning—has taken place.

This work is useful in so far as it opens the door to a recognition of the influential role of tacit learning, and indeed, to a more critical, transformative kind of social learning that acknowledges the significance of reflection to learning itself. But it has largely been developed to better understand and reform instrumentally oriented organizations and thus stops short of the kind of critical perspective that such concepts otherwise imply. The point can be illustrated through Argyris's own approach to double-loop thinking in organization theory and management education.

Focusing on how managers and their employees can and need to reflect on basic assumptions, beliefs and values, organizational participants, in Argyris's (1990) view, engage in "critical learning" when they explore the assumptions that shape managerial decisions with regard to the accuracy of their understanding of market realities. In the process, as Brookfield (2005: 11) describes it, "inferential ladders are scrutinized for false rungs that lead business teams into, for example a disastrous choice regarding the way in which a brand image upsets a certain group of potential customers." The intended outcome of the reflective exercise is an increase in productivity and thus profits, as well as a decline in problematic outcomes such as employee absenteeism or workplace dissatisfaction.

Approached in this way, the basic structures and functions of the economic form upon which the organization is embedded—capitalism and the free market—are *not* part of the discussion. That is, the learning is necessarily truncated because the structural characteristics and ideological premises of the underlying system are left unexamined. In effect, they are outside the bounds of the intended learning and thus go unchallenged.

Put another way, from the perspective of transformational learning, one cannot truly engage in a process of critical learning without examining workplace activities in the context of the larger system of which they are a part. Such learning, for example, would necessarily involve identifying and analyzing topics such as the specific conditions under which profits are generated and how they are distributed; efforts to weaken or even prohibit the activities of labor organizations and unions; practices of moving plants offshore where wages are lower; efforts to avoid environmental standards, and the like. At the same time, such critical learning would also seriously consider other organizational models, such as worker-managed firms and cooperative workplace democracy, and take up opportunities for workplace learning focused on extending workers' creative abilities, in particular the ability to think through such problems on their own terms. This does not suggest that no learning occurs under double-loop thinking. It is to acknowledge the limitations of that learning, a point to which we will return.

Deliberation as transformative learning

We can gain a better understanding of what an even fuller, more complex and respective vision and experience of "learning" looks like by turning to the work of progressively oriented educational theorists who've sought to develop the theory and practices of "transformative learning." Geared in large part to adult education theory and practices, transformative learning is based on a constructivist understanding of action-oriented knowledge and social meaning. Rather than understanding learning as a process in which—in keeping with the Freierean banking model—teachers fill students' minds (construed as empty vessels) with the contents of their expert narratives about which the learners are supposedly either ignorant or misinformed, the teacher and students collaborate to create knowledge about the social world and develop courses of action geared to their own goals and interests related to that world (Shor 1996; Daloz 1999; Herman and Mandell 2004). In a transformational approach, the postempiricist teacher/professional and his or her student/clients cooperatively seek the justification of social knowledge in the sociocultural realm in which it is created. In this understanding, a claim is accepted or rejected as a result of shared discourses, in which social actors negotiate the meanings attached to information, stories, events, objects, and symbols. In effect, meaning is created through the knowledge that is constructed.

Transformative learning thus seeks to move learning from what Bateson (2000) described as first-order to second-order learning. Stated more concretely, such a re-thinking involves shifting the discussion from the particular context in which everyday learning occurs to the larger social order of which it is necessarily a part. Teachers become guides—facilitators—who assist learners in understanding and interpreting their own experiences within the framework of the economic and social forces that have shaped them (hooks 1994). Mills (2000) referred to the task as the "imaginative" process of "translating" biography into history; or, as Williams (1983) put it, through the process of learning, students come to understand the ways that the "structure of feeling" reflects the material and cultural bases of society.

For Mezirow (1991, 2000), the key theorist of transformational learning, the crucial task in creating social meaning—that is, in learning itself—is "becoming critically aware of one's own tacit assumptions and expectations and those of others and assessing their relevance for making an interpretation" of the ongoing social narratives, both one's own and those of others (Mezirow and Associates 2000: 4). Toward this end, he differentiates between meaning "perspectives" and meaning "schemes." The former constitute broadly conceived frameworks that provide an individual with basic orientations to objects, events, and ideas in the social world. Much like ideologies, they provide basic narrative understandings of how the world works and how it should work. Uncovering meaning perspectives requires a deeper form of self-reflection than the kind of thought upon which we rely in everyday life. Transforming a meaning perspective thus involves a process of becoming critically aware of how and why our assumptions have come to shape and constrain the way we perceive, narrate, and feel about our world, and thus changing the structures of habitual expectation to make possible a more inconclusive, discriminating, and integrative story upon which action can be based. Often this involves critical reflection upon so-called "distorted" premises sustaining one's underlying structure of understandings and expectations. Given the embeddedness of meaning perspectives in the very core of self-definition, such reflection is quite challenging; it often encounters significant resistance, including deeply felt emotional resistance.

Meaning schemes, on the other hand, are more concrete sets of understandings that emerge from meaning perspectives. They are oriented to specific beliefs, attitudes, and emotional reactions and can more easily be thought about and corrected. As such, they seldom require the kind of critical self-reflection necessary for the uncovering and exploration of meaning perspectives. As indicated earlier, it is at the level of the meaning schemes that most discussions of organizational learning take place. Following Revans (1982), the distinction can be understood as a difference between "objective reframing" and "subjective reframing." Objective reframing involves reflection on the assumptions of others as they self-evidently present themselves in specific narratives or in action-oriented problem-solving. That is, such assumptions are examined on their own terms. Subjective framing, on the other hand, involves deeper critical reflection on one's own assumptions about narratives pertaining to economic, political, cultural, and interpersonal systems. This deeper level of reflection necessarily touches on a less available, in effect, on a tacit level of knowing.

Here one can illustrate Mezirow's delineation of meaning by returning to Argyris's concept of double-loop learning. Within a particular meaning perspective, an active process of learning can confront particular beliefs, norms, and values related to first-order loop learning. Such learning examines these beliefs and norms that are part of a subordinate meaning scheme; it examines these beliefs and practices in terms of their instrumental or contributory implications for achieving a given set of organizational goals, such as making profits in the example above. But for "critical" learning to occur in the genuine sense of the term, such beliefs and values also have to be scrutinized against second-order learning criteria (Fischer 1995). Here they would be examined as well in terms of their implications for society more generally, particularly their implications for the way of life they offer to its members. That is, the very assumptions grounding the first-order ideas or understandings normally taken-for-granted would be identified and called into question.

Although transformative theory is not formally a theory of developmental stages, it does emphasize the importance of movement toward reflectivity in adulthood through educational interventions geared to the learner's ability and experience. Wildemeersch and Leirman (1988), for example, identify three phases in the development of transformation. The first is a "narrative dialogue," which tells a story or describes an action, characterizes interpersonal communication, and ensures the otherwise self-evident character of the social life-world by affirming or reaffirming our subjective and objective reality—that is, by making actions seem true and normal. This narrative dialogue focuses on the experienced world, which most actors take to be self-evident. In this world, there can be an intellectual and emotional apprehensiveness that seemingly settled issues may actually turn out to be unsettled, and thus new ideas can be seen as potential threats rather than welcome opportunities.

The second phase involves a threatening situation in the individual or group's life-world. In transformational theory, this is understood as the "dilemma" and becomes the very object of exploration. The task is to make apparent the narrative contradictions related to the anxiety-producing dilemma, or what has been called the "manifest situational contradictions." Here, conflict is the result of a disorienting dilemma. During this phase, a "transactional" conversation takes place, involving an analytic dialogue about the evidence and arguments pertaining to alternative viewpoints.

The third phase involves a critical discourse that consciously explores the relationship between the person's or group's own problematic situation and similar themes related to other places and possibilities. In this phase of transformational development, the learner perceives these problems and conflicts in the context of the larger social framework of which they are a part. Through such a process, the participants develop their reflective capacities to identify and interpret different, often competing, perspectives from alternative theoretical points of view. It holds out the possibility of the learner gaining an insight into the "ruptured situation" that can lead to a new perspective, even worldview, and a narrative to convey it (Loder 1981). As such, it involves a "revised narrative-dialogic process" through which disordered beliefs come to make sense. The result is a new story capable of better explaining the problematic situation, how it came to be, and what to do about it.

At this higher level, critical learning involves an essential epistemological component, or what Kitchener (1983: 230) calls "epistemic cognition." Such cognition refers to reflection on the nature of knowledge itself, its limits, degrees of uncertainty, and the criteria for knowing. It also involves learning to understand the ways in which deeper social meanings and the assumptions based on them structure the very ways the participants look at problems and issues. Participants, in short, learn to appreciate the normative undersides of knowledge otherwise simply taken for granted or, put in other terms, tacitly accepted as facts. In organization and policy, such reflection at times closely resembles discussions of how to best approach ill structured problems (those which do not have correct or best solutions).

From a transformative perspective, the basic task of the professional—as educator of students, clients, and citizens—is to facilitate a learning process which, once set in motion, can proceed on its own. The process has to be carefully designed in ways that help learners enlarge their own abilities to pose questions that concern and interest them and to assist in connecting them to the kinds of information and resources needed to aid them in finding answers. As Friere and Faundez (1989) describe it, "learning to question," or as Herman and Mandell (2004: ch. 3) put it, "asking questions" is central to the professional's repertoire. So too, Brookfield (1986: 3) describes facilitating transformational learning as a process of "challenging learners with alternative ways of interpreting their experience" and presenting them with "ideas and behaviors that cause them to examine critically their values, ways of acting, and the assumptions by which they live . . . " Teachers and students, experts and citizens "bring to the encounter experiences, attitudinal sets, and alternative ways of looking at their personal, professional, political, and recreational worlds, along with a multitude of differing purposes orientations and expectations."[15]

There is no specific textbook methodology for engaging in this kind of transformative learning.[16] Different practitioners discuss it in different terms, based in significant part on their own experiences. At the same time, it is generally agreed that an authentic, democratic discursive process depends on particular conditions for its realization. To participate fully and freely, people have to find themselves in situations in which they are free of coercive pressures, have accurate information, are able to assess arguments and examine evidence, can be empathetically open to others' points of view, are able to carefully attend to how others think and feel, and have equal chances to participate in the deliberative process

[15] The medium of this interaction is a complex dialogic examination of the dominant narratives available to explain an existing reality and the problems it poses. Recognizing that "the personalities of the individual involved, the contextual setting for the educational transformation, and the prevailing political climate affect the nature and form of learning," such a dialogue can be likened to the development of a dramatic story in which the philosophies and priorities of the "chief players interact continuously to influence the nature, direction and form of learning" (Brookfield 2005). Encouraging and sustaining this kind of narrative interaction becomes the "educator's" challenge, one that can be supported by a range of strategies, all of which need to encourage dialogue, questioning, and critical reflection on what is taken for granted.

[16] There is, in short, no single way to approach this process of deliberation—of transformational learning. Basically, it is agreed that any approach has to be imaginatively conceived and based on the particular circumstances of the situation to be dealt with, in terms of experiences and educational levels of the participants, cultural assumptions, institutional power dynamics, and the like. Beyond this, its one common element is discourse, understood as the specialized use of dialogue in search of common understandings and assessments of interpretations or beliefs. It involves assessing reasons—both normative and factual—advanced for supporting evidence and arguments and by examining alternative meaning perspectives. When such discourse is both encouraged and nourished, and thus becomes the very stuff of deliberation, it can tap individual and collective experiences in ways that lead to deeper understandings and more informed judgments.

(Mezirow and Associates 2000: 13). Put in yet other terms, such conditions of "ideal speech" can never be fully realized, but the criteria can be used to judge some discursive spaces as better than others, and to assess whether or not enough of the conditions are met to even enter into such a process.[17]

But discourse in transformational learning is more than epistemology; it is grounded in ontological considerations as well. In this regard, as Kegan (1994) writes, discourse is essential to the basic human yearning for social recognition and identity and the related desire for a sense of agency. Discourse, as such, provides a forum in which social actors can "find their voice" within a community of participants. Indeed, as a precondition for free and full participation, participative deliberation and agency are inherently dependent on the beliefs and traditions of the social community. For this reason, discourse always reflects the more general patterns of social and political relationships in the society. That is, the very issues that critical learning seeks to open up are, in important ways, already embedded in the process of discourse itself.

Freire (1970, 1974, 1998), the most influential innovator of critical pedagogy, approaches such discourse through what he calls "problematization," or problem-posing, which is basic to opening up narrative contradictions. For Freire, problematization is the direct antithesis of the kinds of technocratic problem solving that has long defined professional expertise. In the technocratic approach, the expert establishes some distance from reality, analyzes it into component parts, devises means for resolving difficulties in the most efficient way, and then dictates the strategy or policy to be followed. Such problem solving, as Freire makes clear, distorts the totality of human experience by reducing it to those dimensions that are amenable to treatment, as mere difficulties to be solved, or as impediments to be overcome. To problematize, on the other hand, is to help people codify into narrative symbols an integrated story of reality that, in the course of its development, can generate a critical consciousness capable of empowering them to alter their relations to both the physical and social worlds.[18]

---

[17] For a practical application of transformative learning as communicative learning in the context of resource management, see Sims and Sinclair (2008).

[18] Problem-posing represents a fundamental challenge to the traditional-student/professional relationship. As Freire (1973: 67) puts it, in the context of critical dialogue, "the teacher-of-the-students and the students-of-the-teacher cease to exist and a new term emerges: teacher-students with student-teachers." No longer is the teacher merely the one who narrates his or her knowledge to passive students. Now, the teacher him/herself also becomes one who

Essential to the facilitation of empowerment, then, is the creation of institutional and intellectual conditions that help people pose questions in their own ordinary or everyday language and decide the issues important to them. The central focus of such models is to innovate discursive problem-posing procedures that assist learners in the exploration of their own problems and interests. An inquiry, in this regard, is understood to be something that learners take up on their own or with others who share those interests or who are grappling with similar kinds of questions. From a critical/transformational learning point of view, with increased access to relevant information, with greater freedom to question, and with more opportunities to explore issues and dilemmas pertinent to them, learning of all sorts will become more authentic and will deepen.

The facilitation of critical learning, to be sure, involves some difficult questions pertaining to interests, ethics, and ideology. Although clearly political in regard to process, content and outcome, a commitment to such dialogue is not in and of itself to be confused with a commitment to a specific doctrine or ideology. For the facilitator committed to democratic values, educational facilitation and political proselytizing are geared to fundamentally different objectives. Political ideologists accept their beliefs as the one true way of thinking about the world—proselytizing with a predetermined definition of the successful outcome. From such a perspective, divergent views are simply dismissed as wrong thinking, bad faith, or false consciousness. By contrast, the facilitator may passionately advance ideas about how people "should" learn and act, but such views must themselves be presented to learners as objects of critical scrutiny, indeed, of the same kind of critical questioning to which the educator has subjected other views of which he or she is personally critical. The end of the encounter, in other words, is not acceptance by the participants of a set of preordained values and beliefs. Rather, such educational experiences (in whatever social context they might occur) pose myriad problems and questions for critical dialogue and group consensus-formation.

Reorienting professional practice

At this point, one might raise the question: Can this discussion of the foundations of a critical pedagogy be transferred to the practices of

is taught in an ensuing dialogue with the students who, at the same time, are learning how to teach. Jointly responsible for the learning process, they become "co-producers of knowledge."

the policy-oriented professionals? The task is not as difficult as some might imagine. There are, in fact, a number of contributions to the literature on policy and the professions that already open up the topic. Perhaps the best know examples in the mainstream literature on professional expertise are found in the writings of Donald Schön (1983). Writing about "the crisis of confidence in professional knowledge," Schön set out an alternative concept of problem-setting that recognizes both the role of normative assumptions and of tacit knowledge. Problem-setting, as he spells it out, is quite analogous to Freire's concept of problematization or problem-posing. Although he does not take the critical stance that Freire espouses, the implications of Schön's analysis for the professional-client relationship are remarkably similar.

Schön is fundamentally concerned about the lack of an open and authentic expert-client interaction that has characterized the practices of the organizational and policy sciences. For him, recognition of this lack is key to the reconstruction of expert practices. Like Freire, Schön attributes the failure of professional policy expertise to its outmoded adherence to the technical model of rationality and to the superior-subordinate expert–client relationship that it requires. Giving rise to one-dimensional, distorted communications between practitioners and their clients, the relationship impedes the activity most critical to affect practices, what Schön refers to as "problem-setting."

Problem-setting is non-technical in nature and contrasts sharply with problem-solving. Whereas the latter involves technical knowledge and skills, such as those typically associated with policy science methodologies (e.g. cost-benefit analysis, systems analysis, program evaluation), problem-setting is fundamentally normative and qualitative. In technical analysis, values and goals are taken as given; in problem-setting, analysis focuses on their discovery and identification. Indeed, at times, problem-setting involves the consensual shaping of new value orientations. An inherently creative exercise, problem-setting can neither be explained nor taught from the technical (positivist) perspective, which informs much of professional practice. In this sense, problem-setting is better understood as an art than a science.

In more specific terms, problem-setting concerns two interrelated tasks: the determination of the relevant problem situations to be addressed and the theoretical normative "frames" that structure and shape our basic understandings of and discourses about particular policy issues, including the criteria appropriate for their evaluation (Schön and Rein 1994). Analytically preceding technical problem solving, problem-setting requires professionals to initiate what Schön calls a "conversation with the situation." Focusing in particular on naming situations and defining the problems that arise in them, "reflection" necessitates a new epistemological orientation. The quantitative mode of reason that shaped policy inquiry must, in short, make room for more interpretive and narrative modes of qualitative reasoning. Toward this end, Schön (1983: 296–7) calls for a new "reflective contract" between the professional and his or her clients. In this contract, the client and the practitioner agree to enter into a joint inquiry (in effect, a collaboration) relevant to a situation for which the client is seeking help.

Around the same time that Schön was developing these ideas, another appeal to critical learning was put forward by Hirschhorn (1979). Similarly directing attention to the "crisis of the professions" and what to do about it, Hirshhorn's work deals more with the socio-institutional aspects of collaborative inquiry in the social service professions. He argued that such professionals should facilitate the ability of their clients to determine their own interests and to engage in strategies to help them find their own solutions. Focusing in particular on the social, intellectual, and emotional distance that separates the professions from their clients' experiential lifeworlds, Hirschhorn has argued for the need for experts to get closer to the interests and concerns of those they serve. Indeed, the expert's "distance" from the client has often been the source of strident disagreements when it comes to defining the client's social situation, as well as identifying who should have the responsibility for determining the problem. Such struggles invariably raise the question of social control, often leading to acrimonious polemics about the professional's role in the service-to-delivery process.[19]

Essential to the facilitation of empowerment, then, is the creation of institutional and intellectual conditions that help people pose questions in their own ordinary or everyday language and decide upon the issues important to them. Theorists interested in developing these concepts have most typically turned to models of social learning and discourse. The

---

[19] For Hirschhorn, the expert must become a facilitator of authentic client learning. This involves understanding "the conditions for client learning," in particular, designing and facilitating "the environment within which clients develop their own conceptions of satisfactory roles." In short, "professionals must become experts in how clients learn, clarify and decide." The "emphasis is on establishing the institutional conditions within which clients can draw on their own individual and collective agencies to solve their problems." The important exchange in this process is the one conducted between group members. Much like the critical educator/facilitator/mentor described above, Hirschhorn's (1979: 187) "professional acts as programmer, mobilizer of resources and consultant to a self-exploration and learning process on the part of groups members."

central focus of such models is now to innovate "inquiring systems" that assist learners in the "problematization" and exploration of their own problems and interests.[20]

Some will point out the difficulties, even authority, of public administrative agencies to engage in such activities. Given the traditional emphasis on top–down authority and on technical rationality and instrumental analysis, this criticism cannot simply be dismissed. But for those who challenge this orientation by calling for more participatory forms of public administration and policymaking, such a citizen-oriented model is an important step toward democratizing modern governance.

Even here, though, there are other relevant groups in the policy process that are uninhibited by such constraints. Indeed, much of the work related to second-order problem posing (or "conscientization" as Freire calls it) has been the product of efforts of social movements. It is one of the reasons that the discussion of participatory inquiry and transformative learning was stronger in the1970s and early 1980s than it is today. Those were periods when social movements—civil rights, environmental, feminist, and peace movements in particular—and movement intellectuals experimented with such alternative practices. As noted in Chapter 2, in the conservative years that have followed, social movements have largely faded from public attention. But, at the same time, another set of independent actors, partly spawned by the earlier movements, have come to play a central role in the newer focus on governance. Many of these "nongovernmental actors" (NGOs) are free of the outmoded kinds of constraints that still define public administration. In fact, many of them are not only open to such participatory experiments, they actively engage in them. They have become potentially significant consumers and practitioners of transformative learning and of its collaborative practices.

---

[20] Another way to understand the logic of the process is through Fischer's (1995) model of policy deliberation and reflection referred to earlier in Part II. This work offers a specific framework for understanding the epistemological connections involved in shifting the emphasis from first-order meanings and arguments, constituted as "technical verification" and "situational validation," to second-order meanings specified as "societal vindication" and "ideological critique." In the context of policy evaluation, this work shows how the task of a comprehensive evaluation of an action requires the examination of particular policies, programs and practices in terms of both their functional consequences and implications for the larger system of which they are part, as well as in terms of the values and ideological beliefs which undergird that system. The process involves an assessment that ranges from concrete actions situated in particular contexts up through the critiques of a particular social system and the alternative ways of life they might replace. Fischer (2000, 2003) then attaches this logic to a practice of "participatory policy analysis," in which citizens and experts collaboratively pursue the discursive implications of the informal logic underlying the level of evaluation.

Professional education and training

Transformative learning poses some sophisticated challenges for professional education. One concerns the educational curriculum. Once we recognize that this kind of teaching (whatever its context) is more a creative art than a science, we venture into unknown pedagogical territory. Scientific methodology texts can be organized like simple cookbooks. An art form is different. Not only are there no formulas, but also less is known about the creative impulse itself and about the kinds of experiences in which it might be nourished. How, for example, do we educate policy analysts to appreciate the range of human virtues or the boundaries of folly? How do we develop practitioners who can intuitively sense openings and opportunities to gain insights into complex human affairs? How do we convince professionals that their expertise is often only tentative, that grappling with questions and a wide-range of meanings and interpretations is at the very heart of their work? How do we encourage policy analysts to recognize and take seriously the fact that their clients, too, bring their own valuable knowledge to the table? If there are answers to these kinds of questions, they no doubt include greater exposure to the creative arts, to history, literature, and to an array of cultural studies. They certainly imply the need for serious exploration of areas well beyond what is typically included in the "education," or even more narrowly, the "training" of a professional.

Included among these areas of necessary inquiry is one requirement that is relatively straightforward. In very immediate terms, the professional–client collaboration requires the expert to have special knowledge of the citizen/client's needs, interests, values, understandings, and lived experiences. Toward this end, procedural knowledge about how to approach this work has been gained from numerous projects designed to re-socialize professional to the client's "natural setting." Gottlieb and Farquharson (1985), for example, have spelled out the elements of a pedagogical strategy designed to accommodate the student/practitioner to the ways citizens handle their own health and welfare needs. Most important is "the need first to undermine the professional's trust and beliefs in the ascendancy to technology, and force a reexamination of a professional enterprise that casts nonprofessionals into the subservient role of client or patient." Specifically, professionals must gain first-hand knowledge of encounters with self-help groups and other collective projects. They must "get acquainted with local residents who have animated and enabled others to take into their own hands the responsibility for effecting change;" and they must learn firsthand "the empowering impact of a mutual-aid group." And often, such knowledge and insight comes only with patient listening; it does not come quickly or easily.

Acknowledging the interests, the world views, the ways of thinking, and especially the concerns and questions of the nonprofessional—in effect, acknowledging both the professional and nonprofessional as adult learners—involves accepting a more egalitarian relationship, which places unique social-psychological demands on the professional (Shor 1996). This consideration is deeply rooted in our basic socialization and is not to be underestimated. Intellectuals and professional knowledge workers generally are in their positions by virtue of economic and social status as much as a result of any particular aptitude. Although they are the ones who have to provide the leadership (or perhaps more appropriately here, the guidance) in critical learning, such people can also suffer from inflated egos and from their own exaggerated and sometimes distorted views of their own expertise. Moreover, their commitment to social causes can be quite fragile in the face of new attractive career opportunities higher up the professional ladder. All of this illustrates just how difficult it is to question the very hierarchy upon which professional education itself is based. (Emotional dimensions of these complex relations are further examined in Chapter 10.)

This is to say that if such new forms of cooperative learning are to work, they have to be conducted by people with high levels of personal awareness, a willingness to accept the tentativeness of their own conclusions, and with an interest in acknowledging and evaluating their tacit assumptions. This work also requires a tolerance for ambiguities, a desire to listen to ideas and feelings often very different from what they best know, and, overall, a genuine reflective spirit. Indeed, one of the most important but often overlooked psychological dimensions is the ability or skill of finding ways to avoid one's own defensive responses to the difficult process of self-reflection. It means confronting the social, emotional, and intellectual distances that separate the professional from the client's experiential life-world. If we take seriously the various levels of resistance introduced above and the power of the tacit dimension to mold our basic ways of seeing and being, the "training" to teach such interpersonal skills, or what Torbert (1991) defines as "transformational leadership," will need to be rigorous. It is a formidable task.

In curricular terms, then, alternative professional training means building-in educational experiences that bring professionals into closer contact with clients' everyday experience, language, and culture. Such experiences must be designed to wean professionals away form their faith in technique, their adherence to hierarchy, and their reliance on the ideologies of expertise that they use to give legitimacy to their feelings of superiority over those with whom they need to collaborate.

The role of the educator-as-facilitator has to be *learned*, especially given the patterns of socialization that members of contemporary society have internalized. Professional practitioners of all kinds not only have to learn how to make topics and materials more accessible to the client, but also to learn how to act to help move the discussion along in meaningful and constructive ways. There is nothing simple about this, as it requires a form of artful orchestration and imaginative structuring that avoids subtle condescension and sometimes rather overt manipulation. The situation is made even more difficult by the fact that discussions touching upon social-political problems and policies often move progressively toward ideological critique. It is difficult to enter this territory without being accused of advancing a particular ideological perspective.[21]

Although clearly political, as noted throughout this discussion, a commitment to on-going dialogue is not to be confused with a commitment to a specific doctrine or ideology. For the transformative practitioner, for the professional committed to the guiding of a deliberative process who is firmly committed to democratic values, educational facilitation and political proselytizing are geared to fundamentally different objectives. Yet, although neither the educator nor the student can foresee the outcomes of the deliberative process, nor the specific ways in which the actions resulting from the process might be risky to those involved, assuming that they are possible, the initiation and facilitation of transformative learning must follow a set of ethical guidelines that, themselves, need to be articulated, debated and agreed upon. Perhaps as a starting point one can say this: Such a learning process is ethical as long as the educator does not attempt to force or manipulate learners/participants into accepting his or her own perspective, but instead encourages learners to choose freely from among a wide range of relevant viewpoints, some of which the teacher/professional him/herself might never have considered. However, such a professional educator is not bound to help learners carry out actions that conflict with the educator's own code of ethics, even if the learners decided upon these actions after rational discourse.

---

[21] Thus, for example, those who focus on the critique of capitalism as the basic social form within which policies of all kinds are situated can be easily identified as proselytizers. This raises subtle and not so subtle ethical questions that can easily close off important conversations that need to take place.

In this regard, adult educators need to have sufficient self-knowledge and sensitivity to others to be able to help learners deal with common personal and interpersonal conflicts in meaning perspectives that often create barriers to negotiation of difficult issues and life transitions. And, too, educators need to be able to distinguish between these participants and those whose personal problems require professional psychotherapeutic attention. Learning to acknowledge and work within the limits of one's understanding and one's role is, no doubt, a key element in the ongoing development of any transformative professional.

Conclusions

This chapter has explored a number of key issues relevant to the theory of deliberative democracy, notably the ways the very nature of deliberation needs to be better linked to how we think about learning. Through these issues, the discussion has sought to shed light on the self-transformative potentials of citizen deliberation. Three strands of thinking have, in this regard, received special attention. The first is the postempiricist recognition that there are hidden dimensions behind our social constructions and that, following Polanyi's lead, it is crucial to become aware of the ideas, values, logic, commitments that ground what professional experts, politicians, and citizens do and take-for-granted. That is, for Polanyi and others, the very creation of knowledge is bound up in intersubjective understandings that frame the thinking and activities of a particular "fiduciary community" and which, in most instances, remain at the "tacit" level. Such commonly shared tacit knowledge is not only necessary to all scientific work (and thus, too, to the work of social and policy analysts), but also to communities and organizations that necessarily depend upon such taken-for-granted learning.

The second strand taken up in the chapter has concerned the possibility that the workplace, the organization, the community group—deliberative bodies of all kinds—can serve as sites, discursive spaces, for a different kind of learning, for so-called "transformational" learning; that is, for the careful reflection upon the very tacit level that most often goes unnoticed. By "problematizing" what is taken for granted and by opening up discourse to new interpretive possibilities, participants are empowered to ask questions and to explore problems and concerns from which their voices had previously been excluded. To re-imagine such experiences as inherently educational, as opportunities for critical dialogue and new learning, suggests that such a democratization of knowledge can potentially begin a process of citizen education that can transform social relations of all kinds.

Finally, we have suggested that transformative learning cannot be carried out through the structures and relations of teaching and learning upon which we most often rely. Here again, the tacit needs to be made explicit by an ongoing process of rethinking the role of the educator, the trainer, the analyst, and of the policymaker. Instead of a hierarchical model steeped in simple dichotomies of teacher/student or expert/client, new models introduce the role of the facilitator (or in other contexts, the "mentor"), whose task is not to preach, perform or dictate, but rather to shape conversations, mediate discussions, and structure opportunities for deepening dialogue.

Such a direction is challenging because institutions and identities depend upon systems of authority, of monologue, and of rigid divisions between who knows and who needs to learn. We have tried to show that it is also difficult because training itself will have to change in order to make room for the kind and breadth of new learning necessary for professional development. And central to cooperative, dialogical forms of training (and to the interdisciplinary thrust that any new professional curriculum needs to incorporate) is an abiding theme: that whatever the particular form and content of the training will be, its goal must be a fuller and more critical view of the role of the professional, as well as a deeper appreciation of the ideas, motivations, interests, and emotions of those we are claiming to want to understand and help.

In the remaining two chapters we explore the implications of these issues in more detail. Before taking up the complicated and least understood questions pertaining to the role of emotion in the deliberative process, the topic of the final chapter of the book, we next explore the ways such factors tacitly influence the intersubjective dynamics of deliberative spaces.

9

Deliberative Empowerment: The Cultural Politics of Discursive Space

In earlier chapters the focus was mainly on the theoretical issues related to participation, expertise, and deliberation in civil society. But we also saw in the discussion about deliberative research in Chapter 2 that there are practical lessons to learn from concrete cases. One of the most influential and much discussed attempts to analyze these experiences has been the work of Fung and Wright (2001, 2003). They have examined a range of cases designed to promote active political involvement of the citizenry and have labored to sort out what works and what does not. Acknowledging that complexity makes it difficult for people to participate in policy deliberation, they speculate that "the problem may have more to do with the specific design of our institutions than with the task." Toward this end, they have explored a range of empirical responses to this challenge that constitute real-world experiences in the redesign of democratic institutions. They have looked at deliberative innovations that elicit the energy and influence of ordinary people (often drawn from the lowest strata of society) in the pursuit of solutions to the problems that plague them.[1]

---

[*] This chapter elaborates and extends a theoretical perspective that draws in part on materials that appeared in Fischer (2000) and Fischer (2006) "Participatory Governance as Deliberative Empowerment: The Cultural Politics of Discursive Space," The American Review of Public Administration, 36: 24–31.

[1] They have focused on five participatory projects: community groups in Chicago that have substantial power over public schools and neighborhood policing; a regional job training partnership in Wisconsin that brings together a number of organizations in an effort to provide training that helps workers turn jobs into meaningful careers; a habitat conservation planning project under the US Endangered Species Act that convenes stakeholders to empower them to develop ecosystem governance arrangements; the participatory budgeting process of Porto Alegre, Brazil that enables citizens to participate directly in determining the city budget; and local participation reforms basic to the planning process in Kerala and West Bengal, India.

Even though these reforms vary in their organizational designs, policy issues, and scope of activities, as the authors note, they all seek to deepen the abilities of ordinary citizens to participate effectively in the discussion of programs and policies relevant to their own lives. From their common features they isolate a set of characteristics that they define as "empowered participatory governance." The principles they draw from these cases are designed to enable the progressive "colonization of the state" and its agencies. Relying on the participatory capacities of empowered citizens to engage in reason-based action-oriented decision-making, the strategy and its principles are offered as a radical political step toward a more democratic society.

As a product of this work, they isolate three political principles, their design characteristics, and one primary background condition. The background enabling condition states that there should be rough equality of power among the participants. The political principles refer to (1) need of such experiments to address a particular practical problem; (2) that the deliberation rely upon the empowered involvement of ordinary citizens; and (3) that each experiment employs reasoned deliberation in the effort to solve the problems under consideration. The institutional design characteristic specify (1) the devolution of decision-making and the powers of implementation power to local action-oriented units; (2) that these local units be connected to one another and to the appropriate levels of state responsible for supervision, resource allocation, innovation, and problem-solving; and (3) that the experiments "colonize and transform" state institutions in ways that lead to the restructuring of the administrative agencies responsible for dealing with these problems. The political power of these local units to implement the programmatic results of their discussions will thus come from state authorization itself.

Fung and Wright contrast these procedural features of empowered participatory governance with the more fleeting democratic experiences of elections or social movements that mobilize citizens for a particular purpose and then fade away. The goal, as they spell it out, is to learn how to create spaces in which citizens can meaningfully engage in shaping decisions together with state actors through durable forms of practice that advance more responsive governance. Although such procedural principles are commendable in themselves, they also have to be judged by their consequences, in particular their contribution to the effectiveness of state action, social equity, and sustained participation. Toward this end, Fung and Wright set out an empirical agenda for further testing and refining the principles of deliberative design. The remainder of this chapter is an effort to help contribute to that research agenda by examining more specifically one of their cases, that of participatory governance in Kerala. Seeking to further the advance of such deliberative empowerment, it illustrates the ways such structures depend on political-cultural preconditions.

Deliberative Space: Social meaning and identity politics

The approach here is not to deny the importance of Fung and Wright's contribution to the discussion of participatory governance, but rather to argue for the need to supplement the structural and procedural design principles with an examination of the underlying social and cultural realities in the political contexts to which they are applied. It is, in fact, an argument that applies to much of the theory and research about deliberative democracy. If one sets aside their more progressive political goals for the moment, Fung and Wright's basic focus is not dissimilar to that taken by other researchers dealing with deliberative democracy. In large part, the emphasis is on the design of deliberative institutions, in particular the distribution of rights and powers. These questions pose more specific procedural issues about who gets to participate in a deliberative process, what they can or will talk about, how the the topic is approached, when they will do it, and the like. With regard to basic goals, attention has been given to a mix of issues: increasing public participation, increasing the legitimacy of the policy decision-making process, providing officials with information, holding public official accountable, generating effective policies, improving the political skills of citizen participants, and the like. Much less prevalent, if not missing, has been attention to the sociocultural and social psychological dimensions of deliberations, particular under conditions of conflict (Warren 2008).

Acknowledging the importance of institutional structures and procedures within a given territory or space, it is argued here that deliberative investigation needs to also understand the sociocultural practices that give meaning to these spaces for the social actors in them. While it is important to analyze the material and procedural factors that enable participation, it should not be done at the expense of the underlying social conditions that are inherently necessary for participatory governance to work. Deeper political and subjective factors related to the intersubjective aspects of participation have to be included.[2] As the very different literatures of both postmodernism and participatory research show, the kinds of design structures and procedures suggested by Fung and Wright can offer an opening for participatory empowerment, but they cannot ensure such participation itself. These literatures, through their emphasis on social movements, identity struggles, and the politics of resistance, show successful empowerment to be determined by the kinds of intersubjective understandings and normative politics that take place within a social space. Here we discover what might be called the "microcultural politics of social space." This is largely an intersubjective politics of meaning driven in significant part by a politics of social identity.

The connection between political governance, identity, and space is introduced to mainstream political science by March and Olsen (1995: 6). In their view, political governance "is organized through the interdependent obligations of political identities." The governance of political space, whether large or small, is about "affecting the frameworks within which citizens and officials act and politics occurs, and which shape the identities and institutions of civil society." Even more important for present concerns, however, is the emphasis of identity and space in the literatures on social movements and NGOs. In these discussions the "civil society," defined as the space between government and citizens, is typically the focus of the exploration. It denotes "the sphere of private institutions, organizations, associations, and individuals protected by, but outside the scope of state interventions" (Nash 2000: 273). Much of the analysis concentrates on efforts to create spaces, make room for different voices to be heard, and to enable people to occupy spaces that were previously denied to them. But it is in the more explicitly postmodern literature that we find the most fully developed understanding of identity politics and the creation of social space. In this work, an understanding of the dynamics of the participation requires a more qualitative and subjective conceptualization of space. Political space, from this perspective, is not just filled up with competing interests, but rather is understood as something that is created, opened, and shaped by social understandings.

The postmodern perspective thus more fully shifts the understanding of politics to culture, social meaning, and identity politics. Where standard political analysis examines the structures, practices, and methods of state institutions that organize the play of power, postmodern "cultural

---

[2] In a discussion of Fung and Wright's contribution, Mansbridge (2003: 188–9) also points to the need to take into account the role of emotion in deliberation. It is the topic to which we turn in the next chapter.

politics" emphasizes more fundamentally the discursive construction of the meanings and identities of the actors, institutions, and practices inherent to it (Jordan and Weedon 1995). Through an analysis of discursive practices it focuses, for example, on how particular discourses and narratives make some things important and others insignificant, how they include some participants and exclude or marginalize others. Moreover, where traditional political analysis separates politics and culture, cultural politics denies the separation. Cultural politics, as such, explores the signifying practices through which identities, social relations, and rules are contested, subverted, and possibly transformed. It understands these struggles, although less visible and often latent, to be primary concerns underlying and shaping the other more visible and manifest topics and issues under discussion.

Fundamental here is the interplay of power and difference in the making of social spaces and the microcultural politics of the interactions within them. In this view, space is essential to the exercise of power (Bourdieu 1977; Foucault 1986: 252; Lefebvre 1991). Never socially neutral, space enables some actions—including the possibility of new actions—and blocks or constrains others. It is a perspective that calls attention to the importance of analyzing the underlying and implicit assumptions about social and political relations that organize and constitute spaces for participation.[3] To speak only of structural arrangements, such as centralization and decentralization, neglects the very different kinds of understandings that can configure the construction of a decentered space.[4]

More specifically, the meanings that constitute a space are carried and conveyed through discourses which produce and replicate power relations

[3] Social relations, in this theoretical framework, exist only in and through space—having no reality outside the sites in which they are lived, experienced, and practiced. Attention is drawn to how spaces come to be defined, perceived, and animated. Particular ways of thinking about society are seen to be played out in the ways that spaces are organized and occupied, as well as in how they are conceived and perceived. The works of theorists such as Lefebvre thus call attention to the importance of analyzing the underlying and implicit assumptions about the social and political relations that organize and constitute spaces for participation.

[4] Especially interesting is the way Lefebvre shows how the traces of the production of a space are etched into that space. Or, as Bourdieu argues, the traces of prior interaction are so ingrained in a social space and generally unquestioned that they can be understood to be literally embodied in a particular context. "Officialized spaces," to use Bourdieu's (1977) term, such as those created for public consultation or user groups, always exist alongside unofficial spaces and the spaces of everyday life, just as invited spaces exit alongside those claimed and shaped by a range of other actors. Indeed, people bring with them into a new space the collection of associations and experiences they have gained from their encounters in other spaces and employ them to decide what the new space is about and how they should orient themselves to it.

within the spacial context.[5] By formally or informally specifying whose knowledge and meanings count, the discourses in a particular space enable or hinder what is said and how it is understood in a particular space (Foucault 1986; Fraser 1989). For example, the way "participation" is used and understood in a particular discourse determines what "subject positions" are available for participants to take up within particular spaces, thus bounding the possibilities for both inclusion and agency. Whether they are constructed as "citizens," "beneficiaries," "clients," or "users" influences what people are perceived to be entitled to know, to decide or contribute, as well as the perceived obligations of those who seek to involve them. Moreover, the kinds of narratives, artifacts, analyses, and action plans emerging out of these spaces may tell, and indeed be *made* to tell, very different stories.

A good deal of the literature on creating spaces is focused on relocating the poor within the prevailing order and elucidating the ways in which socially imposed identities can be resisted. The location of the socially marginal is taken, as such, to be a site for radical possibilities; it is a "space of resistance." Haraway (1991) speaks of the "marginal perspective" and local knowledge as sources of insight. Spaces that repress or marginalize people become transformed into spaces in which they recognize, assert, and expand their own identities.

Social spaces, then, can be understood as woven together by a set of discursive relationships that determine the meanings and understandings of the identities within them. Through these discursive practices the power relations of the surrounding societal context are brought into the social space. Toward this end, it is necessary to make explicit the less visible discursive power configurations that permeate and produce these and other spaces. The first and most obvious question in the assessment of participatory initiatives is to ask who determines the form of participation that takes place in a given space—who initiates, chooses the methods, and

[5] Focusing on the "architecture" of social space, Foucault (1986) has demonstrated how the discursive replication of the relations of power within an institutional space is a means of controlling it. To take a simple but familiar illustration, the way in which space in a newly created arena is managed—sitting in rows, for example, with the women at the back of the room—makes it easier for some people to speak and be heard than others. Similarly, his work makes clear that the different associations people might have of a particular place will often produce different dynamics. The participatory event held in a different location can easily produce different effects, as the introduction of a prayer or an address by a local leader can, for instance, influence the shape of a deliberation. Through such spatial manipulations political leaders can subtly reproduce the old rules of the game within spaces, such as political committees or public consultations, restricting the engagement of people without status, confidence, or familiarity.

takes part. But the second and more difficult question concerns what the people who enter these spaces bring with them. What are their thoughts and beliefs about what is "really going on" in the space and how do they strategically orient themselves to these understandings? Beyond official statements of intentions to participate, what do the people want to gain, what are their expectations, how do they perceive the costs and benefits associated with the activity? Here one needs something akin to the situational logic of phenomenology. The deliberative situation itself has to be entered to uncover these real but unspoken meanings shaped by larger political relations (class, race, and gender relations, among others) in society (Scott 1986, 1990).

The social-subjective side of deliberation: Informal rules and practices

Beyond these kinds of theoretical understandings of space, we also begin to find empirical research that identifies the importance of such intersubjective relationships. Goersdorf (2006, 2007), for example, found that many of the participants in a scenario workshop spent a good deal of time to thinking about the intersubjective relationships that shape and guide the deliberative process. Although they didn't use words like "intersubjective," they often devoted as much or more time to thinking about and discussing subjectively oriented questions related to social recognition, identity, status, and power underlying the workshop's procedures than they did the substantive topic at hand.

This finding was based on Goersdorf's participatory observations of a scenario workshop in Germany that focused on future developments in biomedical research and their societal implications, particularly as they pertained to commercialization of biomedical procedures and products. Funded by the German Federal Ministry of Education and Research, the project invited thirty-four people to "an experiment on how to start a conversation at eye level between experts and lay citizens," the results of which were to be publicly presented, discussed by invited journalists and politicians, and published online and in journals. Formally stated, the workshop's goal was to assist the participants in dealing with a complicated scientific issue. In the course of their deliberations over a specific period of time, they were to develop their own policy positions on the goals and uses of biomedical science. From the perspective of the ministry and the researchers it engaged to organize and facilitate the workshop, as Goersdorf explains, "the objective was to better understand the conditions for citizens to articulate their point of view drawing on their own abilities and resources." The hope was to understand society's resources by assessing laypeoples' potentially valuable "webs of knowledge' and the ways they might be made available for policy decisionmakers.

At the outset, the organizers provided a clear set of formal rules for structuring and guiding the inquiry, including specific procedural steps that the participants were to follow at each stage of the deliberation. All of this seemed straightforward in the beginning. In the course of following these prescribed rules, however, tensions emerged between the objectives as stated by the organizers and various intersubjective experiences that arose in carrying them out. Although the formal procedures were designed to facilitate communication about the topic, and to anticipate disputes among participants about specific substantive issues, the participants' efforts to express divergent social perspectives gave rise to conflicts about their social status, in particular about individual recognition and the social identities of lay participants and experts. The possibility of such conflicts had been either ignored or suppressed by the formal procedures.

Specifically, the tension emerged as a result of two competing mandates, one formal and the other informal. On the formal side, the assignment of the participants was to bring their own individual social perspectives to bear on the process, which most were enthusiastically eager to do. More informally, however, practical aspects of various unwritten procedures related to time and consensus formulation pressured members of the group to act less individualistically in an effort to produce a common or collective report. In an effort to stay on plan, the organizers regularly urged the participants to move expediently through the procedural steps, leaving too little time for an adequate expression of their own personal views. This left more than a few people with alternative opinions or unsettled issues feeling shut off. Beyond time pressures, some felt that their views didn't fit into various descriptive social categories introduced by the planners. There was thus a general sense that decisions were taken at each step without sufficient discussion of the issues as they saw them.

The result was a feeling among these participants that they weren't being taken seriously, which in turn generated frustration. Feeling "marginalized" and "unrespected," they began seriously to criticize the process in terms related to social status and power: Who was in charge? Who was permitted to say what, and so on? A development that might be likened to Wolin's (1994) concept of "breakout democracy," these concerns encouraged a form of social resistance that raised basic questions about the deliberative process, even portending at points to put the whole workshop in jeopardy. In face of such disappointment, more than a few participants threatened to drop out only half way through the project. Having begun the workshop with the sense of being empowered—"this is our chance to say what we think, our opportunity to be heard"—they ended up feeling misunderstood and alienated. It led some to conclude that the project had failed.

This is only one case, as the author himself notes, but it did uncover the sort of thing that would be anticipated by a social-subjective conceptualization of discursive space. Where most research on deliberation has focused on its outcomes—Could the participants understand the issues? Were the findings informative? Were the outcomes used by policy decision-makers?—Goersdorf uncovered a need to broaden the researchers' focus to include the social-subjective realities underlying the process. Only then could a better understanding be gained of what is actually going on in deliberative fora such as the scenario workshop. As Goersdorf contends, future research needs to open up the black box and look at the less visible, often less openly spoken micro dynamics of deliberation. Stated more simply, investigators need to understand how the participants relate subjectively to the objective dimensions of the process. How do they enact their own subjectivities? How are they reflected through the stories they more covertly tell one another about their experiences and impressions?[6] And the like.

Goersdorf concludes by offering some prescriptions for the designers of deliberative processes. Most importantly, they should focus on the ways in which their embedded assumptions can differ from expectations and suppositions that the participants bring with them or develop over the course of the event. After they have created the initial discursive arrangements, they must be careful to consider how the participants might rightly or wrongly interpret the underlying assumptions differently. When such subjectivities go unattended, as his research shows, emerging discrepancies can silently evolve into major tensions that jeopardize the process. To avoid this, he argues, organizers must do more than just act as discursive facilitators of the ongoing substantive discussions. In addition, they need to incorporate time and space for the participants to reflect on and discuss their intersubjective experiences with the exercise. It should constitute a reflexive examination of the dialectic relationship between the established objective structures and procedures and the subjective experi-

---

[6] Cobb (2004) has developed a narrative approach to understanding and dealing with identity-based conflicts in deliberative processes. She speaks of the need for "narrative facilitation."

ence of them. Toward this end, the process should be flexible enough to include and promote procedural negotiations that can be adjusted for the kinds of tensions that reveal themselves in the course of such reflection. If these intersubjective relationships are not problematized, the deliberative process can easily confront difficulties, even fail.[7]

In a quite different context, Polletta (2002) shows how more established, enduring deliberative organizations discover the need to manage this intersubjective realm. After analyzing participation and deliberation in a range of social movements, she also found that formal deliberative rules alone could not explain participatory decisions. Providing "insufficient guidance" to determine who participates and how, formal rules, as she writes, seldom actually determine "what kinds of concerns can be brought up, how they should be framed, what kinds and degree of emotions should be displayed in debates, how breaches in the formal rules should be dealt with, and so on." What she uncovered was that both the organizers and participants in such movement organizations tended informally to adopt "associative modes" of interaction that attend to these otherwise intersubjective concerns arising during—or as a result of—deliberative processes. The participatory arrangements that she studied depended on a sophisticated set of normative understandings that accompanied the formal rules. Serving as a kind of "etiquette" of deliberation, they functioned to routinize communicative interaction, civilize the expression of emotions, and to generate understanding among the participants, the result of which was often to increase trust. Successful participation in civil rights, women's liberation, and pacificist movements, among others, was organized by political activists who combined formal rules and ideology with noninstitutionalized, nonpolitical models of association. Indeed, she found that the reliance on such models of social interaction were far more important than instrumental considerations in organizing the deliberations that guided such groups.

In particular, she found three primary deliberative styles emerging from the different movements that she studied, which she identified as religious or Christian fellowship, a tutorial model of interaction, and friendship. Pacifist organizations, for example, tended to rely on informal norms characteristic of religious fellowship or personal conscience to guide their deliberative practices. Both religious and secular pacifist organizations anchored the authority of the "rightness" of their political decisions to an emphasis on moral reason.

---

[7] For a discussion of "democratic subjectivity" see Norval (2007).

By way of contrast, in the case of civil rights movements and radical community organizing groups, she found a "tutorial" model of association supplying the informal communicative groundwork. Activist leaders, in these instances, generally took the lead in organizing the meetings, introducing an issue or problem for discussion, but asked volunteers to take responsibilities for specific tasks. They encouraged community participants to take charge of the discussions and deliberate the matter at hand, both in terms of the various pragmatic options available and the relationship of their decisions to the movement's larger political agenda. Typically, they rewarded those who assumed this role with praise. These discussions, as Polleta put it, had something of a "guided character."

The third interactional model based on friendship featured far less guidance. In her analysis of participatory decision-making in SDS (Students for a Democratic Society) and women's liberation movements, Polletta found the salient character of these friendship patterns of communication to be the "informal quality of decision-making," at times even "intimate" in nature. As she wrote, "discussions were made by informal consensus, and tasks were allocated or volunteered for on the basis of a combination of participant preference and skills." Deliberative disputes were frequently heated, but they seldom carried over from one meeting to the next. Unilateral decisions on the part of particular members of the group that might otherwise have appeared to be an effort to gain power or control were often written off as unimportant or excused as a well-meaning mistake.

Noting that these informal rules have seldom been discussed in the scholarship of social movements, she acknowledges that her associational models are generalizations about participatory deliberation, and she examined the variations throughout her book. Putting the particular models aside, however, she succeeds in demonstrating the necessity of taking these informal understandings into account. In this regard, it is not so much the particular associational models that are important here, but rather that such informal, unwritten models play an important role in organizing and guiding deliberations. In addition, she found that the efforts on the part of the participants to establish such informal foundations for dialogue and deliberation give the process something of an experimental character. Similar to Goersdorf, she illustrates how participants' attention to the nature of deliberative process itself can be a source of conflict, even among groups who otherwise differ little on matters related to interest and preference. And, interestingly from the perspective of expertise, the cases tended to show a general tendency to accept expert skills in the group as unproblematic if the informal relations succeeded in establishing a workable model of deliberative interaction.

This sociocultural perspective on the politics of participatory deliberation demonstrates then that a formal theory of design for participation is not possible. It does this by making clear that the structures themselves are social relationships interpreted by those within the spaces. Rather than something like the walls of a room, such spaces are constructed around normative understandings about meanings, intentions, and relationships. For this reason, the practices of design can take on different meanings in different places. Evidence for this normative understanding of space, in fact, is found in other cases in the literature. One such case is that of Kerala, India, drawn upon by Fung and Wright as well. Toward this end, the discussion turns to an illustrative examination of the deliberative project in Kerala, drawing on field interviews conducted by the author (Fischer 2000).[8]

The people's campaign in Kerala: Political empowerment and participatory governance

We examine here the success of the citizens'assemblies in Kerala, taking a closer look at the essential role of the intervening social movement, "The People's Science Movement" of Kerala (widely known as KSSP, short for Kerala Sastra Sahitya Parisha). The activities of KSSP were central to the animation of the decentralized structures. While KSSP's involvement in this story does not go unrecognized, the unique nature of its activities needs to be drawn out more specifically to fully grasp their significance for the process. Geared to the developmental and intrinsic benefits of empowerment, the main contribution of KSSP was to establish the local political-cultural ownership of these deliberative spaces. First, however,

[8] The discussion is in part based on interviews conducted in 1999 with people who were both supportive and critical of the People's Campaign. Especially helpful were Dr. John Kurien and Dr. K. J. Joseph of the Center of for Development studies in Trivandrum, Kerala, R. Radhakrishnan, then president of KSSP; N. C. Narayanan, former KSSP activist, Babu Ambat of the Centre for Environment and Development in Trivandrum, Dr. Ajaykumar Varma of the Science, Technology, and Environment Department of the state of Kerala, and T. M. Thomas Isaac, prominent member of the LDF, the State Planning Board during the Campaign, and KSSP activist. Through interviews, related literature, and campaign documents of various sorts, they offered extensive information on both the politics and practices of the Campaign. Thanks also go to citizens who participated in the deliberative forums, staff members of the Kerala State Planning Board, and students at the Center for Development Studies, all of whom generously took time to explain the project as they experienced or perceived it. In addition, several local journalists made available articles that both praised and criticized the Campaign.

it is important to provide some background on Kerala's "People's Planning Campaign" more generally.

Kerala has been widely celebrated in the development literature for its progressive social and economic redistributive policies in earlier decades.[9] But it is also recognized in more recent times for its important innovation in participatory governance, which is offered by writers such as Fung and Wright as a model of empowerment. Briefly explained, the story of Kerala's decentralized system of participatory development planning begins with India's efforts to reform its overly centralized political system. In 1996, the newly elected Left Democratic Front (LDF) initiated a "People's Campaign for Decentralized Planning" (People's Campaign) to empower the local panchayats (roughly equivalent to a rural county in the United States) and other municipal bodies to draw up the Ninth Five-Year Plan to be submitted to the planners in New Delhi (Isaac and Franke 2000) as part of the country's overall planning process.[10] The "People's Campaign" was specifically designed to engage local citizens in the development of the state's Five Year Plan.[11] As a first step toward citizen participation, Kerala's State Planning Commission made an unprecedented announcement that 35 to 40 percent of the planning activities for the Five-Year Plan would be

[9] Located on the southwestern coast of India, the state government of Kerala has since the middle-to-late 1970s pursued social and redistributive policies that have impressed many students of development (Frank 1993; Heller 1999). As a consequence, its citizens enjoy a level of social development that can be favorably compared with many more developed middle-income countries. It also has one of the highest rates of literacy among all of the states of India.

[10] A primary reason that the LDF shifted its focus to governance was the opportunity that it offered to deal with the failure of long-term efforts on the part of the central and state governments of India to make good on an earlier federal constitutional amendment requiring decentralized planning. Since the 1950s, India has regularly engaged in a five-year planning process based initially on the Soviet model borrowed by Nehru. Much like the experience elsewhere, however, centralized planning proved a disappointment. In response, the central government passed a number of constitutional amendments designed to facilitate the devolution of the governing process to the local level but there were few serious efforts at the state level to decentralize the process and planning activities remained highly centralized and bureaucratic.

[11] One of the primary reasons for the failures of decentralization was the absence of popular representative administrative structures below the state level. Local institutions, moreover, were seldom given the power or financial resources to enable serious development interventions. New Delhi also contributed to the failure by refusing to devolve more powers to the states while continuing to thrust on them one new centrally sponsored program after another. These failures gave rise to a national study commission on decentralized governance, which led a debate throughout India, followed by several constitutional amendments that officially empowered the local level with a mandated role in the planning process. Nonetheless, the general experience following these provisions was not encouraging. In many cases, the mandates were simply ignored by the local political officials, especially those supported by powerful and often exploitative landowners, most of whom benefited both financially and politically from denying their peasant workers a voice in local affairs.

formulated and implemented from below and allocated to the local level an equivalent share of the planning resources. To carry this out, the LDF drew on an extensive network of voluntary organizations and social movements in Kerala, often considered unique to the culture of the state. The goal of these organizations was to make people aware of the People's Campaign and to motivate them to participate. After this first step, the government brought these citizens together with local representatives, officials in the various line departments, and governmental and nongovernmental experts relevant to the local planning process. The officials of the government departments, along with relevant professionals, were instructed to decentralize their planning responsibilities and to cooperate in the new democratic project. Along with the citizen groups, they were offered extensive training programs designed to forge cooperative working relationships for the participatory planning assignments. In the process, public administrators, civic groups, and local representatives, many of whom had heretofore been little more that the passive objects of development planning, were mobilized to work to improve the daily lives of the average citizens of Kerala.

To carry out the planning itself, the state organized a hierarchy of deliberations that moved from the local wards ("grama sabhas") of the panchayats upwards to the district level, and then to the State Planning Board (Isaac and Heller 2003). In and of itself, this was an impressive achievement. Few people, whether they agreed with the Campaign or not, have denied the significance of the "popular assemblies." As argued below, however, the realization of this process was much more than a matter of calling on the citizens. It involved active efforts as well to create the political and social context that made the assemblies work.

To establish a political environment conducive to the process, civic organizations were enlisted to assist in mobilizing their members through publicity strategies and the Science for the People movement introduced empowerment-oriented "conscientization programs" based on the work of the Brazilian educational theorist Paulo Freire (1970, 1973). The goal of these empowerment programs was to employ such didactic techniques to heighten the political consciousness of local community members in particular by assisting them in understanding and interpreting their place in the social and political structures of Kerala and in developing action-oriented initiatives in their own communities. In the local areas of Kerala this meant, among other things, understanding the forces that had been denying them a voice more generally and hindering the mandates for decentralization more specifically.

Toward this end, a range of electronic and print media were called upon to help stimulate citizen involvement, including a public media center that initiated specific programs toward this end. Drawing on approaches developed in the KSSP's earlier and highly successful campaign for "total literacy," dances and local festivals sensitive to the local cultural milieu were held to interest and encourage citizens to take part, and a range of other audio-visual cultural approaches based on folk arts were employed. They also used participatory street theater based on dramatic techniques for political enlightenment and agitation developed by Bertolt Brecht (1965) to advance the socialist movement in Weimar, Germany of the 1920s and 1930s.[12] Passersby would witness the acting out of scenes in which local landowners were exploiting the local peasants, with the peasant farmers uprising to take control over their own situation (Fischer 2000).

Other practical steps were taken as well to maximize participation. The popular assemblies were scheduled to take place on work holidays, and squads of local volunteers visited each household to explain the program and urge their participation at the assemblies. The goal was to encourage at least one member of each household to attend the meetings. The actual process, which can only be summarized briefly here, commenced with the formation of various groups to deal with specific issues, such as agriculture, schools, and environment.

Present in each group were trained "resource persons" who served as discussion facilitators to guide the deliberations. Information about the local area and its people was gathered, including the relevant "local knowledge," and specific development problems were identified. The citizens were then assisted in analyzing these problems on the basis of their own social experiences, knowledge, and understanding, and to make suggestions for solutions. The deliberations of each group were combined and summarized in report form for the plenary session of the local convention. The meetings concluded with the selection of representatives to take these local plans and proposals to the deliberations of the "development seminar," which constituted the next higher stage. The task of the resources development seminar was to come up with "integrating solutions" at the district level for the various problems identified at the lower-level conventions. The district plans then constituted the basis for discussions

[12] Brecht did not want the audience to identify or sympathize with the characters on stage, as was the approach in the classical tradition of theater. Instead, the viewers were to think politically and socially and to judge the actions of the players accordingly. His characters confront both one another and the audience in ways designed to promote critical thought.

about the overall state plan (Isaac and Heller 2003). After the plan was adopted, the state then allocated resources to the local levels to carry out its implementation.

The people's science movement: Critical pedagogy, deliberative space, and participatory inquiry

The People's Science Movement is a genuinely unique sociocultural movement. Established in 1962, it was the product of a number of scientists and social activists in Kerala who were concerned that scientific information was basically inaccessible to the majority of the people of the state. After a decade of success in translating scientific books and articles into the local language and making them available to schools and citizens, the movement adopted the motto "Science for Revolution," and opened the door to what was to become a mass movement with some sixty thousand members. In the process, the emphasis of KSSP shifted to more active efforts to generate a "scientific questioning" attitude in the population as a whole, the underlying goal of which was self-empowerment and change. As result, interest and involvement jumped, reflected in two other major efforts that drew national attention. One was the movement's opposition to the building of a proposed hydroelectric dam, which Indira Gandhi was later compelled to cancel, and the second was a literacy campaign in the City of Cochin that employed progressive educational techniques to increase dramatically the literacy rate in the area. In these educational efforts, both in Cochin and other parts of Kerala, people were taught to read through materials and methods that promoted a questioning attitude toward their own social positions in the society, the forces that shaped their circumstances, and what might be done about it. Such methods, as developed by the practitioners of critical pedagogy, transformed an otherwise abstract or rote activity of learning to read into a project that poignantly took on relevant everyday meanings in the lives of the students, adult learners in particular.

Given the impressive nature of these educational achievements, KSSP received widespread attention in both India and abroad. The movement, for example, was awarded the "Alternative Noble Prize" in 1996 by the Swedish foundation that has bestowed the prize for some years. The active role of KSSP was thus much more than another component in a story explaining the success of the People's Campaign. Both its skills and reputation were central factors in generating public commitment and participation.

The KSSP's early involvement in the People's Campaign is easy to explain. Beyond its reputation generally, many members of the LDF and the State Planning Board were also members of KSSP. Turning to KSSP for assistance was for them an obvious move. To fully grasp KSSP's activities, however, requires an understanding of the philosophy behind them. Basic here are the educational philosophy and pedagogical approach of Paolo Freire (1970) and the methods of participatory research that have been motivated by them (Reason 1994; Chambers 1997). Working with people who have never participated—people who typically begin with the belief that they do not have the capacities to contribute to a deliberative process—the main contribution of the approach was to make clear a basic message: these fora were for the people on their own terms.

Such pedagogical praxis, emphasizing the developmental and intrinsic benefits of participation, begins by drawing out the relevant community histories and local knowledge. By "problematizing" the social marginality of the community members, particularly peasant farmers, these narrative stories are then used to assist them in examining their own beliefs and identities in ways that help them reflect on established understandings of the existing social-structural relationships (Fischer 2000). In the process of learning and discussing the symbols and artifacts through which the social order is communicated, experienced, reproduced, and explored, they are assisted in exploring the cultural politics that define and solidify their own "subject positions" in the dominant discourses of those who exercise social and political power.[13] Through the construction of alternative understandings the participants fashion networks of solidarity, build confidence in their own knowledge and capabilities and, in the process, develop a sense of their own abilities to address their interests and needs. These new understandings and sense of agency shape the assumptions that socially valorize the deliberative space. In Kerala, as we see in the next section, the specific vehicle for engaging these issues was the deliberative inquiry designed for the decentralized planning.

---

[13] In many ways, the process is like opening up the deeper, more difficult kinds of questions that a critical analysis of power would raise (Luke 2005). To what degree do more powerful people shape or influence the consciousness of inequalities of the less powerful and induce them to accept a sense of powerlessness. Whereas the speaker in a deliberation is normally expected to respond only to what has been explicitly said, a critical pedagogical discourse includes questions about "who is saying it and why." Is that person in a position to tell them what s/he tells them? Does s/he have first-hand knowledge and experience of the realities of the situation? Does s/he actually speak for someone else? That is, it concerns identity questions concerned with, as the phrase goes, 'where the speaker is coming from.' In the process, it opens the discussion to questions pertaining to the individual or group's relations to the larger social system—issues including social standing, money, privilege, and the like.

Although critical pedagogy and participatory research come from different intellectual traditions than does postmodernism, both methods pursue many of the same kinds of issues associated with social space, political identity, social meaning, marginality, and resistance. These concepts are basic to the frameworks that both methods employ in their efforts to design environments for social learning. Although not postmodernist per se, participatory research can easily be described as a closely related practice for postempiricist inquiry.

To facilitate the kind of openness and authenticity required for such deliberation, emphasis is placed on restructuring the professional/teacher–participant/learner relationship to minimize the social, emotional, and intellectual distance that typically separates professionals from the participant's experiential life world.[14] Stressing the unique demands placed on those who seek to initiate such an egalitarian—even radically egalitarian—participatory process, the practitioners of such participatory inquiry work to deal with the potential problems of intellectual elitism that can undermine such projects. As one of the leading theorists of participatory research puts it, in so far as "movements for social change are normally led by intellectuals who are in a position to provide leadership not because of any particular aptitude but because they are privileged by their economic and social status," there are "many dangers of relying on an elite leadership for social transformation: the dangers of inflated egos, the fragility of the commitment in the face of attractive temptations; the problems of the growth in size of the elite class as a movement grows and the danger of attracting new adherents holding altogether different commitments," as well as the self-perpetuating nature of institutions established to supply such leadership (Rahman 1995: 84). These were just the kinds of considerations that KSSP leaders insisted on keeping at the forefront of the efforts.

KSSP: Social commitment and local knowledge

After the Campaign's decentralized participatory structures were developed, the project confronted a more specific question: what would be

---

[14] Such participatory inquiry, as an enlightenment strategy for raising the consciousness of ordinary citizens with common interests and concerns, emphasizes the political dimensions of knowledge production and the role of knowledge as an instrument of power and control, as well as the politics of the citizen-expert relationships. It takes human beings to be co-creators of their own reality through the cognitive and emotional experiences—thinking, imagining, and acting—that they gain through participation (Reason 1994: 324).

the basis of the discussions in the decentralized deliberations? Much of the information needed to assess the physical and social characteristics of the local areas was unavailable. To deal with this KSSP combined the methods of critical pedagogy with techniques of rural resource mapping to develop a more specific practice for gathering the information needed for the deliberations. The bridge across these two activities—pedagogy and resource mapping—was the community members' "local knowledge" of their panchayats, social as well as physical. It became a vehicle for both the data collection and the cultural valorization of the political context that enlivened the deliberations of the popular assemblies.

More specifically, the KSSP labored to integrate an established method of evaluating local development that offered quick but *reasonably* accurate assessments of rural resources—"participatory rural appraisal" (or "transect walks")—with more rigorous scientific approaches and participatory pedagogical practices. Those concerned with the didactic methods worked this out with the help of the movement's own members at the Center for Earth Science Studies (CESS) in Trivandrum, an institution long engaged in rigorous scientific research related to resource management and planning. The result was a innovative procedure that combined community based mapping techniques with the more rigorous scientific mapping techniques practiced by the environmental and resource planners of the CESS, while, at the same time, integrating these methods with the local knowledge and social understandings that made the data collection and planning processes relevant to the everyday life of community members (Fischer 2000). Reflecting the pedagogical practices, the goal was described as "land literacy."

Approaching the mapping process as a sociocultural tool for communication among planning experts and local community members, the KSSP and CESS sought to answer three basic local questions: What were the economic, environmental, and social resources in the areas? Where were they located? And how were they located? In economic and environmental terms, these concerns were built around questions pertaining to the terrain of the land, water resources, and the uses of both. With regard to land, the planners sought information on the specific form of the terrain. For example, does it slope? What type(s) of soil does it have? In terms of water, they focused on characteristics such as streams or ponds, whereas land use raised questions concerned with the type of crops planted and how much land is under cultivation. All were questions for which accurate information was unavailable, the absence of which made it difficult to think systematically about development planning.

To this end, the staff developed a "base map" from information gathered from local revenue maps and official documents about landholdings in each village. To these physical questions the CESS staff overlaid the questions about the social infrastructure. That is, what had already taken place in the area—were there roads, schools, and other community facilities, and if so, where precisely were they located? Once the basic design of the planning process was in place, CESS planners turned back to the People's Science Movement, which then took over the assignment of identifying community volunteers for the project, as well as developing and conducting a training program for local data collection.

The approach to data collection was designed to bring the local citizens themselves into the research process and through their activities initiate and animate discussions about the community and its problems among its members themselves. Toward this end, KSSP identified a team of five to eight volunteers for each village in a particular district. In selecting the local volunteers, it was decided that formal educational background needed not be a decisive requirement for participation. For example, the questions about physical terrain could be formulated in ways that permitted the local characteristics to be identified through a scheme of color-coding. After the training, the volunteers were sent to the village wards to be mapped. Each group chose a leader and a ward office (usually someone's home), and established a schedule or work plan for the actual mapping. In addition to the physical information, the volunteers and other villagers assembled relevant social data such as numbers of people in households, earnings, and employment. Throughout the collection of both the physical and social data, the questions were presented in local, rather than scientific terminology. They were formulated in ways that helped people understand in their own lay languages the findings and their economic and social implications.

Upon completion of the physical and social mapping by the volunteers, CESS planners returned to include other parameters, less visible to the naked eye, that required expert measurement—for example, the location of underground water sources. The results were seven sets of maps that integrated the physical and social data, five of which were constructed by the volunteers, two by the planners. The analytic task was to overlay these maps. Onto the physical land use maps were added relevant survey information about "primary" production and "secondary" social sectors. At the end of the process, the approach to data collection had not only brought the local citizens themselves into the research process, it served to initiate and animate discussions about the community. The result of these efforts

was a "development report" that became the basis for community deliberations aimed at formulating an "action plan," which in turn served as a
component of the larger planning process.

Up to one hundred pages in length, the development reports offered
detailed pictures of local development. Their dozen chapters combined a
discussion of local social and cultural history with assessments of various
resources, such as agriculture, education, health, energy, and water supply.
An emphasis on the importance of social mobilization for community
change was combined with a presentation of problems and an action
plan. The action plans specifically emphasized several questions: What
were the economic and social problems? What were the future prospects?
And what were the gaps between the two? In the context of social and
political understandings worked out by the communities, these issues
were then discussed in the decentralized deliberative forums. From these
deliberations emerged a sense of the barriers that stood in the path of
solving the communities' problems, strategies that could be developed to
do something about them, and a heightened sense of motivation to deal
with these issues on terms relevant to communities' own interests. In
short, there were now grounds for critical discussion, especially mutual
discussions among community members, the KSSP facilitators, and the
planning experts.[15]

In an effort to spread the lessons of the project, KSSP developed in later
years a guidebook for use by some five hundred or more other local areas in
India that have sought implement the model or a variant of it. This
material emphasizes the need to take the particular local social and cultural context into consideration; the Kerala model, it asserts, will not work
everywhere. In most cases, it at least requires local adjustments. Toward
this end, the guidelines point out that there can be no hard and fast

---

[15] To inform and assist the local planning efforts, the state planning office made available to
the panchayats information about all of the ongoing development programs in the state, and
the line department offices of the government prepared a review of their respective development sector programs already being implemented in the panchayats, emphasizing in particular
those relevant to the development of their local plans. To further facilitate discussion about
formulation of the integrated programs at the level of the development seminars, a series of
manuals on topics such as watershed management, education and schools, sanitation, drink-
ing water, total energy programs, and environmental protection were prepared and distributed
among resource persons. In order to give the panchayats confidence in their practicality, care
was taken in the manuals to ensure that they were based on actual local field experiences.
Moreover, experts were appointed on a volunteer basis to serve in—but only in—an advisory
capacity during the local deliberations. The deliberative bodies could, if they so desired, avail
themselves of the advice drawn from the full range of sectors, such as agriculture, education,
and environment. It is also important to note that an "expert" was defined in a very broad
sense—it not only included the civil engineer, but also the "wise farmer."

265

blueprints for participatory governance; any serious effort at such reform will require a good deal of trial and error and learning-by-doing. Continuing their own experimentation, it should also be added, KSSP has augmented the popular assemblies through the organization of smaller neighborhood groups of forty or fifty families into mini-popular assemblies that offer more extensive opportunities to discuss local priorities, issues, and plans than do the grama sahbas. Designed to add an additional layer of democratic governance, KSSP has in fact organized a campaign to spread these grass-roots groups throughout the state as a whole.

KSSP and the sociocultural cultivation of deliberative space

From the outset, as we saw, attention to the sociocultural realities underlying and conditioning the acceptance of the People's campaign and its deliberative assemblies were basic to the success of the program. It began with the LDF coalition putting forth the decentralized planning project statewide from the top down. It did this through party meetings, media events, street theater, and folk festivals. In the process, it emphasized the instrumental benefits of citizen participation, namely the empowerment of citizens to deal themselves with local developmental issues such as environmental protection, agricultural modernization, education, health care, and the like. Toward this end, the project was an explicit challenge to powerful landholders and others who had long ignored the various constitutional amendments mandating citizen participation. The message of the Campaign conveyed through the media and public events was clear: It was to give a voice to community members in an effort to wrest away local political control from local landowners who had long exploited these districts with little or no opposition. Given that the LDF had previously helped many of these poor and relatively uneducated peasant farmers through their earlier redistributive efforts, the vast majority of them were enthusiastic political supporters, which was no small consideration in generating the enthusiasm and energy needed to carry out the process.

Equally important, after having laid the groundwork for the project, the LDF turned to the Science for the People movement to socially valorize the deliberative spaces constructed for the discussion of the local plans. KSSP did this by bringing the campaign door-to-door to local citizens, laying the pedagogical groundwork for the inquiry process, organizing the deliberative assemblies, and training resource facilitators to assist with the deliberations. Indeed, the facilitation techniques were informed by Freireian pedagogical techniques for adult education and participatory action research. Together, these efforts established a highly motivated constituency that could, with the kind of local knowledge gathered through the processes of participatory research, meaningfully deliberate and formulate action plans for their local areas.

The crucial contribution of the KSSP was thus to establish the local political ownership of these deliberative spaces, introduce innovative methods for participatory data collection, and develop the deliberative culture. As a result, the assemblies were infused with the message that they were for the local participants and to be conducted on their own terms. The materials that provided the basis for developing this context included local knowledge and community narratives, examined and reinterpreted in terms of the people's position and identity in the prevailing order and the political and material forces that held them there. Thus, in the same process of interpreting the local narratives, the formal and informal rules of communicative interaction were worked out.

Basically, the KSSP understood that the participatory process had to be organized and cultivated. It could not simply be left to the citizens. In this respect, the Kerala campaign underscored an important finding of participatory inquiry more generally, namely the need for someone with expert skills to assist the community in organizing their struggles, to help them to understand the situation, and to develop alternative strategies (Fischer 2000). The goal was to establish autonomous participatory practices in the local communities, but it was recognized that they would first have to be cultivated before they could be successfully institutionalized.

To cultivate the empowerment process, KSSP innovatively organized the participatory mapping process, which not only collected local information and knowledge but cognitively built community members into the activity. The model of participatory resource mapping offered an impressive procedure for facilitating an interaction between scientific experts and the local citizens. The development of the overlapping maps can be seen as an important contribution to the practices of both critical pedagogy and participatory research. For the politics of participatory governance, it showed how the inquiry of the citizens and scientists can be systematically integrated in ways that augment one another, as well as how participatory research can be built into the larger political-making structure. The Kerala State Planning Board has demonstrated how such local empowerment efforts, rather than just remaining a grassroots problem-solving strategy, can meaningfully be connected to higher-level deliberative processes in the formation of the state plan. These contributions of People's Campaign offer lessons from which participatory governance efforts everywhere can benefit.

Deliberative empowerment: Drawing general lessons

For deliberative empowerment this experience suggests that a participatory project at the bottom of the political structure needs to have strong political support from above. In the case of Kerala, the government itself initiated the empowerment project and shaped a political climate at both the state and local levels conducive to its successful implementation. While detailed comparisons are beyond the scope of this paper, the same phenomenon can be seen in the participatory budget project in Porto Alegre, the Brazilian city ruled by a progressive socialist party that established it (Baiocchi 2003). It also did this at the local level, it should be noted, with the assistance of didactic methods based—to a greater or lessor degree—on the pedagogical theory and practices of Freire. If genuine empowerment in the public sector is taken to mean transformative politics, both political support from above and the facilitation of the local activities appear as essential ingredients of success.

This is not to say that other grass-roots or bottom-up projects would be without impact. But in the absence of broader support, both political and pedagogical, deliberation is much more likely to, if not necessarily, become another forum for strategic struggle, rather than citizen empowerment *per se*. While the principles of deliberative empowerment offered by Fung and Wright are presented as a strategy for colonizing the state, it is difficult to find convincing reasons to believe that deliberation in spaces created by the state would permit—at least not for long—the kinds of transformative or emancipatory discourses characteristic of decentralized deliberation in Kerala. This is not to say that state cannot play a role. Indeed, Sirianni (2008) offers a number of case studies to illustrate the case for the state taking on the role of "government as civic enabler." Without denying the value of such a redesign of government practices, however, much of this work in the contemporary state operates within the basic parameters of the capitalist imperatives and thus serves to strengthen instrumental, problem-solving capacities rather than a more fundamental transformative role. One can also easily make the point with regard to the case studies presented as examples of deliberation in empowered participatory governance.[16] This empirical question needs to be added to the research agenda.

Beyond strong support from above, there is also a need for those advancing empowerment actively to enter the discursive space itself. Even when a local participatory project has political support, it cannot be assumed that the citizens will themselves take up the opportunity and turn it into a forum for political emancipation. Not only is it important to recognize that all parties at the local level will not share the same political interests or social consciousness, but also to see that such fora need to be organized pedagogically. Participatory facilitators need to establish the conditions and procedures that make deliberative empowerment possible. Toward this end, we need to more thoroughly research the material and cognitive conditions that make this possible, as well as the practices themselves.

Given the absence of political consensus supporting genuine deliberative empowerment in Western nations, such participatory projects are more likely to continue to evolve in civil society, supported in particular by social movements such as Science for the People. Given that the state exists as the product of competing political interests, the preconditions for groups with common interests and concerns to deliberate meaningfully among themselves are more likely to be found or established in civil society. Although the task will remain difficult, as much of civil society itself is beset with divisions of class, ethnicity, and race, the relative openness of civil society offers better chances for citizens to create spaces in which they might engage in non-strategic discourse about basic choices involving how they want to live together, the practices of governance needed to advance and support such decisions, and the political strategies that can help to bring them about. With the exception of the presence of a socially progressive government, as in Kerala or Porto Alegre, it is mainly in civil society that social spaces can be shaped free of the kinds of implicit

---

[16] Fung and Wright (2003), for example, include in their work the case of the Habitat Protection Program set up by the US Congress and a Wisconsin state industry council for job development. It is doubtful that deliberations about habitat protection in this setting would seriously entertain the discourses of radical ecology, or that an industry council established in conjunction with a state government would be willing to accept talk about transforming the capitalist labor market. To help people "turn jobs into careers" in the existing industrial system is scarcely the kind of transformative discourse that might subversively colonize the state. There is good reason, given the extensive co-optation of participatory reforms, to suspect that the latter cases would be targets for manipulation by the state in pursuit its own interests. These cases are thus more likely to be characterized by the kinds of hidden resistance discussed by Foucault or Scott than open empowerment discourses. Such resistance is by no means unimportant, but the political limits of such a politics have to be understood and theorized differently.

coercion built into official governance structures. It is a point clearly recognized in the emancipation-oriented literature of participatory research, empowerment and self-governance. The progressive projects of self-governance reported there are typically to be found in spaces located outside of the formal state. Removed from the state, the task is to use critical pedagogy to facilitate the development of transformative perspectives that can serve as the basis for solidarity and political opposition to particular state policies and practices. Indeed, to approach it otherwise would seem to neglect the reasons for the emergence of civil society-oriented social movements and NGOs over the past decades.

From this perspective, then, the pedagogical role in deliberative empowerment becomes a primary consideration. While basic preconditions for such empowerment in government depend on broader political developments in society, the pedagogical cultivation of discursive spaces poses an important task for the social sciences. Toward this end, the pedagogical dimension needs to receive more attention on the research agenda of empowered participatory governance. Social scientists need to examine more carefully the kinds of epistemic relationships that govern such deliberation, in particular the sorts of issues that we have examined in the previous chapters. Moving beyond the formal design of decentralized structures, there is a need to engage in experimentation about the nature of communication and learning in these settings. It is a task that should be elevated on the research agenda. A place to begin is the wealth of information from an extensive range of projects devoted to participatory research and empowerment.

Conclusions

The discussion in this chapter has underscored the significance of Kerala's People's Campaign for decentralized governance. It was seen to be a very important—even unpredecented—move toward participatory governance in Kerala, or elsewhere for that matter. In this light, the discussion explored the sociocultural dynamics that underlaid the process. In particular, the issue raised here was that while structural decentralization was a political precondition for the successful implementation of the People's Campaign, in and of itself, the specific decentralized design of the institutions cannot explain this impressive achievement. Every bit as important was the social valorization of the deliberative spaces created by decentralization. In addition to the progressive politics of the ruling coalition, the pedagogically oriented interventions of the People's Science movement played a critical role in shaping the popular assemblies. Drawing on the methods of critical pedagogical inquiry, it mediated between the top–down orientation of the LDF and the local people. Setting up the programmatic machinery, the movement both facilitated the gathering of local knowledge through forms of participatory research and it empowered citizens through an emphasis on the local ownership of the deliberative spaces and the trust it generated.

This discussion of the sociocultural dimension of deliberative space brings us to the final chapter. We next take up the question of emotional expression in deliberation. Always a difficult problem for deliberative theorists, we need to address the fact that the social and cultural dimensions of politics and public deliberation are grounded in deeper emotional commitments that both condition and motivate the discussion of political action.

10

Passionate Participants: Rethinking Emotion in Public Deliberation

Everyone knows that emotion and passion are basic to the political process.[1] Indeed, people seldom enter the political fray without emotional convictions of one sort or another, whether they involve passionate political beliefs, deep-seated animosities toward foreign enemies, ethnic cultural commitments, or religious faith. Electoral research, in fact, shows that most voters make emotional, intuitive responses in choosing which candidates to support; they then later offer post-hoc rationalizations to explain these decisions, at times below the level of conscious awareness. Others respond similarly to emotional fears and anxieties created by political realities such as terrorism, impending economic hardship, ethnic conflicts, and the like. Given the centrality of emotion to such decisions, it is more than a little curious that the social and policy sciences have failed to develop an analytical language capable of dealing with this basic dimension of social and political life.[2]

This neglect, in fact, has deep roots. Emotion and the kinds of impassioned rhetoric associated with it have long been portrayed as the enemy of rationality. An issue extending back to Plato, emotion has been defined as the very opposite of reason. For Plato, and a long list of philosophers after him, emotional passion is a problem for which rational thought is the solution (Meyer 1991: 38). Following this line of reason, the social sciences have from the outset tried to eliminate or reject the role of emotional rhetoric by replacing it with an even-handed, neutral language

[1] Most everyone can speak about emotions in a rather general way; typically they refer to feelings. But a more specific discussion of emotion quickly becomes complex (see Goldie 2000).
[2] For illustrations of this failure as they pertain to the study of social movements, see Goodwin *et al.* 2001: 1–24.

of objectivity. Although passionate speech is a basic aspect of the everyday human realities that neo-Kantian social scientists have sought to understand, they have attempted to substitute it with their own mode of empirical-analytic reason.

In significant part, this denigration and neglect of emotion is a product of modernity (Goldie 2000: 9–10). Various prominent social theorists have, in fact, characterized this avoidance of emotion as basic to the processes of rationalization associated with the development of modern society (Weber 2007). Interpreters of modern social systems from Comte to Weber, Elias, and Habermas have identified the de-emotionalization of public behaviour as an essential precondition for the technical and cultural rationalization that has defined essential aspects of modernity. Indeed, Elias (1997) has described the process of modern civilization as nothing less than the learning of emotional control. Civilization, he has argued, involves a dampening of the forms of pre-modern emotional expression, emphasizing in their place interests and the reservation of feeling and affection. Feeling and passion, as Hirschman (1997) has explained, were replaced in economic and political life by the concept of interests.[3]

Today, however, some have pointed to a re-emergence of emotional expression. They see it as a by-product of "postmaterial values" (Ingelhart 1977). Whereas the traditional values associated with industrialization and urbanization were heavily related to material needs, the postmaterial welfare state shifted people's attention to the quality of life and an emotional sense of social well being. Closely related to such quality life issues have been social movements, typically involving a passionate style of politics (Goodwin *et al.* 2001). Others call attention to the nature of contemporary politics itself. They speak of an emotionalization of politics that has become a structural feature of contemporary media politics. Here writers refer to "feel-good-factors" identified with a "personalization of politics," often described in Europe as the "Americanization" politics. In a highly commercialized society such as the United States, the political electorate is steadily transformed into an "audience" for a form of political entertainment, or what one German political theorist has referred to as "politainment" (Doerner 2001).

---

[3] Hirschman (1997: 20–56) has described how eighteenth-century political and economic philosophers sought to "tame" passions by translating them into interests. Whereas passion and desires were unpredictable, interests could be objectively identified. They thus became the cornerstone of political and economic analysis.

It is difficult in this regard to understate the role of the media in modern social and political processes. Via the mass media, television in particular, emotions have become an integral aspect of the communication of social and political knowledge. Since the introduction of and reliance on a commercially oriented entertainment format, the news itself becomes something of a *production* of reality. In this context, truth is increasingly measured by the degree to which it *feels* authentic.

One of the primary responses to this apparent re-emotionalization of social and political life has been an effort to again reassert the role of reason. In the realm of technology and environmental policy we see this in efforts to emphasize rational techniques of risk assessment and we recognize it in politics more generally through the call for rational argumentation in public deliberation. Today, as then, the emphasis is on rational and deliberate thought, understood as dampening down the role of emotion. Much of the analysis in this tradition, as a consequence, pays only scant attention to emotional expression in politics and policy-making; the emphasis in deliberation and argumentation is still on factual statements and the empirical analysis of them.

To be sure, political and sociological analyses have always acknowledged the role of emotions. The issue has to do more with the way that social-scientific analysis has dealt with it. The problem is in large part the abstract language that is typically used to describe emotionally grounded events and behaviours. Social scientists import emotional behaviour into their analytic models without adequately capturing its affects on thought and action. Public opinion and electoral research, for example, refer to the "intensity" with which particular political and policy beliefs are held by citizens, but such investigation seeks to measure it in ways that empirically objectify its causal effects. In this work, the tendency has been to conceptualize emotions as predictable behaviours resulting from psychological processes (Abu-Lughod and Lutz 1990: 2–3). This fails to understand the ways emotion more broadly conditions and motivates political and social action. Rather than causes that govern actions per se, emotions serve to orient actors to the external conditions confronting them. Motivating and mobilizing thought and action, in short, precedes deliberation. Only after actors have oriented themselves generally, can they determine particular strategies. While the action of choosing is the task of deliberation, the emotionally conditioned orientation indicates the general direction and thus the acceptable alternatives that might be discussed.

274

Reconsidering emotion: Its relationship to reason

But what should we do with our general understandings about emotions? How might we bring emotion into the analytical study of the policy process? The question is surely not new. Emotion, as "pathos," was a major component of Aristotle's rhetoric. Along with "logos" (factual argumentation) and "ethos" (concerned with ethics and virtue), pathos is recognized as an integral and unavoidable part of public debate. Whereas logos presents—inductively and deductively—the relevant empirical considerations, pathos is geared to the mobilization of the audience. In the interest of action, it seeks to generate support for the position advanced by the particular argument. Emotions are thus more than just a diversion from rational argument; they are "all those feelings that so change men as to affect their judgment" (Aristotle 1991). It is a view which has regained the attention of a number of theorists; they appeal for a return to Aristotle's theory of rhetoric, particularly as updated by philosophers such as Perelman (1984) and Toulmin (1958).

In classical rhetoric, there is thus an inherent connection between emotion and reason. Thought and belief are to be understood as the efficient cause of emotion and, as such, emotional responses need to be interpreted as intelligent reactions that can be dealt with through reasoned persuasion. Fortenbaugh (1975: 17) has captured this understanding in these words: "When men are angered, they are not victims of some totally irrational force." Instead, "they are responding in accordance with the thought of unjust result." The beliefs they hold "may be erroneous and their anger unreasonable, but their behaviour is intelligent and cognitive in the sense that it is grounded upon a belief which may be criticised and even altered by argumentation."

However, rhetoric as a formal discipline has not succeeded in carrying the day. Indeed, the very idea of rhetoric has long been cast in a negative light. In arguments that date back to Aristotle's famous teacher, Plato, rhetoric has been rejected as seductively manipulative, the stuff of propaganda, in large part because of its relationship to passion. Even in politics today one refers negatively to his or her opponent's self-serving rhetoric. During the past decade, however, there have been other promising signs of renewed interest in emotion and passion that seem to side-step the baggage of rhetoric while, at the same time, affirming its central significance for reason itself. A growing number of political theorists have sought to move beyond the negative interpretations traditionally associated with this unknown emotional landscape. Often revisiting Hume's

Treatise on Human Nature (1978), in particular his recognition that reason itself cannot motivate us to act, they have begun to rethink the relationship between reason and passion. A fair amount of this writing, moreover, has emerged in critical response to work on deliberative democracy and its dominant emphasis on rational argumentation.

The critics of deliberative democracy have observed that its theorists have, despite their distrust of the passions, tended to smuggle in emotional expression through the concept of "commitment" to democracy, loosely defined as a willingness to deliberate with others. Without a commitment to deliberate, it is recognized, deliberative democracy will not occur, or at least not successfully (Cohen 1996). Citizens "committed" to resolving problems through public reasoning must have the moral sensibility or a desire to be fair; they have to share a disposition to abide by the principles of reciprocity, publicity, and accountability. Although this contention is uncontroversial, critics argue that it is largely stated in a way that obscures the fact that the commitment is grounded in basic emotional dispositions. Young and others, disputing the assumption that the better argument will win the day, point to other good reasons not to participate that are grounded in different emotional dispositions. Mouffe (1999: 755–6) goes even further. In a critique of deliberative democracy, she argues that "the prime task of democratic politics is not to eliminate the passions ... but to mobilise these passions towards the promotion of democratic designs." These passions, she argues, are rooted in and energized by core identities. The goal of her alternative position, "agonistic pluralism," is to recognize the underlying force of core identities and to support the expression of the passions associated with them.

Some critics have drawn on a postmodern willingness to embrace openly the subjective (Ahmed 2004). Often focused on the marginal perspective of the outsider, this literature emphasizes the relationship between emotion and storytelling. Given that stories are carriers of feeling, narrative analysis is seen to provide an approach for bringing emotion back into the analysis of political reason and public deliberation.

These writers seek to correct the positivist take on storytelling. In the same way that emotion has been excluded from rationality, as they point out, storytelling has been falsely portrayed either as the opposite of reason, or at least an inferior form of it. In part, this has resulted from a failure to recognize storytelling's basic function. Unlike reason-giving, as the study of rhetoric makes clear, storytelling is designed to persuade by moving people both intellectually and emotionally. Stories appeal to values as well as facts, emotions as well as reasons. The power of a story, as such, often derives from the narrator's persuasive ability rather than the reasonableness of the claims. For this reason, advocates of strict argumentative rationality often dismiss the value of storytelling to public discourse. While worries about the manipulative potentials of persuasion need to be taken seriously, it is a mistake to overlook the essential contribution of storytelling.

This perspective can, however, swing too far away from reason. Emphasizing the narration and its subjective foundations, rational reason all too often seems to drop out of these discussions Another group of theorists has sought to accept the subjective emotional side of thought but focus on its relationship to reason. Instead of simply accepting emotional expression as one of the components of rhetoric, they have sought to clarify the way reason actually rests on emotion. Here Nussbaum's (2001) work is of seminal importance.

Employing an extensive range of sources—philosophy, literature, poetry, music, religion, social science, and more—Nussbaum demonstrates the various ways that the emotions shape the inner landscape of our lives, both mental and social. Drawing in particular on Proust, she illustrates how emotions function like "geographical upheavals," marking "our lives as uncertain, uneven, and prone to reversal" (p. 1). In this regard, there are good emotions (love and compassion) that play constructive roles and bad ones (anger and hate) that lead to destructive consequences. Whereas philosophers and social scientists have long taken emotions to be rooted in animal-like impulses, mainly emphasizing the destructive capacities of emotions, Nussbaum points to the central role of positive feelings for the social solidarity and harmony of a society. Toward this end, she has interestingly developed principled criteria for differentiating between "legitimate" and "illegitimate" emotions (Nussbaum 2004). We need to ask, in this regard, if it is reasonable to deeply value the object to which the emotion is attached. From this perspective, some emotional passions have no place in public deliberations. Here she refers to sentiments such as shame and disgust. These should always be avoided. On the other hand, emotions such as compassion and commiseration can play essential roles in helping people to understand each other and come to acceptable decisions that help them move forward. Even appropriate levels of anger can at times be seen to have useful effects.[4]

---

[4] In just this regard, Gambetta (1998: 20) notes that a productive conversation does not need to avoid expression of emotion. Citing remarks by Stephen Holmes, he writes that "people who are too cool, analytical, and impartial may generate distrust or may fail to rally

Especially important for the present discussion, Nussbaum sees emotions as having an intrinsic connection to basic thought processes. Indeed, she persuasively argues that our emotions are themselves suffused with a form of tacit intelligence and acumen. Emotions are, in her view, composites of feelings and beliefs (2001). As such, they function as a deep, underlying source of human awareness, critical judgment, and social understanding. In her "cognitive-evaluative" conception of emotions, they are seen to "always involve thought of an object combined with thought of the object's salience or importance; in that sense, they always involve appraisal or evaluation." It is an understanding that harks back to Hume's (1975: 209) work on emotion. As he argued, a particular passion "points immediately to . . . [an] object and constitutes it our good or happiness."[5]

Hall (2006), following Nussbaum, has elaborated on the way the evaluation of alternatives in deliberation rests on a commitment to particular standards and norms. Deliberation, as she explains, means weighing alternatives. It involves a careful balancing of the various options before rendering a judgment. To deliberate is to attend to consequences and their implications for a proposed action, as well as to clarify intentions behind them. It is a process that requires considering what *matters* most to us, which is determined by establishing the relations of decisions to one's values, goals, and intentions. To be sure, reason plays an important role in such deliberation, but so does passion. No such deliberation takes place unless people are motivated to do so and it is passion that does the motivating. People respond passionately when the outcomes of the decision process matter to them.

In short, to say that things matter to people is another way of saying that they "care." As Hall (2006: 19) explains, the language of preferences, interests, and commitments sounds so rational and steady as to nearly hide the fact that feelings are involved. To have "a passion is to be keenly drawn toward something that one perceives as valuable and, consequently, to have some kind of commitment to pursuing and/or sustaining that thing." One must, in this view, decide what matters to one most and this can only be done by determining one's deepest passions. A person's thought processes thus move in the direction of his or her feelings and

people around issues. A passionate style can lead to extremes, but this is not always a bad thing. It can generate the energy to sustain harder thinking about issues."

[5] Hume illustrated his position this way: "If I have no vanity, I take no delight in praise: if I be void of ambition, power gives me no enjoyment: if I be not angry, the punishment of an adversary is totally indifferent to me."

passions. Individuals bring interests and preferences to the deliberative process, but it is their personal passion and commitment for dealing with problems through public reasoning that is their commonly shared passion for democratic governance (Hall 2006: 19).

Similarly, Krause (2006: 11) argues that "to engage the faculty of public reason in deliberation is essentially to frame one's arguments and make one's evaluations in terms of principles and evaluative standards that are constitutive of the polity and are therefore sources of common commitment to things that citizens *care* about." In this regard, "public reasons reflect the shared horizons of concern that are implicit in the political culture of a particular community." As conflicts over these concerns arise, they have to be discussed in terms of other components on the general horizon of issues and concern that are agreed upon at the time. This contestability of common concerns, she argues, points to the need for "perspective-taking." To ascertain which concerns are common is to consult the sentiments of those affected. It means that deliberating citizens have to take into consideration the perspectives and positions of the other members of the community. In the best of situations these citizens learn to empathize with one another.

Emotion and reason: Evidence from neuroscience

From a very different point of view, Marcus (2002) has also argued that our understanding of the relationship between reason and emotion in political science needs to be revised. He turns instead to contemporary research in neuroscience.[6] Here we discover that emotions, at least in important cases, actually trigger rather than hinder reason. Neuroscience, we learn, has identified two interrelated components of our emotional system, the dispositional and the surveillance subsystems. Thanks to the requirements of survival throughout the evolution of human species, these basic emotional processes became part of an inner warning or alarm system intricately involved in stimulating cognitive thought and deliberation. At the risk of dramatic over-simplification, the dispositional system attends to the everyday sensory stream; it receives all of the immediate information from the surrounding environment. Possessing an associative memory containing learned responses to different situations, it processes this information in terms of established categories. As such, it provides feedback

---

[6] Also see Thiele (2006), who connects practical wisdom and narration to neuroscience.

on the success or failure of current ongoing encounters and actions. In many of these cases, the power of the brain is not used all that much. Many of the responses simply trigger relative automatic behaviours based on learned habits and their cues. They do not really have to be thought about. And, in the course of such an action, the dispositional system relies on emotional markers to indicate the success or failure of each element at each stage of the plan of action as it unfolds. When things are either going well or failure is evident, we experience higher or lower levels of the relevant mood marker.

The second system, the surveillance system, works in conjunction with the dispositional system. It moves into action when circumstances or events do not correspond to the expectations and habits of the dispositional system. Specifically, the surveillance system monitors the courses of information in the brain. When it finds nothing unusual in the normal course of mundane events, it does not intrude either on the dispositional system or the activities of the mind. But when something novel or threatening does intrude, the surveillance system interrupts the ongoing behaviour, inhibits it, shifts awareness away from its current engrossed state toward the intrusion, and prepares the body for action. The surveillance system thus alerts us to the inappropriateness of continuing with what we are doing and shifts our attention toward the new and unfamiliar or threatening thing that has made its appearance. Threat or novel intrusions are marked by elevated levels of particular moods (such as concern, disquiet, or surprise), which in turn can trigger anxiety. And this is where the correction to traditional theory comes into the picture. If the surveillance system triggers anxiety, this anxiety sets the processes of reason in motion. Although the emotional system does not directly interact with the processes of reason at this point, it prepares the way for it. It lets the mind take over.

Marcus shows that these finding can be used to support and explain a good deal of research about political behaviour.[7] First, because there is too much going on in the political world for people either to grasp or stay on

---

[7] Westen (2007), also drawing on neuroscience, has more recently sought to demonstrate the way emotion plays a central role in electoral politics. In his book, *The Political Brain*, he argues that reason and rationality are not nearly as important as emotion in political decision processes (asserting that dispassionate reason by itself permits us to predict no more than three percent of the important decisions made by politicians and citizens). Given that the book focuses on the emotional dimensions of American political campaigns, it not surprisingly captured the attention of the political pundits. Arguing that Democratic Party politicians lose because they rely on logical policy arguments, and Republicans win by appealing to the heart, he was for a while a regular guest on the TV talk circuit. Some have argued that he has neglected the interrelationship of emotion to reason.

top of, they rely on the leaned habits of their dispositional systems. Citizens depend on the habits of the dispositional system, as "condensed forms of learning," to decide if something requires their attention or not. They tend, for example, to follow the lead of their party or political reference groups on particular issues. If those groups are not concerned, they don't get worried. Whereas many analysts have taken this to be a sign of apathy, it is seen in this light as a way of dealing with an otherwise overwhelming number of issues, many of them complicated and time-consuming. When some events don't fit into the expected patterns, however, the surveillance function switches on and they take interest. As Marcus (2002: 138) writes, "when the public feels anxious about something important, it stops relying on habit and learns about the alternatives, gets better informed about the issues, and when it comes time to take a judgment the public forswears reliance on simple likes and habitual cues for calculated consideration of the most promising alternatives that satisfy its calculated interests." Indeed, he argues, that "the strictly rational citizen without emotion ... will not react when presented with spectacle and therefore will not invest in learning what significance the situation may hold." He further points to other research that demonstrates that unemotional reason, even when it achieves a complete understanding of the problematic situation, will not lead to action. For the political activist this means finding ways of jarring people away from their political habits and getting them to see things differently—that is, to break out of their reliance on learned "rules of thumb" that rather autonomously govern their decision and actions (or inactions). Put differently, it involves creating the kind of anxiety that will trigger surveillance and, in turn, deliberative reason.

From these contributions we clearly see the need to rethink our epistemological understanding of the relation of reason to emotion.[8] Scarcely being antithetical to one another, they are discovered to work together in important ways. But what does this mean for social practices? How might we best use this information? Can it be incorporated into real-world decision-making? There are several suggestive lines of work to be considered here. One relates to the attempt to introduce and employ the concept of emotional intelligence in guiding social interaction and the other more specifically relates to emotion in deliberation.

---

[8] One should also see the pioneering works of Ciompi (2001) and Damasio (2005). Damasio analyzes the role of emotion from the perspective of practical judgment. He does it within an evolutionary perspective that focuses on each emotion in terms of its functional contribution to social adaptation.

Emotional intelligence and empathy

Whereas Nussbaum the philosopher and Marcus the political scientist have pointed to the ways that emotion is intricately bound up with various forms of knowing, psychologists have for some time researched what today they refer to as "emotional intelligence." Indeed, in recent times the idea of emotional intelligence and the interpersonal competencies to which is seen to give rise have been popularized in fields such as organizational psychology and educational testing.[9]

First coined by Salovey and Mayer in 1990, emotional intelligence refers to "a form of social intelligence that involves the ability to monitor one's own and others' feelings and emotions, to discriminate among them, and to use this information to guide one's thinking and action." Goleman, a trained psychologist and former science writer for the *New York Times*, popularized the term somewhat later. Drawing on research from social psychology and neuropsychology, Goleman (1995, 1998) calls attention to the fact that cognitive abilities are shown to play a relatively limited role in accounting for why some individuals are more successful than others. Not only does emotional intelligence relate to the ability to manage feelings and handle stress, it also involves knowing when and how to express emotion.[10] Studies demonstrate that effective leaders are people who tend to be sociable, warm, outgoing, and emotionally expressive. While much of this work shows that emotional intelligence alone is not a strong predictor of successful performance, it is seen to offer a foundation for competencies that are. One of those competencies is empathy, the ability to perceive and understand what other people are feeling.

Empathy is basic to interpersonal relations in all aspects of social life, including political deliberation (Goldie 2000: 176–219). Stated simply, it is the ability to stand in someone else's shoes and experience things the way

---

[9] The topic, however, is not new. It dates back to the research of psychologists such as Thorndike and Stein (1937) and Wechsler (1940) in the later 1930 and 1940s. Such work was largely forgotten until Gardner 1983) began to write about multiple forms of intelligence in the 1980s (Cherniss 2000).

[10] Emotional knowledge, in Goleman's view, is in large part the ability to understand, evaluate, adjust to, and influence the emotional behaviour of others. Much of this discussion of emotional knowledge has been applied to organizations and how to manage them. This application has led some to worry about superficial uses to this idea, especially as Goleman invents what he call the "Emotional Intelligence Quota" and the need to develop the appropriate skills to manage such knowledge. The idea that some might be able to manipulate emotions is scarcely new as all of the flags after the 9/11terrorist attack in New York have suggested. But the attempt to go into the business of measuring emotional intelligence as we do IQs strikes many as a worrisome orientation to an otherwise useful contribution to our understanding of the role of emotions.

they do. As the ability to take the perspective of the other person, it is the mental process that makes possible understanding others with whom one communicates, thus enabling meaningful interactions. Empathy, in short, refers to the capacity to emotionally know what another person—a "foreign" consciousness—is experiencing from within the frame of reference of that person.[11]

When people empathize with one another, the process tends to connect their senses of identity, a process that also facilitates social trust. Trust, in turn, is basic to building the kinds of social capital that make it possible for members of communities to work together effectively. Beyond its role in everyday life, empathy is also a psychological mechanism that psychotherapists have long used to help patients see other ways of viewing a situation in an effort to break through emotional blockages hindering new ways of dealing with problems (Bohart and Greenberg 1997).

To take an example, consider the role of empathy in foreign affairs, a realm often steeped in deep-seated emotional commitments to forms of nationalism, some of which have led to disastrous consequences. History books are loaded with stories of failure to understand the enemy. Such experiences show that there is no bigger mistake in foreign policymaking than an insensitivity or neglect of the nationalist sentiments of one's opponents. Indeed, former Secretary of Defence Robert McNamara (1995, 1999) identifies the US's—and his—biggest failure during the Vietnam War to have been a failure to understand not only what the Viet Cong was thinking but also what they were feeling. He has argued in various places for the need to learn to empathize with the enemy, to learn to perceive and understand the conflict.[12] In Vietnam then, the US government was not sensitive enough to how the country's actions registered emotionally with its adversaries, a neglect that has often led to

---

[11] Interestingly, the German word for empathy, "Einfuehlung," is translated as "feeling into."

[12] McNamara personally illustrates this point through a set of discursive exchanges organized with his former counterparts in North Vietnam. More than thirty years after the Vietnam War, he brought together the various political and military leaders pursuing each other as enemies at the time and, in an unprecedented move, conducted a series of discussions between them. During the war, the "Domino Effect Theory" was seen to be the central problem, namely that if the Vietnam fell to the communists, other states would also fall. But, as the former officials of North Vietnam clarified, the war had little to do with communism. It was rather about defence of their land which had been occupied for decades by various powers, a fact that gave rise to and supported a deep-seated nationalist passion that sustained their determination to continue their resistance even until the harshest of circumstances. Moreover, there was nothing in the statistical analyses of the Pentagon that could capture the intensity of these sentiments. In addition to his writings on the period, as well as these later discussions, the topic is the subject of a film about McNamara as Secretary of Defense during the war, "Fog of War."

an exacerbation of the intensity of such conflicts. One can say the same of the Bush Administration's understanding of the Iraqi people, as witnessed by the opposition in the post-Saddam phase of the war. In these cases, military occupation, particular military bases on foreign soil, have escalated nationalist emotions to levels that clearly contributed to embarrassing defeats.

Or take the role of human rights in foreign policy. Hunt (2007) has advanced the thesis that the contemporary emphasis on human rights can be traced to the rise of empathy in eighteenth-century European society, in particular in France. A new capacity for empathy, resulting for a complex set of reasons, rendered "self-evident" to many a belief in the equal distribution of human rights. Interestingly enough, she argues that the dramatic expansion of novel reading during that period significantly magnified this emergence of emotional empathy across national, gender and social class lines. Literary novels, she argues, helped people see that "foreign" others also had inner feelings and were thus basically similar in one of the most important human dimensions. Importantly, this led people to reject human cruelties, in particular forms of torture, that had in earlier centuries largely gone unquestioned. Although others have suggested that this increase in the reading of literature may have been more the result than the cause of the new feelings of sympathy and empathy, she has succeeded in demonstrating its emergence at that point in history (Woods 2007).

Both of these examples suggest the need to introduce policymakers to special sorts of communicative encounters in which adversaries learn more than the arguments of their opponents; they learn as well how they more fundamentally perceive and feel about the issues at hand, a point to which we return later in the chapter. But it is not only policymakers who need this kind of emotional intelligence. The same goes for the citizen, especially the citizen of a democratic society. If democracy is a set of institutions and practices designed to help citizens create and pursue ways of harmoniously—or at least managebly—living together, they need the ability to understand each other. If they are to democratically deliberate the issues, make choices and to act together, they have to be able to take account of each others' perspectives in their understanding of the problems the community faces and what responses to those problems might be most viable and just. In fact, it is just this consideration that has led many postmodern theorists to emphasize the importance of differences over a rather narrow understanding of consensus in deliberative politics. Citizens, it is argued, need to learn to deal with differences—political, cultural, ethnic, and religious—and the tensions and conflict to which they give rise with tolerance and respect. These sorts of political practices, as Hall writes, depend on citizen's abilities to cultivate generous forms of "reason-passion."

How do citizens learn this? They do it through empathy. They learn, in short, to stand in the other fellow's shoes and to see and feel the world from that perspective. Rather than merely dealing with facts, they need to get inside the worldview and emotional landscape of the other and to learn to empathize with him or her. One of the primary functions of literary writing, novels, films and plays, is to facilitate this vicarious dimension. As Nussbaum illustrates in detail, the narrative form is a primary vehicle that permits people to experience the lives of others and to exercise the art of empathy. She and others have stressed the need for more specific training in empathetic learning in schools.

There are, of course, concerns associated with attempts to more formally introduce such emotional learning. Some argue that it can easily be misused to promote destructive feelings and passion, such as racism, hostility to foreigners, or militaristic patriotism. Further, this would be especially worrisome if fostered by the state, as the consequences of Hitler's Germany and Stalin's Soviet Union made all too clear. In this regard, such education has to focus on the more constructive emotions that support and foster community among those involved, such as justice, tolerance, a passion for democratic ideals, and the like.

At this point, we turn back to deliberation and explore in more detail what emotion and empathy mean more specifically for policymaking and its analysis. In particular, how might we more formally deal with emotions in the design and facilitation of processes.

Emotion as discursive performance

Gottweis (2006) has pointed to the close relationship between rhetoric and the performative nature of communication and suggested that we apply the concept to the play of politics and public policymaking.[13] Indeed, historians have shown the close connection between Aristotle's rhetoric and the rise of public theatre and performance. From this perspective, emotions belong to "the repertoire of rhetoric," with verbal

---

[13] Gottweis (2005) illustrates the relationship in the case of stem cell research. Smullen (2007) demonstrates the way policy is rhetorically shaped in different political cultures.

statements and the display of passion coexisting as separate but combinable aspects of argumentation (Gottweis 2006). Such a position permits us to examine how language supplies a vehicle through which emotions have effects. Emotional expression can be approached, in Lutz and White's (1986) conceptualization, as a communicative performance in the context of argumentation. Emotion, in this view, is itself a discursive practice.

Hajer (2005), examining various forms of discursive practices, has explored the performative dimensions of policy deliberation by combining Goffman's ethnographical approach to public interaction with Austin's work on language. Toward this end, he emphasizes the importance of the dramaturgy in deliberative settings, in particular the way spoken words and the feelings attached to them are translated into the theatre of everyday life. Yet others have sought further insights from the work of French theorists on "scenography," concerned with the ways speech is constructed in particular public contexts and how performative strategies are discursively employed in such interactions (Caron 1983; Adam 1999; Gottweis 2006).

Performativity, as discursive practice, helps us recognize that different policy issues give rise to different scenarios of discursive engagement. The arena for a policy deliberation, differing discursive vocabularies, and the role of timing, have important—sometimes decisive impacts—on the responses elicited from citizens and politicians. Over time, particular styles of argumentation are seen to set in—e.g. rational argumentative, pragmatic-instrumental, or emotive; they establish different locations and roles in the policy decision-making process. One can compare, for example, the technocratically oriented debates about energy power or military affairs, typically executive dominated politics, with the emotionally laden argumentation surrounding abortion or stem cell research, with people frequently taking to the streets to protest. Despite the fact that such scenarios are politically contested over time, and do at times change, they constitute important explanatory factors in the decision-making processes of dealing with policy issues.

But much of this work is at a fairly high level of theoretical abstraction. While it offers considerable promise in opening up our understanding of policy rhetoric and performativity, we still need case studies that more carefully indicate the nature of scenographies. How, for example, might the planner or policy analyst employ dramaturgy in real world practices? Sandercock (2003) and Hoch (2006) have argued that planners have to recognize emotional expression to be an important aspect of efforts to bring about progressive change. Planners, Sandercock argues, need to focus on the ways emotions hinder or facilitate the sorts of work involved in transforming institutions and values.[14] Whereas the language of planning has traditionally centered around techno-rational discourse, explicitly ruling out emotional expression, planners have failed to understand that their efforts to bring about such change are inherently linked to both the fears and hopes of the members of the community.[15] For instance, when a housing project or a park is the issue at stake, the more hidden emotional and symbolic issues are often much more important. This can especially be the case for the less fortunate, fearing that their very presence in the area is threatened. In just such cases, what otherwise might seem to many like a small concern is actually about big issues such as civic identity, cultural history, and social injustice.

In such situations, we need to carefully consider the ways in which deeply felt concerns and beliefs are related to basic social identities, whether those of a community or the specific individuals who live in it. The point is particularly important for organizing deliberative fora, as we saw in discussion of the scenario workshop in the preceding chapter. When it comes to heated deliberation, more comes into play than just the topics under discussion; the very protection of the individual's self is at stake. In the process of expressing their preferences and interests, as Blaug (1999: 153) explains, participants often take challenges to their ideas as a criticism of themselves and, in the process, assess the views of other participants in just the same way. The hurt feelings that easily result, as he points out, can make "deliberative fora . . . dangerous places" for some people, "and if they become too dangerous, they will, quite rationally, be avoided by participants."[16] Not everyone will be comfortable with such interpersonal clashes. Many participants will exclude themselves from the exchanges; others will be excluded by the group, the result of which undercuts the legitimacy of the deliberative process. For this reason, how to manage emotional issues becomes an essential question. As we saw in Goersdorf's discussion of the scenario workshop, the organizers of such fora need to make crucial decisions about how to deal with these

[14] Hoch (2006: 378) offers a number of sketches that illustrate the way planning processes are laden with emotional considerations and points to the need for planners to develop "an effective tool for grasping the systematic relationships between institutional conditions or organizational practices and emotional response."

[15] See Baum's (1997) concept of "the organization of hope."

[16] Failure to attend to emotional considerations can easily bog down decision processes. As Blaug (1991: 154) writes, "groups who avoid emotional questions find, ironically, that they must deal with them more and more, even to the point of having those issues erupt in such a way as to cause the demise of a deliberative outbreak."

intersubjective issues in the early stages of deliberative design. They need to build in opportunities for the participants to express and process their feelings. As Blaug (1999: 154) puts it, "people need to speak of such matters, receive support and feel safe, if they are to remain members of the group." It is a dimension of deliberation that the activists of the Science for the People movement recognized in their efforts to socially valorize the deliberative fora of the People's Campaign.

We also gain important insights into how to approach such emotional conflict from several planning experiences reported by Sandercock (2003). We turn to them in the next and final section of the chapter.

Emotional performativity in planning: Notes for practice

Planners, Sandercock (2003: 153) maintains, have largely neglected the deep-seated fears and hopes involved in community building, especially in depressed areas. To illustrate this, she points to Frug's (1999) work on the "fear of the stranger," the black stranger in particular, that often blocks constructive urban re-development. Whereas most approaches to community development deal with the "hardware" of planning—physical structures, secure buildings, safe parks, and property protection—the focus needs to turn as well to what she calls the emotional "software" of fear itself.

The progressive planner's efforts to bring about social change, Sandercock argues (p. 153), are bound up with organizing hope, negotiating fears, mediating memories, and facilitating community soul searching. The process requires getting people to deal with the fears that immobilize them, and in the process, to confront the prejudices that distort their basic humanity. Generating community engagement, as she sees it, means breaking through this despair and passivity. Although it will strike some as beyond the realm of the planner, she suggests the need for a "therapeutic approach" (p. 152). A better term, in my view, would be an "empathetic approach"; it is employed below.[17]

In contrast to rational deliberation, an empathetic approach would start with an understanding and analysis of the emotional context at the heart of the particular issue or problem; it would then focus on developing processes for confronting the emotional barriers to effective community

---

[17] In the context of urban planning, "therapy" has awkward connotations. It strikes some as implying that the planner is putting community members in the same category as patients. Moreover, planners seldom have psychological training.

collaboration. The goal is to move from the possibility of a "merely workable solution"—defined as "getting to yes" in contemporary jargon—to the broader considerations of public welfare (Sandercock 2003: 160). Beyond offering "band-aid solutions," the task is to transcend the kinds of strategic, conflictual behavior associated with interest group bargaining through processes of social learning capable of facilitating transformational change.

Social transformations in politics, as with successful therapy, require political-psychological breakthroughs capable of opening up new pathways to individual growth and social engagement. The process involves confronting the underlying social relationships that structure and manage co-existence in the shared spaces of local communities. Only by carefully working through the understandings—often tacit understandings—that define such spaces can the possibility of the collective emerge. Transformative learning, as we saw in Chapter 8, involves processes of public learning aimed at shifting social values and the institutional practices that embody them. Although there is no guarantee of success, such processes appear to be the only way forward in cases where deep-seated social conflicts have long stymied conventional techniques of conflict negotiation.

There is no better illustration of this process than the South African Truth and Reconciliation Commission (Sandercock 2003: 161). Nothing was easy about the work of the Commission, but it did go considerable distance toward shifting the social climate of hatred to a sense of forgiveness— at least enough forgiveness—which facilitated the rebuilding of the country after years of brutal apartheid and all of the social injustices that were associated with it. The Commission, in short, performed a "cathartic function" for citizens who long carried inside deep-rooted feelings of anger, fear, and betrayal; it permitted others whose hearts and minds had been shut off from the cruel realities to hear the full emotional expression of those who suffered. So profound was the experience that even those of us who had the opportunity to simply observe some of the hearings could personally feel the dramatic transformative power of this cathartic process.

It is not that a mere display of emotion is enough. Here, in ways strikingly similar to the processes of neurochemistry, the goal is to trigger reason and deliberation as a response to heightened levels of emotional expression. What is needed, then, is a model for staging such social confrontations. As Sandercock put it (2003: 159), when the conflicting parties "involved in a dispute have been at odds for generations, or come from disparate cultural traditions, or where there is a history of marginalization, something more than the usual methods of negotiation and mediation are needed. An approach is needed that complements but also transcends the highly rational processes typical of the communicative action model" and its emphasis on argumentation. (p. 159). In "situations where direct, face-to-face meetings are unthinkable or unmanageable because of histories of conflict and of marginalization," discursive design processes are needed that offer the parties opportunities to uncover problems and issues that are difficult to approach—if at all approachable—through rational-deliberative processes (Sandercock 2003: 159). When emotional intensity hinders a more formal deliberation, participants need a forum that allows them to tell the stories that convey their feelings.

Sandercock founds her argument on several cases in which planners confronted emotional fears and anxieties in just this way. Basic to these cases was the need to have an expressive stage before moving on to deliberation and negotiation. In one of the cases, this involved a first phase devoted to a cathartic, emphatic out-letting of the kinds of deeper emotional realities that do not or cannot get expressed in a more deliberative, argumentative setting. In this initial forum, participants got a chance to air their own feelings about a situation or project.

Such a process best begins with a series of preparatory meetings in which a planning team meets separately with the conflicting groups. Focused on the hopes and fears of those involved, such meetings—which might usefully include a community psychologist—would best take place in emotionally security settings, such as the living rooms of the various parties. In one of the cases Sandercock reports on, the process also included discussions with the children and teenagers of the families involved.

The activity in this initial phase is primarily storytelling, just as the residents tell the stories to themselves, with the planners listening to them with minimal intervention. Such gatherings might best be organized with the assistance of a local moderator. Specifically, the goal is to learn about the cultural histories of the residents, their local experiences, and their own understandings of their social identities. During such discussions, the planners might hear a particular group express anger and resentment over increasing numbers of foreigners or poor ethnic groups moving into the neighborhood, to whom they attribute rising crime rates in the streets and playgrounds, often drug related. In a typical scenario, they would most likely tell how they struggled hard to come to the neighborhood and to buy a house, all with great hopes and expectations that their children would be able to make a better life for themselves. Now they have seen how all of this has downgraded the local schools their children attend. Anger and hostility pour out as they criticize local political officials for now wanting to turn one of the parks into a high-rise housing project for more of these same people.

After these preparatory discussions, a speak-out can be organized in which each of the groups would be encouraged to participate (Sandercock 2003: 159). The goal is to get community groups to say how they feel before the discussion turns to specific plans or programs. It is to encourage people to say in the presence of the other groups what they feel—to speak the unspeakable—no matter how unpleasant or how painful it might be for the others to hear. A full expression of painful feelings would be heard by those whose hearts and ears have been closed (Forester 2000). Designed as a cathartic experience, this speaking out can serve to generate empathy among those carrying destructive anger, fear of betrayal, grievances over previous losses, and the like. It is not that conflicts would be altogether eliminated, but rather that the "speak out" can be used to reduce the levels of tension enough to make possible a workable level of discussion.[18] Organizing this airing of underlying concerns can create a basis for building a new trust capable of encouraging the participants to engage in the kinds of discussion that can make new agreements possible and move the community forward.

After the speak-out, the process then shifts to holding joint group discussions pursued through the more standard kind of negotiation-oriented deliberations. These discussions would focus on creating the sorts of agreements that would make possible future meetings about planning issues, and eventually meetings in which specific plans could be drawn up. Here, as in the early stages, the guiding principle is not to force closure before there is the possibility of a genuine agreement, one that proves to be more than an unhappily accepted deal.

This kind of work, combing confrontation and dialogue across the divide of cultural differences, requires the practitioner to be knowledgeable and fluent in various modes of communication, from storytelling and listening to interpreting visual and body language. The initial phases can

---

[18] Blaug (1999: 153) refers to this as a discursive "management problem." As he put it, "When people engage in agonistic debate, there is a tremendous outpouring of emotion, and while this can be both enjoyable and empowering, it also presents the group with a significant management problem" (defined not in terms of control but rather coping). The failure to manage the emotional content of such interactions poses a threat to their ability to survive as a workable entity.

also employ the kinds of participatory research techniques that we have discussed in the two previous chapters. Indeed, Sandercock tells of a case in which the planners did just that. Participatory research was used to help the local residents identify their community's sense of identity, even to recreate a new identity based on the community's own multi-cultural history. By getting the citizens themselves to collect and tell their own narratives, planners succeeded in helping the participants both to build a new narrative and rename the area based on it. This active process of reconstructing a new narrative and urban identity proved useful in setting the stage for turning the area around. Not only did it motivate the residents by relating problematic stories to an optimistic vision of the future, but it also gave them a new sense of hope. In short, identities got translated into a promising vision that became the basis for action. It is an example of Throgmorton's conception of "planning as persuasive storytelling."

The message from the kind of work that Sandercock reports on is clear. The planner, like Marcus's political activist, has to find ways of jarring community members away from destructive habits and beliefs; through the processes of catharsis and empathy they need to encourage participants to see and think about each other in a different light. There is, to be sure, little or nothing in contemporary planning or policy curricula that offers any sort of training or guidance that would be useful in helping prospective practitioners to think through and implement such a strategy. Indeed, it is more typically the kind of activity that might best be conducted with the assistance of a psychologist. Much of it is more closely related to the practices of educational psychologists engaged in the sort of transformational learning discussed in Chapter 8. A few psychologists engaged in the study and practice of conflict mediation have begun to work on techniques for dealing with the interpersonal, emotional sides of deliberation (Leary 2004). Such work offers useful insights into how we might proceed in developing fora and practices for an empathetic approach.[19] How to work this into the practice of planning constitutes a formidable intellectual challenge.

[19] Leary (2004), for example, has used the methods of ethnography and oral history to examine micro level interactions in conflictual negotiations. She identifies "critical moments" in discursive process, as seen by the participants themselves, that are basic to intersubjective change and the productive attitudinal shifts that can accompany them. Of special importance in bringing them about are the relational interactions between the facilitators and the participants.

Conclusion

This chapter has explored one of the seriously neglected topics in both the theory of deliberation and the methods of the social sciences more generally. Not only has the role of emotion been neglected, emotional expression has been defined as the enemy of rational deliberation. As we have seen, there has been in more recent years a renewed interest in this topic in some quarters; a number of scholars have begun to rethink the relationship of reason to emotion and passion. The discussion showed the ways Nussbaum's writings have brought the topic to the fore for detailed scrutiny. Rather than the enemy of reason, her work demonstrates the ways in which emotions actually function in tandem with rational thought processes. In addition, the arguments of Hall and Krause were presented to demonstrate that a commitment to rational discourse, as well as to the objects of such discourse, are grounded in emotional commitments. In a very different but supportive light, Marcus's contribution was seen to show neuroscience to offer grounds for the same basic conclusion. To that we added psychological evidence from studies of emotional intelligence.

From these discussions we come to understand argumentation as occurring within specific emotional landscapes across which it does not easily travel. If the emotional terrain is settled, specific objects can be singled out and successfully deliberated. However, if the terrain is uncertain or turbulent, argumentation often only generates further conflict, as emotions churn up the undersides of the discussion that otherwise remain hidden, sometimes tacitly so. Under such circumstances various discursive points will be emotionally expressed in ways that can be counterproductive from the perspective of rational argument.

An awareness of this relationship, however, still leaves open the practical question of how to deal with the interrelationship between the two. One route, as we have seen, is to return to Aristotle's rhetoric, which brings reason and emotion into close contact with one another. The approach suggests the need for different arenas for these modes of expression, which dramaturgy and scenography can help us to better understand. While these discussions move us forward, they are still seen to remain too abstract. We were then able to take another step with the assistance of practical insights offered by illustrations from planning experiences. As Sandercock has shown, such work suggests something of a two-stage process, involving first the outletting of emotion as a precondition for more rational deliberation. Depending on the outcome of that process—or what she calls a "speak-out"—it can secondly be possible to engage in a more formal kind of deliberation based on reasoned argumentation. Emotions, to be sure, do not disappear, but the disruptive excitement that often blocks deliberation can potentially be constructively channeled, thus permitting people to deal at specific points with particular ideas and proposals. Without denying or attempting to eliminate emotional commitments, it can at least get participants talking to one another.

There are, of course, no guarantees in such processes. But it is, at the same time, important to have a better awareness of the emotive processes at work. In the absence of such recognition, as countless failed efforts to deliberate demonstrate, an essential component of the process is not brought into play. If not confronted, such emotional tensions typically only remain at bay to return problematically at a later phase of a controversy. That is, they don't simply go away.

The foregoing discussion, as such, makes clear that a deliberative process is not finished until the emotional reactions that occur in the course of the exchange have come to rest. This necessarily involves building in openings for their expression at the outset of discursive processes and then again later to make sure that everyone feels alright about any decisions that emerge from the process. Little is gained in the long term by formally winning an argument if all of the parties are not comfortable with the outcome. An outcome that leaves bad feelings carries forward problems—perhaps only latent at first—that easily give rise to an active opposition to the initial results. In policy politics, this typically occurs in the process of implementing the decision.

Finally, we conclude by again underscoring that there is nothing simple about emotions. But we are no strangers to them in everyday life. Indeed, we deal with them all day long. And some people do it better than others. When we come to a more careful consideration of their role, however, they reveal themselves to be a complex and uncertain phenomenon. Now that some have begun to open the door to their consideration, it is time to begin examining their role more systematically. This chapter, to be sure, is only a preliminary effort to encourage such work. It is offered in the hope of playing in some small way a role in furthering this effort.

Afterword

The preceding chapters have examined the relation of expertise to citizen deliberation and the implications for deliberative democratic politics, both in theory and practice. In large part the work has been normative and, as such, a contribution to theory. It recognizes that we do not live in a deliberative democracy, although there is plenty of deliberation going on. Addressing practices that have yet to be fully worked out, it attempts to bring these two realities closer together. The discussion has thus been designed to help us think about how we might move forward in doing this. Much of it, to be sure, remains more useful in the experiential setting. But that is one of the ways change works. We need ideas and models for the efforts to bring it about.

The position taken here also recognizes that an attempt to expand democratic practices must concede a basic political fact: Throughout the history of democratic struggles, the idea of democracy has remained as much a vision that has guided efforts to extend participation over centuries as it has been a reality. But the vision has not been without progressive consequences—a woman is the Chancellor of Germany and a black man is now the president of the United States. It is important, in this regard, not to overlook the function of such democratic principles and concepts in the critically important realm of political discourse. The virtue of democratic theory is to be found in the legacy of standards it has bequeathed. Although political theorists will continue to debate the proper application of such standards, they nonetheless provide valuable criteria to which political movements can appeal and against which political practices can be discussed and judged. The very purpose of democracy is to establish a framework for engaging in open discourse and, in turn, for judging its quality. As public philosophy, democratic principles are essential to the processes of free and candid discussion in public affairs.

Nonetheless concepts such as "town hall democracy" strike many as overly idealistic in a complex modern society. What can participatory democracy mean under contemporary circumstances? Given the rapid pace of technological and social change, the idea that it might be democratically guided and controlled through citizen participation is no simple contention. While current realities pose difficult questions—and such change is surely based on ideals scarcely shared by all—this study has attempted in all cases to ground the arguments in practices that have already emerged. That is, the ideas put forward here are anchored to more than a theorist's speculation.

One of the important anchors for the position here, as we have noted throughout, has been the developments in the field of New Democratic Governance. Indeed, the policy politics associated with governance has in important ways already begun to move to the forefront of the struggles to revitalize democracy (Warren 2008). In just this respect, we find public administrative theorists working out new conceptions of the public administrator as facilitator of communities of participation based on citizen engagement (Feldman and Khademian 2007). At the same time, others speak of a new value-oriented public service, the public administrator and policy planner as facilitator, discursive approaches to public decision-making and collaborative planning, and new concepts of public value (Forester 1999; Stoker 2006; Denhardt and Denhardt 2007). While these approaches do not constitute the mainstream perspective, they are now widely recognized. And there are few theoretical discussions in policy or administration that can be judged more interesting.

In view of the challenge, this study has approached the issue of participation cautiously. It has worked, as such, from a realistic assumption—namely, that not everyone must—or even can—participate in the deliberation of all matters. In a complex socio-technical society this is as impossible as it is undesirable. The chapters have posed, in this regard, a more appropriate—but nonetheless pressing—question: How can we lessen the substantial gap between elite decision-making centers and the vast majority of citizens largely left out of the process? Can we, toward this end, build participatory institutions that establish and mediate procedural and discursive relationships between elite decisionmakers, professional experts, and the more actively interested members of the public? Is it possible to design participatory political arrangements at the community levels of a complex society that can, in turn, be authentically linked to higher level decision processes of a representative government, as we saw in the case of Kerala? And can the citizens of these communities in fact meaningfully engage the complex policy issues at hand?

The focus throughout has been on a critical dimension of such delibera-tive participation—one that has regularly failed to receive enough attention in democratic theory—namely, the role of expertise. In the "knowledge society," where professional experts move to the center of the policymaking processes, the political role of expert discourses becomes increasingly evi-dent. Policy analysts and planners—like experts generally—have largely been committed to the art and science of their discourses. As Gouldner (1979) has argued, it is a culture of discourse that defines and unites the technical intelligentsia itself. While their instrumental discourses have often had detrimental consequences for the advance of democratic deliberation, it is the emphasis on discourse itself that offers an opening for those who challenge the orientation. The professional preoccupation with their own discourses—albeit rationally codified discourses—makes it difficult for ex-perts to ignore altogether the wider realm of discourse, including the com-peting discourses of democratic political and social theory. At the same time, however, democratic theorists who wish to engage technical experts in discursive exchanges must also confront the challenge of technological society. Not longer can they limit themselves to the task of theoretical critique. To effectively undermine the technocratic position, they must also show the ways in which democracy can be made compatible with technical complexity. Democratic theorists must take up the "nuts and bolts of democracy" (Fischer 1990; Sclove 1995). At this level, theorists must focus more specifically on the operant political theories that underlie contemporary institutions and their expert practices. Needed is a democratic theory capable of moving from critique to social reconstruction.

Rethinking the practices of expertise has not meant here entirely redefining what the professions do; all experts do not need to engage all of the time in participatory inquiry. But the book has called for a re-orientation back to the public and for a new specialization concerned with the policy epistemics that would inform it. This new orientation, geared to deliberative empowerment, is not designed altogether to turn professional policy practices upside down, but rather to extend the assign-ment to include a new responsibility. It would be *one* of the specializations that constitute the field of policy inquiry, particularly as it is manifested in policy analysis and planning. Such a specialization would emphasize more broadly the role of public enlightenment.

Toward this end, the work here has focused on citizen empowerment. Taking up Dewey's earlier challenge, we have sought ways that experts might facilitate citizen deliberation, including their competencies to do so. One aspect of such deliberative empowerment involves developing and designing discursive settings, finding out more about how citizens learn, and ways to mobile the kinds of resources that help them do that (Hirschhorn 1979). From this perspective, the role of policy science extends to assisting in constituting the political-discursive community itself. To this end, we have examined the possibilities by exploring a range of theories and practices. In the realm of social and political theory, we have looked in particular at the traditional understanding of the professional's relationship to the communities they serve, the potentials of deliberative democracy, and the possibilities of participatory governance. In terms of knowledge and expertise, we have turned to work in the social studies of science, social constructivism in particular. It is seen to open up professional expertise in ways that can benefit from public input. This was explored in terms of the epistemologies that differentiate the technical/instrumental and political realms and the sociopolitically constructed nature of public policy, followed by discussions of the role of narratives, tacit knowledge, the intersubjective empowerment of deliberative spaces, and the complicated question of the role of emotion in public deliberation. All of these issues pertain to deliberative empowerment; none of them suggest that the task is easy. It is thus important to have a better grasp of the terrain ahead.

Nowhere are the implications of this postempiricist oreintation more important than in the contemporary policy curriculum. One issue for educational training has do with the epistemics of knowledge and practice; another has to do with professional conduct, in particular as it relates to the social-psychological orientation of the client or citizen. With regard to education, a primary issue for the curriculum has to do with epistemology. Still largely dominated by an outmoded conception of scientific knowledge, the social and policy sciences ill-equip their doctoral students for the world they are sent out to confront. Armed with empirical research designs and statistical methods, many often have little or no training in understanding either the normative and interpretive foundations of the tools they have learned to rely upon, or the social and political settings to which these techniques are to be applied. Some, to be sure, recognize these interpretive dimensions of the practice, but for reasons of examination and employment are compelled to concentrate on empirical methods. As students come to see the limits of these methods, the disciplinary neglect of these issues and concerns can breed more than a little cynicism. Some simply are turned off; others go through the academic ritual but turn away from—if not against—these methods after jumping over the requisite set of hurdles.

For a long time the argument against changing the curricular focus has turned on the problem of alternatives. Given the absence of credible alternatives, so the argument has gone, it is better to hang on to the traditional—albeit problematic—methods than to step into a methodological void. This, however, no longer needs to be the case. As we have shown here, postempiricism outlines the foundations of a new orientation. Not only does it offer a theory and epistemology of the social and policy science that is readily identifiable in our existing practices, it also incorporates new methods and approaches rather than simply rejecting old ones. In particular, it helps us explore a form of practical public knowledge that interactively brings together the technical and the social. By giving new life to methods and practices, it opens the way to a richer and more productive approach to social and policy inquiry.

Beyond the methodology curriculum, important implications for professional conduct and the public understanding of scientific expertise flow from a postempiricist, discursive model of inquiry. Holding out the possibility of realizing a policy science of democracy, it calls for participatory institutions and practices that open democratic spaces for citizen deliberation of empirical outcomes, contextual assumptions, and the social meaning of conclusions. The ultimate success of a postempiricist policy science will depend upon political and institutional reforms. The goal of such an approach thus remains bound to progress in the struggle to further democratize political decision-making.

This, of course, is more than a matter of changing decision practices; it is even more fundamentally a matter of political culture—namely, bringing about a genuinely democratic political culture. Such change, to be sure, does not take place overnight. But basic to moving it along, we have argued here, has to be a more democratic attitude on the part of policy professionals, rather than the more common top–down, often elitist orientation. We raised the need for a different kind of socialization of professionals in Chapter 8, one that brings them closer to their clients. A participatory orientation, however, requires as well a stronger democratic culture and the mentality that goes with it.

Given that many professionals will find the idea of innovating more participatory approaches unrealistic—if not foolish—introducing these practices into the established professions is no small consideration. Flying in the face of the standard technical rationalities and hierarchical structures that govern the knowledge professions and their practices, bringing such a participatory approach into the established professions might not be much easier today than it proved to be in the 1960s and 1970s, as we saw in the opening chapter. With the exception of a small number of progressive professionals devoted to innovating alternative practices, a citizen or client's role in professional practice is generally treated as a challenge, if not threat, to professional status and authority.

The orientation adopted here, however, is different. Not only is it less strident, it is based on a considerable amount of political experience and social learning since those earlier years. Perhaps most importantly, it recognizes from the outset that establishing participatory inquiry in the professions will depend as much on cooperative support from social and civic movements outside the universities. In this respect, the possibilities are as much a matter of politics as they are methodological innovation. But it is also a matter of education, political education in particular. Democracy, as Dewey argued, is as much a way of life—a set of social relationships among citizens—as it is a set of institutional and electoral relationships, not to overlook political struggles. From this view, education for democratic life is the most fundamental goal of a properly designed educational system. Beyond the democratic education of all citizens, as we have argued here, professional education would have to be re-designed to fit the society which it exists to serve.

In so far as the needed changes are significantly connected to matters of education, it is important to recognize that professionals are themselves the products of an extensive education, and that many of them remain educators makes the terrain, if not the task, familiar. Given that education remains a primary vehicle, the challenge is to change its content. Today professionals are taught to work from the top–down. The goal is not to flatten out expertise, as we saw in Chapter 5, but rather to extend the playing field. Instead of top–down, we need to interconnect the top and the bottom.

Finally, the society we live in is techno-bureaucratic in form and there are big rewards for serving this system. Much of what goes on inside the university is aimed at facilitating the technocratic system of expertise—indeed, this is what is marketed to the students. At this stage, what is needed is a politics of expertise inside the disciplines that reflects the kinds of concerns raised in the chapters here, as well as the related issues of the progressive movements beyond the walls of the university. In all cases, these concerns and the politics associated with them should be taken on as part of the agenda of those in the policy professions committed to democratic decision-making in a more egalitarian society. Making participatory policy inquiry poses, in this respect, one of the important challenges of our time.

References

Abdelrahman, M. M. (2004). *Civil Society Exposed: The Politics of NGOs in Egypt.* London: Tauris Academic Studies.

Abu-Lughod, L. and Lutz A. C. (1990). "Introduction: Emotion, Discourse, and the Politics of Everyday Life," in L. Abu-Lughod and A. C. Lutz (eds.), *Language and the Politics of Emotions.* Cambridge: Cambridge University Press, 1–23.

Ackerman, B. and Fishkin J. (2004). *Deliberation Day.* New Haven: Yale University Press.

Adam, J-M. (1999). *Linguistique texteulle et analyse des pratiques discursives.* Paris: Nathan.

Ahmed, D. (2004). *The Cultural Politics of Emotion.* London: Routledge.

Alcamo, J. (2001). *"Scenarios as Tools for International Environmental Assessments."* Environmental Issue Report, No. 24. Copenhagen: European Environmental Agency.

Alcoff, L. and Potter, E. (eds.) (1993). *Feminist Epistemologies.* New York: Routledge.

Almond, G. and Verba, S. (1963). *The Civic Culture.* Princeton, NJ: Princeton University Press.

Americans Talk Issues Foundation (1994). "Steps for Democracy: The Many Versus the Few," 24, 9–19 January.

Andersen, I. E. and Jaeger, B. (1999). "Scenario Workshops and Consensus Conferences: Towards More Democratic Decision-Making," *Science and Public Policy,* 26: 331–40.

Andrews, M. (2007). *Shaping History: Narratives of Political Change.* Cambridge: Cambridge University Press.

Arendt, H. (1968). *Between Past and Future: Eight Exercises in Political Thought.* New York: Viking Press.

—— (1972). *Crises of the Republic.* New York: Harvest Books.

Argyris, C. (1990). *Overcoming Organizational Defense—Facilitating Organizational Learning.* Needham, MA: Allyn and Bacon.

—— and Schön, D. A. (1996). *Organizational learning II: Theory, Method and Practice.* Reading, MA: Addison-Wesley.

Aristotle (1991). *On Rhetoric. A Theory of Civic Discourse.* Newly translated with introduction, notes, and appendixes by G. A. Kennedy. Oxford: Oxford University Press.

References

Backstrand, K. (2004). "Scientisation vs. Civic Expertise in Environmental Governance: Eco-feminism, Eco-Modern and Postmodern Responses," *Environmental Politics*, 13 (4): 695–714.

Bahro, R. (1987). *Logic der Rettung: Wer kann die Apokalypse Aufhalten?* Stuttgart: Weitbrecht.

Baiocchi, G. (2003). "Participation, Activism, and Politics: The Porto Alegre Experiment," in A. Fung and E. O. Wright, *Deepening Democracy*. New York: Verso Press: 45–76.

Barber, B. (1984). *Strong Democracy*. Berkeley: University of California Press.

Barth, T. J. (1996). "Administering the Public Interest: The Facilitative Role for Public Administrators," in G. L. Wamsley and J. F. Wolf (eds.), *Refounding Democratic Public Administration*. Newbury Park, CA: Sage, 168–97.

Bast, J. H. *et al.* (1994). *Eco-Sanity*. Lanham: Madison Press.

Bateson, G. (2000). *Steps to an Ecology of Mind: Collected Essays in Anthropology, Psychiatry, Evolution, and Epistemology*. Chicago: University of Chicago Press.

Baum, H. D. (1997). *The Organization of Hope*. Albany: State University of New York Press.

Baum, H. S. (1999). "Forgetting to Plan," *Journal of Planning Education and Research*, 19: 2–14.

Baumgartner, F. and Jones, B. (1983). *Agendas and Instability in American Politics*. Chicago: University of Chicago Press.

Beck, U. (1985). *Ecological Politics in an Age of Risk*. London: Polity Press.

—— (1992). *The Risk Society*. Newbury Park, CA: Sage.

—— (1995). *Ecological Enlightenment*. Atlantic Highlands, NJ: Humanities Press International.

Beder, S. (1999). "Public Participation or Public Relations?" in B. Martin, (ed.), *Technology and Public Participation: Science and Technology Studies*. Wollongong, Australia: University of Wollongong, 169–192.

Bell, D. (1960). *The End of Ideology*. New York: The Free Press.

Benhabib, S. (1996). "Towards a Deliberative Model of Democratic Legitimacy," in S. Benhabib (ed.), *Democracy and Difference: Contesting Boundaries of the Political*. Princeton: Princeton University Press.

Berger, P. and Luckmann, T. (1966). *The Social Construction of Reality: A Sociology of Knowledge*. London: Penguin Books.

Berger, T. (1977). *Northern Frontier, Northern Homeland: The Report of the Mackenszie Valley Pipeline Inquiry*, Vols. 1–2. Ottawa: Supply and Services.

—— (1985). *Village Journey: The Report of the Alaska Native Review Commission*. *New York*: Wang and Hill.

Bernstein, R. J. (1976). *The Restructuring of Social and Political Theory*. New York: Harcourt Brace Jovanovich.

—— (1983). *Between Objectivism and Relativism: Science, Hermeneutics, and Praxis*. Philadelphia: University of Pennsylvania.

Berube, M. (1996). "Public Perceptions of the Universities and Faculty," *Academe*, 82 (4), July–August: 10–17.

Bessette, J. (1994). *The Mild Voice of Reason: Deliberative Democracy and American Constitutional Government*. Chicago: University of Chicago Press.

Best, J. (2007). *Social Problems*. New York: W.W. Norton.

Bevir, M. (2006). "Democratic Governance: Systems and Radical Perspectives," *Public Administration Review*, May/June: 426–36.

Blais, A. R., Carter, K., and Fournier, P. (2008). *Do Citizens' Assemblies Make Reasoned Choices?* in M. E. Warren and H. Pearce (eds.), *Designing Deliberative Democracy: The British Columbia's Citizen Assembly*. Cambridge: Cambridge University Press: 127–44.

Blaug, R. (1999). *Democracy, Real and Ideal*. Albany: State University of New York Press.

Bledstein, B. J. (1976). *Culture of Professionalism: The Middle Class and the Development of Higher Education*. New York: Norton.

Bohman, James. (1996). *Public Deliberation: Pluralism, Complexity, and Democracy*. Cambridge: Cambridge University Press.

Bobbio, N. (1987). *The Future of Democracy*. Minneapolis: University of Minnesota.

Bocking, S. (2004). *Nature's Experts: Science, Politics, and the Environment*. New Burnswick: Rutgers University Press.

Bohart, A. C. and Greenberg, L. S. (eds.) (1997). *Empathy Reconsidered: New Directions in Psychotherapy*. Washington, DC: American Psychological Association.

Bohman, J. (1996). *Public Deliberation: Pluralism, Complexity, and Democracy*. Cambridge, MA: MIT Press.

—— (1998). "The Coming of Age of Deliberative Democracy," *The Journal of Political Philosophy*, 6: 400–25.

Bohman, J. and Rehg, W. (eds.) (1997). *Deliberative Democracy*. Cambridge, MA: MIT Press.

Bordo, S. (1987). *The Flight to Objectivity: Essays on Cartesianism and Culture*. Albany, NY: SUNY Press.

Bourdieu, P. (1977). *Outline of a Theory of Practice*. Cambridge: Cambridge University Press.

—— (1993). *The Field of Cultural Production*. New York: Columbia University Press.

Bozeman, B. (1986). "The Credibility of Policy Analysis: Between Method and Use," *Policy Studies Journal*, 14: 519–39.

Brecht, A. (1959). *Political Theory: The Foundations of Twentieth-Century Political Thought*. Princeton, NJ: Princeton University Press.

Brecht, B. (1965). *Schriften zum Theater*. Ost Berlin: Aufbau Verlag.

Brint, S. (1994). *In an Age of Expertise*. Princeton: Princeton University Press.

Brodbeck, M. (1960). "Review: *Personal Knowledge*," *American Sociological Review*, August: 583.

References

Brookfield, S. D. (1986). *Understanding and Facilitating Adult Learning*. San Francisco, CA: Jossey-Bass.

—— (1988). *Developing Critical Thinkers: Challenging Adults to Explore Alternative Ways of Thinking and Acting*. San Francisco, CA: Jossey-Bass.

—— (1995). *Becoming a Critically Reflective Teacher*. San Francisco, CA: Jossey-Bass.

—— (2005). *The Power of Critical Theory: Liberating Adult Learning and Teaching*. San Fransciso, CA: Jossey-Bass.

Brown, N. (1977). *Perception, Theory and Commitment: The New Philosophy of Science*. Chicago: Precedent Publishing.

Brown, P. (1990). "Popular Epistemology: Community Response to Toxic Waste-Induced Disease, " in P. Conrad and R. Kern. (eds.), *The Sociology of Health and Illness in Critical Perspective*. New York: St. Martin's Press, 77–8.

—— and Mikkelsen, E. J. (1990). *No Safe Place: Toxic Waste, Leukemia, and Community Action*. Berkeley: University of California Press.

Brown, R. H. (1977). *A Poetic for Sociology: Toward a Logic of Discovery for the Human Science*. New York: Cambridge University Press.

Bruner, J. (1986). *Actual Minds, Possible Worlds*. Cambridge: Harvard University Press.

Buethe, T. (2002). "Taking Temporality Seriously: Modeling History and the Use of Narratives as Evidence," *American Political Science Review*, 96: 481–93.

Burbules, N. (1993). *Dialogue in Teaching: Theory and Practice*. New York: Teachers College Press.

Burke, K. (1945). *The Grammar of Motives*. New York: Prentice-Hall.

—— (1950). *A Rhetoric of Motives*. New York: Prentice-Hall.

Callon, M. (1995). "Four Models for the Dynamics of Science," in S. Jasanoff, G. E. Markle, J. C. Petersen, and T. Pinch (eds.), *The Handbook of Science and Technology Studies*. Thousand Oakes, CA: Sage, 29–63.

—— (1999) "The Role of Lay People in the Production and Dissemination of Scientific Knowledge," *Science, Technology and Society*, 4 (1): 81–94.

Caplan, L. (1993). "The Lawyers Race to the Bottom," *New York Times*, August 6: A29.

Carolan, M. (2006). "Science, Expertise, and the Democratization of the Decision-Making Process," *Society and Natural Resources*, 19: 661–8.

Caron, J. (1983). *Les regulations du discours*. Paris: Presses Universitaires de France.

Carr-Saunders, A. M. and Wilson, P. A. (1964). *The Professions*. London: Frank Cass.

Carter, N. (2002). *The Politics of the Environment*. Cambridge: Cambridge University Press.

Chambers, R. (1997). *Whose Reality Counts? Putting the First Last*. London: Intermediate Technology Publications.

—— (2002). *Participatory Workshops: A Sourcebook of 21 Sets of Ideas and Activities*. London: Earthscan.

Chambers, S. (2003). "Deliberative Democratic Theory," *Annual Review of Political Science*, 6: 307–26.

—— (2007). *Public Reason and Deliberation*. London: Routledge.

Charity, A. (1995). *Doing Public Journalism*. New York: Guilford.

Chen, D. and Deng, C. (2007). "Interaction between Citizens and Experts in Public Deliberation: A Case Study of Consensus Conferences in Taiwan," *East Asian Science, Technology and Society.* 1 (1): 77–97.

Cherniss, C. (2000). "Emotional Intelligence: What It is and Why It Matters," Paper presented at the Annual Meeting of the Society for Industrial and Organizational Psychology, New Orleans, LA, April 15.

Chodorow, N. (1994). *Femininities, Masculinities, Sexualities: Freud and Beyond* Lexington, KY: University Press of Kentucky.

Chomsky, N. (1989). "Interview by B. Moyers," in B. Moyers (ed.), *A World of Ideas.* New York: Doubleday.

Churchman, C. W. (1971). The *Design of Inquiring Systems*. New York: Basic Books.

Ciompi, L. (2001). *Gefuehle, Affekte, Affektlogic*. Wien: Picus Verlag.

Cobb, S. (2004). "Fostering Coexistence in Identity-based Conflicts: Toward a Narrative Approach," in A. Chayes and M. Minow (eds.), *Imagine Coexistence*. San Francisco, CA: Jossey-Bass: 294–310.

Coburn, J. (2005). *Street Science: Community Knowledge and Environmental Health Justice*. Cambridge, MA: MIT Press.

Cohen, J. (1996). "Procedure and Substance in Deliberative Democracy," in S. Benhabib (ed.), *Democracy and Difference*. Princeton, NJ: Princeton University Press.

Conway, M. (2000). *Political Participation in the United States*. Washington, DC: CQ Press.

Collins, H. M. and R. Evans (2002). "The Third Wave of Science Studies: Studies of Expertise and Experience," *Social Studies of Science*, 32 (2): 235–96.

—— (2003). "King Canute Meets the Beach Boys: Responses to the Third Wave," *Social Studies of Science*, 33 (2): 435–52.

—— (2007). *Rethinking Expertise*. Chicago: University of Chicago Press.

Cooke, B. and Kothari, U. (2001). *Participation: The New Tyranny?* London: Zed Books.

Cordes, C. (1998). "Community-Based Projects Help Scholars Build Public Support," *Chronicle of Higher Education*, April.

Cornwall, A. (2002). "Making Spaces, Changing Places: Situating Participation in Development,". Working Paper No. 170. Sussex: Institute for Development Studies.

—— and Gaventa, J. (2002). "From Users and Choosers to Makers and Shapers: Re-positioning Participation in Social Policy," *IDS Bulletin*, 31 (4): 50–62.

—— and Jewkes, R. (1995). "What is Participatory Research?" *Soc. Sci. Med.*, 41 (12): 1667–76.

Crosby, N. (1995). "One Solution for Difficult Environmental Questions," in O. Renn, T. Webler, and P. Wiedemann (eds.), *Fairness and Competence in Citizen Participation*. Boston: Kluwer.

References

Crosby, N. and D. Nethercut. (2005). "Citizen Juries: Creating a Trustworthy Voice of the People," in F. Gastil and P. Levine (eds.), *The Deliberative Democracy Handbook*. San Francisco, CA: Jossey-Bass, 111–19.

Crouch, C. (2004). *Post-Democracy*. London: Polity Press.

Czarniawska, B. (1997). *Narrating the Organization: Dramas of Institutional Identity*. Chicago: University of Chicago Press.

—— (1998). *A Narrative Approach to Organizational Studies*. Thousand Oaks, CA: Sage.

Dahl, R. (1989). *Democracy and Its Critics*. New Haven: Yale University Press.

Daloz, L. A. (1999). *Mentor: Guiding the Journey of Adult Learners*. San Francisco, CA: Jossey-Bass.

Damasio, A. R. (2005). *Decartes's Error: Emotion, Reason, and the Human Brain*. New York: Penguin.

Davidoff, P. (1965). "Advocacy and Pluralism in Planning," *Journal of the American Institute of Planning*, 31 (4): 335.

deLeon, P. (1988). *Advice and Consent: The Development of the Policy Sciences*. New York: Russell Sage Foundation.

—— (1997). *Democracy and the Policy Sciences*. Albany: SUNY Press.

Deleuze, G. and Guatarri, F. (1987). *A Thousand Plateaus*. London: Athlone.

Deliberative Democracy Meets Dispute Resolution: Reflections and Insights from the 2005 Workshop on Deliberative Democracy and Dispute Resolution, Cambridge, Mass. Program on Negotiation at Harvard Law School Clearinghourse: A Resource for Negotiation Education (www.pon.org).

DeParle, J. (2007). "Kerala's Poor Lack Nothing but Jobs," *International Herald Tribune*, September 9: 1.

de Tocqueville, A. (1969). *Democracy in America*, J. P. Meyer (ed.). Garden City, NY: Doubleday.

Delli Caprini, M. X., Cook, F. L., and Jacobs, L. R. (2004). "Public Deliberation, Discursive Participation, and Citizen Engagement: A Review of the Empirical Literature," *Annual Review of Political Science*, 7: 315–44.

Denhardt, R. B. and Denhardt, J. V. (2007). *The New Public Service: Serving, Not Steering*. New York: M. E. Sharpe.

Dewey, J. (1927). *The Public and its Problems*. New York: Swallow.

DeWitt, J. (1994). *Civic Environmentalism*. Washington, DC: Congressional Quarterly Press.

Dienel, P.C. (1992). *Die Plannungszelle: Eine Alternative zur Establishment-Demokratie*. Opladen: Westdeutcher Verlag.

Diesing, P. (1962). *Reason in Society: Five Types of Decisions in Their Social Contexts*. Urbana: University of Illinois Press.

—— (1967). "Noneconomic Decision-Making," in M. Alexis, and C. Z. Wilson (eds.), *Organizational Decision Making*. Englewood Cliffs, NJ: Prentice-Hall, 16–25.

Doerner, A. (2001). *Politainment. Politik in der medialen Erlebnisgesellschaft*. FrankFurt/M: Surkamp.

Dryzek, J. S. (1982). "Policy Analysis as a Hermeneutic Activity," *Policy Sciences*, 14: 309–29.

—— (1990). *Discursive Democracy: Politics, Policy, and Political Science*. Cambridge: Cambridge University Press.

—— (2000). *Deliberative Democracy and Beyond: Liberals, Critics, Contestations*. Oxford: Oxford University Press.

—— (2001). "Legitimacy and Economy in Deliberative Democracy," *Political Theory*, 29 (5): 651–69.

Dzur, A. (2004). "Democratic Professionalism: Sharing Authority in Civic Life," *The Good Society*, 13 (1): 6–14.

—— (2008). *Democratic Professionalism*. University Park: Penn State Press.

Earle, W. (1959). "Review: *Personal Knowledge*," *Science*, 129, March: 831–2.

Ebrahim, A. (2003). *NGOs and Organizational Change: Discourse, Reporting and Learning*. Cambridge: Cambridge University Press.

Edelman, M. (1971). *Politics as Symbolic Action: Mass Arousal and Quiescence*. New York: Academic Press.

—— (1977). *Political Language: Words that Succeed and Policies That Fail*. New York: Academic Press.

—— (1988). *Constructing the Political Spectacle*. Chicago: Chicago University Press.

—— (2001). *The Politics of Misinformation*. Cambridge: Cambridge University Press.

Edelstein, M. R. (1988). *Contaiminated Communities*. Boulder, CO: Westview Press.

Ehrenreich, B. (1989). *Fear of Failing: The Inner Life of the Middle Class*. New York: Pantheon Books.

Elias, N. (1997). *Ueber den Prozess der Zivilisation*, Vol. 2, Frankfurt/am Main.

Eliasoph, N. (1998). *Avoiding Politics: How Americans Produce Anxiety in Everyday Life*. Cambridge: Cambridge University Press.

Elm, M. and Bertilsson, M. (2003). "Consuming, Engaging, and Confronting Science: The Emerging Dimensions of Scientific Citizenship," *European Journal of Social Theory*, 6 (3): 233–51.

Elster, J. (ed.) (1998). *Deliberative Democracy*. Cambridge: Cambridge University Press.

Epstein, S. (1996). *Impure Science: AIDS, Activism, and the Politics of Knowledge*. Berkeley: University of California Press.

Ericsson, K. A. and Smith, J. (eds.) (1991). *Toward a General Theory of Expertise: Prospects and Limits*. New York: Cambridge University Press.

—— Chambers, N. Hoffman, R. and Feltovich, P. J. (eds.) (2006). *Cambridge Handbook of Expertise and Expert Performance: Its Development, Orgaization, and Content*. Cambridge: Cambridge University Press.

Erlandson, D. A., Harris, E. L., Skipper, B. L., and Allen, S. D. (1993). *Doing Naturalistic Inquiry: A Guide to Methods*. Newbury Park, CA: Sage.

Estlund, D. M. (2007). *Democratic Authority: A Philosophical Framework*. Princeton, NJ: Princeton University Press.

References

Eulau, H. (1977). *Technology and Civility: The Skill Revolution in Politics*. Stanford, CA: Hoover Institutions.

Everts, J., Mieg, H. A., and Feldt, U. (2006). "Professionalization, Scientific Expertise, and Elitism: A Sociological Perspective," in Ericsson, *et al.*, (eds.), *Cambridge Handbook of Expertise and Expert Competence*. Cambridge: Cambridge University Press: 105–26.

Ezrahi, Y. (1990). *The Descent of Icarus: Science and the Transformation of Contemporary Democracy*. Boston, MA: Harvard University Press.

Falk, R. (1998). "The Decline of Citizenship in an Era of Globalization," www.transnational.org/forum/meet/falk_citizen.html

Fallows, J. (1989). *More Like Us: Making American Great Again*. Boston: Houghton-Mifflin.

Fay, B. (1996). *Contemporary Philosophy of Social Science*. Oxford: Blackwell.

Fearson, J. (1998). "Deliberation as Discussion," in J. Elster (ed.), *Deliberative Democracy*. Cambridge: Cambridge University Press: 44–68.

Feldman, M. S. and A. M. Khademian (2007). "The Role of the Public Manager in Inclusion: Creating Communities of Participation," *Governance*, 20 (2): 305–24.

Ferkiss, V. C. (1969). *Technological Man: The Myth and the Reality*. New York: George Braziller.

Fischer, F. (1990). *Technocracy and the Politics of Expertise*. Newbury Park, CA: Sage.

—— (1992). "Participatory Expertise: Toward the Democratization of Policy Science," in W. Dunn and R. Kelly, (eds.), *Advances in Policy Studies since 1950*. New Brunswick: Transaction Press, 351–76.

—— (1995). *Evaluating Public Policy*. Belmont, CA: Wadsworth.

—— and Hajer, M. (eds.) (1999). *Living with Nature: Environmental Politics as Cultural Discourse*. Oxford: Oxford University Press.

—— (2000). *Citizens, Experts, and the Environment: The Politics of Local Knowledge*. Durham: Duke University Press.

—— (2003). *Reframing Public Policy: Discursive Politics and Deliberative Practices*. Oxford: Oxford University Press.

—— (2004). "Professional Expertise in a Deliberative Democracy: Facilitating Deliberative Inquiry," *Good Society*, 13 (1): 21–7.

—— and Black, M. (eds.) (1995). *Greening Environmental Policy: The Politics of a Sustainable Future*. New York: St. Martin's Press.

—— and Forester, J. (eds.) (1987). *Confronting Values in Policy Analysis: The Politics of Criteria*. Newbury Park, CA: Sage.

—— (eds.) (1993). *The Argumentative Turn in Policy Analysis and Planning*. Durham: Duke University Press.

Fisher, W. R. (1989). *Human Communication as Narration: Toward a Philosophy of Reason, Value, and Action*. Columbia: University of South Carolina Press.

Fishkin, J. S. (1996). *The Voice of the People: Public Opinion and Democracy*. New Haven, CN: Yale University Press.

—— and C. Farrar. (2005). "Deliberative Polling: From Experiment to Community Resource," in J. Gastil and P. Levine (eds.), *The Deliberative Democracy Handbook: Strategies for Effective Civic Engagement in the 21st Century*. San Francisco, CA: Jossey-Bass, 68–79.

Flyvbjerg, B. (2000). *Making Social Science Matter*. Cambridge: Cambridge University Press.

Foreman, C. (1998). *The Promise and Peril of Environmental Justice*. Washington, DC: Brookings.

Forester, J. (1999). *The Deliberative Practitioner: Encouraging Participatory Planning Processes*. Cambridge: Cambridge University Press.

—— (2000). "Multicultural Planning in Deed: Lessons from the Mediation Practice of Shirley Solomon and Larry Sherman," in M. Burayidi (ed.), *Urban Planning in a Multicultural Society*. Westport, CN: Praeger.

Forsyth, T. (2007). *Critical Political Ecology*. London: Taylor & Francis.

Fortenbaugh, W. W. (1975). *Aristotle on Emotion*. London: Duckworth.

Foster, J. (1980). "An Advocate Role Model for Policy Analysis," *Policy Studies Journal*, 8 (6) Summer: 958–64.

Foucault, M. (1986). "Of Other Spaces," *Diacritics—A Review of Contemporary Criticism*, 16 (1): 22–7.

—— (1991). "Governmentality," in G. Burchell *et al.* (eds.), *The Foucault Effect: Studies in Governmentality*. Chicago: University of Chicago Press.

Fox Keller, E. (1985). *Reflections on Gender and Science*. New Haven: Yale University Press.

Frank, A. (2002). "Why Study People's Stories? The Dialogical Ethics of Narrative Analysis," *International Journal of Qualitative Methods*, 1 (1), Winter.

Franke, F. (1993). *Life is Better*. Boulder, CO: Westview Press.

Frankenfeld, P. J. (1992). "Technological Citizenship: A Normative Framework for Risk Studies," *Science, Technology, and Human Values*, 17 (4): 459–84.

Fraser, N. (1989). *Unruly Practices: Power, Discourse, and Gender in Contemporary Social Theory*. Minnesota, MN: University of Minnesota Press.

Friedland, L. A. and Nichol, S. (2002). *Measuring Civic Journalism's Progress: A Report Across a Decade of Progress*. New York: Pew Center for Civic Journalism.

Friedson, E. (1986). *Professional Powers: A Study in the Institutionalization of Formal Knowledge*. Chicago: University of Chicago Press.

Freire, P. (1970). *Pedagogy of the Oppressed*. New York: Seabury Press.

—— (1973). *Education for Critical Consciousness*. New York: Seabury Press.

—— (1974). *Education as the Practice of Freedom*. Harmondsworth: Penguin Books.

—— (1978). *Pedagogy in Process: The Letters to Guinea-Bissau*. New York: The Seabury Press.

—— (1998). *Pedagogy of Freedom: Ethics, Democracy, and Civic Courage*. Lanham, MA: Rowman and Littlefield.

—— and Faundez, A. (1989). *Learning to Question: A Pedagogy of Liberation*. New York: Continuum.

References

Frug, G. (1999). *City Making: Building Communities without Building Walls*. Princeton, NJ: Princeton University Press.

Fuller, S. (2006). "The Constitutively Social Character of Expertise," in E. Selinger and R. P. Crease (eds.), *The Philosophy of Expertise*. New York: Columbia University Press: 342–57.

Fung, A. (2003). "Survey Article: Recipes for Public Spheres: Eight Institutional Design Choices and Their Consequences," *The Journal of Political Philosophy*, 11 (3): 338–67.

—— and Wright, E. O. (2001). "Deepening Democracy: Innovations in Empowered Local Governance," *Politics and Society*, 29 (1): 5–41.

—— (2003). *Deeping Democracy: Institutional Innovations in Empowered Participatory Governance*. New York: Verso.

—— (2006). "Varieties of Participation in Complex Governance," *Public Administration Review*, 36: 65–74.

Galbraith, J. K. (1967). *The New Industrial State*. Boston: Houghlin Mifflin.

Gambetta, D. (1998). " 'Claro!' An Essay on Discursive Machismo," in J. Elster (ed.), *Deliberative Democracy*. Cambridge: Cambridge University Press, 19–43.

Gardner, H. (1983). *Frames of Mind*. New York: Basic Books.

Gastil, J. and Levine, P. (eds.) (2005). *The Deliberative Democracy Handbook: Strategies for Effective Civic Engagement in the 21st Century*. San Francisco, CA: Jossey-Bass.

—— Deess, E. P., and Weiser, P. (2002). "Civic Awakening in the Jury Room: A Test of the Connection Between Jury Deliberation and Political Participation," *Journal of Politics*, 64: 585–95.

Gavelin, K. and Wilson, R. (2007). *Democratic Technologies? The Final Report of the Nanotechnology Engagement Group*. London: Involve.

Gaventa, J. (2006). "Towards Participatory Governance," *Currents*, 29: 29–35.

—— and Valderrama, C. (1999). "Participation, Citizenship and Local Governance," www.ids.ac.uk/partic

George, A. (1972). "The Case of Multiple Advocacy in Making Foreign Policy," *American Political Science Review*, 66: 761–85.

Giddens, A. (1990). *The Consequences of Modernity*. Palo Alto, CA: Stanford University Press.

Gilligan, C. (1993). *In a Different Voice: Psychological Theory and Women's Development*. Cambridge, MA: Harvard University Press.

Giovannoli, R. (2000). "The Narrative Method of Inquiry." www.somic.net~rgiovan/essay.2.ht

Goersdorf, A. (2006). "Inside Deliberative Experiments: Dynamics of Subjectivity in Science Policy Deliberations," *Policy and Society*, 25 (2): 177–206.

—— (2007). *Die 'Weisheit der Laien' als politicische Ressource*. Berlin: VDM Verlag Dr. Mueller.

Goleman, D. (1995). *Emotional Intelligence*. New York: Bantham.

—— (1998). *Working with Emotional Intelligence*. New York: Bantam.

Goldie, P. (2000). *The Emotions: A Philosophical Exploration*. Oxford: Oxford University Press.

Goodwin, J. Jasper, J. M., and Polletta, F. (eds.) (2001). *Passionate Politics: Emotion and Social Movements*: Chicago: University of Chicago Press.

Gottlieb, B. and Farquharson, A. (1985). "Blueprint for a Curriculum on Social Support," *Social Policy*, Winter: 31–41.

Gottweis, H. (1995). "Genetic Engineering, Democracy, and the Politics of Identity," *Social Text*, 42: 127–52.

—— (1998). *Governing Molecules: The Discursive Politics of Genetic Engineering in Europe and the United States*. Cambridge, MA: MIT Press.

—— (2005). "Regulating Genomics in the 21st Century: From Logos to Pathos?" *Trends in Biotechnology*, 23: 118–21.

—— (2006). "Rhetoric in Policy Making: Between Logos, Ethos, and Pathos," in F. Fischer *et al.* (eds.), *Handbook of Public Policy Analysis*. New York: Taylor & Francis, 237–50.

Gouldner, A. W. (1979). *The Future of Intellectuals and the Rise of the New Class*. New York: Seabury Press.

Gross, P. R. and Levitt, N. (1997). *Higher Superstition: The Academic Left and its Quarrels with Science*. Baltimore: Johns Hopkins University Press.

Guba, E. G. (1990). *The Paradigm Dialog*. Newbury Park, CA: Sage.

—— and Lincoln, Y. (1989). *Fourth Generation Evaluation*. Newbury Park, CA: Sage.

Gusfield, J. (1981). *The Culture of Public Problems*. Chicago: University of Chicago Press.

Gutmann, A. and Thompson, D. (1996). *Democracy and Disagreement*. Cambridge, MA: Harvard University Press.

—— (2004). *Why Deliberative Democracy?* Princeton: Princeton University Press.

Haas, T. (2007). *The Pursuit of Public Journalism: Theory, Practice and Criticism*. New York: Routledge.

Haber, S. (1964). *Efficiency and Uplift*. Chicago: University of Chicago Press.

Habermas, J. (1973). *Legitimation Crisis*. Boston: Beacon Press.

—— (1987). *The Theory of Communicative Action, Volume 2*, T. McCarthy (trans.). Boston: Beacon Press.

—— (2006). "Political Communication in the Media Society: Does Democracy Still Enjoy an Epistemic Dimension," *Communication Theory*, 16: 411–26.

—— (1996). *Between Facts and Norms: Contributions to a Discourse Theory of Law and Democracy*, W. Rehg (trans.). Cambridge, MA: MIT Press.

Hacking, Ian (1991). "How Should we Do the History of Statistics?" in G. Burchell, C. Gordon, and P. Miller (eds.), *The Foucault Effect*. Chicago, IL: University of Chicago Press, 181–95.

—— (1992). "The Self-Vindication of the Laboratory Science," in A. Pickering (ed.), *Science as Practice and Culture*. Chicago, IL: University of Chicago Press.

References

Hajer, M. (1995). *The Politics of Environmental Discourse*. Oxford: Oxford University Press.

—— (2003). "Policy without Polity: Policy Analysis and the Institutional Void," *Policy Sciences*, 36 (2): 175–95.

—— (2005). "Setting the State: A Dramaturgy of Policy Deliberation," *Administrative and Society*, 36: 624–647.

—— and Wagenaar, H. (eds.) (2003). *Deliberative Policy Analysis: Understanding Governance in the Network Society*. Cambridge: Cambridge University Press.

Hall, C. (2005). *The Trouble With Passion: Political Theory Beyond the Range of Reason*. New York: Routledge.

—— (2006). "Deliberative Democracy and the Public Use of Reason," Paper prepared for delivery at the annual meeting of the American Political Science Association, Philadelphia, PA, August: 31–3.

Haraway, D. (1991). *Simians, Cyborgs, and Women*. London: Free Press.

Hardy, C. and Leiba-O'Sullivan, S. (1998). "The Power Behind Empowerment: Implications for Research and Practice," *Human Relations* 51 (4): 451–83.

Harwood, R. C. (1991). *Citizens and Politicians: A View from Mainstreet America*. Dayton, OH: Kettering Foundation.

Haskell, T. L. (1984). *The Authority of Experts*. Bloomington, IN: Indiana University.

Hawkesworth, M. E. (1988). *Theoretical Issues in Policy Analysis*. Albany, NY: SUNY Press.

Hays, S. P. (1964). "The Politics of Municipal Government in the Progressive Era," *Pacific Northwest Quarterly*, October: 157–69.

—— (1987). *Beauty, Health and Permanence: Environmental Politics in the United States, 1955–1985*. Cambridge: Cambridge University Press.

Healey, P. (2006). *Collaborative Planning: Shaping Places in Fragmented Societies*. London: Palgrave Macmillan.

Heater, D. (1999). *What is Citizenship?* Cambridge: Polity Press.

Heclo, H. (1972). "Review Article: Policy Analysis," *British Journal of Political Science*, 2: 83–108.

Heller, P. (1999). *The Labor of Development: Works' Transformation of Capitalism in Kerala, India*. Ithaca: Cornell University Press.

Hendriks, C. (2005). "Consensus Conferences and Planning Cells: Lay Citizen Deliberations," in F. Gastil and P. Levine (eds.) *The Deliberative Democracy Handbook*. San Francisco, CA: Jossey-Bass: 80–10.

Hendriks, C., Dryzek, J. S., and Hunold, C. (2007). "Turning Up the Heat: Partisanship in Deliberative Innovation," *Political Studies*, 55: 362–83.

Herman, L. and Mandell, A. (2004). *From Teaching to Mentoring: Principles and Practice, Dialogue and Life in Adult Education*. London: Routledge.

Heron, J. (1981). "Philosophical Basic for a New Paradigm," in P. Reason and J. Rowan (eds.), *Human Inquiry: A Sourcebook of New Paradigm Research*. Chichester: John Wiley.

—— (1996). *Co-operative Inquiry*. London: Sage.

Hibbing, J. R. and Theiss-Morse, E. (2002). *Stealth Democracy: America's Beliefs about How Government Should Work*. Cambridge: Cambridge University Press.

Hill, S. (1992). *Democratic Values and Technological Choices*. Stanford: Stanford University Press.

Hills, M. and Mullett, J. (2000). *Community-Based University Research: Collaborative Action for Health and Social Change*. Victoria, BC: Community Health Promotion of Victoria Press.

Hirschhorn, L. (1979). "Alternative Service and the Crisis of the Professions," in J. Case and R. C. Taylor (eds.), *Co-ops, Communes and Collectives: Experiments in Social Change in the 1960s and 1970s*. New York: Pantheon, 153–93.

Hirschman, A. O. (1997). *The Interests and the Passions*. Princeton: Princeton University Press.

Hoch, C. (2006). "Emotions and Planning," *Planning Theory and Practice*, 7 (4): 367–82.

Hoffman, L. (1989). *The Politics of Knowledge: Activist Movements in Medicine and Planning*. Albany: State University of New York Press.

hooks, b. (1994). *Teaching to Transgress: Education as the Practice of Freedom*. New York: Routledge.

Horvath, J. (1999). "Tacit Knowledge in the Profession," in R. J. Sternberg and J. A. Horvarth (eds.), *Tacit Knowledge in Professional Practice: Researcher and Practitioner Perspectives*. Mahwah, NJ: Lawrence Erlbaum Associates Publishers, ix.

Howlett, M. and Rayner J. (2006). "Understanding the Historical Turn in the Policy Sciences: A Critique of Stochastic, Narrative, Path Dependency and Process-Sequencing Models of Policy-Making Over Time," *Policy Sciences*, 39: 1–18.

Hoyt, M. (1995). "Are you Now, or Will You Ever Be, a Civic Journalist? *Columbia Journalism Review*, 34: 27–30.

Hudson, W. E. (1995). *American Democracy in Peril: Eight Challenges to America's Future*. Chatham, NJ: Chatham House.

Hume, D. (1975). *Enquiries Concerning Human Understanding and Concerning the Principles of Morals*, in L. A. Selby-Bigge, (ed.). Oxford: Oxford University Press.

Hume, E. (1978). *A Treatise of Human Nature*, L. A. Selby-Bigge (ed.). Oxford: Oxford University Press.

Hunt, L. (2007). *Inventing Human Rights: A History*. New York: W.W. Norton.

Illich, I. (1989). *A Celebration of Awareness: A Call for Institutional Revolution*. Garden City, NY: Doubleday.

Inglehart, R. (1997). *Modernization and Postmodernization: Cultural, Economic, and Political Change in 43 Countries*. Princeton: Princeton University Press.

Innes, J. J. (1990). *Knowledge and Public Policy* (2nd edn.). New Brunswick, NJ: Transaction Books.

—— (1998). "Information in Communicative Planning," *Journal of the American Planning Association*, 64 (4): 412–23.

References

Innes, J. J. and Booher, D. E. (2003). "Collaborative Policymaking: Governance Through Dialogue," in M. A. Hajer and H. Wagenaar (eds.), *Deliberative Policy Analysis*. Cambridge: Cambridge University Press, 33–59.

Irwin, A. (1995). *Citizen Science: A Study of People, Expertise, and Sustainable Development*. New York: Routledge.

Isaac, T. H. and Franke, R. (2000). *Local Democracy and Development: People's Campaign for Decentralized Planning in India*. New Delhi: Left World Press.

—— and Heller, P. (2003). "Democracy and Development: Decentralized Planning in Kerala," in A. Fung and E. O. Wright (eds.), *Deepening Democracy*. New York: Verso, 77–102.

Jasanoff, S. (2003a). "Breaking the Waves in Science Studies," *Social Studies of Science* 33 (3): 389–400.

—— (2003b). "(No?) Accounting for Expertise," *Science and Public Policy*, 30 (3): 157–62.

—— (2004). "The Idiom of Co-Production," in S. Jansanoff (ed.), *States of Knowledge: The Co-Production of Science and Social Order*. New York: Routledge, 1–12 (page 2 is cited in text)

—— (2005). *Designs on Nature: Science and Democracy in Europe and the United States*. Princeton: Princeton University Press.

—— (2006). "Science and Citizenship: A New Synergy," *Science and Public Policy*, 31 (2): 90–94.

—— (1990). *The Fifth Branch: Science Advisors as Policymakers*. Cambridge: Harvard University Press.

—— Markle, G. E., Petersen, J. C., Pinch, T. J. (eds.) (2001). *Handbook of Science and Technology Studies*. Newbury Park: Sage, new edn.

John, D. (1994). *Civic Environmentalism: Alternative to Regulation in States and Communities*. Washington, DC: Congressional Quarterly Press.

Joly, P. (2005). "Debates and Participatory Processes: Lesson from the European Experience." Forum Science in Society, Brussels, March 9–11.

Jones, E. and Gaventa, J. (2002). *Concepts of Citizenship: A Review*. Sussex: Institute for Development Studies.

Jordon, G. and Weedon, C. (1995). *Cultural Politics: Class, Gender, Race, and the Postmodern World*. London: Blackwell.

Jorgensen, M. S., Hall, D., and Hall, I. (2004). "How Can Science Shops Contribute to Governance," *Living Knowledge*, 3, July: 7–10.

Joss, S. (1995). "Evaluating Consensus Conferences: Necessity or Luxury," in S. Joss and J. Durant (eds.), *Public Participation in Science: The Role of Consensus Conferences in Europe*. London: Science Museum, 89–108.

—— and Durant, J. (eds.) (1995). *Public Participation in Science: The Role of Consensus Conferences in Europe*. London: Science Museum.

Kanigel, R. (1998). "Angry at Our Goods," *Columbia* (October): 23–35.

Kaplan, T. J. (1986). "The Narrative Structure of Policy Analysis," *Journal of Policy Analysis and Management*, 5: 761–78.

—— (1993). "Reading Policy Narratives: Beginnings, Middles, and Ends," in F. Fischer and J. Forester (eds.), *The Argumentative Turn in Policy Analysis and Planning*. Durham, NC: Duke University Press.

Kegan, R. (1994). *In Over our Heads: The Mental Demands of Modern Life*. Cambridge, MA: Harvard University Press.

Kennedy, J. F. (1963). "Commencement Address at Yale University," *Public Papers of the President of the United States: John F. Kennedy, 1962*. Washington, DC: Government Printing Office, 470–75.

King, G. (1989). *Unifying Political Methodology*. Cambridge: Cambridge University Press.

—— Koehane, R. O., and Verba, S. (1994). *Designing Social Inquiry: Scientific Inference in Qualitative Research*. Princeton: Princeton University Press.

Kitchener, K. (1983). "Cognition, Metacognition and Epistemic Cognition," *Human Development*, 26: 222–3.

Kivisto, P. and Faist, T. (2007). *Citizenship: Discourse, Theory and Transnational Prospects*. London: Blackwell.

Kluver, L. (1995). "Consensus Conferences at the Danish Board of Technology," in S. Joss and J. Duran (eds.), *Public Participation in Science*. London: Science Museum, 41–49.

Knight, L. (2006). *Citizen: Jane Addams and the Struggle for Democracy*. Chicago: University of Chicago Press.

Kogut, B. and Zander, U. "Knowledge of the Firm, Combinative Capacities, and the Replication of Technology," *Organizational Science*, 3: 383–97.

Krause, S. (2006). "Public Deliberation and the Feeling of Impartiality," Paper Prepared for Delivery at the American Political Science Association, Philadelphia, PA, August 31–September 3.

Kretzmann, J. and McKnight, J. (1993). *Building Communities from the Inside Out*. Evanston, IL: Center for Urban Affairs, Northwestern University.

Kritzer, H. M. (1996). "The Data Puzzle: The Nature of Interpretation in Qualitative Research," *American Journal of Political Science*, 40: 1–32.

Krumholz, N. and Clavel, P. (1994) *Reinventing Cities: Equity Planners Tell their Stories*. Philadelphia: Temple University Press.

Kuhn, T. (1962). *The Structure of Scientific Revolutions*. Chicago: University of Chicago Press.

Kuklinski, J. H. (2007). "The Limits of Facts in Citizen Decision-Making," *Extensions*, Fall: 5–8.

LaForest, R. and Phillips, S. (2006). "Citizen Engagement: Rewiring the Policy Process," in M. Orsini and M. Smith, (eds.), *Critical Policy Studies*. Vancouver: UBS Press, 67–90.

Laird, F. (1993). "Participatory Policy Analysis, Democracy, and Technological Decision Making," *Science, Technology, and Human Values*, 18: 341–61.

Lasch, C. (1991). *The True and only Heaven: Progress and its Critics*. New York: W.W. Norton.

References

Lasswell, H. (1951). "The Policy Orientation," in H. Lasswell and D. Lerner (eds.), *The Policy Sciences*. Stanford: Stanford University Press.

Latour, B. (1987). *Science in Action: How to Follow Scientists and Engineers Through Society. Cambridge*. MA. Harvard University Press.

—— (1993).*We have Never Been Modern*. Hemel Heampstead: Harvester Wheatsheaf.

—— (2005). *Reassembling the Social*. Oxford: Oxford University Press.

Laudan, L. (1977). *Progress and its Problems*. Berkeley: University of California Press.

Leary, K. (2004). "Critical Moments as Relational Moments: The Centre for Humanitarian Dialogue and Conflict in Aceh, Indonesia," *Negotiation Journal*, April: 311–338.

Lebessis, N. and J. Paterson. (1999). "Improving the Effectiveness and Legitimacy of EU Governance." Forward Studies Unit Working Papers: Brussels, European Commission.

Leib, E. J. (2004) *Deliberative Democracy in America: A Proposal for a Popular Branch of Government*. University Park: Pennsylvania State University.

Leis, H. R. and Viola, E. J. (1995) "Towards a Sustainable Future: The Organizing Role of Ecologism in the North–South Relationship," in F. Fischer and M. Black (eds.), *Greening Environmental Policy: The Politics of a Sustainable Future*. New York: St. Marks: 33–49.

Lefebvre, H. (1991). *The Production of Space*. London: Verso.

Lejano, Raul P. (2006). *Frameworks for Policy Analysis: Merging Text and Context*. London: Routledge.

Levine, A. (1982). *Love Canal: Science, Politics, and People*. Boston: Lexington.

Liberatore, A. and Functowicz, S. (2003). "Democratising Expertise, Expertising Democracy: What does this Mean, and Why Bother?" *Science and Public Policy*, 30 (3): 146–550.

Lieberman, J. (1972). *Tyranny of Expertise*. New York: Walker.

Lin, A. C. (1998). "Bridging Positivist and Interpretive Approaches to Qualitative Methods," *Policy Studies Journal*, 26 (1): 162–84.

Lindblom, C. E. (1990). *Inquiry and Change: The Troubled Attempt to Understand and Shape Society*. New Haven: Yale University Press.

Lindeman, M. (1997). "Building Diversified Deliberative Institutions: Lessons from Recent Research," Paper prepared for presentation at the annual meeting of the American Political Science Association, Washington, DC, August 28.

Lincoln, Y. S. and Guba, E. G. (1985). *Naturalistic Inquiry*. Newbury Park, CA: Sage.

Lippmann, W. (1922). *Public Opinion*. New York: Macmillan.

Lister, R. (1998). "Citizens in Action: Citizenship and Community Development in Northern Ireland Context," *Community Development Journal*, 33: 226–35.

Living Knowledge: International Journal of Community Based Research (www.Living-knowledge.org) The International Science Shop Network.

Lizza, R. (2008). "Making It: How Chicago Shaped Obama," *The New Yorker*, July 21: 49–65.

Loder, J. I. (1981). *The Transforming Moment: Understanding Convictional Experiences*. San Francisco: Harper and Row.

Luje, T. W. (2005). "The Death of Environmentalism or the Advent of Public Ecology," *Organization and Environment*, 18 (4): 489–94.

Luke, S. (2005). *Power: A Radical View*. London: Macmillan.

Luke, T. (1999). "Eco-Managerial Power: Environmental Studies as a Power/Knowledge Formation," in F. Fischer and M. Hajer, (eds.), *Living with Nature: Environmental Politics as Cultural Discourse*. Oxford: Oxford University Press, 103–20.

Lutz, C. and White, G. M. (1986). "The Anthropology of Emotions," *Annual Review of Anthropology*, 15: 405–35.

Macedo, S. (ed.) *Deliberative Politics*. Oxford: Oxford University Press, 211–39.

McCloskey, D. N. (1985). *The Rhetoric of Economics*. Madison: University of Wisconsin Press.

—— (1990). *If You're So Smart: The Narrative of Economic Expertise*. Chicago: University of Chicago Press.

—— (1994). *Knowledge and Persuasion in Economics*. Cambridge: Cambridge University Press.

MacDonald, K. M. (1995). *The Sociology of the Professions*. London: Sage.

MacIntyre, A. C. (2007). *After Virtue: A Study in Moral Theory*. South Bend, IN: Notre Dame Press.

MacRae, D., Jr. (1976). *The Social Function of Social Science*. New Haven, CT: Yale University Press.

McNamara, R. S. (1995). *In Retrospect: The Tragedy and Lessons of Vietnam*. New York: New York Times Books.

—— (1999). *Argument Without End: In Search of Answers to the Vietnam Tragedy*. New York: Public Affairs.

McNeil, M. (ed.) (1987). *Gender and Expertise*. London: Free Association Books.

Majone, G. (1989). *Evidence, Argument, and Persuasion in the Policy Process*. New Haven: Yale University Press.

Mansbridge, J. (1999). "On the Idea that Participation Makes Better Citizens," in S. Elkin and K. Soltan (eds.), *Citizen Competence and Democratic Institutions*. University Park: Pennsylvania State University Press.

—— (1999). "Everyday Talk in the Deliberative System," in S. Marcedo (ed.), *Deliberative Politics*. Cambridge: Cambridge University Press.

—— (2003). "Practice-Thought-Practice," in A. Fung and E. O. Wright (eds.), *Deeping Democracy*. New York: Verso, 175–99.

—— (2007). "Deliberative Democracy or Democratic Deliberation," in S. Rosenberg (ed.), *Deliberation, Participation and Democracy: Can People Decide?* London: Palgrave Macmillan, 251–71.

Marcedo, S. (ed.) (1999). *Deliberative Politics: Essays on Democracy and Disagreement*. New York: Oxford University Press.

March, J. and Olsen, J. (1995). *Democratic Governance*. New York: Free Press.

References

Marcus, G. E. (2002). *The Sentimental Citizen: Emotion in Democratic Politics.* University Park, PA: Penn State University Press.

Marshall C. and Rossman, G. (1999). *Designing Qualitative Research*, 3rd edn. London: Sage.

Martell, L. (1994). *Ecology and Society.* Amherst: University of Massachusetts Press.

Mason, E. S. (ed.) (1964), *The Corporation in Modern Society.* Cambridge, MA: Harvard University Press.

Maynard-Moody, S. and Kelly, M. (1993). "Stories Public Managers Tell About Elected Officials: Making Sense of the Politics-Administration Dichotomy," in B. Bozeman (ed.), *Public Management: The State of the Art.* San Francisco, CA: Jossey-Bass.

Mercer, C. (2002). "NGOs, Civil Society and Democratization: A Critical Review of the Literature," *Progress in Development Studies*, 2 (1): 5–22.

Merritt, D. (1998). *Public Journalism and Public Life: Why Telling the News is Not Enough.* Mahwah, NJ: Lawrence Erlbaum Associates.

Mezirow, J. (1991). *Transformative Dimensions of Adult Learning.* San Francisco, CA: Jossey-Bass.

—— and Associates. (1990). *Fostering Critical Reflection in Adulthood: A Guide to Transformative and Emancipatory Learning.* San Francisco, CA: Jossey-Bass.

—— (eds). (2000). *Learning as Transformation: Critical Perspectives on a Theory in Progress.* San Francisco, CA: Jossey-Bass.

Miller, D. (1988). "The Ethical Significance of Nationality," *Ethics*, 98: 647–62.

Miller, H. T. and Fox C. J. (2006). *Postmodern Public Administration.* Thousand Oaks, CA: Sage.

Mills, C. W. (1959). *The Power Elite.* Oxford: Oxford University Press.

—— (2000). *The Sociological Imagination.* Oxford: Oxford University Press.

Mishler, E. G. (1990). "Validation in Inquiry-Guided Research: The Role of Exemplars in Narrative Studies," *Harvard Educational Review*, 60: 415–42.

Mitroff, I. I. (1971). "A Communications Model of Dialectical Inquiring Systems–A Strategy for Strategic Planning," *Management Science*, 17, June: B634–B648.

—— and Pondy, L. (1974). "On the Organization of Inquiry: A Comparison of Some Radically Different Approaches to Policy Analysis," *Public Administration Review*, 34: 513–20.

Morrison, R. (1995). *Ecological Democracy.* Boston: South End Press.

Mottier, V. (1999). "Narratives of National Identity: Sexuality, Race and the Swiss 'Dream of Order,' " Paper presented at the European Consortium of Political Research.

Mouffe, C. (1999). "Deliberative Democracy or Agonistic Pluralism?" *Social Research*, 66: 745–58.

—— (1992). "Democratic Citizenship and the Political Community," in C. Mouffe (ed.), *Dimensions of Radical Democracy: Pluralism, Citizenship, Community.* London: Verso.

Moynihan, D. P. (1965). "The Professionalization of Reform," *The Public Interest*, Fall: 6–16.

Murphy, J. and Levidow, L. (2006). *Governing the Transatlantic Conflict over Agricultural Biotechnology*. London: Routledge.

Nagel, J. (1987). *Participation*. Englewood Cliffs, NJ: Prentice-Hall.

Nash, K. (2000). *Contemporary Political Sociology*. Oxford: Blackwell.

National Research Council (1996). *Understanding Risk: Informing Decisions in a Democratic Society*. Washington, DC: National Academy Press.

Nelson, R. and Winter S. (1982). *An Evolutonary Theory of Economic Change*. Cambridge, MA: Harvard University Press.

Neuman, R. W. (1986). *The Paradox of Mass Public: Knowledge and Opinion*. Cambridge, MA: Harvard University Press.

Nonaka, I. and Takeuchi, H. (1995). *The Knowledge Creating Company*. New York: Oxford University Press.

Norris, P. (1999). "Introduction: The Growth of Critical Citizens?" in P. Norris (ed.), *Critical Citizens: Global Support for Democratic Governance*. Oxford: Oxford University Press, 1–27.

Norton, A. and Stephens, T. (1995). "Participation in Poverty Assessment." Environmental Department Papers Participation Series, Social Policy and Resettlement Division, World Bank, Washington, June.

Norval, A. J. (2007). *Aversive Democracy*. Cambridge: Cambridge University Press.

—— (2008). "Beyond Deliberation: Agnostic and Aversive Grammers of Democracy: The Question of Criteria," Paper presented at the Workshop on Decentered Governance: Democracy, Conflict and Participation, University of Essex, June 23–4.

Novotny, H. (2003). "Democratizing Expertise and Socially Robust Knowledge," *Science and Public Policy*, June, 30 (3): 151–6.

Novotny, P. (1994). "Popular Epidemiology and the Struggle for Community," *Capitalism, Nature, and Society*, 5 (2): 29–42.

Nussbaum, M. C. (2001). *Upheavals of Thought: The Intelligence of Emotions*. Cambridge: Cambridge University Press.

—— (2004). *Hiding from Humanity: Disgust, Shame, and the Law*. Princeton: Princeton Univesrity Press.

Oels, A. (2000). *Evaluating Stakeholder Participation in the Transition to Sustainable Development: Methodology, Case Studies, Policy Implications*. Muenster: LIT Verlag.

Offe, C. (1996). *Modernity and the State: East, West*. Cambridge: Polity Press.

Ophuls, W. (1977). *Ecology and the Politics of Scarcity*. San Francisco, CA: Freeman.

Orsini, M. and Scala, F. (2006). "'Every Virus Tells a Story': Toward a Narrative-Centered Approach to Health Policy," *Policy and Society*, 25 (2): 109–30.

Paehlke, R. and Torgerson, T. (1992). "Toxic Waste as Public Business," *Canadian Public Administration*, 35, Fall: 339–62.

Paller, B. (1989). "Extending Evolutionary Epistemology to 'Justifiying' Scientific Belief," in K. Halweg and C. A. Hooker (eds.), *Issues in Evolutionary Epistemology*. Albany: SUNY Press, 231–57.

Parkinson, J. (2006). *Deliberating in the Real-World: Problems of Legitimacy in Deliberative Democracy*. Oxford: Oxford University Press.

References

Parsons, T. (1968). "Professions," *International Encylopedia of the Social Sciences*, Vol. 12, D. L. Sills (ed.). New York: Macmillan-Free Press.

Patel, V. L, Arocha, J. F., and Kaufman, D. R. (1999). "Expertise and Tacit Knowledge in Medicine," in R. J. Sternberg and J. A. Horvath (eds.), *Tacit Knowledge in Professional Practice*. Mahwah, NJ: Lawrence Erlbaum Associates, Publishers, 75–99.

Perelman, C. (1984). "Rhetoric and Politics," *Philosophy and Rhetoric*, 17 (3): 129–34.

Perkins, H. (1989). *The Rise of the Professions: England Since 1880*. London: Routledge.

Perry, D. K. (2003). *The Roots of Civic Journalism*. Washington, DC: University Press of America.

Pierre, J. (ed.) (2000). *Debating Governance: Authority, Steering, and Democracy*. Oxford: Oxford University Press.

Price-Chalita, P. (1994). "Spatial Metaphor and the Politics of Empowerment: Mapping a Place for Feminism and Postmodernism in Geography," *Antipode*, 26 (3): 236–54.

Plough, A. and S. Krimsky (1987). "The Emergence of Risk Communication Studies: Social and Political Context," *Science, Technology, and Human Values*, 12 (3–4): 4–10.

Polletta, F. (2002). *Freedom is an Endless Meeting: Democracy in American Social Movements*. Chicago: University of Chicago Press.

Polanyi, M. (1958). *Personal Knowledge: Towards a Post-Critical Philosophy*. London: Routledge and Kegan Paul.

—— (1966) *The Tacit Dimension*. Garden City, NY: Doubleday.

—— (1974). *Personal Knowledge: Towards a Post-Critical Philosophy*. Chicago: University of Chicago Press.

Porter, R. B. (1980). *Presidential Decision Making: The Economic Policy Board*. Cambridge: Cambridge University Press.

Posner, R. A. (2003). *Law, Pragmatism, and Democracy*. Cambridge, MA: Harvard University Press.

Price, D. (1965). *The Scientific Estate*. Cambridge, MA: Harvard University Press.

Purcell, M. (2008). *Recapturing Democracy: Neoliberalism and the Struggle for Alternative Urban Futures*. New York: Routledge.

Putnam, R. (2000). *Bowling Alone: The Collapse and Revival of American Community*. New York: Simon and Schuster.

Qvortrup, M. (2007). *The Politics of Participation*. Manchester: Manchester University Press.

Rabe, B. G. (1991). "Beyond the Nimby Syndrome in Hazardous Waste Facility Siting: The Albertan Breakthrough and the Prospects For Cooperation in Canada and the United States," *Governance*, 4, April: 184–206.

—— (1992). "When Siting Works, Canada-Style," *Journal of Health Politics, Policy and Law*, 17: 119–42.

Radaelli, C. M. (1999). "Harmful Tax Competition in the EU: Policy Narratives and Advocacy Coalitions," *Journal of Common Market Studies*, 37 (4): 661–82.

Rahman, M. D. A. (1995). *People's Self-Development*. London: Zed Books.

Rampton, S. and Stauber, J. (2001). *Trust Us, We're Experts!* New York: Penguin.

Ravetz, J. (1999). "What is Post-Normal Science," *Futures*, 31: 627–35.

Rawls, J. (1971). *A Theory of Justice*. Cambridge, MA: Belknap Press.

—— (1993). *Political Liberalism*. New York: Columbia University Press.

Reardon, K. (1997). "Participatory Action Research and Real Community-Based Planning in East St. Louis, Illinois," in P. Nyden, *et al.* (eds.), *Building Community: Social Science in Action*. Thousand Oaks, CA: Pine Forge, 233–9.

—— (2003). "Ceola's Vision, Our Blessing: The Story of an Evolving Community-University Partnership in East St. Louis, Illinois," in B. Eckstein and J. A. Throgmorton (eds.), *Story and Sustainability.*Cambridge, MA: MIT Press, 113–42.

Reardon, K. M., Welsh, J., Kreiswirth, B., and Forester J. (1993). "Participatory Action Research from the Inside: Community Development Practices in East St. Louis," *American Sociologist*, 24: 69–91.

Reason, P. (1994). "Three Approaches to Participatory Inquiry," in N. K. Denzin and Y. S. Lincoln (eds.), *Handbook of Qualitative Research*. London: Sage.

—— and Rowan, J. (eds.) (1981). *Human Inquiry: A Sourcebook of New Paradigm Research*. New York: John Wiley.

Reber, A. (1989). "Implicit Learning and Tacit Knowledge," *Journal of Experimental Psychology: General*, 118: 219–35.

Revans, R. (1982). *The Origin and Growth of Action Learning*. Bickly, Kent: Cartwell-Gratt.

Rhodes, R. (1996). "The New Governance: Governing without Government." *Political Studies*, 44: 652–67.

—— (2007). "*Understanding Governance*: Ten Years On." *Organization Studies*, 28 (8): 1243–64.

Richardson, H. S. (2002). *Democratic Autonomy: Public Reasoning about the Ends of Policy*. Oxford: Oxford University Press.

Riessman, C. K. (1993). *Narrative Analysis*. Thousand Oaks, CA: Sage.

Rip, A. (2003). "Constructing Expertise in a Third Wave of Science Studies?" *Social Studies of Science*, 33 (3): 419–34.

—— and Pierre-Benoit, J. (2004). "*Multi-Actor Spaces and the Governance of Science and Innovation in the ERA.*" Prime-TN, Workpackage 2. Unpublished manuscript.

Roberts, N. C. (1997). "Public Deliberation: An Alternative Approach to Crafting Policy and Setting Direction," *Public Administration Review*, 57 (2): 124–32.

Roe, E. (1994). *Narrative Policy Analysis*. Durham, NC: Duke University Press.

Rorty, R. (1979). *Philosophy and the Mirror of Nature*. Princeton, NJ: Princeton University Press.

Rosen, J. (1996). *Getting the Connections Right*. New York: Twentieth Century Fund Press.

—— (2001). *What Are Journalists For?* New Haven: Yale University Press.

Rosenberg, S. W. (2003). *The Not so Common Sense: Differences in How People Judge Social and Political Life*. New Haven: Yale University Press.

—— (ed.) (2007). *Deliberation, Participation and Democracy: Can the People Govern?* London: Palgrave Macmillan.

Rothblatt, S. (1968). *The Revolution of the Dons*. London: Faber.

Rouse, J. (1988). *Knowledge and Power: A Political Philosophy of Science*. Ithaca, NY: Cornell University Press.

—— (1996). *Engaging Science*. Ithaca: Cornell University Press.

Rowe, G. and Frewer, L. J. (2000). "Public Participation Methods: A Framework for Evaluation," *Science, Technology and Human Values*, 25 (1): 3–29.

—— (2004). "Evaluating Public Participation Exercises: A Research Agenda," *Science, Technology and Human Values*, 29 (2): 512–57.

—— (2005). "A Typology of Public Engagement Mechanisms," *Science, Technology and Human Values*, 30: 251–90.

Ruddick, S. (1989). *Maternal Thinking: Toward a Politics of Peace*. Boston: Beacon Press.

Ryfe, D. M. (2003). "The Principles of Public Discourse: What is Good Public Discourse?" in J. Rodin and S. Steinberg (eds.), *Public Discourse in America: Conversation and Community in the Twentieth-First Century*. Pennsylvania: University of Pennsylvania Press, 163–77.

Sabatier, P. A. (1988). "An Advocacy Coalition Framework of Policy Change and the Role of Policy-Oriented Learning Therein," *Policy Science*, 21: 129–68.

Salamon, L. M. (1993). "The Global Associational Revolution: The Rise of the Third Sector on the World Scene," Occasional Papers 15. Institute for Policy Studies, John Hopkins University, Baltimore.

Sale, K. (1995). "Setting the Limits on Technology: Lessons from the Luddites," *The Nation*, June 5: 785–8.

Sandal, M. (1998). *Liberalism and the Limits of Social Justice*. Cambridge: Cambridge University Press.

Sandercock, L. (2003). "Dreaming the Sustainable City: Organizing Hope, Negotiating Fear, Mediating Memory," in B. Eckstein and J. A. Throgmorton (eds.), *Story and Sustainablity: Planning, Practice, and Possibility for American Cities*. Cambridge, MA: MIT Press, 143–64.

Santos, B. S. (ed.) (2005). *Democratizing Democracy: Beyond the Liberal Canon*. London: Verso.

Sarbin, T. R. (ed.) (1986). *Narrative Psychology: The Storied Nature of Human Conduct*. New York: Praeger.

Sardell, A. (1988). *The U.S. Experiment in Social Medicine: The Community Heath Movement Center Program, 1965–1986*. Pittsburgh, PA: University of Pittsburgh Press.

Schaffer, J. and Miller, E. D. (1995). *Civic Journalism: Six Case Studies*. Washington, DC: Pew Center for Civic Journalism/Poynter Institute for Media Studies.

Schiffen, D. (1985). "Everyday Argument: The Organization and Diversity of Talk," in Teun van Dijk (ed.), *Handbook of Discourse Analysis: Discourse and Dialogue*, Vol. 3, London: Academic Press, 35–47.

—— (1990). "The Mangement of a Cooperative Self During Argument: The Role of Opinion and Stories," in A. D. Grimshaw (ed.), *Conflict Talk: Sociolinguistic Inverstigations of Arguments in Conversations*. Cambridge: Cambridge University of Press 1990, 241–59.

—— (1994). *Approaches to Discourse*. Oxford: Blackwell.

Schiffrin, D., Tannen, D., and Hamilton, H. (eds.) (2001). *The Handbook of Discourse Analysis*. Oxford: Blackwell.

Schlozman, K. L. (2002). "Citizen Participation in American: What do we Know? Why Do We Care?" in I. Katznelson and H. Milner (eds.), *The State of the Discipline*. New York: W.W. Norton, 432–61.

Schneider, A. L. and Ingram, H. (eds.) (2006). *Deserving and Entitled: Social Constructions and Public Policy*. Albany, NY: SUNY Press.

Schor, I. (1996). *When Student have Power: Negotiating Authority in a Critical Pedagogy*. Chicago: University of Chicago Press.

Schram, S. F. (1993). "Postmodern Policy Analysis: Discourse and Identity in Welfare Policy," *Policy Sciences*, 26: 249–70.

Schram, S. and Neisser, P. T. (eds.) (1997). *Tales of the State: Narrative in Contemporary U.S. Politics and Public Policy*. New York: Rowman and Littlefield.

Schumacher, E. F. (1973). *Small is Beautiful*. New York: Harper.

Schön, D. (1983). *The Reflective Practitioner*. New York: Basic Books.

—— and Rein, M. (1994). *Frame Reflection*. New York: Basic Books.

Sclove, R. (1995). *Democracy and Technology*. New York: Guilford Press.

Scott, J. C. (1986). *Weapons of the Weak*. New Haven: Yale University Press.

—— (1990). *Domination and the Arts of Resistance: Hidden Transcripts*. New Haven: Yale University Press.

Scriven, M. (1987). "Probative Logic," in F. H. van Eemeren *et al.* (eds.), *Argumentation: Across the Lines of Discipline*. Amsterdam: Foris.

Shapiro, I. (2005). *The State of Democratic Theory*. Princeton: Princeton University Press.

Shor, I. (1996). *When Students have Power: Negotiating Authority in a Critical Pedagogy*. Chicago: University of Chicago Press.

Sillitoe, P. (ed.) (2007). *Local Science vs. Global Science: Approaches to Indigenous Knowledge in International Development*. New York: Berghahn.

Simon, R. I., Dippo, D., and Schenke, A. (1991), *Learning Work: A Critical Pedagogy of Work Education*: Westport, CT: Bergin and Garvey.

Sims, L. and Sinclair, A. J. (2008). "Learning Through Participatory Resource Management Programs: Case Studies from Costa Rica," *Adult Education Quarterly*, 58 (2): 151–68.

Sirianni, C. (2008). "Investing in Democracy: Government as Civic Enabler," Unpublished manuscript.

Sirianni, C. and Friedland, L. (2001). *Civic Innovation in American: Community Empowerment, Public Policy and the Movement for Civic Renewal*. Berkeley: University of California Press.

References

Skelcher, C. (2003). "Jurisdictional Integrity, Polycentricism, and the Design of Governance," Presented at the Transatlantic Policy Consortium Conference on Liberalisation and Democratic Governance, German University of Administrative Sciences, Speyer, Germany, June 17.

Skocpol, T. (2003). *Diminished Democracy: From Membership to Management in American Civic Life*. Norman, OK: University of Oklahoma Press.

Smullen, A. (2007). "Translating Agency Reform: Rhetoric and Culture in Comparative Perspective." Doctoral dissertation, Department of Political Science, Erasmus University Rotterdam.

—— (forthcoming 2010). Rhetoric and Culture in Public Agency Reform: Compatative Perspectives. Basington Stoke: Palgrave Macmillan.

Sokol, A. (1996). "A Physicist Experiments with Cultural Studies," *Lingua Franca*, 62–4.

Sorensen. E. and Torfing, J. (2007). *Theories of Democratic Network Governance*. London: Palgrave.

Sternberg, R., Wagner, R., Williams, W., and Horvarth, J. (1995). "Testing Common Sense," *American Psychologist*, 50 (11): 901–12.

Stilgoe, J. (2004). "Experts and Anecdotes: Shaping the Public Science of Mobile Phone Health Risks." PhD dissertation, University College London, London.

—— Irwin, A., and Jones, K. (2006). *The Received Wisdom: Opening Up Expert Advice*. London: Demos.

Stockman, N. (1983). *Anti-Positivist Theorists of the Sciences: Critical Rationalism and Scientific Realism*. Dordrecht: D. Reidel.

Stoker, G. (2000). "Urban Political Science and the Challenge of Urban Governance, " in J. Pierre (ed.), *Debating Governance: Authority, Steering, and Democracy*. Oxford: Oxford University Press.

—— (2006). "Public Value Management: A New Narrative for Governance?" *American Review of Public Administration*, 36 (1): 41–57.

Stone, D. (1988). *Policy Paradox and Political Reason*. Glenview, IL: Scott, Foresman and Company.

—— (1989). "Causal Stories and the Formation of Policy Agendas,". *Political Science Quarterly*, 104: 281–300.

—— (2002). *Policy Paradox: The Art of Political Decision-Making*, 2nd edn. New York: W.W. Norton.

Strand, K. J. *et al.* (2003). *Community-Based Research and Higher Education: Principles and Practices*. San Francisco, CA: Jossey-Bass.

Sullivan, W. M. (1995). *Work and Integrity: The Crisis and Promise of Professionalism in America*. New York: HarperCollins.

—— (2004). "Can Professionalism Still be a Viable Ethic?' *Good Society*, 13 (1): 15–20.

Sullivan, P. and Goldzweig, S. (1995). "A Relational Approach to Moral Decision-Making: The Majority Opinion in Planned Parenthood v. Casey," *Quarterly Journal of Speech*, 81: 167–90.

Tannen, D. (1985). *Analyzing Discourse: Text and Talk*. Washington, DC: George-town University Press.

—— (1989). *Talking Voices: Repetition, Dialogue and Imagery in Conversational Discourse*. Cambridge: Cambridge University Press.

—— (1998). *The Argument Culture: Moving from Debate to Dialogue*. New York: Random House.

Tawney, R. H. (1921). *The Acquisitive Society*. New York: Harcourt Brace.

Taylor, P. (1961). *Normative Discourse*. Englewood Cliff, NJ: Prentice Hall.

Thiele, L. P. (2006). *The Heart of Judgment: Practical Reason, Neuroscience, and Narrative*. New York: Cambridge University Press.

Thompson, J. (1998). "Arguing for Deliberation: Some Skeptical Considerations," in J. I. Elster (ed.), *Deliberative Democracy*. Cambridge: Cambridge University Press, 161–84.

Thorndike, R. L. and Stein, S. (1937). "An Evaluation of the Attempts to Measure Social Intelligence," *Psychological Bulletin*, 34: 275–84.

Throgmorton, J. A. (1993). "Survey Research as Rhetorical Trope: Electrical Power Planning Arguments in Chicago," in F. Fischer and J. Forester (eds.), *The Argumentative Turn in Policy Analysis and Planning*. Durham, NC: Duke University Press, 117–44.

Tirtanadi, A. (2006). "National Deliberative Democracy," *The Good Society*, 15: 241–5.

Torbert, W. (1991). *The Power of Balance: Transforming Self, Society, and Scientific Inquiry*. Newbury Park, CA: Sage.

Torff, B. (1999). "Tacit Knowledge in Teaching: Folk Pedagogy and Teacher Education," in R. J. Sternberg and J. A. Horvath (eds.), *Tacit Knowledge in Professional Practice*. Mahwah, NJ: Lawrence Erlbaum Associates, Publishers, 195–214.

Torgerson, D. (1995). "The Uncertain Quest for Sustainability: Public Discourse and the Politics of Environmentalism," in F. Fischer and M. Black (eds.), *Greening Environmental Policy: The Politics of a Sustainable Future*. New York: St Martin's Press, 3–20.

—— (2006). "Promoting the Policy Orientation: Lasswell in Context," in F. Fischer, G. Miller, and S. Sidney (eds.). *Handbook of Public Policy Analysis: Theory, Politics and Methods*. New York: Taylor & Francis Group: 15–28.

Toulmin, S. (1958). *The Uses of Argument*. Cambridge: Cambridge University Press.

—— (1983). "The Construal of Reality: Criticism in Modern and Postmodern Science," in W. J. T Mitchell (ed.), *The Politics of Interpretation*. Chicago: University of Chicago Press.

—— (1990). *Cosmopolis: The Hidden Agenda of Modernity*. Chicago: University of Chicago Press.

Turnbull, N. (2006). "How Should We Theorise Public Policy? Problem Solving and Problematicity," *Policy and Society*, 25 (2): 3–22.

References

Turner, S. (2006). "What is the Problem with Experts?" in E. Selinger and R. P. Crease (ed.), *The Philosophy of Expertise*. New York: Columbia University Press, 159–86.

van Eeten, M. M. J. (2006). "Narrative Policy Analysis," in F. Fischer *et al.* (eds.), *Handbook of Public Policy Analysis*. New York: Francis and Taylor, 251–69.

van Riper, P. P. (1958). *History of the United States Civil Service*. Evanston, IL: Row, Peterson and Co.

Verba, S., Schlozman, K. L., and H. Brady (2006). *Voice and Equality: Civic Voluntarism in American Politics*. Cambridge, MA: Harvard University Press.

Wagner, P. (2006). "Public Policy, Social Science and the State: An Historical Perspective," in F. Fischer, *et al.* (eds.), *Handbook of Public Policy Analysis*. New York: Francis and Taylor.

Walzer, M. (1999). "Deliberation, and What Else?" in S. Marcedo (ed.), *Deliberative Politics*. New York: Oxford, 59–69.

Warren, M. E. (2002). "What Can Democratic Participation Mean Today?" *Political Theory*, 30 (5): 667–701.

—— (2007). "Institutionalizing Deliberative Democracy," in S. Rosenberg (ed.), *Deliberation, Participation and Democracy: Can the People Govern*. London: Palgrave MacMillan, 272–88.

—— (2008). "Governance-Driven Democratisation: Opportunities and Challenges," Plenary Address at the 3rd Annual Conference in Interpretive Policy Analysis, University of Essex, UK, June 19.

Warren, M. and Pearce, H. (eds.) (2008). *Designing Deliberative Democracy: The British Columbia Citizens' Assembly*. Cambridge: Cambridge University Press.

Weber, F. (2007). "Emotionalisierung, Zivilitaet und Rationalitaet," *Osterreichische Zeitschrift fuer Politikwissenschaft*, 36 (1): 7–22.

Webler, T. (1999). "The Craft-and-Theory Dialectic of Public Participation," *Journal of Risk Research*, 2 (1): 55–71.

Wechsler, D. (1940). "Non-Linguistic Factor in General Intelligence," *Psychological Bulletin*, 37: 444–5.

Weiss, C. (1972). "Research for Policy's Sake: The Enlightenment Function of Social Research," *Policy Analysis*, 3, Fall: 553–65.

—— (1990). "Policy Research: Data, Ideas or Arguments?" in P. Wagner *et al.* (eds.), *Social Sciences and Modern States*. Cambridge: Cambridge University Press.

Wenger, E., McDermott, R., and Snyder, W. M. (2002). *Cultivating Communities of Practice*. Boston: Harvard Business School Press.

Westbrook, R. B. (1991). *John Dewey and American Democracy*. Ithaca, NY: Cornell University Press.

Westen, D. (2007). *The Political Brain: The Role of Emotion in Deciding the Fate of the Nation*. New York.

Wiebe, R. (1967). *The Search for Order: 1987–1920*. New York: Hill and Wang.

Wildavsky, A. (1997). *But is it True? A Citizen Guide to Environmental Health and Safety Issues*. Berkeley: University of California Press.

Wildermeersch, D., and Leirman, W. (1988). "The Facilitation of the Life-World Transformation," *Adult Education Quarterly*, 39: 19–30.

Willard, C. A. (1996). *Liberalism and the Problem of Knowledge: A New Rhetoric for Modern Democracy*. Chicago: University of Chicago Press.

Williams, R. (1983). *Culture and Society: 1780–1950*. New York: Columbia University Press.

Wineman, S. (1984). *The Politics of Human Services: A Radical Alternative to the Welfare State*. Boston: South End Press.

Winner, L. (1989). *The Whale and the Reactor: A Search for Limits in an Age of High Technology*. Chicago: University of Chicago Press.

Withhorn, A. (1984*). Serving the People: Social Services and Social Change*. New York: Columbia University Press.

Wolin, S. 1994. "Fugitive Democracy," *Constellations*, 1 (1): 11–25.

Woods, G. S. (2007). "Natural, Equal, Universal," Sunday Book Review, *New York Times*, April 8: 1.

World Bank (1994). *The World Bank and Participation*. Washington, DC: Operations Policy Department.

Wynne, B. (2003). "Seasick on the Third Wave: Subverting the Hegemony of Propositionalism," *Social Studies of Science*, 33 (3): 401–17.

Yankelovich, D. (1991). *Coming to Public Judgment: Making Democracy Work in a Complex World*. Syracuse, NY: Syracuse University Press.

Yanow, D. (2000). *Conducting Interpretive Policy Analysis*. Newbury Park, CA: Sage.

—— and Schwartz-Shea, P. (eds.) (2006). *Interpretation and Method: Empirical Research Methods and the Interpretive Turn*. Armonk, NY: M E Sharpe.

York, R., and Rose, E. A. (2003). "Key Challenges to Ecological Modernization Theory," *Organization and Environment*, 16 (3): 273–88.

Young, I. M. (1990). *Justice and the Politics of Difference*. Princeton, NJ: Princeton University Press.

—— (1999). "Justice, Inclusion, and Deliberative Democracy," in S. Marcedo (ed.), *Deliberative Politics*. Oxford: Oxford University Press, 151–8.

Young, S. C. (2000). *The Emergence of Ecological Modernisation: Integrating the Environment and the Economy?* London: Routledge.

Zolo, D. (1992). *Complexity and Democracy: A Realist Approach*. Cambridge: Polity Press.

Zukin, C., Keeter, S., Andolina, M., Jenkins, K., and Delli Carpini, M. X. (2007). *A New Civic Engagement: Political Participation, Civic Life, and the Changing American Citizen*. New York: Oxford University Press.

Index